The Forty-Three Presidents

The Forty-Three Presidents

What They Said To and
About Each Other

Nero James Pruitt

iUniverse

The Forty-Three Presidents
What They Said To and About Each Other

iUniverse books may be ordered through booksellers or by contacting:

iUniverse
1663 Liberty Drive
Bloomington, IN 47403
www.iuniverse.com
1-800-Authors (1-800-288-4677)

ISBN: 978-1-4917-6309-4 (sc)
ISBN: 978-1-4917-6310-0 (e)

Library of Congress Control Number: 2015910604

Print information available on the last page.

iUniverse rev. date: 08/03/2015

Table of Contents

Introduction

The first American president was born in 1732 and took office in 1789. **George Washington** was followed in the next two centuries by 42 individuals. The latest is **Barack Obama** who was born in 1961 and took office in 2009.

These are the forty-three Presidents with the dates of their administrations and the dates of their lives:

President	Years Served	Years Lived
George Washington	1789 -1797	1732 -1799
John Adams	1797 -1801	1735 -1826
Thomas Jefferson	1801 -1809	1743 -1826
James Madison	1809 -1817	1751 -1836
James Monroe	1817 -1825	1758 -1831
John Quincy Adams	1825 -1829	1767 -1848
Andrew Jackson	1829 -1837	1767 -1845
Martin Van Buren	1837 -1841	1782 -1862
William Henry Harrison	1841 -1841	1773 -1841
John Tyler	1841 -1845	1790 -1862
James Knox Polk	1845 -1849	1795 -1849
Zachary Taylor	1849 -1850	1784 -1850
Millard Fillmore	1850 -1853	1800 -1874
Franklin Pierce	1853 -1857	1804 -1869
James Buchanan	1857 -1861	1791 -1868
Abraham Lincoln	1857 -1865	1809 -1865
Andrew Johnson	1865 -1869	1808 -1875
Ulysses S. Grant	1869 -1877	1822 -1885
Rutherford B Hayes	1877 -1881	1822 -1893
James Garfield	1881 -1881	1831 -1881
Chester Alan Arthur	1881 -1885	1829 -1886

Grover Cleveland	1885 -1889 and 1893-1897	1837 -1908
Benjamin Harrison	1889 -1893	1833 -1901
William McKinley	1897 -1901	1843 -1901
Theodore Roosevelt	1901 -1909	1858 -1919
William Howard Taft	1909 -1913	1857 -1930
Woodrow Wilson	1913 -1921	1856 -1924
Warren Harding	1921 -1923	1865 -1923
Calvin Coolidge	1923 -1929	1872 -1933
Herbert Hoover	1929 -1933	1874 -1964
Franklin Roosevelt	1933 -1945	1882 -1945
Harry Truman	1945 -1953	1884 -1972
Dwight Eisenhower	1953 -1961	1890 -1969
John F. Kennedy	1961 -1963	1917 -1963
Lyndon Johnson	1963 -1969	1908 -1973
Richard Nixon	1969 -1974	1913 -1994
Gerald Ford	1974 -1977	1913 -2006
Jimmy Carter	1977 -1981	1924 -
Ronald Reagan	1981 -1989	1911 -2004
George HW Bush	1989 -1993	1924 -
Bill Clinton	1993 -2001	1946 -
George W Bush	2001 -2009	1946 -
Barack Obama	2009 -	1961 -

Although all have been males, all except **John F. Kennedy** have been Protestant and all except **Barack Obama** have been white, there is more diversity than one might expect among them. We have had a President in a wheel chair (**Franklin Roosevelt)** and one for whom English was a second language (**Martin Van Buren** grew up speaking Dutch.) Two US Presidents have been Unitarians (**Millard Fillmore** and **William Howard Taft**) and two were Quakers (**Herbert Hoover** and **Richard Nixon**). People of **James Buchanan's** time thought he was gay.

This is not a book about Vice Presidents but one had a common-law black wife (Richard Johnson who served under **Martin Van**

Buren) and another grew up on an Indian reservation (Charles Curtis, **Hoover's** Vice President).

The first president (**Washington**) and the sixteenth (**Abraham Lincoln**) are recognized as among the greatest people of world history. Others – **Thomas Jefferson, James Madison**, and **Franklin Roosevelt** - are seen as near-great. Others – **Andrew Jackson, Theodore Roosevelt** and **Ronald Reagan** come to mind - greatly influenced their eras and changed the direction of American history. The rest were good, mediocre, poor, or awful. But each has occupied the position that has become the most recognized office in the world.

It is the most recognized, but that is not because of the length of tenure in office by any individual. Due to term limits, first voluntary or determined by elections, and later mandatory, only one served more than eight years. Other institutions are different. **George Washington** was followed by 42 successors but King George III by only eight. During the two hundred twenty-six years that the forty-three presidents have served, only seventeen popes have been in office. In the 129 years since 1886 when the American Federation of Labor was formed there have been nine presidents of the AFL and only six if we count only those who served for more than one year. In that time period twenty-two US Presidents have been in office. In short, kings, popes and union leaders tend to be lifetime appointments but the American people move our Presidents along. Ten have been rejected by the voters when they sought a second term and others didn't run because they knew it would be a lost cause.

But our system has provided stability. Here's a comparison: Mexico had twenty presidents between 1840-48. During this period the US had four:

- **Van Buren** who was finishing his term.
- **William Henry Harrison** who served for a month.
- **John Tyler** who served for nearly four years.
- **James Knox Polk** who served for four years.

There are plenty of Americans greater than the vast majority of the forty-three presidents. Here are some: Alexander Hamilton for his joint authorship of the *Federalist Papers* and development of the American financial system, John Marshall for establishing the precedent of judicial review and Thomas Edison for developing devices like the light bulb and the phonograph. The historian Garry Wills argues that the **Kennedy** era was really the Martin Luther King era. Besides the "43" there are near-misses. They include: an Ohio politician named Ben Wade who but for one vote in **Andrew Johnson's** impeachment trial in 1868 would have elevated to the presidency (Wade once said that **Abraham Lincoln** was "born of poor white trash"), Samuel Tilden who lost an election most deemed as fraudulent in 1876 to **Rutherford B Hayes**, Elihu Root, the powerful cabinet member whom President **Theodore Roosevelt** considered endorsing in 1908 but instead picked another cabinet member, **William Howard Taft** and in our time Al Gore whose defeat by **George W Bush** in 2000 was not final until court action and Hillary Clinton who lost an epic race for the Democratic nomination by a tiny amount of votes to **Barack Obama** in 2008.

By the third century of the constitutional order in the US, the presidency is a worldwide phenomenon, a proof of American exceptionalism. The world responds to polls on the American presidential election and, to put in crudely, sweats out the outcome. Nelson Mandela is honored for his role in South Africa by being called the **George Washington** of South Africa. **Nixon** was honored in China long after his resignation. The capital city of Liberia is named after **James Monroe**. A department (state) and its capital in Paraguay are named for **Rutherford B Hayes.**

The forty-three presidents stand alone as a group and trillions of words have been written about them. This book uses their quotes to show what they said about each other, what they thought about each other, what they thought about similar topics and how they were connected - both in life and across time. This book analyzes the statements and interactions of presidents, even if they occurred long before (or after) their presidencies.

This book is based on the thesis that the forty-three individuals are united as are no others for two reasons:

First, they are united because they took the following oath, first given in 1789:

"I do solemnly swear (or affirm) that I will faithfully execute the Office of President of the United States, and will to the best of my ability, preserve, protect and defend the Constitution of the United States." (**Washington** added to the inaugural oath in 1789: "so help me God" and this phrase, although not in the Constitution, has been consistently uttered by each new President. In the confusion following President **Kennedy's** assassination in 1963 **Lyndon Johnson** took the oath of office aboard *Air Force One* with his hand on a Catholic prayer book belonging to **Kennedy** that he thought was a Bible. The judge administering the oath read from the constitutional text and then added out loud "so help me God" which **Johnson** then repeated.)

Second, and remarkably, they are united because they took that oath in an orderly ceremony often attended by their rivals as an expression of the evolving American democracy. They took it in quiescent years like 1805 (**Thomas Jefferson**) or 1905 (**Theodore Roosevelt**) or 1993 (**Bill Clinton**) and they took it during times of crisis like 1801 (**Jefferson**), 1861 (**Lincoln**), 1945 (**Franklin Roosevelt** and **Harry Truman**) or 1969 (**Richard Nixon**).

What kind of country?

Consider the different environments in which these forty-three Presidents served.

John Adams left Braintree Massachusetts for Philadelphia in 1774. Letters to and from his wife Abigail took two to three weeks to traverse the four hundred miles. **Adams** wrote her: "Is there no way for two friendly souls to converse together although their bodies are four hundred miles off? Yes, by letter. But I want a better communication." He could not have imagined a world with the

Internet, E-mail, texting and tweeting. In 1775 **Adams** wrote Abigail from the Second Continental Congress of the danger she faced in the Boston area. "In Case of real Danger, fly to the Woods with our children." Instead, she took **John Quincy Adams** to witness the Battle of Bunker Hill. Over the next forty years cities like Boston, Detroit, New York were occupied by the British and Washington DC was burned.

In an era when letters took 2-3 months to cross the ocean the **Adams** family struck a friendship with **Thomas Jefferson** in Paris. In effect, the **Adamses** took in **Jefferson** and **John Adams** and **Thomas Jefferson** bonded as diplomats in a way that modern diplomats would not.

The country they were founding was huge by the communication standards of the era. In the *Federalist Papers* **Madison's** insight was that an "extensive Republic" could help manage the diverse population. (He and his colleagues were mostly concerned with religious differences.) In 1786 **James Monroe** wrote **Thomas Jefferson** his concern about the settlement of the West - that land between the Appalachians and the Mississippi River. **Monroe** wrote that their "interests will be opposed to ours." **(Jefferson** was of the same mind writing in 1804: "Whether we remain in one confederacy or form into Atlantic confederations, I believe not very important to the happiness of either part.") In 1790 **Jefferson**, **Madison** and **Monroe** decided to rebut some political charges of Alexander Hamilton. The drafting fell to **Madison** and **Monroe**. For several days messengers on horseback delivered drafts and revisions between their estates in Charlottesville and Montpelier. This was a distance of about fifty miles. The essays that resulted and the responses by Hamilton were early signs of a system of a two-party government that has dominated American politics ever since then.

The great historian Henry Adams - himself the grandson and great-grandson of presidents - wrote in the late 1800s that **Jefferson** thought political unity was "not very important" beyond the Alleghany mountains. Instead, Henry Adams wrote: "to escape the tyranny of Caesar by perpetuating the simple and isolated lives of their fathers was the sum of their political philosophy; to fix upon the National Government the stamp of their own idyllic conservatism was the height of their ambition."

It was one hundred miles between Monticello and Washington DC traveled in early America by stagecoach. **Jefferson** wrote in 1801: "Of eight rivers between here and Washington, five have neither bridges nor boats." Henry Adams later wrote of that period: "If Americans agreed in any opinion, they were united in wishing for roads..."

Wages in the cities were low. Money was scarce. In the countryside the great majority of people probably lived on sand covered floors surrounded by bare walls. It took 4-6 days to travel from Boston to New York by stagecoach. At the time of the first constitutional government Pittsburgh was the westernmost town of any consequence with 500 people. My ancestor Abraham Pruitt was born in South Carolina in 1787 and died in Kentucky in 1856, illiterate.

The majority of workers were farmers. Their diversions included dog fighting – a larger one tied to a stake against a pack of smaller ones - or cock fighting. Other "sports" in the Virginia of 1800 included horse-racing, betting and drinking, and the rough-and-tumble fight which was a no-rules mayhem. Life expectancy was about 40. Church membership was very low. Another of **Madison's** guarded views and the reason that he deserves mention in world history is that he thought that the collective wisdom of such people would best guide the country through the House of Representatives in the new government. Most elites had no desire to create a system where common people voted in the laws.

Dueling was an accepted issue-resolution process. In 1797 **Monroe** and Alexander Hamilton edged toward a duel. It arose out of Hamilton's affair with a married woman a few years earlier in which her husband blackmailed Hamilton into paying hush money and in which **Monroe** accused Hamilton of certain financial irregularities. **Jefferson** and **Madison** met and concluded that the duel challenge should be resolved. Within ten years Hamilton lost his life in another duel, the most famous in American history with Aaron Burr who was Vice President of the US at the time. Hamilton's son had been killed in a duel earlier. Hamilton's wife lived for another fifty years after her husband's death. She stoutly defended her husband's reputation on all controversies and even demanded a complete apology from **Monroe** which he would not give although he met with her to reconcile differences. **William Henry Harrison** as a young military officer discouraged dueling. **Andrew Jackson** fought in at least three duels. The practice of dueling was slow to die out. In 1854 during acrimonious congressional debates future Vice President John Breckinridge was challenged to a duel by another congressman. As the challenged party Breckinridge was allowed to choose the weapons and he chose rifles. President **Franklin Pierce** worked behind the scenes to settle the duel. **Pierce's** ambassador to Spain fought a duel while there with the French ambassador using guns and the US ambassador's son fought one with swords.

European powers wanted to keep the US weak. They believed the US would fail, some thought within five years. According to one British statesman, the size of the US worked against it. The US capital moved frequently from Philadelphia, to Boston, to Annapolis, to Trenton and New York. It eventually settled in what is now Washington DC but as late as 1808 Congress debated moving the capital back to Philadelphia. There were difficult negotiations with Spain which tried to pit the Northeast against the West by offering a commercial treaty (which the Northeast coveted) in return for the US waiving access to the Mississippi River for twenty-five years (strenuously opposed by the West).This tentative treaty caused talks of secession. A twenty-something member of the Congress in the Articles of Confederation period, **James Monroe** helped calm this issue.

The new Constitution was shaky and so was the office of the Presidency. When a shooting war at sea started between the United States and revolutionary France in 1798, President **John Adams** wrote his predecessor, **George Washington** offering to resign so that **Washington** could resume the job. In 1799, when confronted by Federalist allies over his diplomatic efforts toward France, **Adams** threatened to resign again which would have made **Thomas Jefferson** President. Burr, by then a former Vice President, was tried for treason.

When Congress met on December 6, 1802 with a potential crisis looming of French occupation of New Orleans, a quorum wasn't available until December 15.

In 1803 **Jefferson** sent **Monroe** to Europe on a crucial diplomatic mission. The British ambassador who was on good terms with the US at the moment offered **Jefferson** British transport for the **Monroe** mission but it was realized that a month or two of delay would be necessary. After the Louisiana Purchase of 1803 which more than doubled the land mass of the US, **Jefferson** knew that on the frontier the Indian tribes were allying with the British in the north and the Spanish in the south and that no spot between New Orleans and Mackinaw was safe. Consider also the conditions in Europe: In late 1804 **Monroe** traveled by coach from Paris to Madrid. It took three weeks. He arrived New Years Day. He traveled through barren country where inns were irregular.

Zachary Taylor grew up in Kentucky. As a young officer he served in Wisconsin, Minnesota, Missouri, Illinois and Indiana in the early 1800s. (For nearly two centuries of perspective, contrast that coming-of-age experience with that of **Barack Obama** who left Hawaii in the 1980s for school in California and then New York.) In **Taylor's** era enlisted men in these outposts got $6 per month. They spent it on alcohol, candy, raisins, spices, tobacco, soap, etc.

In 1809 **John Quincy Adams** left the US to be ambassador to Russia. He later served in Ghent in modern Belgium negotiating the end to the War of 1812. He left his two older sons, ages 6 and 8 with relatives and took his two-year-old, Charles Francis Adams. He did not see his older sons for the next six years and did not return to the US for eight years. Both older sons died as young adults in tragic circumstances of alcoholism and estrangement. The two-year old grew up to be a famous statesman.

A war raging within the borders of the US could be ignored by most of the population. As Henry Adams later wrote about the US during the War of 1812: "The country was vast, and quiet reigned throughout the whole United States." The army was filled by enlistments for a five-year period at $5 per month, a $16 bonus and, upon discharge three months pay and 160 acres of land. Day-laborer wages were about $9/month so the money was not a motivation for military service. State militias were another source. But in a population of about 7 million less than ten thousand entered the military service. In 1814 **Monroe** ordered **Jackson** from Mobile to New Orleans. **Monroe** and **Madison** were alarmed at **Jackson**'s slow movements as well as his incursions into Spanish Florida. Their worry: was **Jackson** a backcountry Napoleon?

In 1817 **Monroe** went on a four tour of the Northeast as far as Detroit. A few years later after **Monroe** took a tour of six southern states, octogenarian **John Adams** remarked: "What a Precedent is **Monroe** establishing for future Presidents? He will make the office the most perfect slavery that ever existed - The next president must go to California."

Rutherford B Hayes was born in Ohio in 1822 just as it was moving past its pioneer era. As a child he smelled sugar-making and cherry tree blossoms. He heard the smashing of apples in cider presses. Children in the area had pet birds, squirrels and rabbits. At 12 he went to visit relatives in Vermont. At 15 he went to school in Connecticut. In the late 1820s Congressman **Polk** and his wife traveled from Tennessee to Washington DC by stagecoach. According to the custom of the day they lived in a boarding house in Washington with upstairs apartments and a downstairs parlor and common eating area.

Garfield was born in 1831 in the Western Reserve. It was a fertile land covered by forests. The city of Cleveland a few miles away had a population of about one thousand.

In 1830, Chicago had about twelve families living around a fort and a fur station. (In 1860, the population was 100,000 and it hosted the Republican convention.) Wrestling was a popular frontier sport. When **Fillmore** got to Washington as a congressman in 1833 a few dilapidated boarding shacks were at the base of the national capitol.

In the 1840 campaign **William Henry Harrison** complained about receiving an average of twenty-four letters per day. "(I) f I were to answer all this correspondence I should have no time for anything else." **Harrison** was the first president to be photographed in 1841. During the presidential transition in 1845 the statehood of Texas was an issue. The incoming President **Polk** considered altering some of his predecessor **Tyler's** instructions to Texas officials but that would have involved sending a fast horse to catch up with couriers.

In 1847 President **James K Polk** traveled by train from Washington DC to his *alma mater,* the University of North Carolina at Chapel Hill. A local dignitary noting that **Polk** had entered the university thirty years before said to him: "What changes have come over the world in thirty years!" He claimed that those thirty years had seen more change than the previous three hundred, noting steam power and electricity.

The Whig Party convention in Philadelphia in 1848 nominated **Zachary Taylor**. **Taylor** was not at the convention. Officials sent a letter to him in Louisiana informing him that he had been selected by the party. **Taylor** did not reply for a month because the letter didn't have postage and had been tossed in the dead letter file by the local postmaster. **Grant** was born in 1822. As a young officer in 1848 he was ordered to report to Detroit. When he and his wife arrived he was reassigned under protest to **Madison** Barracks in Sackets Harbor, New York 450 miles away. By winter his protest was upheld and he was reassigned to Detroit. But the lake was frozen and his return was delayed until spring.

In 1849 **Polk** wrote in his diary that **Taylor** believed that California and Oregon could set up "an independent government" since they "were too distant to become members of the Union." **Hayes** in frontier Cincinnati in 1850 socialized by attending literary societies, plays, lectures and meeting young women. Politics in the 1850s involved torchlight parades, muddy streets lit by gas lamps, sometimes a brass band. Many participants were drunk. In 1851 businessmen in New York gave **Fillmore** a splendid coach with two horses. It cost $1500. **Franklin Pierce** elected in 1852 was the first president to hire a full-time bodyguard. In 1852 **Grant's** unit was transferred from New York to the Pacific Coast to provide order during the Gold Rush. It took 2 months to sail to Panama, cross the isthmus and arrive in San Francisco. He didn't see his wife for two years.

In 1861, the telegraph lines stopped in Missouri. It took dozens of pony express riders about 7 days to get copies of **Lincoln's** inaugural address speech to California. Because **Grant** had risen from obscurity in the western theater during the Civil War **Lincoln,** governing from Washington DC, did not know him until 1864 when he summoned the general to the East. **Lincoln** greeted **Grant** at a White House Party with these words. "Why, here is General **Grant**! Well, this is a great pleasure, I assure you." During the next year **Lincoln** rode 10 miles by horse with **Grant** to visit the front. The population at the time of the Civil War was about thirty million.

Henry Adams wrote of Washington DC that "as in 1800 and 1850, so in 1860, the same rude colony was camped in the same forest, with the same unfinished Greek temples for workrooms, and sloughs for roads." This was not just quaint. This disarray symbolized the intrinsic weakness of the society. "The Government had an air of social instability and incompleteness that went far to support the right of secession in theory as in fact." Famously, Adams said of Washington DC in 1861 that there was nothing to learn there except "bad tempers, bad manners, poker and treason." He described a "summer village about La Fayette Square in 1869."

In 1863 a contractor was hired to help ready the Gettysburg battle site for the dedication. He exhumed the bodies from shallow graves and reinterred them. He charged $1.59 per grave.

In the 1870s when **Garfield** was in Congress, Members did not have offices so they conducted their business from their desks on the floor. They each had one secretary. **Grant** appointed **Chester Alan Arthur** to the New York Custom House head in 1871; at more than $50,000 per year **Arthur** was the highest paid federal official in the country.

The US industrialized after the Civil War. It changed from an agricultural country to one with mills and factories. Modern finance arose. A railway system emerged. Stock speculation began. In 1875 **Grant** became the first president to travel as far west as Salt Lake City. News of the controversial election of 1876 was transmitted by wire, across the whole continent, brought to court houses, party headquarters or gathering places and posted on bulletin boards and read aloud. This was also the year of Little Big Horn. In 1880 **Hayes** became the first president to make it to the West Coast.

In **Hayes'** White House of 1877-81, typewriters were not widely utilized; he had clerks summarize letters he received and clip newspaper stories into scrapbooks by subject as a sort of news digest. (President **Obama** probably has a different system.) The telephone (1876), and the electric light began to change life in that decade. **Grant**, **Arthur** and **Benjamin Harrison** traveled and spoke for **Garfield.**

In presidential elections in the late nineteenth century candidates stayed at home and received visitors while surrogates campaigned. The concept was that the office sought the man rather than the other way around. In 1880 **Garfield** and Winfield Scott Hancock followed this pattern. **Garfield** had a telegraph machine installed at his farm in Ohio. Both nominees wrote a "letter of acceptance" which was the method of responding to the party platform. President **Rutherford B Hayes** advised **Garfield** as did Robert Ingersoll and Mark Twain. In that election, a six-year-old **Hoover** saw a torchlight parade.

Citing progress in 1884 Senator **Benjamin Harrison** said about the Dakotas: "The emigrant who is now seeking a home in the West does not now use as his vehicle a pack-train, a Conestoga Wagon, or even a Broad Horn. The great bulk of the people who have gone into Dakota have gone upon the steam-car...." When the White House got electric lighting **Harrison** who served from 1889 – 1893 and his family left the lights on for fear of being electrocuted. An engineer would arrive in the morning to turn off the lights. **Theodore Roosevelt** was the first president to leave the country while he was president and he was the first to drive his own car. When **Warren Harding** died in 1923 Vice President **Calvin Coolidge** was visiting his father in Vermont. There was no phone at the farm house. A messenger from the post office brought the telegram during the night. He was sworn in by his father by the light of a kerosene lamp. **Coolidge** was the first president to effectively use radio. His broadcasts reached tens of millions of people in a single speech. By contrast **TR** reached an estimated 13 million in all the speeches he gave in his career. **Truman** was the first president to have a television set in the White House.

Decades pass and **Barack Obama** like millions of Americans uses a Blackberry or an iPhone, a small box about the size of a pack of cigarettes to send and receive messages all over the world. This concept would probably have been as foreign to **Lyndon Johnson** who died in 1973 as it would have been to **James Madison** who wrote to **Thomas Jefferson** regarding the state of Georgia in 1787 that "Of the affairs of Georgia, I know as little as those of Kamskatska" (which is in the Russian Far East).

The presidents associated with celebrities of their day and who these celebrities were reminds us of the passage of two centuries. Daniel Boone (1734-1820) was with **George Washington** in 1755 in military action in western Pennsylvania. After the War of 1812 **William Henry Harrison** was befriended in Washington by author Margaret Bayard Smith. Author Washington Irving who was born in 1783 and named for **George Washington** was a friend of **Van Buren** and may have based some of his characters including Ichabod Crane on people in **Van Buren's** home town, Kinderhook, New York. **John Tyler** sent Irving to Spain as ambassador and **Fillmore** became a friend of Irving. **Van Buren once** saw Junius Booth, father of John Wilkes Booth, perform on stage. Charles Dickens met with **Tyler** and said: "He looked somewhat worn and anxious, and well he might be, being at war with everybody." An aged **John Quincy Adams** met Dickens at about the same time. Later Dickens met **Andrew Johnson** and recognized him as a person of presence and

14

wrote that no one could meet him without concluding that he was an extraordinary man. (Well, some could.)

In the 1830s **Franklin Pierce** took a law student into his legal practice in New Hampshire. This student's younger sister was Mary Baker Eddy, founder of the Christian Science Church. **Pierce** attended school with Nathanial Hawthorne and Henry Wadsworth Longfellow - both Americans who are probably better-known that he. In 1837 **Pierce** helped Hawthorne get a government job to survive financially. The job was in the Boston Custom House. In the early 1840s **Pierce** secured another Custom House job for Hawthorne. **Pierce** commissioned a portrait of Hawthorne which he hung in the White House and he appointed him to a diplomatic post in England. Hawthorne described his friend **Pierce** as "deep, deep, deep" and **Pierce** was with him when he died. (Hawthorne supported the **Jackson** campaign of 1828.) In 1860 John Greenleaf Whittier (Massachusetts) and William Cullen Bryant (New York) were **Lincoln** electors. (In the early 1900s **Richard Nixon** lived as a child in a California town named for the former as did Lou Henry the future wife of **Herbert Hoover.)**

Ulysses S. Grant's *Memoirs* is the best military memoir of the Civil War and regarded by many historians as the best presidential autobiography ever written. It was written to meet pressing financial needs as he was dying. Mark Twain defended **Grant** from the British critic Matthew Arnold. Twain read from Arnold's review of **Grant's** *Memoirs* and said in 1887: "To read that passage a couple of times would make a man dizzy; to read it four times would make him drunk." Twain admired **Grant** and called him "the simple soldier." Twain knew **Grover Cleveland** of whom he said "the verdict for you is rock and will stand." He also knew **TR** and called him "the Tom Sawyer of the political world of the 20th century."

In the disputed election of 1876 General Lew Wallace went to Florida on behalf of **Hayes** to observe the canvassing boards. He took statements and offered counsel. He and others were called "visiting statesmen." He wrote his wife: "If we win, our methods are subject to impeachment for possible fraud. If the enemy win, it is the same thing exactly." After the election **Hayes** appointed him governor of the New Mexico territory where he wrote *Ben-Hur* and oversaw the execution of Billy the Kid. **Garfield** later appointed Wallace ambassador to the Ottoman Empire noting that he thought Wallace could "draw inspiration from the modern east for future literary work." **Benjamin Harrison's** campaign biography in 1888 was written by Wallace, a personal friend. Rudyard Kipling once wrote American friends about **TR**: "Take care of him. He is scarce and valuable." After **TR** was shot during the campaign, Frank James, brother of Jesse James, offered to form a bodyguard for **TR** if he resumed his campaign. Bat Masterson said to **TR** at the time: "The bullet has not yet been molded that can kill a man of your strength and character." **TR's** response: "Bully for you, Bat."

Thomas Edison supported **TR** in 1912: "I'm a natural born Bull Moose. I believe in change because all progress is the result of change... The Americans are experimenters; we want to try experiments in government.... **Roosevelt** would win easily if there were not so many sheep in the world who won't think." **Coolidge** once told the famous actress Ethel Barrymore: "I think the public wants a solemn ass as president and I think I'll go along with them." When Babe Ruth was introduced to **Calvin Coolidge** in a ball park on a steamy day he said, "Hot as hell, ain't it, Prez?" Babe Ruth met or corresponded with every president from **Wilson** to **Truman** and in 1948 was photographed with **George HW Bush** and the Yale baseball team.

In 1912 Jim Thorpe played a celebrated football game for the Carlisle Pennsylvania team coached by Pop Warner against the West Point team that included **Dwight David Eisenhower**. **Nixon's** second cousin who also lived in his home town was the author Jessamyn West. **Reagan** was the co-master of ceremony at the grand opening of Disneyland in 1955 and he introduced Walt Disney. When he was president, **Reagan** called the baseball player, Pete Rose, to congratulate him on becoming team manager and to ask him to come to a campaign appearance. Rose declined but told **Reagan**, "Anytime you wanna call, though, I'd be happy to talk to ya." **Bill Clinton** had Hollywood friends Linda and Harry Thomason who helped him with campaign videos.

Celebrities have opposed the Presidents. Harry Belafonte called President **George W Bush** a slave master. Actress Jessica Lange said: "I hate **Bush**. I despise him and his entire administration – not only because of its international policy, but also the national. Today it makes me feel ashamed to come from the United States. It is humiliating." **Harriet Beecher Stowe** went to the Bible to display her contempt for **Buchanan**: "The fool has said in his heart there is no God." During the Civil War Stowe called **Pierce** an "arch-traitor." A famous actor killed **Lincoln**. Longfellow said that **Andrew Johnson** was "capable of any iniquity."

World leaders and would-be leaders outside of the United States have opined about the American presidents. In 1783 King George III said about **George Washington** that if he gave up power he would be the greatest person in the world. Of course **Washington** did give up the command of the Continental Army and later the presidency itself. As **Thomas Jefferson** said: "**George Washington** was one of the few in the whole history of the world who was not carried away by power." In 2009 Fidel Castro, said that **Obama** looked "conceited" on television. Thus, for the most part, dictators have not understood the American people's presidents. It's really not that difficult: they serve as head of the executive branch of a constitutional government for a prescribed amount of time until, as required in our 1787 settlement, the people choose again.

In this historical context, the forty-three presidents had ample occasion to talk to and about each other. The presidents have been long-term allies (For example, **Jefferson** and **Madison**), running mates (For example, **Franklin Roosevelt** and **Harry Truman**; **Eisenhower** and **Nixon**). They have been intra-party competitors (For example, **Pierce** and **Buchanan** in 1852 and 1856; **Theodore Roosevelt** and **Taft** in 1912; **Kennedy** and **Lyndon Johnson** in 1960; **Nixon** and **Reagan** in 1968. **Herbert Hoover, Warren G. Harding** and **Calvin Coolidge** were all dark horses at the 1920 Republican convention.) They have run against each other in the general election (I count twenty-one of the forty-three men who have been President as at one time running against another President. The first two were **John Adams** and **Thomas Jefferson**. The most recent were **George HW**

Bush and **Bill Clinton**.) There have been fathers who lived until the presidencies of their sons (**John Adams** and **George HW Bush)**. They have served under one another in military command (**Grant** under **Taylor**; **William McKinley** under **Hayes**). They have hated each other (**John Quincy Adams** and **Jackson**). They have written about each other even when separated by generations. (**Theodore Roosevelt** about **Tyler**; **Nixon** about **Woodrow Wilson**; many of them about **Lincoln** and **Washington**) Historian David McCullough has written that history for **Harry Truman** was part of life. "Often when he spoke of **Andrew Jackson** or **John Quincy Adams** or **Abraham Lincoln** it was as if he were talking about someone he knew." In a similar way, **Abraham Lincoln** reflected on **Andrew Jackson** during the Civil War, **Theodore Roosevelt** reflected on **Thomas Jefferson** as he worked to build up the Navy and **Barack Obama** reflected on **Lincoln** as he assumed the presidency.

Style and Organization

I have grouped presidential interactions into these chapters:

- Jobs
- Affinity
- Historical Perspectives
- Transitions
- Rivalry
- The Icons
- The Constitution
- Policy
- Religion
- Political Parties
- Race
- Summary

In each chapter I have three sections:

- Overall context
- Moving Forward. In some instances, I have sub-divided this section but generally I have followed a chronological approach
- A review: What is the Point of All This?

The *Overall Context* serves as an introduction to the topic. The *Moving Forward* section is mainly chronological although I have made at least one type of exception to a straight-through-the-years approach. When one president has said something to or about another that is uncannily like what another president said later or even when they address the same issue, I have sometimes made a linkage. For example, **John Adams** tried to discount **Thomas Jefferson's** claim of authorship of the Declaration of Independence and in 1896 **Theodore Roosevelt** cited **John Quincy Adams** as the real author of the **Monroe** Doctrine. For another example, in 1808 **James Buchanan** was expelled and then reinstated at Dickinson College for participating in drunken revelry at local taverns. Later **Buchanan** wrote that he was not "dissipated" but had taken part so that he would be thought of as "a clever and spirited youth." In 1992 **Clinton** was asked if he had ever broken international law. He responded: "When I was in England, (as a student in the 1960s) I experimented with marijuana a time or two, and didn't like it. I didn't inhale and I didn't try it again." The *What is the Point of All This?* section draws lessons and is the briefest part of the chapter – sometimes very brief – because the words of the presidents speak for themselves.

Also: I have **bolded** the names of the presidents and usually put in first names in those instances in which names are repeated: the **Adamses, the Harrisons,** the **Johnsons** (the only two in this group who are unrelated), the **Roosevelts** and the **Bushes.**

Chapter 1

Jobs

Overall context

The presidents gave each other jobs and assignments. These show patterns of mentorship, the setting of long-range policy, affinity or random chance.

As president, **Monroe** had no relationship more important than that with his Secretary of State, **John Quincy Adams**. **William Henry Harrison** took jobs from several presidents. He was appointed by **John Adams** as secretary of the Northwest Territory, then as governor of Indiana and re-appointed by both **Jefferson** and **Madison. Jefferson** gave **Harrison** the authority to negotiate treaties with Indian tribes. (**Harrison's** job searching attracted some criticism. **John Quincy Adams** once said of **Harrison** that he was someone whose "thirst for lucrative office is absolutely rapid" and that he "has withal a faculty of making friends, and is incessantly importuning them for their influence in his favor.")

James Buchanan declined some jobs. In 1838 **Buchanan** turned down **Van Buren's** offer of Attorney General. He accepted an appointment by **Polk** to the position of Secretary of State but later turned down at least one offer from **Polk** to be on the Supreme Court. At the outbreak of the Mexican-American War, **Pierce** was selected by **Polk** as a general in part because he was a Democrat. But he did not play politics and was loyal to his commanding officer, Winfield Scott, a Whig whom he ran against four years later. In early 1848 after combat service **Pierce** returned to the US and reported to **Polk**.

In 1852 **Buchanan** lost the nomination to **Pierce** and declined the vice presidential nomination. **Pierce** then appointed him ambassador

21

to England. This new job was fortuitous for **Buchanan's** career as he was out of the country when a sectional crisis emerged over the Kansas-Nebraska Act and thus politically viable to get elected president in 1856 after more than a decade of trying.

In 1871 **Arthur** was appointed to the head of the US Custom House in New York by **Grant**. That Custom House brought in one-third of all government revenue. It was housed in big marble building on Wall Street with columns, a rotunda, and hundreds of small offices for clerks and officials. All of these staff members were appointed by the head of the Custom House who thereby controlled more patronage opportunities than many cabinet members. **Arthur's** role there was to lead to one of the important developments in post-Civil War relationship between the presidency and the Congress.

In 1880 at a tumultuous Republican National Convention, Indiana politician **Benjamin Harrison,** came to the room of dark horse **James Garfield** and asked **Garfield** if, in the event of a deadlock, under what conditions might he accept the nomination? Later that week, **Garfield** became the first person nominated for the presidency while attending his party's convention.

In the **Arthur** administration, **Taft** was appointed collector for internal revenue.

Benjamin Harrison appointed **Taft** solicitor general in 1890. Then **Harrison** appointed him to the Federal Court of Appeals. **Herbert Hoover's** international reputation was established in World War I as the Chairman for Relief in Belgium with responsibility for food shipments. **Wilson** appointed **Hoover** Food Administrator in the wartime US in 1917 and after the war **Wilson** ordered **Hoover** to convert the Food administration into an agency for relief and reconstruction in Europe. **Truman** tapped **Hoover** to lead a similar commission in 1946. In 1971 **Nixon**, moving toward improved relationships with China, attempted to mollify our ally Taiwan by sending California Governor **Ronald Reagan** as a personal envoy to offer reassurances.

Moving Forward

Presidents have promoted or tried to promote each other into military and political positions and even judicial positions. They have also opposed each other's job possibilities.

Military

Wars shaped future presidents.

Veterans of the War of 1812 who became president included **Monroe** (Secretary of War), **Jackson** (hero of New Orleans), **Harrison** (Tippecanoe), **Tyler** (an officer in the Richmond brigade) and **Taylor** (hero of Fort **Harrison** named for **William Henry Harrison** in present day Terre Haute Indiana.)

Taylor, **Pierce** and **Grant** and all served in the Mexican-American War, the first two as generals. (So did Winfield Scott [Whig Party candidate in 1852], George McClellan [Democrat Party candidate in 1864], Robert E. Lee and Jefferson Davis.) The Civil War had **Grant**, **Hayes**, **Garfield**, **Arthur**, **Benjamin Harrison** and **McKinley** in the ranks. World War II veterans who promoted to the presidency included **Eisenhower**, **Kennedy**, **Johnson**, **Nixon**, **Ford**, **Carter**, **Reagan** and **George HW Bush**. A generation shift was evident in **Clinton's** defeat of two World War II heroes (**George HW Bush** and Bob Dole) and **Obama's** defeat of a Vietnam War hero, John McCain. Intra-generational splits saw **George W Bush** defeat two Vietnam War veterans (Albert Gore and John Kerry.)

Washington, **Grant** and **Eisenhower** were three of the most apolitical generals in American history. They were the only American soldiers to hold both supreme military and political power. **William Henry Harrison** and **Jackson** like **Washington** had experience in civil authority which **Taylor** did not. **Harrison** had been a territorial governor, a member of Congress and on a diplomatic mission. **Jackson** was a territorial governor, a senator, a member of Congress and a judge. **Washington** was chair of the Constitutional

Convention, a member of the Virginia House of Burgesses and had had to deal with the Continental Congress.

In 1775 **Adams** recruited **Washington** to lead the Continental Army against England, one of that era's superpowers. More than twenty years later – after war, independence, a new constitutional arrangement and **Washington's** two terms of office - the XYZ affair in which French officials tried to secure bribes from American diplomats incited war-fever in the US. **John Adams** called **Washington** back into service as commander in chief of the armed forces. **Washington** then named Alexander Hamilton as his second-in-command. **Adams** suggested that he appoint Aaron Burr as a brigadier general. **Washington** responded according to **Adams** much later: "By all that I have known and heard, Colonel Burr is a brave and able officer; but the question is, whether he has not equal talents at intrigue."

Monroe met **Washington** (and **Jefferson**) when he was a college student at William and Mary in Williamsburg in 1774. **Monroe** was under **Washington** in the retreat from New York in 1776. Later he was one of the first to cross the Delaware and **Washington** promoted him from Lieutenant to Captain. In 1777-78 **Monroe** was at Valley Forge. In 1779 **Washington** wrote a letter of recommendation for him: "I take occasion to express to you the high opinion I have of his worth." In 1779 **Monroe** was appointed a lieutenant colonel in the Virginia militia and made an aide to the governor, **Thomas Jefferson.** In 1780 the British took Charleston and Governor **Jefferson** sent 22 year-old **James Monroe** to scout out the military situation in the Carolinas. **Monroe** was instructed to set up a type of express system 40 miles apart so as to get information to Richmond at the rate of 120 miles per day. **Monroe** was gone two months.

William Henry Harrison grew up in a prominent Virginia family and received his military commission from **George Washington**. (During the Revolution his father had been the official correspondent for the Congress with **Washington** in the field.) As territorial governor of Indiana in 1812 **Harrison** went to Kentucky to organize the defense of the West. The governor of Kentucky and other leading citizens including Henry Clay got him appointed general of their military and **Harrison** marched north. When **Madison** heard about the decision in Kentucky he made **Harrison** a brigadier-general giving him orders to re-take Detroit from the British, or, as the War Department directive read: "to regain the ground that has been lost by the Surrender of Detroit..." In late 1812 **Harrison** wrote Acting Secretary of War **Monroe** advising against an attack on British positions at Detroit but the city was regained in 1813 after naval victories on the Great Lakes and **Harrison's** victory at the Battle of Thames.

In 1812 after American were driven out of Fort Dearborn (the future Chicago), Fort Mackinac, and Fort Detroit, Captain **Zachary Taylor** successfully defended Fort **Harrison. Taylor** gave this report to **William Henry Harrison:** "My presence of mind did not for a moment forsake me. I saw, by throwing off part of the roof that joined the blockhouse that was on fire...the whole row of buildings might be saved." As a result, **James Madison** promoted **Taylor** to the status of brevet major. In 1812 **Madison** had considered but then dropped the idea of bringing in **Jefferson** as Secretary of State. Instead, he picked **Monroe** who indicated in a letter to former President **Jefferson** that he discussed with President **Madison** taking a military command in the war with England. **Monroe** ultimately declined because he would only take the position of top commander of the armies. In 1814 **Monroe**, as Secretary of State and from a forward position, advised **Madison** to abandon the capital in the face of a British advance. **Madison** evacuated with valuable national property before the British burned Washington DC. After the burning **Monroe** and **Madison** returned by horse to the city. **Madison** was shaken for months over the destruction. For the first time in their careers **Madison** apparently fell under the control of **Monroe. Monroe**, using petitions from some of the remaining troops, pressured his way to being appointed Secretary of War in what Henry Adams later called a co*up d' etat.* Later that year **Monroe** directed the defense of Baltimore working to raise troops, assemble militias, get supplies, set up communications. He left tactics to the generals. Working around the clock he slept in his office. The British were turned back on September 14, 1814, in a battle that became the inspiration for our national anthem.

In 1812 **Madison** and **Monroe** discussed where to place **Harrison** in the western army. **Harrison** had had some bad publicity from the Battle of Tippecanoe in 1811 from the regular army commander. **Madison** agreed to the "great superiority" of his "qualifications" but believed his military knowledge to be "limited" and thought "a more extensive weight of his character would be of material importance." **Madison** had decided to put **Monroe** in charge to sort this out but then changed his mind when praise for **Harrison** came in. **Monroe** decided to decline anyway. As he wrote **Jefferson**: "I had off'd to proceed...to take command and was on the point of setting out when it was thought best to decline." Ultimately **Harrison** was replaced by **Jackson.** However both **Madison** and **Monroe** purportedly would have preferred that **Harrison** rather than **Jackson** take command in Mobile and New Orleans where **Jackson** made history. **Madison** signed the treaty to end the war without consulting **Jefferson**.

In 1817 **Monroe** recalled **Jackson** to military service to fight the Seminoles.

In the next generation, **Andrew Jackson** by then a former president advised **Polk** that in the event of war with England over issues concerning the Canadian border, **Taylor** should lead American forces. **Polk**, however, appointed **Taylor** to the northern campaign in the Mexican-American War in 1846 but became uneasy with his military performance viewing him as stolid and unimaginative. He thought **Taylor** lacked the "grasp of mind" to command and that he seemed "unwilling to express any opinion or to take any responsibility on himself." But he was stuck with him because he kept winning.

Grant was a young officer serving under **Taylor** in the Mexican-American War. During the early stages of the war, **Taylor's** casual appearance often got him criticism from officers. But Lieutenant **Grant** wrote, "No soldier could face either danger or responsibility more calmly than he. These are qualities more rarely found than genius or physical courage." **Grant** added: "He knew how to express what he wanted to say in the fewest well-chosen words, and would not sacrifice meaning to the construction of high-sounding sentences." **Grant** served under **Taylor** in the North and Winfield Scott at Vera Cruz through Mexico City. He later observed in his *Memoirs*: "Both were pleasant to serve under - **Taylor** was pleasant to serve with." **Taylor** reciprocated the respect. During a maneuver, **Grant** jumped into a river to demonstrate for green troops how to clear some underwater obstacles and received mocking comments from other officers. **Taylor** rode up and said: "I wish I had more officers like **Grant** who would stand ready to set a personal example when needed."

In the Civil War a young **William McKinley** impressed the lieutenant colonel **Rutherford B Hayes**, a generation older, by both his brave conduct and administrative ability and he was made commissary sergeant. They were together at Antietam. **McKinley** remained closely associated with **Hayes** throughout the war. **Hayes** described him as "a handsome bright, gallant boy" and "one of the bravest and finest officers in the army." **McKinley** on **Hayes**: "His whole nature seemed to change when in battle. From the sunny, agreeable, the kind, the generous, the gentle gentleman...he was, when the battle was on...intense and ferocious."

In 1862 **Lincoln** appointed **Andrew Johnson** military governor of Tennessee and commissioned him as a brigadier general. He was later quoted as saying that **Johnson** never embarrassed him. During the Civil War. **Lincoln** had persuaded **Garfield** to resign as a brigadier general and run for Congress.

Garry Wills has reported that "well-focused words were the medium through which **Grant** and **Lincoln** achieved their amazing degree of mutual sympathy and military accord." **Lincoln** explaining why he would not fire **Grant** after the Battle of Shiloh in 1862 said: "He fights." When **Lincoln** got complaints about **Grant** in 1862-3 before the battle of Vicksburg he said: "I think **Grant** has hardly a friend left, except myself." But he sent author Charles Dana to visit **Grant** and check-out rumors of drinking. Dana gave **Grant** a good report. **Lincoln** telegraphed to **Grant** after his victory at Vicksburg in 1863 that although he had had some misgivings about **Grant's** strategy: "I now wish to make the personal acknowledgement that you were right, and I was wrong." After victory at Chattanooga in 1863 **Lincoln** wrote **Grant**: "I wish to tender you, and all under your command, my more than thanks, my profoundest gratitude, for the skill, courage and perseverance with which you and they, over so great difficulties, have effected that important object. God bless you all." **Lincoln** also said about **Grant**. "**Grant** is the first general I have had. You know how it's been with all the rest. As soon as I put a man in command of the army, they all wanted me to be the general. Now it isn't so with **Grant**. He hasn't told me what his plans are. I don't know and I don't want to know." In 1864 **Lincoln** telegraphed **Grant**: "Hold on with a bull-dog gripe, and chew and choke, as much as possible." **Grant** laughed and said: "The President has more nerve than any of his advisors."

In the Congress in 1864 **Garfield** voted against a bill to reestablish the rank of lieutenant-general which had not existed since **Washington** (except by brevet) and the related recommendation urging **Grant** for the rank. (Earlier in the war, **Grant** had removed **Garfield** from a staff position in the army.) Later that year, **Lincoln** promoted **Grant** to lieutenant general. But he delayed the promotion until he was sure that **Grant** would not run for president in 1864 as was another general, George McClellan. (**Grant's** politics were unknown and like **Eisenhower** nearly a century later was courted by both Republicans and Democrats.) A friend of **Grant** brought **Lincoln** a letter from **Grant** disclaiming any intent to run with the specific reason that there was a chance to re-elect **Lincoln**. **Lincoln** said: "You will never know how gratifying that is to me. No man knows when the presidential grub gets to gnawing at him, just how deep it will get until he has tried it; and I didn't know but what there was one gnawing at **Grant**." **Lincoln** was right. **Grant** ran for President in 1868, 1872 and 1880.

In late 1864 William Tecumseh Sherman took Savannah. When **Lincoln** got the news a few days later he congratulated Sherman in writing and said "What next?" Then, catching himself: "I suppose it will be safer if I leave Gen. **Grant** and yourself to decide." In April 1965 he telegrammed **Grant** who was pursuing General Robert E. Lee's army in Virginia: "General Sheridan says, 'If the thing is pressed I think Lee will surrender.' Let the *thing* be pressed." **Grant** did and Lee surrendered a few days later at the Appomattox Court House after which a twenty-two year old **McKinley** was honorably discharged with the rank of brevet major with his commission signed by **Lincoln**.

During the Civil War Mexico repudiated its debts to France and the French invaded in violation of the **Monroe** Doctrine and installed an emperor, answering to Napoleon III. After the war, Mexican nationalist Benito Juarez wanted the Union army to intervene. Upon **Andrew Johnson's** orders **Grant** prepared for an invasion of Mexico to defeat Napoleon's Maximillian. It was unnecessary as the Mexicans toppled the puppet ruler themselves. (However, Union forces were rushed to the Texas/Mexican border under General Phil Sheridan, who made sure that the Mexicans got all the weapons and ammunition they needed to expel the French. American soldiers were discharged with their uniforms and rifles if they promised to join the Mexican Army to fight the French. The American Legion of Honor marched in the victory parade in Mexico City.)

During the latter stages of the Civil War **Hayes** appealed to **Grant** for assistance in prisoner trading with the Confederates. He wrote a relative that **Grant** "rules matters where he really attempts it."

In 1866 the US Supreme Court in *Ex Parte Milligan* voided the convictions of certain southern sympathizers on the grounds that military commissions were illegal when civilian courts were operating. **Garfield**, in his first case as a lawyer helped win this verdict and it is a landmark of constitutional law. One of the convicted southern sympathizers proceeded to sue members of the commission for damages. **Grant** asked **Benjamin Harrison** to represent the officials. **Harrison** argued in court that these southern sympathizers had "protracted the war" by "holding out aid and comfort to the enemy." He lost the case on points of law but won in the court of public opinion as the officials were only assessed five dollars.

After winning the presidency in 1896 **McKinley** was initially doubtful about appointing **Theodore Roosevelt** Assistant Secretary of the Navy: "I hope he has no preconceived plans that he would wish to drive through the moment he got in." **McKinley**, however, went ahead with the appointment. **TR** was a hyper-active Assistant Secretary instrumental in pushing the US to war with Spain.

During the World War II **FDR** sent **LBJ** on a fact-finding mission to the Pacific. **Johnson** received a medal for participation on a bombing mission even though the plane he was in returned to base after a blown generator. He maintained the plane was fired on by the Japanese. Others discounted this.

Stateside in 1942, **Eisenhower** drafted communiqués for **FDR** to send to General Douglas MacArthur who was fighting a holding action in the Philippines. MacArthur blamed **Eisenhower**, **FDR** and George Marshall for the defeat of US forces there that year. In 1943 after the fall of Italian fascist Benito Mussolini, **FDR** still pressed unconditional surrender while **Eisenhower** would have offered more lenient terms to Italy.

In late 1943 **FDR** needed to decide who would lead the reconquest of Europe. Army chief of Staff George C. Marshall had earned the assignment by his masterful buildup of the US military since 1939. **Roosevelt** was in Tunis talking about the issue with **Dwight Eisenhower** who at the time was the American commander in London. **FDR** told him, "**Ike**, you and I know who was chief of staff during the last years of the Civil War but practically no one else knows, although the names of the field generals - **Grant**, of course, and Lee and Jackson, Sherman, Sheridan and the others - every schoolboy knows them. I hate to think that fifty years from now practically no one will know who George Marshall was. That is why I want George to have the big command. He is entitled to establish his place in history as a great general." But **FDR** also felt he needed Marshall in Washington. He knew the world military situation better than anyone. So, ultimately, he picked **Eisenhower** to head-up what became D-Day. He told Marshall, "I feel I could not sleep at night with you out of the country." Marshall who had not campaigned for the job and had only said that he would do whatever **FDR** wanted him to do accepted the decision without any questions or comment. In that role, **Eisenhower** led a cross-channel invasion - a feat that eluded both Napoleon and Hitler.

FDR was negative toward Charles DeGaulle whereas **Eisenhower** was positive. However, **FDR** agreed with **Eisenhower** over Prime Minister Winston Churchill's objections to bomb the French transportation system to isolate Normandy as much as possible before D-Day. In 1950 after the start of the Korean War **Truman** requested that **Eisenhower** take command of NATO. **Eisenhower** who, as a five-star general was always on active duty responded: "I am a soldier and am ready to respond to whatever orders my superiors...may care to issue to me." He insisted that **Truman** "order" him.

Sometimes applications for jobs were denied. After the Battle of Tippecanoe in 1811 **Andrew Jackson** wrote **William Henry Harrison** offering his services. Nothing resulted. When the War of 1812 started **Andrew Jackson** raised a group of 2500 volunteers and offered his command to **James Madison**. It wasn't accepted either, possibly because of a previous association **Jackson** had had with Aaron Burr. In 1911 as conditions in revolutionary Mexico deteriorated, **TR** saw the need for American involvement, writing President **Taft**: "I most earnestly hope that we will not have to intervene... But, if by any remote chance... there should be a serious war, a war in which Mexico was backed by Japan or some other big powers, then I would wish immediately to apply for permission to raise a division of, such as the regiment I commanded in Cuba." He went on in great detail telling the amused President whom he would select for division commanders. In 1913 **TR** stayed on message, warning his cousin, Assistant Secretary of the Navy **Franklin Roosevelt**, of the possibility of war with Mexico or Japan. In 1917 he was still at it. **TR** had been harshly critical of **Wilson's** reluctance to commit the US to the First World War but when war came **TR** volunteered to lead a volunteer unit to Europe. He said to **Wilson**, "Mr. President, what I have said and thought and what others have said and thought is all dust in a windy street, if we can make your message good. Of course, it amounts to nothing if we cannot make it good. But if we can translate it into fact, then it will rank as a great state paper, with the great state papers of **Washington** and **Lincoln**." After making the request **TR** told **Wilson** aide Colonel House: "After all, I'm only asking to be allowed to die." House supposedly responded: "Oh? Did you make that quite clear to the President?" In the Senate, **Harding** worked to get **Roosevelt** appointed to lead the volunteer unit. **Wilson** declined **TR's** request and in an obvious snub bestowed on **William Howard Taft** the honorific of Major General for his service in the American Red Cross. **TR**: "Major General **Taft**! How the Kaiser must have trembled when he heard the news!"

B. Politics

John Adams' hiring policies greatly shaped the county. Not only did he tap **Washington** to lead the Continental Army, he appointed John Marshall Chief Justice of the United States and in 1776 **Adams** asked **Jefferson** to write the Declaration of Independence. Later, **Adams** recounted the conversation with **Jefferson** asserting that Jefferson said that **Adams** should write it. This conversation ensued:

Adams: "I will not,"

Jefferson: "You should do it,"

Adams: "Oh! No."

Jefferson: "Why will you not? You ought to do it."

Adams: "I will not."

Jefferson: "Why?"

Adams: "Reasons enough."

Jefferson: "What can be your reasons?"

Adams: "Reason first, you are a Virginian, and a Virginian ought to appear at the head of this business. Reason second, I am obnoxious, suspected, and unpopular. You are very much otherwise. Reason third, you can write ten times better than I can."

Jefferson: "Well, if you are decided, I will do as well as I can."

Adams: "Very well. When you have drawn it up, we will have a meeting."

In 1782 while serving in Holland, **Adams** sent his 14 year-old son **John Quincy Adams** as a translator for an American diplomat to St. Petersburg, a 1200 mile journey by coach.

George Washington appointed **Thomas Jefferson** as the first Secretary of State. But **Jefferson** was the fourth choice. John Jay had held that position under the Articles of Confederation but he preferred the job of Chief Justice. **John Adams** was Vice President. Benjamin Franklin was old and ill. That left the ambassador to France, **Thomas Jefferson** whom **Washington** then appointed. **Madison** persuaded **Thomas Jefferson** to accept.

At the end of **Washington's** first term, **Jefferson** resigned. Yet, **Jefferson** contributed to one of the most important decisions in the new republic by urging **Washington** to run for a second term and to help keep the country unified. **Washington** offered the Secretary of State job to **Madison** who declined as a sign of his growing distance from **Washington**. **Washington** observed with disfavor the development of pro-French democratic societies and said, "I should be extremely sorry if Mr. **M-----n** *from any cause whatsoever* should get entangled with them, or their politics."

Madison and **Jefferson** began to form an opposition party and **Washington**, after his own retirement, never mentioned **Madison** again in his letters or writing. **Jefferson** suggested in 1795 that **Madison** take the Republican nomination to succeed **Washington**.

In 1794 **George Washington** appointed **John Quincy Adams** age 27 to be ambassador to the Netherlands. **John Adams** wrote his son after he took up his post: "Go on, my son, in your glorious Career and may the Blessings of God crown you with success." **John Quincy Adams** went on assignment from there to London where he courted his future wife. **Washington** then assigned him to Portugal. **George Washington** wrote **John Adams** that: "I give it as my decided opinion that Mr. (**John Quincy**) **Adams** is the most valuable public character that we have abroad, and there remains no doubt in my mind that he will prove himself to be the most ablest of our diplomatic corps if he is now to be brought into that line or into any other public work."

When **John Adams** became president, he re-assigned **John Quincy Adams** to the position of ambassador to Prussia. The younger **Adams** wrote his father that he was worried that people would see this as nepotism saying that his position had a "degraded and humiliating aspect." President **Adams** thought he needed his son in Prussia to report on the upheavals of the Napoleonic Era. After his defeat in 1800 **Adams** recalled **John Quincy Adams** to spare him from being dismissed by the incoming **Jefferson** administration.

In 1794 **George Washington** offered **Madison** the role of ambassador to France but **Madison** declined (and he would later decline **John Adams'** similar offer). **Washington** then appointed **James Monroe** in part to conciliate France - although **Monroe** and **Madison** had suggested Aaron Burr. **Monroe** wrote from France during a period of controversy over the Jay Treaty which he believed favored England over France, "Poor **Washington**. Into what hands has he falled!" For his part, **Washington** called **Monroe** a "mere tool in the hands of the French government" and he was recalled in 1796 with **Washington** citing his "uneasiness and dissatisfaction" with his work and "other concurring circumstances." (**John Adams** had also received reports from his son **John Quincy Adams** who was abroad at the time that **Monroe** was telling the French that the United States had allied with England.)

This issue escalated. By the time **Monroe** got back to the US, **John Adams** was President and he expressed his displeasure at the warm send-off the French government had given the sacked ambassador. **Adams** said in 1797: "that the honor done, the publicity and solemnity given to the audience of leave to a disgraced minister recalled in displeasure for misconduct, was a studied insult to the government of my country." **Monroe** raged at the "dishonorable & unmanly attack of our insane President." He wrote a 400-page treatise in defense of his diplomatic mission to France. **Jefferson** called it "masterful." **Washington** made 40 pages of notes. In these notes **Washington** noted that **Monroe** criticized his address to Congress in 1795 viewing it as unsympathetic to France and mused: "If Mr. **Monroe** should ever fill the Chair of government he may (and it is presumed he would be well enough disposed) let the French minister frame his speeches." As this shows, presidents have trouble seeing others filling their job. In the twentieth century, **Nixon** once said to Governor Nelson A. Rockefeller of New York: "Can you see **Gerald Ford** sitting in this chair?" In an Oval Office conversation that was surreptitiously taped in 1971 **Nixon** said: "With a **Reagan** in here, you could damn well almost get yourself in a nuclear war."

Early in **Jefferson's** first term, **John Quincy Adams** was turned out of a sinecure, a commissioner of bankruptcy, when new legislation placed these positions under the control of the President. **Jefferson,** practicing what another century would call plausible deniability, later said he didn't know that **Adams** was let go.

By 1802 **Jefferson** was under a great deal of pressure to respond to presumed Napoleonic designs on Louisiana which France had just reacquired from Spain. It was difficult to control the Congress and western legislatures were passing resolutions to put soldiers nearby to take Louisiana at the first sign of French troops. A Spanish official had closed New Orleans to American commerce. **Jefferson** wanted to avoid war and wrote his diplomat in Paris that French occupation of New Orleans was not "important enough to risk a breach of peace." But he summed up the whole situation to **Monroe** that "the agitation of the public mind on occasion of the late suspension of our right of deposit at New Orleans is extreme. In the Western country it is natural, and grounded in honest motives; in the seaports it proceeds from a desire for war, which increases the mercantile lottery; in the Federalists generally, and especially those of Congress, the object is to force us into war if possible, in order to derange our finances; or if this cannot be done, to attach the Western country to them as their best friends, and thus get again into power. Remonstrances, memorials, etc., are now circulating through the whole of the Western country, and signed by the body of the people. The measures we have been pursuing, being invisible, do not satisfy their minds.

35

Something sensible, therefore, has become necessary." He then asked **Monroe** to go to Paris to buy New Orleans and the Floridas.

Monroe, however, was reluctant to go but **Jefferson** responded: "The circumstances are such as to render it impossible to decline. ...on the event of this mission depends on the future destinies of the republic." The **Monroe** mission was widely predicted to be an alternative or a last-chance before war with France. **Jefferson's** charge to **Monroe** was to help the other American diplomats already in France in "enlarging and more effectively securing our rights and interests in the river Mississippi and in the territories eastward thereof." **Monroe** went well beyond that charge. At the cost of fifteen million dollars, he gained for the US a territory larger than France, Spain, Portugal, Italy, Germany, Holland, Switzerland and the British Isles – combined. In the 1803-05 period **Jefferson** and Secretary of State **James Madison** relied on **Monroe** working in European capitals to extend the gains of the Louisiana Purchase to try to get West Florida from Spain. In this he did not succeed.

In 1806 **Monroe** was ambassador in England trying to negotiate a new treaty affecting issues like impressments, trade and neutral rights at sea. **Monroe** told the British "that the President wished to postpone the matter until he could include impressment and neutral rights in the treaty; that we must begin *de novo;* that America was a young and thriving country; that in 1794 she had had little experience, since then she knew her interests better; and that a new treaty should omit certain things from that of 1794, and include others. The most urgent part was that which respected our seaman." And yet, from the start of his time as ambassador to England, **Monroe** placed less emphasis on the issue of impressments than did **Madison** and **Jefferson** who seemed to undercut **Monroe** by sending Thomas Pinckney to assist him but with conditions that England would reject. **Jefferson** may not have wanted a treaty and may have wanted to thwart **Monroe's** success so as to assist with **Madison's** ascension to the presidency. **Monroe** and Pinckney ultimately set aside the instructions and negotiated a treaty that **Jefferson** refused to submit to the Senate. From **Jefferson's** perspective, the proposed treaty with Britain failed because it did not resolve impressments.

In late 1807 **Monroe** left Europe for the US. Since the Louisiana Purchase in 1803, most of his efforts had been failures. He had been abroad for four years, shuttling by stage coach between Madrid, Paris and London. He had served under **Washington** in France earlier and now had the experience of having been rejected by both **Washington** and **Jefferson**.

Shortly after he left the presidency **Jefferson** warned **Madison** to never yield on the issue of impressments. He thought it would confirm to England how the US could be bullied in negotiations. "They did it in Jay's case, were near it in **Monroe's**." In 1813 Secretary of State **Monroe's** initial instructions to the peace commissioners who were to join **John Quincy Adams** were that no treaty should be concluded without a stipulation against impressments. In 1814, however, as negotiations with England ending the war got to the crucial stages, **James Madison's** cabinet advised him to refrain from insisting that the British practice of impressments end and **Monroe** instructed the US delegation led by **Adams**: "...you may omit any stipulation on the subject of impressment, if found indispensably necessary to terminate it. You will, of course, not recur to this expedient until all your efforts to adjust the controversy in a more satisfactory manner have failed."

In 1814 the Treaty of Ghent ending the War of 1812 was signed. When the treaty reached the US it got none of the protests of the Jay Treaty or the **Monroe** Treaty of 1806. The only issue was that the American commissioners had signed their names below the British commissioners instead of on a parallel line. Secretary of State **Monroe** wrote **John Quincy Adams** to tell him that this had been noted in the ratification as non-precedent setting.

Madison appointed **John Quincy Adams** ambassador to England, a post previously held by **John Adams**, and **Monroe** and later by **Van Buren** and **Buchanan** (and **Lincoln's** son and **JFK's** father). In 1815-16, congressional caucuses determined the Republican nomination. Some high-level politicking took place. **Jefferson** may have persuaded **Jackson** to withdraw from the race. **Madison,** like **Jefferson** eight years earlier, was outwardly neutral but it was assumed that **Monroe** had his support. When **Monroe** was president and thought of appointing **Jackson** as ambassador to Russia, **Jefferson** said, "Why good God! He would breed you a quarrel before he had been there a month."

In 1817 while he was still in Europe where he had served in key diplomatic posts for 8 years **John Quincy Adams** received by letter **Monroe's** offer to be Secretary of State. **John Adams** urged him "to accept it without hesitation." As Secretary of State **John Quincy Adams** worked well with President **Monroe**. **Thomas Jefferson** wrote: "They were made for each other." In 1819 **John Adams** said: "a more happy combination is not to be expected" and he hoped for **Monroe** to be re-elected. (**John Adams** had obviously mellowed over the previous 25 years.)

In the 1820 election **William Henry Harrison** was an elector for **Monroe**. As he recognized the new Latin American states in 1822 **Monroe** considered sending **Jackson** as an emissary but thought he was too controversial.

Martin Van Buren supported New York Governor DeWitt Clinton over **Madison** in 1812 but said that he doubted Clinton could win the presidency. Already a party man, **Van Buren** thought **Madison** would gain from patriotic war fever and could use patronage to cement his renomination. He supported Clinton only because he felt bound by caucus action taken previously and he stipulated that Clinton should not ally with the Federalists. **Van Buren** supported William Crawford of Georgia over **Jackson** in 1824 while **John Quincy Adams** initially considered **Jackson** as a running mate. After the bitter 1824 election **John Quincy Adams** offered **Jackson** the position of Secretary of War but **Jackson** declined. (He had been considered for that same position under **Monroe** eight years earlier as had **William Henry Harrison**.)

Although they had little in common, **Tyler** was supported by Virginia friends of **John Quincy Adams** in his defeat of John Randolph for the US Senate in 1827 as **Adams** chose between – from his perspective – the lesser of two evils.

Facing personal financial problems in the early 1820s **William Henry Harrison** tried unsuccessfully to get **Monroe** to appoint him ambassador to Mexico. He also hoped for the appointment from **John Quincy Adams**. But **Adams** went with a Congressman recommended by **Monroe**. **Harrison** then sought the ambassadorship to Colombia, writing a friend about the job: "My great object is to save a little money." It paid nine thousand dollars per year. **John Quincy Adams** appointed him but wrote in his diary: "**Harrison** wants the mission to Colombia much more than it wants him, or than is wanted by the public interest."

Harrison served in Colombia only a short amount of time. When **Jackson** was elected he promptly removed **Harrison** from the post. A cabinet member who had served under **Harrison** in the War of 1812 urged **Jackson** to keep **Harrison** saying that, "If you had seen him as I did, at the Battle of Thames, you would, I think, let him alone." **Jackson** replied, "You may be right. I reckon you are, but thank God, I didn't see him there." **Jackson** did not consider this removal as a negative reflection. He wrote **Van Buren**: "Nothing has occurred to the necessity of his early departure."

As he left Colombia **Harrison**, worried about the move to a dictatorship by Simon Bolivar, wrote him: "Are you willing that your name should descend to posterity amongst the mass of those whose fame has been derived from shedding human blood, without a single advantage to the human race? Or shall it be united to that of **Washington** as the founder and the father of a great and happy people?"

When he returned to the US Harrison was accused of fomenting anti-Bolivar plots. He defended himself by writing a pamphlet that included the letter he had written Bolivar. **Madison** wrote him: "Whatever may have been the different views taken of the letter to Bolivar, none can contest the intellectual literary merit stamped upon it, or be insensible to the Republican feelings which prompted it." **Harrison** visited **John Quincy Adams** who wrote in his diary: "The conduct of Bolivar has for many years been equivocal.... **Harrison** was but a short time there, but long enough to get involved in some of their party divisions. It was perhaps impossible to avoid it." **Harrison** called on **Jackson** and was "very graciously" received.

Pierce campaigned for **Jackson** in 1828 and **William Henry Harrison** attempted unsuccessfully to get the vice presidential nomination to run with **Adams** that year. In 1832 **Buchanan** was suggested as a running mate for **Jackson** but **Jackson** chose **Van Buren** and selected **Buchanan** to be the ambassador to Russia. In 1833 **Jackson** named **Lincoln** postmaster of New Salem, Illinois. A decade-and-a-half later **Zachary Taylor** offered **Lincoln** the governorship of Oregon territory but he declined. In 1843 after two cabinet members were killed in the explosion of the ship, the *Princeton*, **Tyler** tried to bring Democrats into his administration. He offered the Navy Secretary to **Polk** who, after consulting with **Jackson,** respectfully declined.

In 1844 **Jackson** opposed his one-time protégé, former President **Van Buren,** in his quest for the nomination in favor of the winner **Polk** because of **Van Buren's** opposition to the acquisition of Texas. In 1845 **Polk** made **Pierce** US Attorney for New Hampshire as reward for supporting him on the annexation of Texas. In 1846 **Polk** offered **Pierce** the position of Attorney General in an unusually warm letter but **Pierce** declined.

As a soldier **Grant** hadn't voted. As a civilian he voted for the first time in 1856. As he wrote his father: "I voted for **Buch.** for President to defeat Freemont (*sic*) but not because he was my first choice." He thought **Buchanan** would more likely be able to preserve the Union. He also said: "I voted for **Buchanan** because I didn't know him and voted against Fremont because I did know him."

As the Civil War neared in 1861 **Pierce** wrote **Van Buren** noting that there were five living ex-presidents and suggesting that **Van Buren** call them together in Philadelphia "where the Constitution was framed" to try to reach some sort of agreement to prevent disunion. He said to **Van Buren**, the most senior: "No man can with propriety summons such a meeting but yourself." **Van Buren** demurred saying that **Pierce** who had more hope for success should call for the meeting adding that if **Pierce** called for it: "I will accept the invitation without hesitation." There the matter was dropped.

Tyler went on to work on a peace commission to try to prevent secession and consulted regularly with **Buchanan**. **Lincoln**, who was soon to take the oath of office told the peace commission: "The Constitution will not be preserved and defended until it is enforced and obeyed in every part of every one of the United States." And, "In a choice of evils, war may not always be the worst." From this, **Tyler** joined the Confederacy.

In 1860 **Fillmore** opposed **Lincoln's** election - as did a future president, a young **Cleveland** - and in the war-time 1864 election the three living ex-Presidents - **Fillmore**, **Pierce** and **Buchanan** - opposed **Lincoln's** re-election. **Fillmore** felt that defeating **Lincoln** was necessary to save the US from "military despotism" and "national bankruptcy." A future president was ambivalent that year: **Hayes** was unconcerned over the possible election victory of George McClellan thinking the war would not be affected. Another future president, **Garfield,** sided with **Lincoln** over his mentor Salmon P. Chase when Radical Republicans who were dissatisfied with **Lincoln's** reconstruction plans sought to replace the President with Chase as the nominee. "The administration is not all I could wish but it would be a national calamity to alienate the radical element from Mr. **Lincoln**..." **Lincoln** appointed Chase Chief Justice. After the 1864 election, **Grant** said: "The overwhelming majority received by Mr. **Lincoln** and the quiet with which the election went off, will provide a terrible damper to the rebels. It will be worth more than a victory in the field both in its effect on the rebels and its influence abroad." In 1866 **Grant** declined **Andrew Johnson's** appointment of him as ambassador to Mexico, correctly perceiving it as a way to get him out of Washington DC. **Grant** averred in a cabinet meeting, looking directly at **Johnson**: "No power on earth can compel me to it." In 1867 **Grant** also declined **Johnson's** appointment as Secretary of War, one of the core events in the impeachment crisis.

Although he formally supported James G. Blaine of Maine for president in 1876, **Garfield** encouraged his fellow Ohioan, **Hayes,** writing him in March of 1876: "We should give you the solid vote of the Ohio delegation and await the break up, which must come when the weaker candidates drop out." **Hayes** got the nomination and the Republican national committee put **Benjamin Harrison** on a speaking tour for him. In the post-election crisis that year **Grant** asked Member of Congress **Garfield** to go to New Orleans to investigate the vote in Louisiana. **Garfield** wrote that "we have only one duty, to ascertain who is elected and see that he is so declared." Once there, **Garfield** gave **Hayes** assurances that he carried Louisiana.

In 1877 **Hayes** wanted **Harrison** for his cabinet but was thwarted by Indiana state politics. That same year **Hayes** urged **Garfield** not to run for the Senate because he figured he would be elected Speaker of the House of Representatives. **Garfield** doubted that he would be elected Speaker but went along with it and in the end got neither and resented being asked to make the sacrifice. **Garfield** put in his diary that **Hayes** wanted him to succeed him.

In 1880, **Benjamin Harrison** went to New York State to campaign because **Chester Alan Arthur** pleaded: "We need General **Harrison**." **Grant** had allowed his name to be put forward against **Garfield** for the Republican nomination that year and his role in the ensuing campaign was at first uncertain. But he soon told **Arthur** who was effectively managing the campaign: "I concluded to break other engagement that might conflict and go at any time you might fix." **Arthur** then proceeded to arrange **Grant's** campaign travel and **Grant** became the first former president to campaign for his party's national ticket.

In a quasi-campaign trip in Buffalo, **Garfield** was joined by **Harrison** and **McKinley.** In 1880-81 **Garfield** tried unsuccessfully to recruit **Lincoln's** one-time secretary John Hay to be his private secretary. In 1882 **Arthur** appointed **Grant** as a commissioner to negotiate a trade agreement with Mexico. (The treaty was negotiated and ratified by the Senate but required enabling legislation by Congress which failed to happen.)

TR campaigned for **Benjamin Harrison** in 1888 and **Harrison** appointed him Civil Service Commissioner. **TR** was zealous in the job. **Harrison** said that **TR** "wanted to put an end to all the evil in the world between sunrise and sunset." Four years later, **Cleveland** reappointed **TR**. Four years out of office, **Benjamin Harrison** traveled and spoke for **William McKinley** in 1896.

In 1902 **Cleveland** advised **TR** on a coal strike. **Cleveland** was the only living ex-president and the strike was **TR's** first major crisis as president. The mayors of more than a hundred of the largest cities in the US called for nationalization of the industry. **Cleveland** had intervened to end the 1894 Pullman strike in the name of free enterprise but to **TR** he counseled patience. The Attorney General of the US also advised **Roosevelt** that he had no constitutional basis to intervene. **TR** disagreed saying that he would not act "on the **Buchanan** principle of striving to find some constitutional reason for inaction."

Cleveland sold his stock in coal at depressed prices and agreed to serve on a commission of inquiry into the strike at **TR's** request: "You rightly appreciate my reluctance to assume any public service" he wrote **TR**. He didn't serve however as coal management rejected **Cleveland** as a member.

In 1902 when **Woodrow Wilson** was appointed president of Princeton University, **TR** said he was "overjoyed" and called **Wilson** "a perfect trump." In retirement, **Cleveland** associated with Princeton and walked with **Wilson** in graduations.

In 1900 **McKinley** appointed **Benjamin Harrison** to a ceremonial seat at the new International Court of the Hague. Later, saying that **Taft** was "just the man for the Philippines," **William McKinley** appointed him Governor General of the islands. **Taft** told him that he was not the right person since he has opposed acquisition of the islands. **McKinley** responded: "We've got them. What I want you to do now is go there and establish civil government." While **Taft** considered the matter **McKinley** wrote a friend: "A commission made up of the men of the character of Judge **Taft** will give repose and confidence to the country and will be an earnest of my high purpose to bring to those peoples the blessings of peace and liberty. ..." **Taft** performed his duties as governor there in a way that led to a good outcome. Consider:

- The build-up to the Spanish-American War was a problem inherited by **McKinley**.
- The war itself was abetted by William Randolph Hearst and Joseph Pulitzer.
- The war was costly. Thousands of men were mobilized who never saw action but who ultimately drew pensions.
- The British and German fleets were near the Philippines at the War's end. The Philippines became a US protectorate.
- Local Philippine leader Emilio Aguinaldo felt betrayed leading to an insurrection which lasted a year-and-a-half and led to the appointment of **Taft**.
- Eventually Aguinaldo was captured. He allied with the US and the military government became a civilian government under **Taft**.
- In 1916 the US announced the intention of granting the Philippines independence as soon as possible. World War II interrupted progress and independence was granted on July 4, 1946.

Taft brought as much foreign policy experience to the presidency as anyone since **John Quincy Adams. Buchanan, Hoover** and **George HW Bush** also brought a great deal of foreign policy experience to the presidency. All five were one-termers.

In 1909 **TR** as ex-president was in London when the king of England died. **Taft** asked him to represent the US at the ceremonies. By 1910 **Taft** and **TR** had drifted apart and **Taft's** allies including his Vice President blocked **TR** from temporary chair of the New York state Republican convention. In 1912 **TR** ran against **Taft** and both lost to **Wilson**.

In 1915 **TR** helped **Hoover** fend off accusations from Henry Cabot Lodge that he was violating the Logan Act which forbade Americans from dealing with an enemy. This was in connection with **Hoover's** work bringing relief to Belgium. **TR** told **Hoover** about Lodge, "I will hold his hand." That same year **Calvin Coolidge** ran for Lieutenant Governor of Massachusetts and was helped by Ohio politician **Warren Harding**.

During World War I at **Wilson's** request, **Taft** served on the War Labor Board. In 1918 both **TR** and **Taft** came to Massachusetts to campaign for **Coolidge** for governor. **TR**: "Mr. **Coolidge** is a high-minded public servant of the type which Massachusetts has always been honorably anxious to see at the head of state government."

In 1920 President-elect **Harding** gave **Hoover** the choice of being Secretary of Interior or Secretary of Commerce. He chose the latter and kept it in 1924 when **Coolidge** offered to appoint him the Secretary of Agriculture.

As a president who had been elevated from the vice presidency upon the death of **Harding** a year before, **Coolidge** was not considered a sure-thing for the 1924 Republican nomination. Other than **TR**, no elevated vice president had been renominated. **Taft** talked with and corresponded with party-insiders on **Coolidge's** behalf. In the campaign **Coolidge's** allies brought out a quote from the late **Theodore Roosevelt** against third-party challenger Robert Lafollette that he was "a most sinister enemy of democracy." **Hoover** used his California connections to defeat a Progressive Senator Hiram Johnson who had challenged **Coolidge** for the Republican nomination.

FDR helped mentor a future president, **Lyndon Johnson**. In 1935 he made **LBJ** director of the National Youth Administration, an agency dedicated to helping young people get training and education. (In 1939 **FDR** offered **LBJ** the directorship of the Rural Electrification Administration. **Johnson** turned him down preferring to stay in the Congress.) On the day after the attack on Pearl Harbor, Congressman **LBJ** who was in the Naval Reserve telegrammed **FDR**: "As a member of the Naval Reserve of the United States Navy, I hereby urgently request my commander in chief to assign me immediately to active duty with the fleet." He got a desk job helping war production and took a "leave of absence" from Congress with his wife running the congressional office. **FDR** then assigned him to visit Douglas MacArthur in Australia. **FDR** later asked all members of Congress to return.

In 1940 **FDR** offered Senator **Harry Truman** of Missouri an appointment to the Interstate Commerce Commission if he would withdraw from his re-election race in the Democrat primary in favor of another candidate. **Truman** stayed in the race and was re-elected.

In 1946 **Harry Truman** appointed **Herbert Hoover** as honorary chairman of the Famine Emergency Committee to address food shortages around the world. **Truman**: "I have a job for you that nobody else in the country can do and you know more about feeding nations and people than anybody in the world." **Hoover** had led a similar effort in World War I. In that same year **Truman** considered **Eisenhower** for Secretary of State. In 1947 **Truman** advised **Eisenhower** to accept the position of president of Columbia University and released him from his Chairman of the Joint Chiefs of Staff position. In 1949 **Truman** tried to get **Eisenhower** to run for the Senate from New York as a Democrat. New York Governor Thomas Dewey offered **Herbert Hoover** the vacant Senate seat. He declined after "prayerful consideration."

Hoover supported Bob Taft (the son of President **Taft**) against **Eisenhower** in 1952. In 1956, **Eisenhower** suggested to his Vice President **Richard Nixon** that he step down from that office and take a cabinet position in the next administration, an idea that went nowhere but did strain their relationship. Later that year **JFK's** father offered to **LBJ** that he would finance a presidential campaign against **Eisenhower** and **Nixon** if **Johnson** would take **JFK** as a running mate. **Johnson** declined because he calculated that **JFK's** father was actually assuming an **Eisenhower** victory and was preparing his son for 1960. In 1960 **Eisenhower** was lukewarm for **Nixon**.

In 1960 a young farmer named **Jimmy Carter** supported **Kennedy**, an unpopular stance in his part of the state of Georgia at the time.

In 1967 with the advocacy of Congressman **Ford** and former Vice President **Nixon**, **George HW Bush** was given a seat on the powerful

Ways and Means committee as a Congressional freshman. In 1967-68 **George HW Bush** campaigned for **Nixon.** Part of his job was to keep a watch on **Reagan** organizing in Texas. This began a **Bush-Reagan** rivalry that lasted until 1980. During this time **Bush's** father Prescott Bush and others tried to lay the groundwork for him to be nominated for Vice President in 1968. **Eisenhower** was persuaded to write **Nixon** suggesting that he give consideration to pick **Bush.** This effort was unsuccessful but with the help of presidents, **George HW Bush** got an impressive array of jobs over the next decade. The significance of these jobs can be seen in that in the seven elections between 1980 and 2004 a **Bush** was on the Republican ticket six times and five of those were Republican victories. (In 2015, Jeb Bush, the son and brother of presidents, was viewed as a top-tier candidate for the Republican nomination for president.)

In 1969 **George HW Bush** discussed with **LBJ** his hopes to leave the House of Representatives and run for the Senate and whether it was worth the risk. **LBJ** said, "Son, the difference between being a member of the Senate and a member of the House is the difference between chicken salad and chicken shit. Do I make my point?" **Nixon** told **George HW Bush** that if he ran and lost for the Senate in 1970 **Nixon** would assure a "soft landing."

Bush did run for the Senate and lost in 1970 and **Nixon** then appointed him UN Ambassador after first offering him the chair of the Republican National Committee. (**Nixon** first offered the UN post to a Democrat, Daniel Patrick Moynihan who accepted it and then withdrew. Moynihan was later appointed UN ambassador by **Ford** and subsequently elected to the US Senate from New York where he served four terms. He always spoke well of **Nixon.**) In 1972 **Nixon** appointed **Bush** to the chair of the Republican National Committee. **Bush** was reluctant and his wife was opposed. He told her, "You can't turn a president down." **Bush** then took over the RNC just as it went into the crisis of the Watergate scandal.

Nixon put **Ford** in a group called the "Political Group for 1970." It had congressional leadership and some of **Nixon's** staff like Patrick Buchanan.

In 1973 when **Nixon** picked **Ford** to be his Vice President, **Ford** was actually his fourth choice. His preferences were:

1. John Connally - but as a recent Democrat not confirmable.
2. **Reagan** - too right to be confirmable.
3. Nelson Rockefeller - too left to be confirmable.
4. **Ford**

Ford placed **George HW Bush** as liaison to China. (In accepting the Republican nomination in 1988 **Bush** reflected on his propensity to take risks such as going into the wartime Navy in 1942 rather than college. Also: "President **Ford** offered me an ambassadorship to England or France - pretty glamorous duty. I opted for China.") **Ford** later made him Director of the CIA. The latter job may have been Defense Secretary Donald Rumsfeld's attempt to sideline a political rival in 1975. **George HW Bush** did not want the appointment to CIA Director. In the confirmation process **Ford** was obliged to rule out selecting **Bush** for his 1976 running mate. In 1976 a thirty-year old **Bill Clinton** worked for the **Carter** campaigning in Arkansas while running for state Attorney General.

During the 1976 campaign **Reagan** was asked if he would put **Nixon** into his cabinet. **Nixon** was by then a couple of years into his forced resignation due to the Watergate scandal. **Reagan** answered loyally, saying that he couldn't respond "until history itself... tells us more about the situation that saw his resignation...unless history gives us a different perspective on Watergate than the one we have now."

Ford endorsed **George HW Bush** over **Reagan** in the 1980 primaries but **Reagan** still considered offering the vice presidency to **Ford** even though **Ford** had served as President.

Reagan sent **Carter** to receive American hostages released by Iran in 1981.

In retirement during **Reagan's** first term **Nixon** thought **George HW Bush** was not adequate for playing the "bad cop" role that he himself had played for **Eisenhower**. He urged **Reagan** to consider dropping **Bush** from the ticket and in 1986 **Nixon** predicted that the Democrats would defeat **George HW Bush** for the presidency. He was wrong.

In 1988 **George HW Bush** surprised the political world by his selection of Indiana Senator Dan Quayle as a running mate. Questions about his draft status during the Vietnam War and his readiness surfaced. **Reagan** stood by **Bush**: "Vice President **Bush** has made an outstanding selection of Senator Quayle as his running mate. I know he will be a great vice president." Nevertheless, **Bush** later admitted in his diary that he had erred. **George W Bush** was stunned at the decision to pick Quayle and tried to get his father to reverse it. In 1989 **Carter** was asked by the **Bush** administration to go to Panama to help oversee important elections. In 1990 **Bush** asked **Carter** to help with elections in Nicaragua. During the next two decades **Carter** observed elections throughout the world.

In the general election in 1988 **Nixon** advised **George HW Bush** to show his toughness by announcing that he would fire all of **Reagan's** cabinet and not to attack his opponent Michael Dukakis directly. "Anyone who tries to show strength by a strong voice and strong gestures conveys the opposite impression. The best way to convey a sense of strength on television is quiet control of power." **Bush** replied by note: "Please keep sending me those Nixonian tidbits." In late 1988 **Ford** and **Carter** urged President-elect **Bush** to drop a "no new taxes" pledge he had made in the campaign but **Nixon** urged him to stick with his pledge.

In 2005 **George W Bush** sent his father and **Clinton** to organize relief following a tsunami that had hit Asian countries. In 2008 **Clinton** opposed **Obama** in the race against Hillary Clinton for the Democrat nomination. In 2010 after an earthquake caused great loss of life and property in Haiti, **Obama** asked **George W Bush** and **Clinton** to organize relief. **Obama**: "This is one of those moments that calls out for American leadership. **Clinton** said, "I'd like to thank President **Bush** for agreeing to do this, and for the concern he showed for Haiti."

In addition to the obvious examples of **John Quincy Adams** and **George W Bush**, the children and close relatives of presidents have played a role in American life. **Van Buren's** son was active in the New York State Democrat Party during the **Pierce** administration as the party split over patronage, causing embarrassment for **Pierce**. **Andrew Jackson's** nephew ran for Vice President in 1856 from the American Party with **Fillmore** at the top of the ticket. **John Quincy Adams'** son Charles Francis Adams served with distinction as ambassador to England in the **Lincoln** administration charged with keeping England neutral in the Civil War. He succeeded. As his political fortunes ebbed in 1866 **Andrew Johnson** considered a cabinet shake-up which would have included placing **Grant** as Secretary of War and Charles Francis Adams as secretary of state.

In 1850 Charles Francis Adams had taken his son, Henry Adams to Washington DC where he met **Zachary Taylor**. This Adams became a great historian and later thought **Taylor** owed his election to **Martin Van Buren** and the Free Soil Party which had siphoned votes from the Democrat ticket.

Henry Adams became an important commentator on Presidents. He japed that **Grant's** initials stood for "uniquely stupid" and that "the progress of evolution from President **Washington** to President **Grant**, was alone evidence enough to upset Darwin." Henry Adams may be responsible for **Grant's** low historical reputation. He wrote: "A great soldier may be a baby politician." When **Hayes** left office Henry Adams said that **Hayes** had been a "most successful" president and he later wrote that **Benjamin Harrison** was the best President since **Lincoln**. Adams wrote that: "**(Theodore) Roosevelt** enjoyed a singularly direct nature and honest intent, but he lived naturally in restless agitation that would have worn out most tempers in a month, and his first year of Presidency showed a chronic excitement that made a friend tremble." He called **TR** "pure act." Later, observing **TR** out of office and moving to the left on social issues, Henry Adams wrote: "His mind has gone to pieces... He is, as **Taft** justly said, a neurotic..."

Lincoln's son Robert Lincoln served as Secretary of War under **Garfield**. The *New York Times* practically endorsed him for the

Republican nomination in 1884. He was also suggested as a vice president nominee. He took himself out of consideration. It is possible that his foes were planning to publicize his mother's insanity trial which had taken place a decade earlier and his role in committing her to a mental institution. He was mentioned again in 1888 and his continual demurrals seemed to add to his attractiveness and he stayed viable. He had appeal for southern blacks. He called the presidency "a gilded prison." President **Benjamin Harrison** appointed him Ambassador to Great Britain from 1889 -1893. Later he was counsel for the Pullman Company during the 1894 strike and still later company president. **McKinley**, **TR** and **Taft** kept Lincoln out of any mention for president until 1912. A scheme at the 1912 convention to get Black delegates (there were 66) to vote as a block for Robert Lincoln in order to forestall a **Taft** win fizzled. Robert Lincoln died in the 1920s. **Lincoln's** last descendant died in 1987.

Grant appointed **William Howard Taft's** father Attorney General in 1876. **Garfield's** son was **TR's** Secretary of the Interior and as such a colleague of **Taft**. In **Taft's** administration this Garfield opposed **Taft** and sided with **TR** on conservation issues. Upon **William McKinley's** death the son of the late **Benjamin Harrison** released a memo his father had written: "Should Mr. **Roosevelt** aspire to become President of the United States, I believe that he will be successful." **TR's** son and namesake was Assistant Secretary of the Navy under **Coolidge**. In 1941 Theodore Roosevelt Jr. then 53 left his business career and entered the army. In 1944 on D-Day he was the ranking officer on the beach with the US landing forces. He died within days of a heart attack. President **Ronald Reagan** visited Normandy in 1984 and laid a wreath at his burial site.

As he was about to assume command of NATO in late 1950 **Eisenhower** offered to Bob Taft, the son of President **Taft,** that he would repudiate a run for the presidency if Taft would support the concept of NATO. Taft demurred and was **Eisenhower's** rival all the way to the 1952 Republican convention. **Eisenhower** was supported by Sherman Adams a descendant of two presidents and this Adams became **Eisenhower's** Chief of Staff and had at best a cool relationship with Vice President **Nixon**. Herbert Hoover Jr. was in the **Eisenhower** administration as Under Secretary of State and in 1956 Eisenhower considered replacing **Richard Nixon** with the younger Hoover. At the 1960 Republican convention the youngest son of **FDR**, John Roosevelt, seconded the nomination of **Richard Nixon**. During the 2000 election **Reagan's** son Ron said that **George W Bush's** only accomplishment in life was that he was no longer a drunk. In 2008 **Kennedy's** daughter Caroline supported **Obama** in the Democrat primaries whereas **Clinton's** daughter Chelsea supported Hillary Clinton, **Obama's** opponent (and her mother). President **Obama** subsequently appointed Caroline Kennedy ambassador to Japan.

Supreme Court

There have been presidents appointed to the US Supreme Court. In 1810 **Madison** appointed **John Quincy Adams** to the Supreme Court and he was confirmed by the Senate. The news took weeks to reach him in Russia where he was ambassador and he declined. Most historians believe that **Adams** preferred living abroad at that time in his life but he cited as the reason his wife's pregnancy. In 1823 **Van Buren** hoped for a Supreme Court appointment from **Monroe**. It did not materialize. **Polk** and **Tyler** offered **Buchanan** appointments to the US Supreme Court. **Buchanan** may have been interested under **Polk** but withdrew twice. **TR** offered **Taft** a position on the Supreme Court in 1902 and in 1903 and 1906. Ultimately, **Warren Harding** appointed **Taft** to the Chief Justice in 1921, a position he held until his death in 1930. He is the only president to have held the Chief Justice position and thus the only president to swear-in other presidents – **Calvin Coolidge** in 1925 and **Herbert Hoover** in 1929. (As an aside, Thomas Dewey who was upset by **Harry Truman** in the presidential election of 1948 was offered the post of Chief Justice by **Richard Nixon** in 1969 but declined.) Chief Justice **Taft** once said, "I do not remember that I was ever President." (As president, **Taft** chose appointees of advanced age. He named Edward Douglass White as Chief Justice at the age of 65, over Charles Evans Hughes who was already on the bench and was only 48. Was **Taft** planning for the future?)

Although the jobs he held make him unique in American history, **Taft's** historical reputation is greatly affected by his landslide loss in 1912 which was the result of a party split.

<u>What is the point of all this?</u>

The forty-three presidents struggled for the rare prizes in American politics, positions of influence and possessing of the opportunities for advancement. They can be seen as teams and they cooperated at times seamlessly. They networked. Elders like **Ford** got a younger **George HW Bush** assigned to various positions. **Jefferson** appointed **Monroe** to key posts. But to use Doris Kearns Goodwin's phrase in a different context, they were often teams of rivals. **Jackson** blocked **Van Buren's** comeback. **Clinton's** relationship with **Obama** is at times strained. No matter. The Founders, the Jacksonian Democrats, the post-Civil War Republicans and the cohorts that led to the **Bushes** all paid attention to each other's careers.

Chapter 2

Affinity

Overall Context

There is much that links the forty-three men who have become the President of the US. Speaking of his relationship with **Bill Clinton** after both were out of office, **George HW Bush** said: "There is an inescapable bond that binds together all who live in the White House." **Franklin Pierce** and **Ulysses S. Grant** were from different political parties and differed greatly in political matters. **Pierce's** presidency is generally considered a failure. But both **Pierce** and **Grant** had served in the Mexican-American War and in his *Memoirs*, **Grant** wrote: "Whatever General **Pierce's** qualifications may have been for the Presidency, he was a gentleman and a man of courage." When **George W Bush** was out of office he wrote a book about his father, **George HW Bush**. He noted that at that point "my father's memory had faded" so it became less a biography and more a personal portrait. He noted that when he started the book, "I knew that many people liked **George HW Bush**. What I did not fully understand is how many people adore him."

In addition, many of the presidents have had some similar personal experiences.

As a boy **Van Buren** hung around his father's tavern in Kinderhook New York in the late 1790s and took in a culture in the same way that **Pierce** hung around his father's tavern in Hillsborough, New Hampshire listening to Revolutionary War veterans (His father had been with **Washington** at Valley Forge.) **Coolidge** was born over his father's store in Vermont in 1872. **Hoover** was an office boy in his uncle's real estate office in Salem, Oregon in the 1880s. **Nixon** worked in his father's gas station in Whittier, California in

54

the 1920s and **Jimmy Carter** was in his father's general store in Plains, Georgia in the 1930s. **Clinton** was in his grandfather's store in Hope, Arkansas in the 1950s. **Clinton** and **George W Bush** were born 44 days apart in 1946.

Some of the presidents had difficult childhoods. When asked by an interviewer about his early days, **Lincoln** said: "'the short and simple annals of the poor.' That's my life, and that's all you or anybody else can make of it." (This refers to a line from Thomas Gray's [1716-1771] "Elegy Written in a Country Churchyard" which was a favorite poem of **Andrew Johnson** and at one time one of the most quoted poems in the English language.) **Grant** was teased by boys in the small village where he grew up in Ohio for making a bad deal in the sale of a horse when he was twelve. ("Papa says I may offer you twenty dollars for the colt, but if you won't take that, I am to offer twenty-two and a half, and if you won't take that, to give you twenty-five.") Later **Grant** said: "Boys enjoy the misery of their companions, at least village boys in that day did, and in later life I have found that all adults are not free from the peculiarity." **Monroe** and **Hayes** both lost fathers and were mentored and financially supported by maternal uncles. **Garfield** also lost his father early and was brought up in pre-Civil War Ohio under very hard circumstances. He later said: "Let us never praise poverty, for the child at least." He wrote to a friend, "It was very bad for my life." **Ford's**, **Reagan's** and **Obama's** fathers were alcoholics. As a very old man, **Ford** was clear about his feelings: "My father was a bad man." (**Ford** was brought up by his mother and step-father whom he loved and respected and for whom he was named.) As a boy **Reagan** had to drag his passed-out-drunk father in from the front yard of their house. Nancy Reagan thought that **Reagan** may have reacted to these childhood experiences by withdrawing into himself and developing a deeply private side. She once said, "There's a wall around him. He lets me come closer than anyone else, but there are times when even I feel that barrier." **Clinton** and **Obama** were both raised without their fathers. (**Clinton** like **Hayes** was born after his father died. **Clinton's** step-father was an alcoholic. When he was 15, his mother and step-father divorced. They remarried about a year later. To show support for his mother's decision, **Bill** legally changed his last name from Blythe to **Clinton**.)

Hillary Clinton said of **Bill Clinton** during a period of time in which he had confessed to an affair: "Yes, he has weaknesses. Yes, he needs to be more responsible, more disciplined. But it is remarkable given his background that he turned out to be the kind of person he is, capable of such leadership. . . . He was so young, barely four, when he was scarred by abuse that he can't even take it out and look at it. There was terrible conflict between his mother and grandmother." Michelle Obama once told a friend that "**Barack** spent so much time by himself that it was like he was raised by wolves."

Obama's parents met in a Russian class at the University of Hawaii on the day of the first **Nixon-Kennedy** debate in 1960. The senior Obama was a student from Kenya. He was a bigamist, a wife-beater, an alcoholic and a highly intelligent man. He never contributed financially to **Obama's** upbringing and after his infancy saw him once. He was kicked out of Harvard and deported from the US. He died in a car crash while driving drunk. In grade school **Obama** told classmates that his father was an African prince.

This is how some of them recalled their own youth. **Hayes** played baseball at Harvard in 1844 although he also went to the theater; he wrote his uncle: "I consider one game of ball worth about ten plays. I am now quite lame, from scuffling, and all my fingers stiffened by playing ball. Pretty business for a law student. Yes, pretty enough; why not? Good exercise and great sport." In the 1870s **Hayes** called baseball "a *manly* game" although he was happy "to hear of (his son's) improvement in foot ball" at Cornell University. In the spring of 1880, Congressman **James Garfield** would get away from the Capitol Building occasionally to watch baseball games at a wooden grandstand near the uncompleted **Washington** monument. In 1947 and 1948 **George HW Bush** played baseball at Yale. In 1952 actor **Ronald Reagan** played the part of baseball player Grover Cleveland Alexander, born during the first **Cleveland** administration. In the 1990s **George W Bush** owned a professional baseball team. There is even a claim in baseball history that in 1860 a committee informing **Abraham Lincoln** that he was the Republican nominee met him at his hometown of Springfield, Illinois and found him on the commons playing in a game that was then called "base ball." **Lincoln** was on the field and sent a message to the committee: "Tell the gentlemen, that I am glad to know of their coming; but they'll have to wait a few minutes till I make another base hit." Another version of that story has **Lincoln** playing a game of fives which was an early version of handball. **Obama** was a good high school basketball player in Hawaii in the 1970s. (At least one biographer wrote that basketball marked the beginning of **Obama's** path toward acculturation to black America.)

TR after he made an ill-advised expedition to the Brazilian jungle following his presidency where he nearly died was asked why he did it. He supposedly said, "It was my last chance to be a boy." (**Wilson** once said of **TR**: "Yes, he is a great big boy. There is a sweetness about him that is very compelling.") **Coolidge** liked to play practical jokes and bestowed nicknames (Much like **George W Bush** eighty years later the giving of nicknames to White House staff was viewed by others as somewhat of a juvenile trait.) **Coolidge** once said: "Do you know I've never really grown up?" **Bill Clinton**: "I was born at 16, and I'll always feel I'm 16." **Monroe** trained for the revolutionary militia while in college. **Pierce** was involved in a student strike at Bowdoin College in Maine in the 1820s. In the 1890s to take a summer job during college **Hoover** walked eighty miles from Stanford University to Stockton California. **Reagan** led a student strike at Eureka College in Illinois in the 1930s forcing the resignation of the college president.

Certain presidents have changed their names. **Grant** was named at birth in 1822 **Hiram Ulysses Grant** but the Hiram was dropped. The Congressman who nominated him to West Point didn't know if he had a middle name and assumed it was Simpson (his mother's maiden name) when he nominated him for West Point in 1839 and entered into the records: **Ulysses S. Grant**. At West Point he picked up the nickname Sam from his initials which his colleagues enlarged to Uncle Sam. **Calvin Coolidge** was born John Calvin Coolidge but dropped his first name. David Dwight Eisenhower later became **Dwight David Eisenhower** just as Leslie Lynch King, Jr. became **Gerald Rudolph Ford** and William Jefferson Blythe III became **William Jefferson Clinton**.

Cleveland legally avoided the draft by paying for a substitute - a 32-year old Polish immigrant who survived the war - and lost to and later defeated a Civil War veteran (**Benjamin Harrison**) in his races for the presidency. **Clinton** avoided the draft in the Vietnam War and defeated two World War II veterans in his races for the presidency. **George W Bush** served stateside in the Air National Guard during the Vietnam War and later defeated two Vietnam veterans for the presidency.

One of the impeachment articles against **Andrew Johnson** was for "intemperate, inflammatory and scandalous harangues." In 1913 **Harding** made a New Year's resolution to "cut out cuss words, except in great need of them." **Nixon** was faulted for obscene language during the Watergate crisis.

In the 1880 campaign there was a rumor that **Arthur** had been born in Canada not Vermont making him ineligible for the presidency or the vice presidency. In 1928 **Hoover's** opponents suggested that he was a British subject. A clerk in London said he was on the voting roles there. **Hoover** had been born in Iowa but had lived abroad for years. In 2008 and beyond, "birthers" asserted that **Obama** was not born in the US but in Indonesia. (**Obama** was born in Hawaii.) Also in the 1880 campaign a forged letter purporting to show that **Garfield** favored the importation of Chinese labor became a late-hitting issue. This was echoed 124 years later when *CBS News* "revealed" that President **George W Bush** had received preferential treatment as a National Guardsman more than thirty years before basing its report of documents widely perceived to be false.

Millard Fillmore taught law clerks in his law offices in Buffalo in the 1830s. **Grover Cleveland** later studied at a firm descended from **Fillmore's** firm. **Clinton** taught law students in the 1970s, **Obama** in the 1990s. In the 1850s **Garfield** and **Arthur** taught in the same small town in Vermont about a year apart. There is no record that they met.

As president, **Arthur** suffered secretly from Bright's disease, a kidney disorder which made it difficult to rid his body of toxins. He was in effect slowly poisoning himself. In 1893 **Cleveland** had a secret surgery to remove a tumor from his mouth. The surgery was performed on a yacht in Long Island Sound. **Cleveland** wanted it secret so as not to panic the country during tough financial times and to avoid the national spectacle that had attended **Grant's** death in 1885. It was concealed from the public until 1917, nearly ten years after **Cleveland's** death.

As for **Kennedy**:

1. He could not have passed a physical exam to get into the military services but used his father's influence.
2. His back troubles were not from football injuries or war wounds, but advanced osteoporosis.
3. He had Addison's disease, an autoimmune destruction of the adrenal glands resulting in low blood pressure, low energy levels and increased complications from infection and needed cortisone injections daily.
4. He had recurring stomach and colon problems and chronic venereal disease he contracted as a teenager.
5. His political biography declared that he studied at the London School of Economics in 1935, but he got sick that year and never attended.
6. In late 1961, his brother Robert Kennedy discovered that **JFK** was taking amphetamines administered by Dr. Max Jacobson, later known as "Dr. Feelgood"
7. He always figured he would die young and lived life in a hurry.

It is well-known that the **Bushes** and the **Adamses** were father-son teams. It is perhaps less well-known that there were other interrelationships between the forty-three presidents. **William Henry Harrison** was **Benjamin Harrison's** Grandfather. **Zachary Taylor** was a second cousin of **James Madison**. FDR was a fourth cousin to Presidents **Ulysses S. Grant** and **Zachary Taylor** (He was also a seventh cousin of Winston Churchill.) The **Roosevelts** were fifth cousins. In 1905 **FDR** married Eleanor Roosevelt, **TR's** niece. Her maiden name was Roosevelt. **TR** gave her away saying to **FDR**:

"There's nothing like keeping the name in the family." **George W Bush** was a distant cousin to **Franklin Pierce** through his mother who was known as Barbara Pierce when she met **George HW Bush** in 1941.

Presidents have often recognized a kinship and support each other in crises.

At the beginning of the bribery scandal in the 1920s known as the Teapot Dome scandal, **Coolidge** couldn't accept that **Harding's** judgment in people could have been so bad and **Taft** agreed. To **Taft**, **Coolidge** criticized the Republicans in the Senate for their weak support: "The Republican senators are a lot of damned cowards." He came to feel differently and supported the investigation of **Harding's** administration. "Some people think they can escape purgatory. There are three purgatories to which people can be assigned: to be damned by one's fellows, to be damned by the court, to be damned in the next world. I want these men to get all three without probation." **Coolidge** was under pressure to fire Attorney General Harry Daugherty who was linked with the scandal. **Taft** favored keeping him and **Hoover** favored firing him. One of **Coolidge's** stated reasons for not acting was what he perceived **Harding's** wishes would have been. He soon got **Taft** to ask Daugherty to resign. This was unsuccessful and eventually **Coolidge** fired Daugherty.

During the 1968 election **Lyndon Johnson** broke into an argument among his staff about the Vietnam War and the coming election saying about a long-time rival: "Mr. **Nixon** shouldn't enter into this in any way. The North Vietnamese feel the same about all of us." A few years later, **Nixon** talked with author Theodore White: "We came in with 43 percent of the vote, with the establishment giving us nothing but a kick in the butt, and the press kicking the beejeezus out of us, the intellectuals against us....those four years weren't an easy period. When I came in, **LBJ** couldn't even leave the White House - he was right, he shouldn't have subjected himself to violence ..."

Presidents have mentored each other. In the early twentieth century, the historian Henry Adams wrote that his grandfather, **John Quincy**

Adams had been **Washington's** protégé. **Jefferson**, the Virginia planter was a mentor to **Van Buren**, a middle-class northerner and one generation younger. **Jackson** was a mentor to **Polk** whom he ultimately favored over **Van Buren**. **Lincoln** formed an easy personal relationship with **Grant** that guaranteed the Union victory. In 1864 he visited his general near the front lines. When he arrived, **Lincoln** said: "I just thought I would jump aboard a boat and come down and see you. I don't expect I can do any good, and in fact I may do harm but I'll put myself under your orders and if you find me doing anything wrong just send me [away] right away." Later that year, he telegraphed **Grant** to say that possibly the general should personally return to defend Washington DC from the Confederates but added: "This is what I think… and it is not an order." **Grant** ended up sending a subordinate. By that time **Lincoln** was instinctively relying on **Grant** for military matters and **Grant** was relying on **Lincoln** to get re-elected. When that occurred, **Grant** telegraphed his superior, Secretary of War Edwin Stanton saying, "Congratulate the President for me." **Hayes** mentored his fellow Ohioan **William McKinley** both in the Civil War and later in politics. In 1888 **McKinley** was a long shot possibility for the Republican nomination for President. When he came up short, **Hayes** told him that he had "gained gloriously" by staying loyal to another candidate. "Men in public life must be ambitious. But the surest path to the White House is his who never allows his ambition to get there to stand in the way of any duty, large or small." **McKinley** gained the presidency eight years later. Besides his own father **George HW Bush** regarded **Nixon** as his most important political mentor. In 1990 **Bush** backed off a pledge not to raise taxes causing lots of criticism from the right. **Nixon** who as noted had advised him to stick with his pledge still supported him, writing **Bush**: "The mark of a great leader is to change his policies to meet new situations even when that means backing away from a campaign commitment. As you know I had to burn a lot of my own speeches and eat a lot of words when I went to China in 1972."

The presidents dealt with alcohol issues. In 1831 **William Henry Harrison** quit the distillery business because of his disgust with the excessive drinking that he witnessed. In 1836 Speaker of the House **James K Polk** defended Congressman **Franklin Pierce** from a rumor concerning **Pierce's** drinking noting that "few men with whom I have been associated in Congress have possessed to a greater extent, the confidence and respect of the political friends with whom he has universally acted." In 1842 **Pierce** promised his wife Jane that he would stop drinking, a pledge he broke during combat service in the Mexican-American War in 1847. In the 1980s **George W Bush** promised his wife he would stop drinking and followed through with this commitment. **Andrew Johnson** apparently drank whiskey before his vice presidential inaugural speech and gave a terrible performance. **Hayes** who had just been elected to the Congress was glad that his wife was not there to witness **Johnson's** conduct. When told about it, **Lincoln** said, "Oh well, don't you bother about **Andy Johnson's** drinking. He made a bad slip the other day, but I have known **Andy** a great many years, and he ain't no drunkard."

In 1842 **John Quincy Adams** spoke to a county temperance society. Alcoholism was in his family and he was a moderate drinker. He said: "To the general cause of temperance throughout the world, I would say, as I would say of all moral reform, God speed you." But he asked them not to forget, "in the ardor of your zeal for moral reform ... the rights of personal freedom." **Lincoln** did not drink, smoke or use profanity but he did not look down on those who did. He said to the Springfield Temperance Society: "Such of us as have never fallen victims, have been spared more from the absence of appetite, than from any mental or moral superiority owner those who have." In 1866 **Andrew Johnson** made a campaign trip trying to get more allies elected to Congress. It took him by train to ten states in about three weeks and was known as the "Swing Around the Circle." **Grant** accompanied him and was apparently drunk at times. Other reports have it that **Johnson** was drinking heavily during this trip. **Hayes** banned alcohol in the White House. This has seen by a recent biographer as a shrewd attempt to keep Prohibition-oriented Republicans from migrating to the Prohibition Party. **Garfield** was a moderate drinker. In the 1880 campaign, Mrs. Garfield caused controversy by saying about her husband: "The general takes great interest in the affairs of our little village. But the general does not believe in total abstinence. Oh, no! He believes every man should have a mind of his own, but not drink to excess...." **Hayes** later wrote that he regarded **Garfield's** intention to "restore wine and liquor to the White House" as a sign that he "lacks the grit to face fashionable ridicule." As a young politico in Buffalo, **Cleveland** drank a lot in beer halls and put on excessive weight. He later admitted that during this period of his life he sometimes drank so much that he was forced to "lose a day." In 1913 **TR** sued a writer who had accused him of alcoholism and won a verdict.

Truman was by no means an alcoholic but on the night of the 1950 elections which went bad for his party, he drunk himself into oblivion. While president, **Eisenhower** had concerns about **Nixon's** drinking. When **George W Bush** was in his 20s and single, he came to his parents' home one night inebriated. "**Dad** was reading a book. He lowered his book, calmly slid off his reading glasses, and stared right at me. Then he put his reading glasses back on and lifted up the book. I felt like a fool. I slunk out of the room."

Certain presidents had early experiences with other presidents. A young **Tyler** met **Jefferson** at a dinner at his father's house in 1809. **Tyler** called it "an extraordinary occasion." **Tyler** also knew **Madison** and **Monroe**. In the 1820s as a young lawyer in a small town in western New York, 24 year-old **Fillmore** supported **John Quincy Adams**. In July 1842 **Fillmore** retired from Congress and returned to Buffalo to work in his legal practice. In 1843 **John Quincy Adams** visited Buffalo. **Fillmore** greeted him with a speech. **Adams** responded: "I cannot forbear to express here my regret at (**Fillmore's**) retirement in the present emergency from the councils of his nation." As a college debater in 1824 **Pierce** supported **Jackson**. In 1833 Congressman-elect **Pierce** met **Jackson** and **Van Buren** when they came to Concord, New Hampshire.

As a fourteen-year-old **Hayes** supported **Harrison** in 1836 in a losing effort. As a student at Kenyon College in 1840 **Hayes** supported **Harrison** again saying that he despised **Van Buren**; at **Harrison's** victory he said, that "I was never more elated by anything in my life." In Harvard law school in 1844 **Hayes** cast his first vote for Henry Clay but won $20 worth of books by betting on **Polk**. In that same election, a teen-age **Chester Alan Arthur** who supported the Whig

Party joined with other young Whigs and fought a brawl against fellow students who supported Democrat **James K. Polk.** In the 1848 election **Hayes** worked "like a trooper" for **Zachary Taylor** who won. Later that year **Hayes** went from Ohio to Texas to visit a friend. He traveled by stage, train, and steamer along the Mississippi and the trip took over a month. Riding down the Mississippi and he saw the President-elect's house near Louisville, Kentucky: a "neat, one-story, long cottage - porch all around - on a pleasant hill."

In the 1852 election between **Pierce** and Winfield Scott, an election fraught with sectional tension over slavery, a twenty-one year old **Garfield** expressed disinterest. One of **Woodrow Wilson's** early memories of his life in Georgia - he was born in 1856 - was of a man shouting, "**Lincoln** is elected and now we will have war." When **Franklin Roosevelt** was seven, his father took him to meet President **Grover Cleveland**. **Cleveland** told him, "My little man, I am making a strange wish for you. It is that you may never be President of the United States."

At the birth of **Hoover** in a small Iowa town in 1874, his father told neighbors: "We have another General **Grant** at our house." **Coolidge** remembered **Benjamin Harrison's** victory over **Cleveland** in 1888 as well received in his high school in Vermont, a Republican state. "Two nights were spent parading the streets with drums and trumpets, celebrating the victory." As a student at Stanford University, **Hoover** criticized **Cleveland's** laissez faire attitude toward the depression of the 1890s and refused to admit **Benjamin Harrison** to a college baseball game until he purchased a ticket. In 1920 a seven-year old **Richard Nixon** celebrated the election of **Harding-Coolidge** with his father. In 1937 after his election to Congress **LBJ** met with **FDR** in Texas aboard **Roosevelt's** train. **FDR** later said that **Johnson** "came on like a freight train." He also told his aide Tommy Corcoran: "I've just met the most remarkable young man. I like this boy and you're going to help him with anything you can." As a young man **Reagan** listened to **FDR's** fireside chats and in his presidency tried to emulate him by talking to the camera and to average citizens. **Reagan**: "His strong, gentle, confident voice resonated across the nation with an eloquence that brought comfort and resilience to a nation caught up in a storm and reassured us that we could lick any problem. I will never forget him for that." (As president, **Carter** more specifically tried to emulate **FDR's** approach by talking about the 1970s energy crisis wearing a sweater seated in the Oval Office before a fire.) As a sports announcer in the 1930s **Reagan** broadcast a University of Michigan football game where one of the players was **Gerald Ford**, an all-American. **Richard Nixon** first saw **Ike** in 1945 as the General led a parade in New York City at the end of World War II. As President, **Nixon** would raise both his arms in a V-salute copying **Eisenhower** in that parade.

As a high schooler, **Clinton** shook hands with **JFK** at an official function. Years later, when he had acquired a reputation as a womanizer **Clinton** was asked what question he would like to ask **JFK** and responded: "I'd want to ask him, you know, how did you do it? How'd you get away with it?" A close **Clinton** friend has said that **JFK** "was the only political hero that he ever had." **George W Bush** was introduced to Senate Majority Leader **Lyndon Johnson** when he was ten years old by his grandfather. **LBJ** shook **Bush's** hand and said: "Pleased to meet you." **Bush** remembered **Johnson** as a very tall man. (**Johnson** was 6' 4." **Lincoln** was the same height.)

Both **Madison** and **Monroe** had closer relationships with **Jefferson** than they did with each other and **Madison** and **Jefferson** who bonded as Virginians determined to protect their state's interest in the national government were the closest. Their relationship began in 1779 when **Madison** went to the Continental Congress and he started trading letters with **Jefferson**, a practice that continued for over forty years. The letters were not limited to politics. When **Jefferson** learned that **Madison's** fiancé had broken off their engagement he wrote him that "no event has been more contrary to my expectations" and that "the world still presents the same and many other resources for happiness."

John Quincy Adams described the **Jefferson/Madison** partnership as a "phenomenon, like the invisible and mysterious movements of the magnet in the physical world." Shortly before he died, **Jefferson** wrote **Madison** that he had been "a pillar of support through life."

That presidential relationship was unique but all or at least most presidents have felt a type of bond with other presidents. **Grant**, for example, grew to intensely dislike **Andrew Johnson** but he was shocked in 1866 when an anti-**Johnson** riot burst out in Indianapolis during a campaign trip. One man was killed. A shot was fired into **Johnson's** room in what **Grant** saw as "a deliberate attempt to assassinate Mr. **Johnson**." A century later a reporter who went to work for **Carter** once told him that he had thought **Ford** was a good President. **Carter** responded: "So did I."

Sometimes the affinity is tepid or self-serving. Two recent examples:

- In the 1976 campaign **Carter** said: "I can see in retrospect what President **Kennedy** meant to the deprived people in this country and abroad... He never really did much for them, but he made them think he cared."
- In 2011 President **Obama** was asked to assess his presidency. He said in part: "... I would put our legislative and foreign-policy accomplishments in our first two years against any president—with the possible exceptions of **Johnson, FDR** and **Lincoln**—just in terms of what we've gotten done in modern history."

What follows are positive comments and experiences grouped by the order of the presidency.

Moving forward

When **John Quincy Adams** age 18, sailed for home from Europe to start Harvard in 1785 he had in his care seven hunting dogs that were a present from Lafayette the French hero of the American Revolution to **George Washington**. **Washington** in time grew close to **John Quincy Adams**. In 1789 **George Washington** visited Massachusetts. When he returned to Philadelphia, he assured Abigail Adams that **John Quincy** was more interested in books than women. **Washington**, who had no sons and who had a habit of furthering the careers of younger men like Alexander Hamilton, had a rapport with the sixth president that he never had with **John**

Adams. After his Farewell Address, while going over a batch of **John Quincy Adams**' letters with **John Adams, George Washington** said "Things appear to me exactly as they do to your son."

In 1794-5 during the Whiskey rebellion **George Washington** stayed at an inn near **Buchanan's** family home in western Pennsylvania favorably impressing the **Buchanan** family. (But many decades later **Buchanan** failed to draw from this example. In the secession crisis of late 1860 he gave his annual message. It was convoluted but he concluded that the Constitution did not empower the president or the Congress "to coerce a State into submission which is attempting to withdraw, or has actually withdrawn." Many disagreed citing **George Washington's** taking to the field against the resisters of the whiskey tax in Pennsylvania in 1794 along with other examples.)

John Adams and **Jefferson** bonded in Paris defending the United States. When **Adams** and his family left Paris for a diplomatic assignment in London in 1785 **Jefferson** wrote that he was "in the dumps" and "my afternoons hang heavily on me." **John Adams** saw in **Jefferson**: "the wisdom of taciturnity." He saw it in **George Washington** too. (**Lincoln** saw it in **Grant** too noting approvingly during the Civil War before he even met him, "He is a copious worker and fighter but a very meager writer or telegrapher." He added that **Grant** was "the quietest little fellow you ever saw." An acquaintance of **Grant** once described him as "a man who could remain silent in several languages." This was obviously a quality that **Lincoln** admired. He once said: "I am rather inclined to silence and whether that be wise or not, it is at least more unusual now-a-days to find a man who can hold his tongue than to find one who cannot.")

John Adams about **John Quincy Adams**: "The world says they should take him for my younger brother." The elder **Adams** was clear, however, on his role. He once said to his son: "You come into life with advantages which will disgrace you if your success is mediocre. And if you do not rise to the head not only of your profession, but your country, it will be owing to your own laziness, slovenliness, and obstinacy." Aboard a ship for Europe in 1778, **John Adams** wrote that **John Quincy Adams** "behaves like a man."

He added: "My little son has sustained this long journey...with the utmost firmness as he did our fatiguing and dangerous voyage." After the losing 1992 campaign **George HW Bush** said of **George W Bush** that it was "a joy having **George** with us - feisty fighter and campaigner if there ever was one." (In his memoir *Decision Points* published in 2010, **George W. Bush** wrote about his father's defeat in 1992 by **Bill Clinton**: "Dad had been raised to be a good sport. He blamed no one; he was not bitter.")

The affinity between the first father-son Presidents was of course indissoluble. In 1815 when **John Quincy Adams** had been in Europe for years, **John Adams** wrote him: "One thing is clear in my mind, and that is you ought to be home..." When **John Adams** learned that **John Quincy Adams had** landed in New York in 1817 after an eight year absence he wrote: "Yesterday was one of the most uniformly happy days of my whole life." In 1824 when **John Quincy Adams** won the presidency, **John Adams** wrote **Jefferson** that "our **John**" had won. "I call him our **John** because when you was at Cul de sac at Paris, he appeared to be almost as much your boy as mine." There was much truth to this observation. In **John Quincy Adams**' diary in the 1780s France he wrote: "Spent evening with Mr. **Jefferson**, whom I love to be with." (In the same decade, **Monroe** said: "Having formed strong attachment to Mr. **Jefferson**... I resolved to purchase a tract of land...in (his) neighborhood.")

As a senator after 1803, **John Quincy Adams** played chess with Secretary of State **James Madison**. Late in life, **John Adams** wrote to a friend that **John Quincy Adams**' marriage to Louisa Johnson was "the most important event" in **John Quincy's** life.

Monroe was something of a protégé of **Jefferson** who was about fifteen years his senior and governor of Virginia when **Monroe** was fighting in the Revolutionary War. In 1780 **Monroe,** by then a veteran of the Delaware-crossing and Valley Forge followed Governor **Thomas Jefferson's** advice and returned to college and read law under **Jefferson's** direction. **Jefferson** wrote to **Monroe** in 1782 suggesting that he was leaving public service: "Nothing could so completely divest us of liberty as the establishment of the opinion

that the state has a *perpetual* right to the services of all its members."
At this time, **Jefferson** had withdrawn from the state legislature to
care for his dying wife but he did not want to discuss the matter.
Monroe tactfully explained the situation to **Jefferson's** detractors
who felt **Jefferson** was shirking public responsibility. In 1784 as
he left for France **Jefferson** fostered a close and confidential
relationship between **Madison** and **Monroe** which then lasted -
with one lapse - for decades by telling **Madison** about **Monroe**:
"The scrupulousness of his honor will make you safe in the most
confidential communications. A better man cannot be." **Jefferson**
wrote to **Madison** about **Monroe** three years later: "Turn his soul
wrong side outwards and there is not a speck on it."

Jefferson felt he had to advise **Madison** regarding personnel matters.
For example, **Jefferson** did not trust his own Vice President, Aaron
Burr and wrote in his diary: "I habitually cautioned Mr. **Madison**
against trusting him too much."

In Indiana Territory in the early 1800s **William Henry Harrison**
founded a town, Jeffersonville. After **Jefferson** reappointed
Harrison territorial governor of Indiana in 1806, **Harrison** wrote him
back: "I received...the new Commission...and I beg you to receive
my warmest thanks for this additional proof of your confidence and
friendship. The emoluments of my office afford me a decent support
and will I hope...enable me to lay up a small fund for the education
of my children. I have hitherto found however that my nursery grows
faster than my strongbox."

In 1811, **Zachary Taylor** age 25 was a young officer in charge of Fort
Knox in Indian Territory. **William Henry Harrison** issued this report:
"Captain **Z. Taylor** has been placed in command of the Garrison near
this. To all the qualities which are esteemed for an amiable man he
appears to unite those which form a good officer. In the short time he
has been a commander he has rendered the Garrison defensible –
before his arrival it resembled anything but a place of defence."

After the British burning of Washington DC in 1814 a 63-year
old **James Madison** was deeply shaken. **Jefferson** tried to

encourage him: "In the late events at Washington I have felt so much for you that I cannot withhold the expressions of my sympathies... Had General **Washington** himself been now at the head of our affairs, the same event would probably have happened." A few months later **Jefferson** wrote **Monroe** in order to cast blame for the disaster on subordinates: "I never doubted that the plans of the President were wise and sufficient. Their failure we all impute, (1) to the insubordinate temper of (Secretary of War John) Armstrong, and (2) to the indecision of (William) Winder."

In 1819 **Monroe** and **Jackson** visited the western military outposts and attended a party that included Lieutenant Colonel **Zachary Taylor** in Kentucky.

John Quincy Adams saw **Monroe's** ability to evaluate advice as a quality "which in so high a place is an infallible test of a great mind." As president, **Monroe** was solicitous of **Jackson's** feelings. **Jackson** reciprocated and credited **Monroe** with "magnanimity of conduct only to be met with in great and good minds..."

In 1817 **Monroe** visited an aged **John Adams** at his home near Boston. **Adams** invited forty guests.

After serving in **Monroe's** cabinet and succeeding him, **John Quincy Adams** remained friendly and loyal. **Adams** said of **Monroe**: that he was "nurtured in the detestation of tyranny."

In 1834 Congressman **Franklin Pierce** gave his first speech in Congress. It was on pension claims emanating from the Revolutionary War era. **John Quincy Adams** also a member of Congress noted that **Pierce** was "a new member and young man from New Hampshire, who spoke about half an hour very handsomely..." In the 1840s, still in Congress, **Adams** noted in his diary that Congressman **Andrew Johnson** had "great native ability." (Henry Adams was not particularly moved by meeting **Andrew Johnson** in 1868 but came to look back on him as "perhaps the strongest [President] he was ever to see.")

John Adams was an elector in 1820 and voted for **Monroe**. In retirement **Monroe** joined **Jefferson** and **Madison** on the board of directors for the University of Virginia. **John Adams** said that the "world will expect something very great and very new from such a noble triumvirate." **Adams** overlooked the animosities between each member of this noble triumvirate and him of a quarter century earlier.

Andrew Jackson and **James Knox Polk**, born twenty-eight years apart, developed a close personal and political friendship. The first time **Polk** saw his future wife since she was a small child was when she was talking with family friend **Andrew Jackson** in 1819 at a ball. She was 16. **Jackson** encouraged **Polk** to marry her. In his early career in Congress during the administration of **John Quincy Adams**, **Polk** would send **Jackson** information from the capital. **Jackson** responded: "I feel greatly obliged to you for the information...and I duly appreciate those feelings of friendship which dictated the communication."

During the dirty campaign of 1828 **Polk** advised **Jackson** not to respond to personal allegations. He sent **Jackson** a letter which said, "Treat everything that has or may be said with silent contempt." **Jackson** appreciated the advice and wrote on the letter: "My friend Col **Polk's** letter to be kept as a token of his real friendship." He replied to **Polk**: "I received my Dr. Sir, your letter as the highest evidence of your sincere friendship, & as such treasured it up." As president, **Polk** helped engineer the sale of a Democrat newspaper to a friendlier owner. **Jackson,** who was not so sure of this, worriedly wrote **Polk**: "But my dear friend, the movement was hasty, and as I think badly advised and I pray my god that it may not result in injury to the perfect unity of the democracy."

Martin Van Buren, a gregarious politician, was a link between generations. **Van Buren**, 42, visited **Thomas Jefferson,** 81, in 1824 for several days. Years later, **Van Buren** wrote, "It may well be imagined with how much satisfaction I listened to Mr. **Jefferson's** conversation. His imposing appearance as he sat uncovered - never wearing his hat except when he left the carriage and often not then – and the earnest and impressive manner in which he spoke of men and things, are yet as fresh in my recollection as if they were experiences of yesterday." In 1842 after his own presidency, **Van Buren** was traveling in Illinois. He was, like presidents after him, on the comeback trail. Local Democrats introduced him to a young Whig, **Abraham Lincoln**. **Van Buren** was 60; **Lincoln** was 33. The two entertained a small gathering one evening with funny stories. **Van Buren** talked of the days of Aaron Burr and Alexander Hamilton. **Lincoln** according to a witness told stories "one following another in rapid succession, each more irresistible than its predecessor. The fun continued until after midnight, and until the distinguished traveler insisted that his sides were sore from laughing." **Van Buren** later said that he had never "spent so agreeable a night in my life." In 1855 **Fillmore** and **Van Buren** were in London at the same time, **Fillmore** on the comeback trail. (He ran for president on a third party ticket a year later.)

Early in **Jackson's** first term he formed a tie with **Martin Van Buren** who wrote a friend, "We are getting along extremely well....The president proves to be in all respects a finer man than I anticipated." **Andrew Jackson** and **Martin Van Buren** reversed protocol and visited the daughter of **Thomas Jefferson**. During this time, **Van Buren** also reached out to establish a relationship with **Jackson's** bitter enemy, **John Quincy Adams**. **Adams** appreciated the gesture but still noted in his diary that **Van Buren** resembled **Jefferson** in "profound dissimulation and duplicity" but that he reminded him of **Madison** in his discretion and disinclination of open conflict.

In the 1830s **Pierce** argued in the Senate for more resources for the military. The Army was fighting a guerilla campaign against the Seminole nation. **Pierce** wondered why staff officers were paid more than line who were fighting in Florida "(w)here the invincible (**Zachary**) **Taylor** overcame the enemy on the Okeechobee..." (In this campaign **Taylor** used canines to track Indians and **John Quincy Adams** wondered sarcastically if those dogs should get military pensions.) In 1838 **Pierce** took Jefferson Davis to meet with President **Van Buren**, giving an early sign that he was a northern man with southern sympathies. In 1844 **Tyler** was worried about Sam Houston's apparent lack of enthusiasm to annexing Texas to the US. Knowing of **Andrew Jackson's** good relationship with Houston he sent he sent **Jackson's** nephew Andrew J. Donelson as US *charge d'affaires* to Texas. **Lincoln** worked his state for **William Henry Harrison** in 1840 over Henry Clay because he thought he was more electable. In the general campaign that year **Lincoln** said **Van Buren** was "in feeling and principle an Aristocrat." He even criticized him for advancing Black voting rights in New York some twenty years earlier. In late 1847 several Whig Members of Congress styling themselves the "Young Indians" started a **Taylor**-for-President club. **Lincoln** was a member.

After the election of 1848 President-elect **Taylor** said of his running mate, "I wish Mr. **Fillmore** would take all of the business into his own hands..." This relationship quickly cooled and **Taylor** did not consult with **Fillmore** in making his cabinet. In 1852 a Jacksonian candidate was supported by past and future Jacksonian Presidents. **Buchanan** campaigned for **Pierce** answering a charge that **Pierce** was a coward by this: "How preposterous!" **Van Buren** who had left the Democratic Party in 1848 supported **Pierce** in 1852 helping to create party unity that year. **Van Buren** said to **Pierce** referring to the New Yorkers who had supported his own Free Soil candidacy in 1848: "I am yet to hear of the first man who will not vote for Mr. (Rufus) King (the running mate of **Pierce**) & yourself." In 1855 a diplomatic crisis emerged with England over illegal recruiting in the US to meet England's military demands during the Crimean War. **Buchanan** was the US ambassador in London but had resigned pending a replacement so as to return home to run for president. **Pierce** asked him to stay on during the crisis to deal with the British government: "Whatever the result of negotiations may be, touching this embarrassing subject, I deem it very important that you 'see it out.' I have been reluctant to urge to remain at London beyond Sept. 30th, but shall never fail to appreciate the high considerations which have prompted your determination."

In February of 1861 **Lincoln** stopped in Columbus Ohio on his way to his inauguration. State Senator **Garfield** apparently did not meet with him but did observe him and noted: "On the whole, I am greatly pleased with him. He clearly shows his want of culture, and the marks of Western life, but there is no touch of affectation in him, and he has a peculiar power of impressing you that he is frank, direct and thoroughly honest. His remarkable good sense, simple and condensed style of expression, and evident marks of indomitable will, give me great hopes for the country."

In 1864 **Lincoln** assured a delegation of skeptical Republican leaders that **Johnson** would be a good running mate: "Don't be concerned. When **Andy** was here last, he said if it were necessary to carry on the war for thirty years, he was for carrying it on." **Lincoln** had genuine respect and affection for **Johnson**. **Lincoln's** party impeached **Johnson** four years later, but in 1864 **Lincoln** said, "No man has a right to judge **Andrew Johnson** in any respect who has not suffered as much or done as much as he for the Nation's sake." In 1866 **Pierce** wrote **Johnson**: "You need no expression of the thanks, which my heart readily acknowledges, for your brave devotion to the Constitution and the Union and for the unanswered & and unanswerable arguments with which you have dumfounded the enemies of both." In the election of 1868 some Republicans tried to make **Pierce** an issue against the Democrats but **Grant** had nothing bad to say about **Pierce** and **Pierce** did not campaign hard against **Grant**. When **Pierce** died in 1869 **Grant** referred to him as an "honored predecessor" adding that **Pierce** had been "eminent in the public councils and universally beloved in private life."

In 1860 **Benjamin Harrison** some 28 years away from the presidency ran for state office in Indiana - reporter of the Supreme Court - and campaigned for **Abraham Lincoln**.

In 1869-70 **Garfield** investigated a gold buying scandal and did not implicate **Grant** who was probably completely innocent, although naïve. **Garfield** noted after it was over: "The President expresses himself under a good many obligations to me for the management of the Gold panic investigation." **Grant's** style of delegating responsibility may have gotten him into trouble in this instance but is typical of the modern Presidency and drew praise from **Rutherford Hayes** who wrote that "**Grant's** leadership and rule is beyond question."

After the 1880 election **Benjamin Harrison** wrote **Garfield**: "You must know how sincerely I rejoice over your success. Outside of your own family I am sure no man in the country can be happier than I am over your elevation to the presidency." **Hayes** wrote to his successor **James Garfield** in January of 1881: "It is generally supposed that (James G.) Blaine will be in the State Department. The saving clause in the whole business is *the faith that you will be President.*" **Garfield** appointed Blaine Secretary of State.

McKinley once said to his Vice President **Theodore Roosevelt**: "You make me envious. You've been able to get so much out of books."

Upon **FDR's** marriage to Eleanor in 1905, **TR** told him: "I like you, and trust you, and believe in you." **TR** once warned **FDR** that if he stayed in politics he might face an assassin and he had better prepare for it. In 1912 when **TR** was a former president, campaigning to return to office, he was wounded by a would-be assassin. His attacker was committed to a state hospital where he lived for the next thirty years without a single visitor or letter. As President-elect, **FDR** was almost killed by a gunman in 1933. The shooter missed **Roosevelt** but killed the Mayor of Chicago who was nearby. The killer was executed about a month after the attack.

Wilson in a private letter on **Hoover** who had done humanitarian work in war-torn Europe: "He is a real man...one of the very ablest we have sent over there (to war-torn Europe.) A great international figure. Such men stir me deeply and make me in love with duty." **Wilson** told his brother-in-law that he wanted **Hoover** to succeed him. In oddly modern language, **Harding** called **Hoover** "the smartest 'geek' I know." Decades later **Nixon** saw **Hoover** as a more intelligent man politically than people usually thought.

Harding liked to compare himself to **McKinley**.

As governor of Massachusetts in 1919, **Coolidge** welcomed **Woodrow Wilson** to Boston in February of 1919: "We welcome him as the representative of a great people, as a great statesman, as one to whom we have entrusted our destinies, and one whom we are sure we will support in the future in the working out of that destiny, as Massachusetts has supported him in the past." **Coolidge** gave this advice to **Hoover** about visitors: "If you keep dead still, they will run down in three or four minutes. If you even cough or smile, they will start up all over again." Chief Justice **Taft** was one of President **Coolidge's** few advisors.

Hoover wouldn't play poker with **Harding** in the White House: "It irks me to see it in the White House." However in 1923 **Hoover** traveled with **Harding** on his last trip through, among other places, Portland, Tacoma, Alaska, and San Francisco. They played cards. **Hoover** later wrote that **Harding** confided in him about the brewing scandal that would eventually destroy his reputation and asked his advice. **Hoover** wrote that he recommended, "Publish it, and at least get credit for integrity on your side." **Hoover** was unaware of the specifics of **Harding's** concerns.

In 1945 after **Harry Truman** invited **Herbert Hoover** to the White House for consultations for the first time in twelve years, the Communist *Daily Worker* criticized **Truman** for meeting with such a "Fascist beast." **Truman** wrote in his diary: "Saw **Herbert Hoover**... and had a pleasant and constructive conversation on food and the general troubles of US Presidents - two in particular." **Hoover** confided that **Truman** added ten years to his life. **Hoover** advised **Truman** in 1946 that the only way to deal with the USSR was to be tough. "Even if he were to present a gold watch, it should be presented in a truculent mood."(A young congressman, **Richard Nixon**, who generally opposed **Truman**, supported the administration's hard line against the Soviets.) **Herbert Hoover** gently chided **Harry Truman** about his amount of vacation time in comparison to other presidents. **Truman** responded: "I guess I'm a damn sight better manager than my predecessors whom you have known."

Truman came to like **Hoover** - in 1947 he reversed an earlier decision by **FDR** and re-named the Boulder Dam on the Colorado the **Hoover** Dam - but said that he was "to the right of Louis the Fourteenth." **Truman** added that **Hoover** "deserves to be treated with respect as an ex-President. **Roosevelt** couldn't stand him and he hated **Roosevelt**. But he...can do some things. No reason to treat him other than with respect." However, **Truman** thought that **Hoover** "doesn't understand what's happened in the world since **McKinley**."

In 1941 **LBJ** ran for the Senate in Texas. The Democrat primary in that time and place was the decisive election. **FDR** told reporters: "I can't take part in a Texas primary (but) if you ask me about **Lyndon** himself I can only tell you what is perfectly true - you all know he is a very old and close friend of mine." In 1948 **LBJ** quoted **FDR**: "**Lyndon**, my boy, it is my observation that the men who serve me best, and the ones I respect the longest, are those who have a passion for anonymity."

During the World War II, **FDR** had visited **Eisenhower** in North Africa and met **Ike's** driver, Kay Summersby. He later confided to his daughter that he thought **Eisenhower** and Summersby were having an affair. Years later, when **Eisenhower** returned to the US and met with **Truman**. **Eisenhower's** Republican opponents were spreading stories about his wife's alleged drinking, an alleged affair with Summersby and about him supposedly being Jewish. **Truman** told him: "If that's all it is, **Ike**, then you can just figure you're lucky." **Eisenhower** denied the affair with Summersby but said she was a "peach." **Ike** died in 1969. Summersby died in 1975 and in her autobiography that came out that year asserted that they did have a relationship but it involved kissing and long walks rather than sex. **Eisenhower's** son was on his staff during the war and said in response to Summersby's book about Summersby's wartime experience: "She was perky and she was cute. Whether she had any designs on the Old Man and the extent to which he succumbed, I just don't know."

Nixon gave General **Eisenhower** a secret briefing on communist influence in the government in 1949. This was his first meeting with **Ike**. In 1950 **Eisenhower** attended a retreat at the Bohemian Grove in Northern California that included his Republican predecessor and successor: **Herbert Hoover** and **Richard Nixon**. Both were impressed with **Ike** but were uncertain whether he had the judgment to be president.

Eisenhower speculated in 1956 that in 1960 the Democrats might nominate "young **John Kennedy**, an attractive guy." **Eisenhower** to **Nixon** on the day after the 1960 election: "We can be proud of these last eight years." **Nixon**: "You did a grand job." **Nixon** later told **Eisenhower** that he had never heard him sound so depressed.

In 1950 when **Nixon** ran for the Senate, **JFK** told him: "**Dick**, I know you're in a pretty rough campaign and my father wanted to help out." He gave him a check. After **Nixon's** win **JFK** wrote a friend: "I was glad to...see **Nixon** win by a big vote." In 1952 when **Nixon** was nominated for Vice President **JFK** wrote him: "I was tremendously pleased that the convention selected you for VP... You were an ideal selection and will bring the ticket a great deal of strength...."

Nixon made his mark as a first-term Member of Congress by his successful pursuit of accused spy Alger Hiss. When Hiss was convicted of perjury in 1950 **Nixon** took credit and blasted the administrations of **FDR** and **Truman**. **Hoover** told him: "The conviction of Alger Hiss was due to your patience and persistence alone. At last the stream of treason that existed in our Government has been exposed in a fashion that all may believe." **Eisenhower** agreed, at the 1952 Republican convention describing **Nixon** as someone "with special talent and ability to ferret out any kind of subversive influence where it may be found and the strength and persistence to get rid of it."

LBJ spoke privately of retiring in 1948 at about age 40. He foresaw an anti-New Deal conservative era. The argument his close supporters used to dissuade him was that he would be "running out on **Roosevelt**." On election night in 1952 **LBJ** called **JFK** to congratulate him on his Senate victory. After the call, **JFK** said to an aide: "That was **Lyndon Johnson** in Texas. He said he just wanted to congratulate me. That guy must never sleep." **Ike** thought that **LBJ** "lacked the inner pressure gauge that told him when to relax. He had no hobbies or interests outside of politics."

LBJ had a heart attack in 1955. Both **Eisenhower** and **Nixon** visited him. **LBJ** thought that the heart attack ended his chances for the presidency. Ironically, he got encouragement when **Eisenhower** himself had a heart attack and went on to get re-elected.

In 1956 Senator **Kennedy** sent Senator and Majority Leader **Johnson** a telegram acknowledging the "the first class job you did for us all this year." He added that it was a "pleasure to be a **Johnson** man." In 1957 **JFK** said to MIT professor Walt Rostow: "The Democratic Party owes **Johnson** the nomination. He's earned it. He wants the same things for the country that I do. But it's too close to Appomattox for **Johnson** to be nominated and elected. So, therefore, I feel free to run." In the late 1950s **Nixon** said of **LBJ** that "He would be a successful President" but that his health and region were against him. In 1959 **JFK** told the National Press Club: "**Lyndon** would make the ablest president of any of us running, but he can't be elected."

At the 1960 Democrat convention in Los Angeles **LBJ** complained to his mentor Sam Rayburn that **JFK** "probably got himself a half dozen starlets." Rayburn told him not to be jealous. **LBJ** responded: "Jealous? Chickenshit. I'm not jealous, I'm just pissed off that I'm working my ass off and he's playing tiddly-winks."

The media covered up **JFK's** sexual infidelity as admitted in later years by journalist Hugh Sidey among others. But **JFK's** sexual activities probably had some effect on how he did his job. His decision in 1961 to retain FBI Director J. Edgar Hoover may have been caused by Hoover knowing about **JFK's** secrets and Hoover may also have been able to use the information to pressure Attorney General Robert Kennedy into approving wiretaps on Martin Luther King. In 1962 National Security Advisor McGeorge Bundy may have waited a day before giving **JFK** the news that surveillance photos revealed Soviet Missile sites in Cuba because **JFK** was tired from a liaison with a woman the night before: Bundy: "I decided that a quiet evening and a night of sleep were the best preparation." **JFK** and San Giancana a Chicago mob figure were both sleeping with a young woman named Judith Campbell Exner. J. Edgar Hoover learned of this in 1962. This story stayed hidden until 1975.

After the 1960 election, **JFK** advised **Nixon** to write his political memoirs which he did and which he titled *Six Crises*. (A decade later Mao Tse-tung told him that he had read and liked the book.) **Eisenhower** knew in 1967, according to **Nixon**, that **George HW Bush** "not only believed in the right conservative principles, but that he had the personality and charisma to win." After the 1964 election, **LBJ** turned more to **Eisenhower** for consultation on the Vietnam War. **Eisenhower's** advice was to go for victory. **LBJ** wrote him: "No one knows better than you the accumulated demands of the Presidency. No one gives more attention than you to the best interests of our country." In late 1967 members of **LBJ's** staff assisted **Eisenhower** and his wife in some matters. **Eisenhower** told them "No one has ever been nicer to me or to us than your president." In 1966, **Reagan** won the Republican gubernatorial primary in California. He went to Gettysburg and visited with **Eisenhower**. **Ike** was asked if **Reagan** would be a viable candidate for president in 1968 if he could beat incumbent Governor Edmund Brown in the fall. His answer: "You can bet."

After both **Nixon** and **Johnson** had died, **LBJ's** daughter said: "President **Nixon** very graciously would have somebody come down and brief Daddy on what was going on. He really did try to keep Daddy in the loop."

Late in life, **Nixon** referred to a recent book on **Woodrow Wilson** that asserted that friends of **Wilson** once paid hush money to a girl friend of **Wilson** to protect his career. **Nixon**: "Of course they paid her off - as they should have." (In the 1912 campaign both **Taft** and **TR** were offered romantic letters that **Wilson** had sent to a woman while he was married. They refused. **TR** joked that "no evidence could ever make the American people believe that a man like **Woodrow Wilson**, cast so perfectly as the apothecary's clerk, could ever play the Romeo.")

After receiving encouragement from **Nixon** while in his job as UN Ambassador, **George HW Bush** wrote in his diary: "This side of **Nixon** is totally unknown to people."

In the 1976 campaign **Jimmy Carter** responded to a memo that had been leaked that accused the **Nixon** and **Ford** administrations of using federal jobs as a dumping ground for defeated Republican candidates. **George HW Bush** was then director of the CIA. **Carter** said: "I happen to think a lot of **George Bush**. I would not include **George Bush** among those who were appointed without qualifications." A generation later, **Carter** was far more critical of **George W Bush** claiming that North Korea built nuclear weapons because **Bush** had labeled it "the axis of evil."

In 1981 American ally, President Anwar Sadat of Egypt was murdered. **Reagan** asked former presidents **Nixon**, **Ford** and **Carter** to represent the US at the Egyptian's funeral. During the trip **Carter** became close to **Ford** and they worked together on various initiatives in the next several years.

There were rumors linking **George HW Bush** to a woman on his staff. These rumors went back to 1974. This staffer had worked with **Bush** at the Republican National Committee and at his diplomatic post in Beijing. In Beijing they would eat together and shop when Barbara Bush was out of town. Once she went with **Bush** alone on an official trip from Beijing to Hawaii. Whether or not their relationship became sexual they did have a close emotional link and Barbara Bush found that hurtful. The rumors resurfaced in the 1988 campaign and **George W Bush** confronted his father and took the answer to *Newsweek* magazine that: "The answer to the Big A question is N-O." This discussion between father and son represented a maturing of their relationship. Laura Bush has said: "If there was any leftover competition with being named **George Bush** and being the eldest, it really at that point was resolved." The rumors of **George HW Bush** and this staffer came up again in the 1992 campaign.

In 1988 Vice President George **HW Bush** greeted **Reagan** upon his return from a trip to Moscow: "You made us proud. This week an American president strode the hard ground of Red Square and reminded the world through the sureness of his step and the lilt of his words what a bracing thing freedom is— what a moving and bracing thing."

On January 17, 1998 **Clinton** was deposed in the in a case involving a woman who had accused him of sexual harassment named Paula Jones. He was asked if he had ever been alone with an intern, Monica Lewinsky. He said that he did not remember, but that he might have been alone with her a few times when she delivered documents to him. He denied that he had sexual relations with her and the term "sexual relations" was broadly defined as contact to include intentionally touching in a sexual manner. During the deposition, **Clinton** studied the definition and indicated that he understood it. Near the end of the deposition, **Clinton's** attorney waived a copy of an affidavit from Lewinsky denying that she had had sex with President **Clinton**. **Clinton** said the affidavit was "absolutely true." In later months, Lewinsky came under an attack from unnamed White House staffers in a campaign that one *New York Times* liberal columnist later called "sickening."

In the next year, incontrovertible biological evidence that the President and Lewinsky had had some type of sexual activity emerged. In August **Clinton** testified before the grand jury over closed-circuit television from the White House. He insisted that he had not testified falsely in the *Jones* case when he denied having sexual relations with Lewinsky. One of the prosecutors pointed to a passage in the January 17 deposition in which **Clinton's** lawyer has asserted that "there is no sex of any kind in any manner shape or form" between **Clinton** and Monica Lewinsky and asked **Clinton** whether this "was an utterly false statement." **Clinton's** famous answer later appeared in *Bartlett's Familiar Quotations:* "It depends on what the meaning of is….is" He went on: "If 'is' means is, and never has been, that is one thing. If it means there is none, that was a completely true statement." Later that day **Clinton** addressed the nation. He acknowledged having had an "inappropriate" relationship with Lewinsky involving "intimate contact."

As **Clinton** then faced impeachment, **Ford** would not comment on **Clinton's** personal problems, and only said that he hoped "respect for the presidency would be restored soon." He consistently tried to downplay the entire issue. **Ford** wrote in the *New York Times* that **Clinton** should be "rebuked" but not impeached, the ultimate position of **Clinton's** supporters. After he was impeached anyway, **Ford** and **Carter** wrote that the Senate should "censure" rather than convict. **Ford** and **Carter** tried to craft a solution to censure **Clinton** but it fell apart.

Ford later recounted a conversation with **Clinton**:

Ford: "**Bill**, I think you have to admit that you lied. If you do that, I think that will help."

Clinton: "I won't do that. I *can't* do that."

Ford: "Well, **Bill**, this conversation must end."

Although **Clinton** was impeached, he survived in office. In essence the public accepted that the sexual contact between the president and Ms. Lewinsky was consensual and the lying was overlooked.

Some years later, Ms. Lewinsky spoke out. She asserted that **Clinton** had lied under oath in the *Jones* deposition and also that he was insincere when he told the public in 1998 that he had wronged her: "I think if he really felt these things – especially given the age difference and where I was in life, so young – at the very least, he would have apologized. Then he would have done something [to rectify the situation.] to me."

(In some ways, the scandal echoed a nineteenth century scandal involving a US president. During the campaign of 1884, it came out that **Cleveland** had fathered a son some ten years earlier with a young widow, Maria Halpin. **Cleveland** acknowledged paternity and his supporters stressed that both he and Mrs. Halpin were single at the time. Mark Twain said, "To see grown men, apparently in their right mind, seriously arguing against a bachelor's fitness for President because he had private intercourse with a consenting widow! Isn't human nature the most consummate sham & lie that was ever invented?" The most famous preacher in America, Henry Ward Beecher supported **Cleveland**. Democratic operatives reported that Ms. Halpin had had sex with several men and that **Cleveland** had accepted paternity to pretect the others, all of whom were married.

However, twenty-first century research has cast doubt on the version promoted by the Democrats that year. An affidavit sworn out in 1884 by Mrs. Halpin read in part about the one-time that Ms. Halpin said there was sexual contact with **Cleveland**: "While in my rooms he accomplished my ruin by the use of force and violence and without my consent. After he had accomplished his purpose he told me that he was determined to ruin me if it cost him ten thousand dollars, if he was hanged by the neck for it. I then and there told him that I never wanted to see him again and would never see him and commanded him to leave my rooms which he did. I never saw him after this until my condition became such that it was necessary for me to send for him some six weeks later to inform him of the consequences of his actions. He came to my rooms in response to my note which I sent him and when I told him of my condition and despair by reason of it, he pretended to make light of it and told me that he would do everything which was honorable and right towards me and promised that he would marry me which promises he has never kept."

Cleveland also survived this scandal with the public focusing on what it assumed was consensual sex instead of rape.)

In 2000 **Ford** said of **Clinton**: "He'll always have a blemish on the grounds of character, but on the other hand, you have to admit he's a hard-working, articulate, bright person who has done his darndest to build up an image. But you can't erase character problems." **Carter** was "deeply embarrassed" by the scandal and later wrote that **Clinton** "had not been truthful in the deposition given in the Paula Jones case or in the interrogation by the grand jury." The elder **George Bush** said on ABC's "This Week" about the possibility of a **Clinton** indictment: "I don't want something bad to happen. He's been through a lot. The country's been through a lot. Let's heal and forget." **Clinton** gave **Ford** the Presidential Medal of Freedom in 1999. In a book published after his death, **Ford** said about **Clinton's** sexual affairs: "Betty (**Ford's** wife) and I talked about this a lot. He's sick. He's got an addiction. He needs treatment."

In the 2000s **George HW Bush** said about **Clinton**. "…he is very considerate of me. I'm, you know, old enough to be his dad." **Clinton**, like **George W Bush**, was born the summer of 1946. His own father died in a car accident before his birth. The elder **Bush** even wondered aloud, to a Houston *Chronicle* reporter, if "I'm the father he never had." In 2004 at the dedication of the **Clinton** library **George HW Bush** said: "**Bill Clinton** proved himself to be more than a good politician In the White House, the whole nation witnessed his brilliance… The president was not the kind to give up a fight. His staffers were known to say that if **Clinton** were the *Titanic,* the iceberg would sink."

In 1990 **George HW Bush**, traveled to Kuwait to have Thanksgiving dinner with American troops who were poised to expel Saddam Hussein's Iraqi forces from Kuwait. In April 1993, an Iraqi plot to assassinate **George HW Bush** was revealed. President **Bill Clinton** responded by ordering a missile attack. In 2003 **George W Bush** traveled in secrecy to share Thanksgiving Dinner with American troops in Baghdad. Later that year, they captured Saddam who was subsequently hanged by the Iraqis.

In a 1998 re-election campaign for governor of Texas **George W Bush** used the term "compassionate conservative." Later **Clinton** said that when he heard that term he knew the Democrats were in trouble. In 2001 following his inauguration **George W Bush** was in the Oval Office. His father, **George HW Bush** said to him. "Mr. President." The son responded, "Mr. President." Both men began to cry. When the younger **Bush** was president, the criticisms of him affected his father more than it did him. He said he frequently had to call **George HW Bush** to get him to calm down. The son had this to say about the father: "His unconditional love inspired me and gave me the confidence necessary to go into public service." **George W Bush** still later said of his father: "**George Bush** set an example as a man who put civility and decency ahead of the ugliness of politics."

After the 9-11 attacks in 2001 **Clinton** said of **George W Bush**: "We should not be second-guessing. We should be supporting him." In 2004 portraits of **Bill** and Hillary **Clinton** were unveiled at the White House. **George W Bush** greeted the couple with, "Welcome home." He noted that his father and he often referred to themselves at "41" and "43" and added: "We're glad you're here, 42.'" **George W Bush** later told an interviewer: "How could you not like **Bill Clinton**?" In the fall campaign that year in which he ran against the Democrat John Kerry, **Bush** called **Clinton** who was in the hospital recovering from heart surgery and told him "This Kerry campaign is the most inept group I have ever seen in politics. Don't let them ruin your reputation." By 2014 **George W Bush had** developed a close friendship with **Bill Clinton** referring to him as his "brother from another mother."

In 1965 a hurricane damaged New Orleans. **LBJ** flew there and used a flashlight to find his way to a shelter where he told people: "This is your president. I'm here to help you." In 2005 **George W Bush** was criticized for a lack of empathy for those suffering from Hurricane Katrina which struck the same city. He later ruefully cited **Johnson's** example of leadership as one he should have followed.

George W. Bush at **Ford's** ninetieth birthday: "Many presidents have stayed longer but few have left the White House with greater respect from the American people, and none ever did more to restore the dignity and credibility of the office of the president than **Jerry Ford**."

In 2005 shortly before being sworn in as a senator **Obama** was in a group that met President **George W Bush** in the White House. **Bush** said, "**Obama**, come here and meet Laura. Laura, you remember **Obama**. We saw him on TV on election night. Beautiful family. And that wife of yours - that's one impressive lady." **Obama** responded, "We both got better than we deserve, Mr. President."

In 2009 President **Obama** attended a community service forum at Texas A&M University hosted by **George HW Bush**. **Obama** took the opportunity to emphasize that, regardless of partisan politics, the government can only do so much with the challenges facing

Americans. "We face threats to our health, our climate and, of course, our security that have left many of our young people wondering what kind of future they will be leaving for their own kids." **Obama** added: "Anyone here thinks that our government always has the solutions, President **Bush** and I will be the first to tell you that you'll be sorely disappointed."

In 2010 **Obama** took the position that the tax cuts put in place under **George W Bush** should not be extended for those earning over $250,000. **Bush** said nothing very negative about **Obama**, just that raising taxes on anyone right at that time would not be a good idea. **Obama** ended up supporting an extension of the **Bush** tax cuts for all taxpayers, a position that **Clinton** also supported.

At the unveiling of his official portrait at the White House in 2012 **George W. Bush** said to President **Obama**: "I am also pleased, Mr. President, that when you are wandering these halls as you wrestle with tough decisions, you will now be able to gaze at this portrait and ask: 'What would **George** do?'"

Obama said of **Reagan** near the centenary of the latter's birth: "Perhaps even more important than any single accomplishment was the sense of confidence and optimism President **Reagan** never failed to communicate to the American people. It was a spirit that transcended the most heated political arguments, and one that called each of us to believe that tomorrow will be better than today. At a time when our nation was going through an extremely difficult period, with economic hardship at home and very real threats beyond our borders, it was this positive outlook, this sense of pride, that the American people needed more than anything."

Wives and mothers express affinity and greatly influence Presidents. Abigail Adams wrote a sixteen-year-old **John Quincy Adams**, "What is it that affectionate parents require of their Children; for all their care, anxiety, and toil on their accounts? Only that they would be wise and virtuous, Benevolent and kind." A few years later she wrote to acknowledge his great opportunities: "How unpardonable would it have been in you to have been a blockhead." Abigail Adams was a domineering mother. While in his twenties **John Quincy Adams** broke off a romance apparently following his mother's insistence. This inveterate diarist did not write about it for over forty years. In 1976 a newspaper opined that "President **Ford** would be a better man and a better leader if he paid more heed to his wife, Betty, who is consistently demonstrating that she has more sense, honesty, and moral courage than the man she married." **George W Bush's** younger sister died in 1953 of leukemia when he was seven. His mother gave more attention to the remaining children. "She kind of smothered me," he said.

In the 1780s, Abigail Adams called **Jefferson** "one of the choicest ones of the earth." She told **Jefferson** that she had seldom seen anyone with whom her husband could associate with "such perfect freedom and unreserve." In 1956 **Hoover** praised **Woodrow Wilson** who by that time had been dead for more than thirty years: "He was "a man of staunch morals. He was more than just an idealist; he was the personification of the heritage of idealism of the American people. He brought spiritual concepts to the peace table. He was a born crusader." He defended **Wilson's** moralism in the Versailles conference arguing that he was trying to deal in a hate-filled atmosphere with his faith in democracy. **Hoover's** 1958 book, *The Ordeal of Woodrow Wilson* was a best seller. **Wilson's** wife said to **Hoover**: "...you really seem to have understood him."

In 1952 **Nixon's** wife Pat urged him to persevere when he was thinking about quitting the Republican ticket amidst a scandal. She told him that if **Eisenhower** wanted to force him from the ballot, then he would probably lose the election but that **Nixon** would soon be vindicated. But if he decided to "crawl away, you will destroy yourself. Your life will be marred forever and the same will be true of your family and, particularly, your daughters." **Nixon** stayed. In 1964 Lady Bird Johnson talked **Lyndon Johnson** out of quitting the presidency telling him he was "as brave a man as **Harry Truman** - or **FDR** - or **Lincoln**." In the early 2000s, Barbara Bush was asked if she was "fond" of **Clinton**. Her response was ambivalent: "Yes. All right. Yes, no, I like him." "I just enjoy being with the guy."

What is the point of all this?

The presidents are in the most select historical club. Their shared experiences drive most to an underlying respect for each other.

The second volume of **Grant's** *Memoirs* which came out in the 1880s had this assessment of **Hayes**: "His conduct on the field was marked by conspicuous gallantry as well as the display of qualities of a higher order than that of mere personal daring. This might well have been expected of one who could write: 'Any officer fit for duty who at this crisis would abandon his post to electioneer for a seat in Congress ought to be scalped.'" **Hayes** said this "brought tears" to his eyes.

In the 1920 campaign, **Harding** was appealing to a country tired of war in Europe and disillusioned. He said of the domestic effects **Wilson's** war policies: "In the name of democracy, we established autocracy." But **Harding's** advisors wanted him to go farther. He replied: "I guess you have nominated the wrong candidate, if this is the plan, for I will never go to the White House over the broken body of **Woodrow Wilson**."

Here is another example of respect. During World War II, the brother of **JFK**, Joseph P. Kennedy Jr., died in action. His father confronted **Truman** in 1944 when **Truman** was running on the Democrat ticket with **Franklin Roosevelt**: "**Harry**, what the hell are you doing campaigning for that crippled son-of-a-bitch that killed my son Joe?" The senior Kennedy went on, saying **Roosevelt** had caused the war. **Truman**, by his later account, stood all he could, then told Kennedy to keep quiet or he would throw him out the window.

At any given time only a few people alive have been president. **Richard Nixon** saw three former presidents die during his years in office – **Eisenhower**, **Truman** and **LBJ** - and for the last two years of his presidency had no living predecessors. On the other end of this spectrum, **Lincoln**, **Clinton** and **George W. Bush** all had, at one time in their presidencies, five living predecessors. This selectivity drives the presidents to make historical pronouncements. From these we learn, if not profundities, at least more about the US.

Chapter 3

Historical Perspectives

Overall Context

In his 1824-25 trip to America the French hero Marquis de Lafayette saw **Jefferson**, **Madison, Monroe**, **John Quincy Adams** and **Jackson** – and the grave of **George Washington**.

Presidents brush up against presidential history. When **Obama** once declared **Ronald Reagan** historically consequential and **Bill Clinton** not, he was in effect saying that he (**Obama**) intended to be the **Reagan** of a new liberalism. **TR** in 1910 felt he had missed a chance at greatness. He told an audience in England: "...if **Lincoln** had lived in times of peace, no one would know his name now." **Grant** graduated from West Point in 1843. In the few years after that he served, among other places at **Jefferson** Barracks near St. Louis, in northern Mexico under **Taylor** and in **Madison** Barracks in Sackets Harbor, New York.

Nixon's favorite twentieth century president was **Wilson** and **Carter's** was **Truman**. In planning his post presidential life **Clinton** studied the lives of **John Quincy Adams** and **Jimmy Carter**.

Presidents have noted the Declaration of Independence:

- In 1776 **John Adams** wrote his wife: "The (date) will be the most memorable Epocha, in the History of America. I am apt to believe that it will be celebrated, by succeeding Generations, as the great anniversary Festival. It ought to be commemorated, as the Day of Deliverance by solemn Acts of Devotion to God Almighty. It ought to be solemnized with

Pomp and Parade, with Shews, Games, Sports, Guns, Bells, Bonfires and Illuminations from one End of this Continent to the other from this Time forward forever more.

- In 1876 President **Grant** opened up an exposition in Philadelphia which subtly signaled the emergence of the US as a world power.
- In 1976 President **Ford** commemorated the Bicentennial and said on July 4 of that year: "In its first two centuries the nation has not been able to right every wrong, to correct every injustice, or to reach every worthy goal. But for two hundred years we have tried, and we will continue to strive to make the lives of individual men and women in this country and on earth better lives – more hopeful and happy, more prosperous and peaceful, more fulfilling and more free. This is our common dedication and it will be our common glory as we enter the third century of the American adventure."

Presidents are concerned with how history will regard them and are anxious to get credit for accomplishments. Even before the Revolutionary War **John Adams** asked Abigail to save his letters and in 1776 he bought a "Folio Book" to keep copies of his letters so that he could preserve a record of "the great Events which are passed, and those greater which are rapidly advancing." He encouraged **John Quincy Adams** to start a journal when they went to France together during the war. A very young **John Quincy Adams** wrote in 1779: "My Pappa enjoins upon me to keep a journal, or Diary of the Events that happen to me, and of objects that I See, and of Characters that I converse with from day to day, and altho I am Convinced of the utility, importance & and necessity of the Exercise, yet I have not patience and perserverence enough to do it Constantly as I ought." The first entry was November 12, 1779 the day before **Adams** began his second voyage to Europe with his father. **Adams** kept it for the next seventy years and it is a source for anyone studying that era. **Jefferson, Polk, Hayes, Garfield, TR, Taft, Wilson, Truman, Eisenhower, Carter, Reagan and George HW Bush** and others all kept diaries.

Moving Forward

Recovering from exhaustion after the War of 1812 **Monroe** read John Marshall's *The Life of George Washington*. It reconciled him to the first President and influenced the rest of his political career.

In 1815 **John Adams** wrote:

"Mr. **Madison's** administration has proved great points, long disputed in Europe and America:

1. He has proved that an administration, under our present Constitution, can declare war.
2. That it can make peace.
3. That, money or no money, government or no government, Great Britain can never conquer this country or any considerable part of it.
4. That our officers and men by land are equal to any (of Wellington's forces) from Spain and Portugal.
5. That our navy is equal...to any that ever floated on the ocean."

In 1817 **Monroe** went on a tour of the Northeast. He and **John Adams** toasted each other at a dinner hosted by **Adams** to cheers and applause. **Adams** wrote Attorney General Richard Rush: "I could write you a volume on the visitation of the president to the eastern states. The result has been highly favorable to the public cause. Not an indiscretion has escaped from him. And his patience and activity have been such as I could never imitate and such as I could scarcely believe feasible."

Some historical clams can be grandiose. **John Adams** wrote to **Jefferson** in 1817: "Not withstand(ing) a thousand Faults and blunders," **Madison's** administration had "acquired more glory, and established more Union than all his three Predecessors, **Washington, Adams, Jefferson,** put together." In 1837 **John Quincy Adams** orated that the Declaration of Independence was second in importance to the history of humanity only to the coming of

Christ. (**Lyndon Johnson** declared on the cusp of the Great Society: "These are the most hopeful times since Christ was born.")

Lincoln lost his first race for the state legislature in 1832 but won his own precinct 222-7. He noted that he was a devout supporter of Henry Clay and the precinct itself was not and that later that year it gave "a majority to Genl. **Jackson** over Mr. Clay."

One of **Polk's** first actions was to hang a portrait of **Jackson** in his office. (He untactfully wrote **Jackson**: "The contrast between your appearance then and now is very great.")

Upon receiving the Whig nomination for Vice President to run with **William Henry Harrison** in 1840 **Tyler** said, "To have my name associated with that of the imminent patriot ... is ...no ordinary honor. The friend and supporter of **Jefferson**, of **Madison**, and of **Monroe**, and the immediate descendant of a signer of the Declaration of Independence, can be none other than true to his early Republican creed..." A few months later he ascended to the presidency and substantially repeated that sentiment: "In the administration of the government, I shall act upon the principles which I have all along espoused - derived from the teachings of **Jefferson** and **Madison**."

Looking back, in 1841 **John Quincy Adams** called **Jackson's** Indian removal policies an "abomination." "It is among the heinous sins of this nation, for which I believe God will bring to them judgment."

In 1847 **Polk** spoke in Philadelphia's independence Hall: "This is the hall in which sat that venerable body of men - here sat John Hancock - here sat **Thomas Jefferson** - here sat your own Franklin and Rush - that venerable, that illustrious body of men, (God bless their memories!) who made the astounding declaration to the world - that a nation of freemen lived!" He noted that it had been seventy years and then "when seventy more years have passed away - when other Presidents shall have enjoyed the honor which I now enjoy of being warmly welcomed by the citizens and municipal government of this city, I would ask - what human sagacity can foresee the prosperity and greatness of my beloved country? May our constitution ever be held sacred, our Union unbroken and inviolate."

In 1840 **Andrew Johnson** called for county Democrats to rally in Greenville Tennessee. They came by horses, carts and wagons and on foot. Someone read resolutions **Johnson** had written. These criticized **John Adams** for the Alien and Sedition Acts of more than forty years earlier. **Thomas Jefferson** by then dead nearly fifteen years was lauded. The so called "Corrupt Bargain" of 1824 that put **John Quincy Adams** in the White House over **Andrew Jackson** was criticized. **Jackson** was praised. **Johnson's** speech also criticized the Hartford Convention of 1815 which was a meeting by New England states with secessionist tendencies. One of **Andrew Johnson's** first acts in Congress was to secure reimbursement to **Andrew Jackson** for a fine that **Jackson** incurred from a New Orleans judge in 1812. This presaged a similar action forty years later. At the very end of his term **Arthur** recommended to Congress a bill which became law to give **Grant** a pension with a special provision that gave him a considerable salary in the last months of his life. **Grant** was being harassed by creditors and dying of cancer.

Lincoln on **Jefferson** at the outbreak of the Civil War: "All honor to **Jefferson**." And, "The principles of **Jefferson** are the definitions and axioms of free society." When faced with secession threats soon turned to reality, **Lincoln** hung a portrait of **Jackson** in his office.

Andrew Johnson, facing challenges in 1866, said that if **Andrew Jackson** knew what was going on in our country today he "would shake off the habiliments of the tomb and declare 'the Constitution and the Union, they must be preserved.'" In this he was quoting a famous toast by **Jackson** in a state dinner in 1830. **Andrew Johnson** instructed his staff not to remove a desk because it had been used by **Andrew Jackson**.

Pierce revered **Andrew Jackson**. In 1868 in New York at a celebration that included **Andrew Johnson** honoring **Jackson's** victory in the battle of New Orleans over fifty years earlier, a letter from **Pierce** was read: "No one can sit at your banquet table without contrasting with painful emotions the condition of our country now with what it was during the eight years that the great defender of the Crescent City (**Jackson**) was at the head of the government."

In 1885 **Chester Alan Arthur** by then a former president was a trustee of the **Grant** Memorial Association charged to build "a great national monument which shall appropriately testify to future ages" for "the grandest character of the century."

In retirement **Hayes** said that all of the Presidents from **Washington** to **Jackson** were "free of the least taint of personal corruption. All were honest men. All were in the best sense gentlemen." He also wrote of **Cleveland** (who was of the opposite party) "I no doubt like him better than the majority of those who elected him. He is sound on the currency, the tariff, and the reform of the civil service." He worried about the lack of tact and friendliness of **Benjamin Harrison.** He had positive feelings about **McKinley.** (Nearly a century later, **Nixon** jotted down similar thoughts: **FDR** – "Charm." **Truman** – "Gutsy." **Eisenhower** – "Smile, prestige." **Kennedy** – "Charm." **LBJ** – "Vitality.") In 1890 **Hayes** wrote in his diary: "**Lincoln** was for a government of the people. The new tendency is "a government of the rich, by the rich, and for the rich."

Truman during the 1948 campaign: "....under that great engineer, **Hoover**, we backed up into the worst depression in history."

TR criticized **Jackson's** "narrow mind" and "bitter prejudices." **TR** criticized **Jefferson** as a "scholarly, timid, and shifty doctrinaire." In 1896, **TR** supported **McKinley** over William Jennings Bryan. It was an era that had seen a great deal of labor strife - the Haymarket bombing, the Homestead Strike - and **TR** compared labor activists to the leaders of the French Revolution. He added: "If Bryan wins, we have before us some years of social misery, not markedly different from that of any South American republic... Bryan closely resembles **Thomas Jefferson**, whose ascension to the Presidency was a terrible blow to this nation." **TR** thought **Jefferson's** foreign policy was "a discredit to my country."

Harding more subtly attacked **Jefferson** by dedicating a statue to Alexander Hamilton in 1923. **FDR** put **Jefferson** at near the very top of the presidents by dedicating the **Jefferson** Memorial in 1943. **Woodrow Wilson** in 1912 on **Grant**: "The honest, simple-hearted soldier had not added prestige to the presidential office.... He ought never to have been made President." In 1922 Vice President **Calvin Coolidge** dedicated the **Grant** Memorial in Washington DC.

Theodore Roosevelt held that **Tyler** was "a politician of monumental littleness and that **Tyler** and **Andrew Johnson** "were the most contemptible presidents we have ever had."

Harding put **Taft's** name into nomination at the 1912 convention which was torn by rivalry between **Taft** and **TR. Harding** called **Taft** "the greatest progressive of the age." He added that **Taft** "was the finest example of lofty principles since the immortal **Lincoln** bore the scourge of vengeful tongues without a murmur from his noble heart." **Coolidge** in 1929 about the **Harding** presidency: "It would be difficult to find two years of peace time history in all of our republic that were marked with more important and far-reaching accomplishments. He listed:

- Higher tariffs.
- Lower taxes.
- A new budget system.
- A postwar peace that **Harding** made with the central powers.

Hoover as President: "This is not a showman's job, I will not step out of character and you can't make a **Teddy Roosevelt** out of me."

Shortly after coming into office, **FDR** gave these views: "**Washington** personified the idea of Federal union. **Jefferson** practically originated the party system as we now know it by opposing the democratic theory to the republicanism of Hamilton. This theory was...reaffirmed by **Jackson**. Two great principles of our government were forever put beyond question by **Lincoln**. **Cleveland**, coming into office after a period of great political corruption, typified rugged honesty. **Theodore Roosevelt** and **Wilson** were both moral leaders, each in his own way and for his own time, who used the Presidency as a pulpit." In an informal setting once, **FDR** asked people present to name four great leaders from history. His own choices were: Benjamin Franklin, **Jefferson** and **TR** and an advisor to Oliver Cromwell.

Harry Truman wrote his wife after two months as president about previous presidents, picturing them as ghosts in the White House: "I can just imagine old **Andy (Jackson)** and **Teddy (Roosevelt)** having an argument over **Franklin (Roosevelt)**. Or **James Buchanan** and **Franklin Pierce** deciding which was more useless to the country. And when **Millard Fillmore** and **Chester Arthur** join in for place and show the din is almost unbearable." **Truman** on **Pierce**: "He was the best looking president the White House ever had, but he ranked with **Buchanan** and **Coolidge** as one of the worst." (Queen Victoria of England never met **Pierce** but she met his predecessor **Millard Fillmore** in London in the mid-1850s after he left the presidency and considered him the handsomest man she had ever met.)

Elected in 1844 **Polk** promised to serve only one term and had four objectives:

- An Independent Treasury System
- Tariff reduction.
- Acquisition of at least some of the Oregon Country. (**Polk's** bargaining position was "Fifty-four Forty or Fight!" but he settled for less.)
- The acquisition of California and New Mexico

By the end of his term, he retired and he was dead within months.

A century later **Truman** said of **Polk**: "He said exactly what he was going to do and he did it." **Truman** on **Jackson**: "He wanted sincerely to look after the little fellow who had no pull and that's what a president is supposed to do." **Truman** said that "in many ways **Wilson** was the greatest of the greats." **Truman** believed that the UN Charter had vindicated **Wilson's** vision of the League of Nations. During the Korean War, **Truman** attempted to prevent a strike by ordering the military to seize steel mills. He justified this action – which the Supreme Court subsequently found "illegal" - by noting that **Lincoln**, **Wilson** and **FDR** had all used their inherent powers in the interests of national security.

In the early 1920s while stationed in Panama, **Eisenhower** was encouraged to read **Grant's** *Memoirs* by his commanding officer. In preparing to write his own memoirs - *Crusade in Europe* - in 1947, **Eisenhower** reread **Grant**. Six decades earlier, **Hayes** read the first volume of **Grant's** *Memoirs* and said it was "intensely interesting and very valuable." He added "It is graphic and simple and as truthful as truth itself." Six decades later **Clinton** tried to model his own autobiography on **Grant's** *Memoirs*. Still later, when **George W Bush** was considering writing his memoirs he consulted historians. Nearly all of them suggested he read **Grant's** *Memoirs* which he did.

In 1937 **LBJ** won his first election to Congress with the motto: "**Franklin D** and **Lyndon B**." In 1969 on his last day in office and as one of his last acts, **Lyndon Johnson** signed a proclamation adding territory to the national park system establishing a "**Franklin Delano Roosevelt** Memorial Park." It was dedicated in 1997 by **Clinton**. **JFK** was surprised that Americans rated **TR** so highly since he had never led the country through any war. **Nixon** titled one of his books *In the Arena* in homage of **TR**. (**Roosevelt** gave a speech in France in 1910 from which portions were written into an article entitled "The Man in the Arena.")

Hoover wrote in 1952 about **Coolidge**: "With his associates there was little of taciturnity. Many times over the five years he sent for men to come to the White House after dinner just to talk an hour or two. He had a fund of New England stories and a fine, dry wit." In 1976 **Carter** compared **Ford** to **Hoover** in failing to provide leadership for the country. The **Kennedy** half-dollar with the image of President **John F. Kennedy** was first minted in 1964, a year after his assassination. **Lyndon Johnson** said that he would order the minting of so many **Kennedy** half-dollars that the market could be saturated and that would force the coins to stay in circulation.

In 1947 **Reagan** as the president of the actors union testified before a congressional committee. He appeared with fellow actors Robert Taylor and Gary Cooper. This was his first meeting with **Nixon** who was on the committee. Although **Reagan** said he abhorred communism he advocated strong labor union action and a civil libertarian approach in combating it. He said, "I believe that, as **Thomas Jefferson** put it, if all the American people know all the facts they will never make a mistake."

In 1959 the Senate refused to confirm **Dwight Eisenhower's** selection for Secretary of Commerce. **Eisenhower** blamed Senate President **Lyndon Johnson**. He said it was the second worst day in the US Senate, second only to when it tried **Andrew Johnson**: "This was the most shameful thing that had happened in the US Senate since the attempt (*sic*) to impeach a president many, many years ago."

In the 1960 campaign, **Kennedy** quoted two of America's greatest presidents:

- "**Franklin Roosevelt** said in 1936 that that generation of Americans had a rendezvous with destiny. I believe in 1960 and sixty-one and two and three we have a rendezvous with destiny."
- "In the election of 1860, **Abraham Lincoln** said the question was whether this nation could exist half-slave or half-free. In the election of 1960, and with the world around us, the question is whether the world will exist half-slave or half-free ..."

On October 27, 1964 **Ronald Reagan** gave a televised speech for Republican candidate Barry Goldwater. Goldwater lost to **Lyndon Johnson** a few days later in a landslide but **Reagan's** speech launched a political career that took him to the California governorship in 1967 defeating an incumbent and to the presidency in 1981 also defeating an incumbent, **Jimmy Carter**. In the 1964 speech, **Reagan** began by quoting **James Madison**:

"I am going to talk of controversial things. I make no apology for this. It's time we asked ourselves if we still know the freedoms intended for us by the Founding Fathers. **James Madison** said, 'We base all our experiments on the capacity of mankind for self government.' This idea — that government was beholden to the people, that it had no other source of power — is still the newest, most unique idea in all the long history of man's relation to man."

Reagan closed this speech by, like **JFK,** quoting **FDR:** "You and I have a rendezvous with destiny. We will preserve for our children this, the last best hope of man on earth, or we will sentence them to take the first step into a thousand years of darkness. If we fail, at least let our children and our children's children say of us we justified our brief moment here. We did all that could be done."

In 1969 **Nixon** told his domestic advisors that "I'd like to see more decisions made by the responsible men. **John Quincy Adams** and **Grover Cleveland** read every bill and almost killed themselves." After he left office **Nixon** said: "Democratic presidents, since **FDR**, had excelled - reveled - in flexing the formidable political muscle that goes with being the party in the White House... So I ended up keeping the pressure on the people around me to get organized, to get tough, to get information on what the other side was doing... I told my staff we should come up with the same kind of imaginative dirty tricks that our Democratic opponents used against us and others so effectively in previous campaigns."

In 1970 **Nixon** spoke to the nation from the White House about a military incursion into Cambodia during the Vietnam War. He cited other presidents: "In this room **Woodrow Wilson** made the great decisions which led to victory in World War I. **Franklin Roosevelt** made the decisions which led to our victory in World War II.... **John F. Kennedy**, in his finest hour, made the great decision which removed Soviet nuclear missiles from Cuba and the Western Hemisphere." In 1972 as he accepted his re-nomination, **Nixon** mentioned his five predecessors - **FDR**, **Truman**, **Eisenhower**, **JFK**, and **LBJ** - in his criticism of isolationism.

In 1973 **Richard Nixon** fired Special Prosecutor Archibald Cox in what came to be called the "Saturday Night Massacre" in a defining moment in the Watergate scandal. The issue had to do with Cox demanding that the White House turn over tapes of presidential conversations in defiance of **Nixon's** refusal to do so. Governor **Ronald Reagan** was asked for a comment. He said: "I will not comment on the issue of Archibald Cox being discharged since it is relatively unimportant." But **Reagan** went on to say that the issue **Nixon** faced with Cox's refusal to follow orders was "the same problem that confronted President **Truman** during the Korean War." **Reagan** was referring to **Truman's** firing of General Douglas MacArthur.

As he considered his 1980 run for the presidency, **Reagan** often reflected on **Madison's** statement that through history people most often lost freedom not in armed conflict but in "gradual and silent encroachment of those in power." **Coolidge** and his traditional conservatism were somewhat of an inspiration to **Reagan** who said: "I happen to be an admirer of **Silent Cal** and believe he has been badly treated by history." **Reagan** was a teenager during the **Coolidge** presidency and put **Coolidge's** portrait and one of **Eisenhower** in the Cabinet Room of the White House (replacing **Jefferson** and **Truman**). In 1981 **Reagan** said of **Coolidge** that "he cut the taxes four times."

Reagan said of **Truman**: "I believe that the President of the United States is what **Harry Truman** called him: he is the people's lobbyist in Washington...the only one there who was elected for all the people. "After he left office **George HW Bush** wrote: "I supported much of **Harry Truman's** foreign policy in the late 1940s. But I didn't like what he and the Democratic Party stood for in the way of big, centralized government..." **George W Bush** said that when **Reagan** left office "people had soured on his administration" but by the time of his death in 2004 "perceptions of him had changed" for the better. In 2003 **Clinton** wrote in the context of his designating national monuments in 2001 that he tried to stick to **Theodore Roosevelt's** conservation ethic to take "the long look ahead."

As he went into office the politician that President **Obama** admired the most was **Bill Clinton**. **Obama** thought that **Clinton** "instinctively understood the falseness of the choices being presented to the American people." **Clinton** "tapped into the pragmatic, non-ideological attitude of the majority of Americans." But **Obama** also said: "**Ronald Reagan** changed the trajectory of America in a way that **Richard Nixon** did not, that **Bill Clinton** did not."

In 2010 **Carter** said, "I feel my role as a former president is probably superior to other presidents." He offered several explanations to support his premise, suggesting his charitable work on the world stage had more impact than that of **George HW Bush**, **Bill Clinton** and **George W Bush**. **Carter** said about the same time: "This country has become so polarized that it's almost astonishing... Not only with the red states and blue states... President **Obama** suffers from the most polarized situation in Washington that we have ever seen - even maybe than the time of **Abraham Lincoln** and the initiation of the war between the states."

In 2010 **George W Bush** released his autobiography to which **Clinton** responded: "**George W Bush** ... gives readers a good sense of what it's like to be president, to take the responsibilities of the office seriously, do what you think is right, and let history be the judge."

In 2013 **Jimmy Carter** talked of asking **George W Bush** to do something about a civil war in the Sudan. **Carter** said that **Bush** set up meetings for him with the Secretary of State. **Carter** concluded: "In January of 2005, there was a peace treaty between north and south Sudan that ended a war that had been going on for 20 years. **George W. Bush** is responsible for that."

What is the point of all this?

When **George Washington** surrendered his military commission to the Congress in 1783 his retirement dinner was attended by **Jefferson**, **Madison** and **Monroe**. That was surely an historical moment and the four Virginia planters, concerned as they were about posterity, may have grasped it. Unconvincingly, however, presidents occasionally minimize their role or even deny that they care about history. **TR** in 1906: "I am not in the least concerned as to whether I will have any place in history and, indeed, I do not remember ever thinking about it." **Taft** in 1912 about his administration: "It is a very humdrum, uninteresting administration, and does not attract the attention or enthusiasm of anybody but after I am out, I think ...I can look back with some pleasure in having done something for the benefit of the public weal."

In many ways, **Rutherford B Hayes** was ahead of his time. In the 1880 campaign he told a veterans group that the Civil War destroyed slavery but "its evils live after it." He argued for education and equal rights and he knew that education in the South and western territories would require federal aid. Or, as he put it in another context: "The first half (of) my active political life was ...to resist the increase of slavery and ...to destroy it... The second half...has been to rebuild, and to get rid of the despotic and corrupting tendencies and the animosities of the war, and the other legacies of slavery." His interests extended beyond race relations and education. In 1888 **Hayes** said: "...I think the time for capital punishment has passed."

Coolidge: "Perhaps one of the most important accomplishments of my administration has been minding my own business." **LBJ** rejected advice from a staffer to give a speech to Congress in 1968 after the assassination of Martin Luther King without a specific program to offer: "Words without actions isn't leadership. I guess **Roosevelt** and **Kennedy** and maybe some of the others could do what you're talking about, but pretty words aren't my style." According to **Clinton**, "two of the great achievements" of his presidency were fighting the Republicans during a government shutdown and surviving impeachment.

In short all or most of the presidents seem to have some interest in the others in their small class. Some probably liked to look back to earlier presidents because they agreed with **Truman** who thought that "the presidents made the highlights of American history, and when you tell about them, you've got it."

Chapter 4

Transitions

The Presidents have perhaps understood each other most at times of transition. Both when a change in presidents occurs and when one dies, presidents are moved to comment and those comments illuminate American history.

Overall Context of Presidential Transitions

In eighteenth century America, it made sense to provide a four month interval between the election and the inauguration of the president. In 1776 it took **John Adams** 15 days by horseback over icy roads sometimes in 20 degree temperature and staying at inns to get from Braintree (near Boston) to Philadelphia. He wrote that it was a "cold journey." Travel in that era meant going on roads that were water-bogged, interrupted by tree stumps and which came to resemble tunnels going through dense forests. During this time interval problems occasionally arose:

- **Madison** to **Jefferson** regarding **John Adams**' last days in office: "Instead of smoothing the path for his successor he plays into the hands of those who are endeavoring to strew it with as many difficulties as possible."
- **Polk** to his diary in 1849: "General **Taylor** is, I have no doubt, a well-meaning old man. He is, however, uneducated, exceedingly ignorant of public affairs, and I should judge of very ordinary capacity. He will be in the hands of others, and must rely wholly upon his cabinet to administer the government." Before the inauguration of **Taylor**, **Polk** ordered his cabinet members not to call on him until **Taylor** first called on **Polk**. The cabinet agreed, overriding the disagreement of Secretary of State **Buchanan**.

- During the period between the election of **Lincoln** and the inauguration, **Buchanan** ineffectively argued that it was unconstitutional for states to leave the union but that he could do nothing about it.
- **Herbert Hoover** in 1933 toward the end of his term looking at the Great Depression and feeling that **FDR** was purposefully let the banking crisis grow: "Perhaps they want a breakdown. That is always the technique of revolution."

Issues like this became an argument for the Twentieth Amendment to the Constitution passed in 1933. It reduced the amount of time between Election Day and the beginning of Presidential term from March 4 to January 20.

Yet, the **Truman-Eisenhower** transition was the most hostile of the twentieth century. **Truman** described **Eisenhower** as "frozen grimness throughout" and added that he tried to give **Eisenhower** advice on how to organize his staff but "I think all this went into one ear and out the other." That last part was accurate. Years later **Eisenhower** wrote in his memoirs that this meeting with **Truman** which lasted about twenty minutes and was the only meeting between the two between the election and the inauguration "added little to my knowledge, nor did it affect my planning for the new administration..."

Many Presidents have expressed great relief at leaving office. However, there are exceptions. Both **TR** in 1909 and **Clinton** in 2001 left office with regrets. **TR** tried for a third term in 1912; **Clinton** helped his wife to a close second in the Democrat primaries in 2008.

Moving Forward

Here are some of the other presidential transitions.

In 1789 when **Washington** accepted the presidency he said he was like "a culprit who is going to the place of his execution." As the inauguration of **John Adams** in 1797, **George Washington** whispered to him: "Ay! I am fairly out and you fairly in! See which of us will be the happiest."

The 1800 election was suffused with bitterness and ended in the defeat of **John Adams** by **Jefferson**. The outgoing president did not attend the inauguration and the two did not correspond for years except that **Adams** sent him this note from Massachusetts: "This part of the Union is in a state of perfect tranquility and I see nothing to obscure your prospect of a quiet and prosperous administration, which I heartily wish you." **Jefferson** noted at the inauguration of **Madison** in 1809 that he had been relieved of a burden and that he was "much happier at the moment than my friend." **John Quincy Adams** about the inaugural ball that year: "The crowd was excessive, the heat oppressive, and the entertainment bad."

Upon hearing that **John Quincy Adams** had been elected in 1824, **John Adams** sent a message that "the multitude of my thoughts and the intensity of my feelings are too much for a mind like mine in its ninetieth year." He called for "the blessings of God Almighty" on his son. **William Henry Harrison** wrote a supporter about **John Quincy Adams'** inaugural address: "The Inauguration Address of Mr. **Adams** has given general satisfaction. You will see that he is *up to the Hub* for internal improvements." In 1829 after his defeat but before the inauguration of **Jackson**, **John Quincy Adams** noted that **Jackson** was in Washington but had not come to see him. He wrote that **Jackson** had "not thought it proper to hold any personal communication with me since his arrival." **Adams** sent a marshal to **Jackson** to let him know that "I should remove my family from the house so that he may, if he thinks proper, receive his visits of congratulations here on the 4th of March." **Monroe** wrote **Adams** at that low point in the latter's life: "I shall always be happy to see you here, and wherever we may chance to meet. I shall through life, take a sincere and great interest in your welfare and happiness."

In 1841 after a rough campaign in which he had been defeated, President **Martin Van Buren** broke tradition by paying President-elect **William Henry Harrison** a return visit and he took his entire cabinet. **Van Buren** said: "The President is the most extraordinary man I ever saw. He does not seem to realize the vast importance of his elevation. He talks and thinks with...much ease and vivacity... He is as tickled with the Presidency as is a young woman with a new bonnet." **Van Buren** offered to leave the White House before the inauguration day and **Harrison** declined with thanks. During the interval **Harrison** was besieged by job-seekers driving him to exhaustion. Member of Congress **Millard Fillmore** observed: "I understand they have come down upon General **Harrison** like a pack of famished wolves." **John Quincy Adams** wrote: "His popularity is all artificial. There is little confidence in his talents of firmness. ... **Harrison** comes in upon a hurricane; God grant that he may not go out upon a wreck." **Adams** added that the inauguration was "showy-shabby, like the campaign" and that the horse **Harrison** rode was "mean-looking." **Harrison** died within a month.

As negotiations over annexation of Texas continued in 1844, **Tyler** who was soon to leave office told the Mexican government that an invasion of Texas would be an act of war against the US. In response, **Andrew Jackson** observed to President-elect **James Polk**: "This is the true energetic course." **John Quincy Adams** agreed, writing that **Tyler** had acted with "intrepity and access." But negotiations stalled and in his very last few days in office **Tyler** had to decide whether to accept a congressional resolution on the annexation of Texas and decided to do so. He sent John Calhoun to inform the incoming President **Polk** of his decision. Calhoun reported back that "**Mr. Polk** declined to express any opinion or to make any suggestion with regard to the subject."

Between his election and inauguration in 1852-1853, **Franklin Pierce** wrote to intra-party rival **James Buchanan** about the cabinet. He said he did not want to meet because it would lead the public to "speculations and groundless surmises." He asked for advice and also said that he intended to appoint men who had "not hitherto occupied cabinet position." This ruled out **Buchanan** who had been Secretary of State under **Polk**. **Buchanan** responded quickly with what he called "by far the longest letter I have written in my life." He gave advice and said about himself that **Pierce's** letter "relieved me from no little personal anxiety. Had you offered me a seat in your cabinet...I would have declined it without a moment's hesitation."

The transition between **Buchanan** and **Lincoln** during the secession crisis of 1860-61 was the most dangerous in the history of the US with the possible exception of the **Kennedy**-to-**Johnson** transition a century later. **Buchanan's** annual message in December of 1860 was convoluted but he concluded that the Constitution did not empower the president or the Congress "to coerce a State into submission which is attempting to withdraw, or has actually withdrawn." He also placed in a state paper this remarkable swipe at **Abraham Lincoln**: "(T)he election of any one of our fellow-citizens to the office of President does not of itself afford just cause for dissolving the Union" even if "the antecedents of the President elect have been sufficient to justify the fears of the South that he will attempt to invade their constitutional rights." (By that time **Buchanan** showed mental strain much like **Wilson** would during his efforts for the League of Nations in the summer of 1919 and **Nixon** would during the Watergate scandal in the summer of 1974.)

During this period, **Lincoln** kept publicly quiet but wrote his concerns to members of Congress. He opposed popular sovereignty, the notion that states could vote slavery up or down and he opposed an extension of the Missouri Compromise of 1820 line. In these he adhered to the Republican Party platform on which he had run. He objected to **Buchanan** giving up forts in South Carolina, writing in a "confidential" letter: "If Mr. **B** surrenders the forts, I think they must be retaken." He told his secretary that if **Buchanan** intended to surrender the forts "they ought to hang him." Two of the forts were abandoned. Only Fort Sumter remained.

The former presidents during this transition weighed in as follows:

- **Van Buren** supported the Crittenden Compromise which called for the extension of the Missouri Compromise of 1820 line. But **Van Buren** also told the press that he had met **Lincoln** some years earlier and thought him "endowed with talents to adorn the nation."
- **Fillmore** urged enforcement of the Fugitive Slave Law. **Fillmore** hosted **Lincoln** who was on his way to the inauguration. They attended services at the Unitarian

church. After services the President-elect and his wife dined at **Fillmore's** home. (However about a year later **Fillmore** called **Lincoln** "a tyrant" who "makes my blood boil.")
- **Pierce** urged the Alabama secessionists to be patient but added: "If we cannot live together in peace, then in peace and on just terms, let us separate." He also said: "How can I urge the men of the South to take a view that I should not take if I were there?"
- Upon the election of **Lincoln** in 1860 **Tyler** said: "I fear that we have fallen on evil times and that the day of doom for the great model republic is at hand." **Tyler** praised **Buchanan's** leadership as a "wise and statesmanlike course." He urged **Buchanan** to remove troops from Fort Sumter. **Buchanan** responded that if he did he would be burned in effigy.

Buchanan said to **Lincoln** after the latter's inauguration: "If you are as happy in entering the White House as I shall feel on returning to Wheatland (his home) you are a happy man." At that inauguration, Charles Francis Adams contrasted **Buchanan's** "tall, large figure and white head" to **Lincoln's** "lank, angular form and hirsute face" and said: "the outgoing President was undeniably the more presentable man of the two." Immediately after his swearing in **Lincoln** was with **Buchanan** in the Capitol. **Lincoln's** secretary John Hay overheard **Buchanan** tell the new President: "I think you will find the water on the right-hand well at the White House better than the left." He added other kitchen-related details. **Lincoln** later told Hay that he hadn't heard a word **Buchanan** had said.

In the next four years **Lincoln** entered world history or, as his Secretary of War Edwin Stanton said upon the assassination: "Now he belongs to the ages." **Hayes'** first thoughts about **Andrew Johnson** after **Lincoln's** assassination were to recollect his apparent drunkenness at the inaugural which had "made the nation hang its head." After meeting with him a few weeks later **Hayes** was more favorably impressed. "He strikes one as a capable and sincere man - patriotic and with a great deal of experience as a public man." This positive feeling did not last.

In 1877 when **Rutherford B Hayes** was elected, **Abraham Lincoln's** secretary John Hay sent him a gold ring that contained a strand of **George Washington's** hair. Hay had obtained the ring from Alexander Hamilton's grandson years earlier. **Hayes** promised to "prize it [and] wear it on special occasions if not constantly." **McKinley** accompanied **Hayes** from Ohio to Washington DC for the inauguration. The outgoing **Grant** told **Hayes** that he "felt like a boy getting out of school." Changing the metaphor, as **Grant** and his wife left the White House in a carriage after the inauguration **Hayes** said: "General, if I had a slipper, I'd throw it after you." **Garfield** reflected: "No American has carried greater fame out of the White House than this silent man who leaves it today."

During their presidential transition period in 1880-81 **Hayes** tried to ease **Garfield's** burden by making certain appointments and other personnel changes. Knowing that **Garfield** could not afford certain equipment for his new position **Hayes** left his carriage and horses. At the inauguration of **Garfield**, **Benjamin Harrison** thought that **Garfield** looked "worn" and that **Hayes** looked "sweet and lamblike." On that occasion, **Hayes** said with a wink, "I am glad to be a freed man." **Garfield** wrote that he saw the presidency as a "bleak mountain" that he needed to climb. His term was to last about six months.

Cleveland has the distinction of leaving the White House twice. When he left the first time in 1889, **Hayes** who was of the opposite party but who liked **Cleveland**, wrote him of the problems of being President: "For them it is no doubt well to leave the high place now. Those who are such a place cannot escape the unfortunate influence on habits, disposition and character. In that envied position of power and distinction they are deferred to, flattered, and supported under all circumstances, whether right or wrong, or wise or foolish, by shrewd and designing men and women who surround them. Human nature can't stand this too long.... A long life in the hothouse atmosphere of the high station would leave an impress which would color unfavorably all of their later years."

Eight years later **Cleveland** left the presidency again. **McKinley** met with him a day or two before his inauguration. The meeting was cordial as **Cleveland** believed that **McKinley's** election had saved the country from the radicalism of William Jennings Bryan. Much of their talk involved avoiding war with Spain over Cuba. **McKinley** told the outgoing **Cleveland** that if he could avoid a war while in office he would be "the happiest man in the world." **Cleveland** later recalled the "settled sadness and sincerity" of the meeting. **Cleveland's** and **McKinley's** policies toward Spain had this difference: **Cleveland** tilted toward Spain, **McKinley** toward the rebels in Cuba.

In 1909 **William Howard Taft** assumed the presidency as much the handpicked successor of an outgoing President (in this instance, **Theodore Roosevelt**), as any president in history. He did not quickly recognize the new relationship between the men, writing **TR** a letter wishing him a good trip overseas that began as follows: "My dear **Theodore**: If I followed my impulse, I should still say 'My dear Mr. President.' I cannot overcome the habit. When I am addressed as 'Mr. President,' I turn to see whether you are not at my elbow."

Anticipating defeat in 1912 **Taft** looked to the future and said: "By and by, people will see who is right and who is wrong." After the election **Taft** gave a toast to **Wilson**: "Health and success to the able, distinguished and patriotic gentleman who is to be the next President of the United States." The transition from **Taft** to **Wilson** was smooth.

At his inauguration in 1921 **Harding** looked much healthier than **Wilson,** the victim of a stroke but **Wilson** outlived **Harding** by six months. (**Wilson**, labor leader Samuel Gompers and Vladimir Lenin all died in 1924.) During the early stages of the 1928 campaign, there was uncertainty about whether **Coolidge** would run again. **Hoover** asked **Coolidge** if he thought he should run and **Coolidge** responded, "Why not?" Later, **Hoover** offered him 400 delegate votes he had accumulated. **Coolidge**: "If you have 400 delegates, you better keep them." When nominee **Hoover** met with President **Coolidge** in 1928 before cameras, the reporters asked for a statement. **Coolidge**: "Let him talk. He's going to be President." **Coolidge** had announced that he would not run for re-election at a time when he was very popular. But he may have had some second thoughts. In 1929 he watched the preparations for **Hoover's** inauguration as if it were - in the words of a chief aide: "the building of a scaffold for his own execution."

During the long interval between the 1932 election and the inauguration of 1933 **Hoover** and **FDR** met. **Hoover** said that **FDR** "was amiable, pleasant, anxious to be of service, very badly informed and of comparatively little vision." **Hoover** said privately that he never wanted to speak with **FDR** again. In 1945, after taking office following **FDR's** death, **Truman** wrote his wife: "It seems like the late president had a positive genius for picking inefficient administrators. His Court appointments are somewhat disgraceful, too."

In 1953, as he was leaving the White House, **Truman** said of **Eisenhower**: "He'll sit here and say, 'Do this! Do that!' *And nothing will happen* – it won't be a bit like the army. He'll find it very frustrating." On **Ike's** first day as president he wrote in his diary: "My first day at the president's desk. Plenty of worries and difficult problems. But such has been my portion for a long time…"

In 1961, four consecutive Presidents stood together at the inauguration:

- **Dwight David Eisenhower** (1953-61)
- **John Fitzgerald Kennedy** (1961-63)
- **Lyndon Baines Johnson** (1963-69)
- **Richard Milhous Nixon** (1969-74)

At the time, **Ike** was apprehensive. He had had reservations about **Nixon** but these were insignificant in comparison to his doubts about **JFK**. He thought the new president "came of bad stock," was "reckless" and would "get America into bad trouble."

A couple of days before he took office **JFK** had met with **Eisenhower**. **Eisenhower** warned him that he would have to take action in Laos. **Kennedy**: "If the situation was so critical why didn't you decide to do something?" **Eisenhower**: "I would have but I did not feel I could commit troops with a new administration coming to power."

(Out of office, in his 1978 memoir, **Nixon** criticized "**Kennedy's** naïve willingness to accept a 'neutralist' coalition regime [in Laos] that was known to be a convenient cover for the Communist Pathet Lao guerrillas.") As **JFK** took office, **Eisenhower** wrote him: "While it is of course well known that in the domestic field there are governmental proposals and programs concerning which you and I do not agree, I assure you that my political views, though strongly held and sometimes vigorously expressed, contain nothing of personal animus on my part." After the Bay of Pigs disaster in 1961, **JFK** told **Eisenhower**, "no one knows how tough this job is until he has been in it a few months." **Eisenhower** replied: "Mr. President, if you will forgive me, I think I mentioned that to you three months ago." (In another account of the time, **JFK** spoke to **Nixon** whom he had defeated a few months previously and said "It really is true that foreign affairs is the only important issue for a president to handle, isn't it? I mean, who gives a shit if the minimum wage is $1.15 or $1.25, in comparison to something like this?" In yet another account, after the failure of the Bay of Pigs when **JFK's** popularity went higher, he said, "It's just like **Eisenhower**. The worse I do, the more popular I get.") **Ike's** nickname for **JFK** was "Little Boy Blue." In 1964 **Ike** said to an author about **Nixon**: "My God, there's the man. We wouldn't have any God damned Bay of Pigs with **Dick** in that damn place. We wouldn't have any of this with **Dick** running the show." During the 1960 campaign **Kennedy** said that seventeen million Americans went to be hungry every night. **Eisenhower** told aides: "They must all be dieting."

Several factors made the transition between **JFK** and **LBJ** following **Kennedy's** murder unique:

- The public was transfixed by the television coverage. Within an hour of **JFK's** death, 68% of all adults in the US had heard about it and by the end of the day that had reached 99.8%. Most Americans watched some aspect of the three-day trauma of the murder, **LBJ's** swearing in, the murder of Lee Harvey Oswald and the funeral of the President.
- **Kennedy's** aides had low regard for **LBJ** possibly emanating from the President.

- The President's brother and key advisor, Robert Kennedy and **LBJ** hated each other. It was one of the great political feuds of American history, rivaling that of Alexander Hamilton and Aaron Burr. (In his 2009 autobiography Edward Kennedy said that President **Johnson** tried to play him off against his own brother, Robert Kennedy. He commented that **LBJ's** attempt was "totally bizarre, since there was no way that a Kennedy would side with an outsider against another Kennedy.")
- As late as the very day of **JFK's** assassination, the news media was investigating **LBJ's** finances and the Congress was beginning an investigation of Bobby Baker, his key aide from his Senate years. These investigations were aborted after November 22.
- **JFK** died later in his term than any other president who had died in office, causing **Johnson** to need to quickly focus on an election campaign.

During the transition to the presidency **LBJ** managed the concern that the USSR and Cuba were behind the assassination of **JFK**. He quickly appointed the Warren Commission of which **Ford** was a member to investigate **Kennedy's** murder. (After his service on the Commission, **Ford** co-authored a book on Lee Harvey Oswald, *Portrait of the Assassin.*) He also used the momentum created by the martyrdom of **Kennedy** and his (**Johnson's**) great legislative skill to get the Civil Rights Act passed. As he told the Congress four days after **JFK's** death: "No memorial oration or eulogy could more eloquently honor President **Kennedy's** memory than the earliest possible passage of the civil rights bill for which he fought so long. We have talked long enough in this country about equal rights. We have talked for one hundred years or more. It is time now to write the next chapter, and to write it in the books of law."

The Civil Rights Act of 1964 resulted. It was part of a crusade that we know as the Great Society. It included the Voting Rights Act of 1965, Medicare and Medicaid, Head Start, Job Corps, Model Cities and more.

This all validated a comment made by **LBJ** within days of **JFK's** assassination when he told one of **Kennedy's** economic advisors that: "Now I want to say something about all this talk that I'm a conservative who is likely to go back to the **Eisenhower** ways.... It is not so.... I am a **Roosevelt** New Dealer. As a matter of fact, to tell the truth, **John F. Kennedy** was a little too conservative to suit my taste."

After the 1968 election **Nixon** said that until the inauguration **Johnson** would speak "not just for this administration but for the nation." He added: "And for the next administration as well." After **Nixon's** first inauguration, **George HW Bush** and Barbara Bush were the only Republicans at Andrews Air force Base to see **LBJ** off to Texas. **Bush** explained to a University of Texas historian who was present and who asked him why he was there: "He has been a fine president and invariably courteous and fair to me and my people, and I thought I belonged here to show in a small way how much I have appreciated him. I wish I could do more." **LBJ** was later told this and responded to **Bush** that he was "deeply appreciative of your words as he quoted them to me. Please know that I value your friendship, as I do your father's, and that I am glad you are one of us down here in Texas." **Bush** may have been hoping to neutralize **LBJ** in an upcoming race he was planning for the Senate.

In 1974 **Gerald Ford** assumed the presidency upon the resignation of **Richard Nixon** in the wake of the Watergate scandal. In 2004 he recalled this exchange with **Nixon** as **Nixon** left the White House for California on August 9, 1974: "I think I said to him, '**Dick**, I'm sorry about this. You did a good job.'" He recalled that **Nixon** said something like "Good luck, **Jerry**." **Ford** offered this comment in his inaugural address: "Before closing, I ask again your prayers, for **Richard Nixon** and for his family. May our former President, who brought peace to millions, find it for himself." In the 1976 general election, **Ford** was challenged by **Carter**. **Nixon** sent this encouragement to **Ford**. "The next two months will be the longest and hardest of your life but I am sure you are ready to give the opposition the fight of their lives." **Carter** won and at his inauguration said: "For myself and for our nation, I want to thank my predecessor for all he has done to heal our land."

After his 1980 defeat by **Reagan**, **Carter** told reporters that history would judge his presidency higher than the election results might suggest. During the transition they met in the Oval Office. **Carter** briefed **Reagan** for about an hour during which time **Reagan** did not take notes or ask questions, even declining **Carter's** offer of a notepad. On November 21, 1980, **Carter** wrote in his diary: "(Secretary of State Edmund) Muskie told me about plans to invite President Chun from South Korea to the inauguration. It's unbelievable to me, but I suspect that dictators around the world are rejoicing because of the outcome of the election." In reality the **Reagan** transition team dealt with the South Korea government to spare the life of a dissident who was scheduled for execution: Kim Dae Jung. **Reagan's** team was successful and about twenty years later Kim was president of South Korea. Chun was never invited to the inauguration although he had asked for that.

President **Jimmy Carter** worked until the last moments of his administration overseeing negotiations with the Iranian government to free American hostages that the Iranians had held for 444 days. **Carter** called **Reagan** at about 6:30am on inauguration day but **Reagan's** staff would not awaken him. **Carter** called back at 8:30am and briefed him on the nearly-completed bargaining with the government in Iran. **Reagan** apologized for his staff's oversight. After **Carter** ended the call his own staff asked him about the conversation and **Carter** bitterly joked that **Reagan** had said: "What hostages?" The two men then rode to the inauguration mostly in silence. Nancy Reagan later said, "Fortunately, it's a short ride." **Reagan** put it this way: "The atmosphere in the limousine was as chilly as it had been at the White House a few days before when Nancy and I had gone there to see for the first time the rooms where we would be living. We'd expected the Carters to give us a tour of the family quarters, but they had made a quick exit and turned us over to the White House staff. At the time, Nancy and I took this as an affront. It seemed rude." By 1989 **Reagan** had a different perspective: "Eight years later I think we could sense a little of how President **Carter** must have felt that day— to have served as president, to have been through the intense highs and lows of the job, to have tried to do what he thought was right, to have had all the farewells and good-bye parties, and then be forced out of the White House by a vote of the people. It must have been very hard on him."

In an act of spite, the Iranians ended up delaying the release of the hostages until minutes after **Reagan** took office.

Afterwards, **Carter** rode to an air force base with his Vice President and their wives to fly home. He noted in his diary: "We made some disparaging remarks about the quality of **Reagan's** inaugural address, but in general it was a pleasant drive."

After his 1992 defeat **George HW Bush** received from **Nixon** a copy of a letter that **Nixon** had received in 1960 from two-time Republican nominee Thomas Dewey. It read in part: "If you are defeated pay no attention to the Monday morning quarterbacks. Everybody knows how to conduct a campaign better after the event. No one could have worked harder with high fidelity to duty and integrity; no one could have done more for Party and Country. You have earned the best and the nation will always be in your debt." **George HW Bush** to President-elect **Clinton** in November 1992: "**Bill**, I want to tell you something. When I leave here, you're going to have no trouble from me. The campaign is over, it was tough and I'm out of here. I will do nothing to complicate your work and I just want you to know that." Sixteen years later, his son offered the same gracious point: "One thing I don't want to do is stay on stage. The spotlight needs to shift to President-elect **Obama**....because he's the president. Therefore, I won't try to get it to shift to me. And I'll be very respectful of him during his presidency."

In December of 1992, the **George HW Bush** administration received a UN mandate to send US troops to Somalia to secure distribution of food. President-elect **Clinton** was very supportive: "I applaud the initiative of President **Bush**..." As **Clinton** prepared to take office **Carter** said in an interview that he was "very disappointed" that **Clinton** was planning to send his daughter to a private school. (Sixteen years earlier **Carter** had sent his daughter to a public school and sixteen years later **Obama** sent his daughters to private school.) At the inauguration, **Clinton** ignored **Carter** while he honored **Reagan.** In 1993 **Ford** said: "I've had a lot of contact with **George** since he left office because I wanted him to know that there's life after the White House."

In 2013 President **Obama** spoke at the dedication of the **George W. Bush** Library. He said of his first day in office: "The first thing I found in that desk the day I took office was a letter from **George.** He knew that I would come to learn what he had learned—that being president, above all, is a humbling job."

What is the point of all this?

Shortly after he left office in 2009, **George W Bush** said: "People were kind of tired of me." They were but also the changing of power required and prescribed by the US constitution is one of the marvels of the political world. In peace time and during war one of the forty-three has left and another has taken his place. There is a reassuring regularity to the process.

Death

Overall context

Presidents often speak of the burden of the office. **Lincoln** said, "I'm a tired man. Sometimes I think I am the tiredest man on earth." **Wilson** said: "Men of ordinary physique and discretion cannot be Presidents and live, if the strain be not somehow relieved." **Truman** wrote, "A superman cannot successfully meet world problems in this age without the help of the people." **Grant** said of the presidency in 1871: "Whoever has the place will have a slave's life." **Monroe** to **Madison** during his presidency: "I have never experienced such a state of things...nor have I personally ever experienced so much embarrassment and mortification." **Monroe** wrote **Jefferson** near the end of his term that "I shall be heartily rejoiced when the term of my service expires...." **Hayes** served one term of office between 1877-81. He said: "The first half of my term was so full of trouble and embarrassments as to be a continual struggle and I do not propose to invite a new season of embarrassment."

In September of 1837 **John Quincy Adams** visited **Van Buren** in the White House. He was impressed by **Van Buren's** "composure and tranquility" but also noted **Van Buren's** description of the "cares and afflictions" of the presidency and his musing "how universal the delusion was that anyone could be happy in it." **Polk** in 1847 noted that two-thirds of his presidency was over. "I...most heartily wish that the remaining third was over, for I am sincerely desirous to have the enjoyment of retirement in private life." In 1849 as he left office after consistently refusing to run for a second term: "I feel exceedingly relieved that I am now free from all public cares." **Garfield** about life in the White House during appointment struggles in 1881: "My God! What is there in this place that a man should ever want to get into it?" **Hoover** came to call the presidency a "compound hell" and as **Lyndon Johnson** said in 1967 it was "tough to carry the burdens of being President." **JFK** when things were going poorly: "I'm going to give the job to **Nixon**."

A sense that they are part of a very small group that has shared a burden has caused feelings of empathy. This empathy extends in most cases across party lines and to death. When **JFK** died, an eighty-nine year-old **Hoover** told **LBJ**: "I am ready to serve our government in any capacity, from office boy up." **Hoover** himself was dead within a year.

Moving Forward

When he heard that **George Washington** had died, **John Adams** said: "I feel myself alone bereaved of my last brother." **Adams** soon took a more critical line: "The feasts and funerals in honor of **Washington** is as corrupt a system as that by which saints were canonized and cardinals, popes and whole hierarchical systems created." (**Washington's** will stipulated that his body "be interred in a private manner, without parade, or funeral oration.") **Jefferson** refused to attend a memorial service for **Washington**. **Madison** was in the Virginia assembly in 1799 when news came of **Washington's** death: "Death has robbed our country of its most distinguished ornament and the world of one of its greatest benefactors."

When **Thomas Jefferson** and **John Adams** died a few hours apart of the fiftieth anniversary of the signing of the Declaration of Independence, many saw the hand of God. The president at the time, **John Quincy Adams,** wrote, "The time, the manner, the coincidences...are visible and palpable marks of Divine favor." **Tyler** as governor of Virginia was writing a eulogy for **Jefferson** when he heard that **John Adams** had died. He added a paragraph: "Scarcely has the funeral knell of our **Jefferson** been sounded in our ears, when we are startled by the death-knell of another patriot, his zealous coadjutor in the holy cause of the Revolution - one of the most foremost of those who sought his country's disenthrallment - of **Adams**, the compeer of his early fame, the opposing orb of his meridian, the friend of his old age, and his companion to the realm of bliss. They have sunk together in death, and have fallen on the same glorious day into that sleep that knows no waking. Let not party spirit break the rest of their slumbers, but let us hallow their memory for the good deeds they have done, and implore that God who rules the universe to smile on our country."

Madison said of **Jefferson** at the time: "He was certainly one of the most learned men of the age. It may be said of him as has been said of others that he was a 'walking Library,' and what can be said of but few such prodigies, that the Genius of Philosophy ever walked hand in hand with him." He added: "[He] will live in the memory and gratitude of the wise & good, as a luminary of Science, as a votary of liberty, as a model of patriotism, and as a benefactor of human kind."

In 1831, after his own presidency and after he had been then elected to Congress, **John Quincy Adams** visited an ailing **Monroe** in New York City. They discussed resignations in **Andrew Jackson's** cabinet which **Adams** called "the recent quasi revolution at Washington" and the violence in Europe. **Monroe** was so ill that **Adams** thought he would never leave his room. **Monroe** wrote **Madison**: "I deeply regret that there is no prospect of our ever meeting again, since so long have we been connected, and in the most friendly intercourse, in public and private life, that a final separation is among the most distressing incidents which could occur..." **Madison** wrote **Monroe** from Virginia: "The pain I feel, associated as it is with the recollections of the long, close and uninterrupted friendship which united us, amounts to a pang which I cannot well express, and makes me seek for an alleviation in the possibility that you may be brought back to us in the wonted degree of intercourse." **Monroe** died on July 4 of that year. **Adams** gave a eulogy citing his nationalism and concluding: "Thus strengthening and consolidating the federative edifice of his country's Union, till he was entitled to say, like Augustus Caesar of his imperial city, that he had found her built of brick and left her constructed of marble."

In 1840 Anna Symmes Harrison upon the election of her husband of 45 years **William Henry Harrison**: "I wish that my husband's friends had left him where he is, happy and contented in retirement." A month into his term in 1841 **Harrison** was near death and delirious. He was destined to be the shortest-serving president in US history. **Harrison** thought **Tyler** was nearby and told him: "Sir, I wish you to understand the true principles of government - I wish them carried out, nothing more." He asked that Psalm 103 be read and at his funeral a section from I Corinthians 15 was also read. **Jackson** uncharitably called **William Henry Harrison's** death: "the deed of a kind and overruling Providence." In 1841 **John Quincy Adams** thought that **Harrison's** funeral "ceremony was performed in a decent and unostentatious manner, with proper religious solemnity and with the simplicity congenial to our republican institutions."

At **Jackson's** death in 1845 his protégé **Polk** said: "**Andrew Jackson** is no more! His country deplores his loss, and will ever cherish his memory." In a private letter he wrote that **Jackson** was "the greatest man in the age in which he lived, a man whose confidence and friendship I was so happy to have enjoyed from my youth to the latest hour of his life." **John Quincy Adams**' observations offered a contrast. He wrote: "**Jackson** was a hero, a murderer, an adulterer...who in his last days of his life belied and slandered me before the world and died." **Jackson** felt about the same way about **Adams**: "He is certainly the basest, meanest scoundrel that ever disgraced the image of his God. Nothing is too mean or low for him to condescend to secretly carry his cowardly and base purposes of slander into effect."

In 1848 the recent death of **John Quincy Adams** may have propelled his son Charles Francis Adams to the vice presidential nomination of the Free Soil party as **Van Buren's** running mate. **Andrew Johnson** wrote a friend in 1848: "**J.Q. Adams** fell dead in the House the other day."

Zachary Taylor on an occasion when he heard a *rumor* of **Polk's** death while **Polk** was in office said: "While I regret to hear of the death of any one, I would have as soon as heard of his death, if true, as that of any other individual." (By that time he thought **Polk** was trying to sabotage his career having been reprimanded by him for the terms he had given the enemy during the Mexican-American War in taking Monterey.) When **Polk** did die, **Taylor** by then president called upon the country "to mourn the loss of one, the recollection of whose long services in its councils will be forever preserved in the tablets of history."

In 1850 **Fillmore** upon hearing that **Taylor** had died and that he faced a national crisis centering on a border dispute between Texas and New Mexico wrote to the cabinet: "I have no language to express the emotions of my heart. The shock is so sudden and so unexpected that I am overwhelmed.... I ...shall appoint a time and place for taking the oath of office...at the earliest moment." **Lincoln** said on that occasion: "We have lost a degree of that confidence...which will not soon...pertain to any successor....I fear that the one great question of the day, is not now so likely to be partially acquiesced in by the different sections of the Union, as it would have been, could Gen. **Taylor** have been spared to us." **Theodore Roosevelt** wrote of **Taylor** that he "was an able and gallant soldier, a loyal and upright public servant, and a most kindly, honest, and truthful man. His death was a greater loss to the country than perhaps people ever knew."

Van Buren knew fourteen presidents starting with **Jefferson**. Upon the death of **Van Buren** in 1862 **Lincoln** ordered ceremonial rituals beyond the norm. Here was his statement on July 25, 1862: "The President with deep regret announces to the people of the United States the decease, at Kinderhook, NY, on the 24th Instant, of his honored predecessor **Martin Van Buren**. This event will occasion mourning in the nation for the loss of a citizen and a public servant whose memory will be gratefully cherished. Although it has occurred at a time when his country is afflicted with division and civil war, the grief of his patriotic friends will measurably be assuaged by the consciousness that while suffering with disease and seeing his end approaching his prayers were for the restoration of the authority of the Government of which he had been the head and for peace and good will among his fellow-citizens." **Lincoln** may well have been thinking of the story-swapping evening years before.

Tyler died that same year loyal to the Confederacy and **Lincoln** took no official notice. **Tyler** was buried next to **Monroe**.

On March 8, 1865 **Andrew Johnson** was in the Washington area after the inauguration and wrote **Lincoln** that the "prostration of my health forbids me visiting you in person." They met for the first time as President and Vice President on April 14, the day before **Lincoln** was assassinated but there is no record of what they discussed. **Pierce's** hometown erupted in fury upon hearing of **Lincoln's** assassination. Knowing that **Pierce** was a political foe of the martyred president, a mob advanced on his house. **Pierce** faced it down from his front porch and refused on principle its demand to put up an American flag. At **Lincoln's** death **Fillmore** who was out of town did not immediately adorn his house with black drapes and a vandal smeared it with black ink. **Buchanan** was warned by a friend to write a statement sympathetic to **Lincoln**. Meanwhile, in **Washington**, rumors began that the lives of **Andrew Johnson** and **Grant** were in danger but **Johnson** walked through the night to **Lincoln's** deathbed. When **Grant** heard that **Lincoln** was dead, he told his wife that he was filled "with the gloomiest apprehension." Newly elected Congressman **Rutherford B Hayes** said at **Lincoln's** death: "Such a loss to the country."

Garfield wrote his wife upon hearing of **Lincoln's** assassination: "My heart is so broken with our national loss that I can hardly think or write or speak." A few days later he said: "It was not one man who killed **Abraham Lincoln**. It was the embodied spirit of treason and slavery, inspired with fearful and despairing hate, that struck him down in the moment of the nation's supremist joy."

Grant wept at the White House at **Lincoln's** funeral maintaining later that it was the saddest day of his life. **Johnson** stood quietly. When **Lincoln's** coffin was transported through Philadelphia on its way to Springfield Illinois **Buchanan** age 70 drove his buggy from his home in Lancaster about seventy miles to join the mourners. **TR** age 6 watched the procession in New York. **Fillmore** and **Cleveland** watched it in Buffalo.

One of **Buchanan's** last statements was: "Whatever the result may be," he said, "I shall carry to my grave the consciousness that I at least meant well for my country." (Only **Nixon** matched **Buchanan's** post-presidency efforts to explain and salvage his presidency and was deservedly far more successful.)

When **Andrew Johnson** died in 1875 **Grant** said: "The solemnity of the occasion which called him to the Presidency, with the varied nature and length of his public services, will cause him to be long remembered, and occasion mourning for the death of a distinguished public servant."

In 1881 **Garfield** was assassinated by Charles Julius Guiteau, a former member of a utopian religious sect who was also probably mentally ill. A letter in Guiteau's apartment was addressed to "President **Arthur**" and gave advice on cabinet members. Guiteau claimed to have shot **Garfield** to make his "friend" **Arthur** president. **Garfield** was alive for over two months after the shooting and at least one modern historian concludes that he died from poor medical care – even for the era - which caused a spreading infection. Although there is no evidence that **Arthur** was involved, conspiracy theorists of that era linked him to **Garfield's** death just as earlier some had linked **Andrew Johnson** to **Lincoln's** murder and a century later extremists linked **LBJ** to **JFK's** murder. **Benjamin Harrison** saw **Arthur** the next day and said: "He showed deep feeling and seemed to be overcome with the calamity." **Arthur** said at the time: "I am an American among millions of Americans grieving for their wounded chief." **Garfield**, when he was informed of the rumor said from his death bed: "I do not believe that." **Arthur** sobbed alone in his library when he heard of **Garfield's** death some two months later. **TR** wrote in his diary: "Frightful calamity of America...this means work in the future for those who wish their country well." **Benjamin Harrison** visited **Garfield's** wife Lucretia after the shooting and was impressed by her calmness. He called her "the most heroic woman I ever knew." Lucretia Garfield lived another 37 years. **Hayes** was dumbstruck: He wrote, "**Arthur** for President!" He called it a "national calamity whose consequences we cannot now confidently conjecture." **Garfield** was shot on July 2. That year many Independence Day speeches quoted his own words as a Congressman two decades earlier upon **Lincoln's** assassination: "Fellow citizens! God reigns, and the government in Washington still lives!"

At the very end of his life, **Grant** reflected on the amazing turn of events that took him from obscurity to world renown. He wrote a friend: "It seems that man's destiny in this world is quite as much a mystery as it is likely to be in the next." At the same time, **Grant** wrote brief notes, some of which survive: "I should prefer going now to enduring my present suffering for a single day without hope of recovery." **Grant's** death in 1885 called forth a stupendous outpouring of national emotion and imagery. A million-and-a-half people gathered in New York for his funeral. In addition there were thousands of memorial services across the US stressing sectional reconciliation. Upon his death Blacks remembered **Grant** as a liberator, the supporter of the Fifteenth Amendment and the prosecutor of the Ku Klux Klan. Whites remembered him for his generous peace terms at Appomattox. **Cleveland** appointed two Confederate generals as pallbearers for **Grant** at the request of **Grant's** family. **Hayes** and **Arthur** came from opposite wings of the Republican Party. **Hayes** had once fired **Arthur** from an important political position but they may have composed their differences at **Grant's** funeral when as ex-presidents they rode in the funeral entourage. **Hayes** said that **Arthur** "proved to be an excellent companion for such a drive." (Eighty years later **JFK's** funeral was the occasion for reconciliation between **Eisenhower** and **Truman**.) **Cleveland's** official proclamation at **Grant's** death described him as an "illustrious citizen and ex-President of the United States" and said, "the destined end has come at last, and his spirit has returned to the Creator who sent it forth."

Hayes who had been born the same year as **Grant** and was to live another eight years said "the interest in General **Grant's** death has been very great." He advocated the building of a memorial that would "be worthy of the Republic, worthy of General **Grant**, and worthy of the righteous cause of which he was the most illustrious soldier." **Grant's** Tomb in New York is the largest tomb in North America. It was dedicated in 1897. **McKinley** and **Cleveland** were in attendance. **McKinley**: "New York holds in its keeping the precious dust of the silent soldier, but his achievements - that he and his brave comrades wrought for mankind - are in the keeping of seventy millions of American Citizens, who will guard the sacred heritage forever and forever more."

Hayes knew every president from **Lincoln** to **Taft**. (He knew **McKinley** and **Taft** when they were boys.) He worked with **TR** in the reform movement. He and **Cleveland** were close. At **Chester Alan Arthur's** death **Hayes** wondered why he wasn't a pall bearer until someone explained to him that **Grover Cleveland** who was President regarded **Hayes** and himself as mourners. As he aged **Hayes** thought of **John Quincy Adams** who did his "best work long after middle life." While seeing friends die he wrote: "As friends go it is less important to live."

Grover Cleveland was the only Democrat president between **Buchanan** in 1861 and **Wilson** in 1913. But he was friendly with his fellow presidents. Upon the death of **Rutherford Hayes** in 1893 he said to his wife: "He was coming to see me but he is dead now and I will go to him." **Cleveland** was criticized by other Democrats for attending **Hayes'** funeral. **Cleveland** at exactly that time was both a former president and president-elect. He is he only president to serve nonconsecutive terms. Governor **William McKinley** of Ohio also attended.

In 1901 when **Benjamin Harrison** died, **McKinley** said that "in the high office of President" **Harrison** had "displayed extraordinary gifts as administrator and statesmen." **McKinley** was shot within six months and lingered for about a week until he died. His final words, "It is useless, gentlemen. I think we ought to have a prayer." **TR** eulogized **McKinley** saying that whereas **Lincoln** and **Garfield** were killed for the kinds of government they stood for, **McKinley** was the victim of a modern kind of assassin, one against government itself. He delivered a tirade against anarchism. **McKinley's** wife Ida McKinley lived another six years after his murder.

Cleveland died in 1908. His last words were, "I have tried so hard to do right." **TR** wrote to **Cleveland's** wife: "Your telegram shocked me greatly. Mrs. Roosevelt joins in very deep and sincere sympathy. I have, of course, abandoned my intention of starting to-day for the New London boat races, so that if the funeral is either Thursday or Friday I can attend. I can also attend if it is Sunday, but if it is Saturday a number of men are coming here from various parts of the country on a business engagement which I cannot well break. Will you direct some one to wire me when the funeral is to be and where?" Mrs. Cleveland lived for nearly forty years after her husband's death. She remarried and took her new husband's name. She met **Dwight Eisenhower** at a reception in 1946. In conversation she happened to mention that she had once lived in Washington DC. **Ike**, who did not know her, responded, "You did? Where?"

TR was in the hospital a few days before he died and he spoke to a friend and exhibited his animosity toward **Woodrow Wilson**: "I seem pretty low now, but I shall get better. I cannot go without having done something to that old gray skunk in the White House." **Theodore Roosevelt's** death in 1919 was a surprise to the public as he had been positioning to run for president in 1920. When **TR** endorsed Charles Evan Hughes in 1916 and refused the nomination of the Progressive Party, **Warren Harding** began to move toward **TR**. He met with him and said: "He made a rather more favorable impression on me then I have ever had heretofore, but I cannot say as to what impression I left with him. My best guess is that the Colonel is looking forward to a candidacy in 1920, and felt that it might not be unwise to be on friendly terms with me..." **Wilson** was in Europe when he was informed of **TR's** death by a telegram. He smiled triumphantly shocking British Prime Minister Lloyd George. **FDR** was aboard ship when he heard the news. He said: "My cousin's death was in every way a great shock, for we heard just before leaving that he was better -and he was after all not old. But I cannot help think that he himself would have had it this way and that he has been spared a lingering illness of perhaps years." **Taft** called **TR** at his death "the most commanding personality in our public life since **Lincoln**."

Before **Harding** left on a cross-continent train trip in 1923 in which he died he made a will.

Coolidge upon being notified of **Harding's** death and his own elevation to the presidency said: "I believe I can swing it." **Woodrow Wilson** was driven to the White House for **Harding's** funeral but was too weak to get out of the car and remained there while the services were conducted inside. **Taft** was forward-looking at the time of **Harding's** death: "My feeling of deep regret (at **Harding's** death) is somewhat mitigated by the confidence I have on the wisdom, conservatism, courage of his successor. Of course, he lacks the prestige and experience, but he is deeply imbued with a sense of obligation to following Mr. **Harding's** policies, especially Mr. **Harding's** purpose to defend the institutions of the country against wild radicals."

Coolidge on **Harding's** death: "I do not know what impaired his health. I do know that the weight of the Presidency is very heavy. Later it was disclosed that he had discovered that some whom he had trusted had betrayed him, and he had been forced to call them to account. It is known that this discovery was a very heavy grief to him, perhaps more than he could bear." **Coolidge** did not want to attend the dedication of the **Harding** memorial and it was postponed until the **Hoover** presidency. In 1931 in Marion Ohio **Herbert Hoover** spoke at the dedication of the memorial. He talked of his last few days with **Harding**: "**Warren Harding** had a dim realization that he had been betrayed by a few of the men whom he had trusted, by men who he had believed were his devoted friends."

Often affinity manifests at time of death. When **Woodrow Wilson** died **Coolidge** and his wife showed up at **Wilson's** home. They were the only ones outside **Wilson's** circle.

In 1944 after his nomination for vice president and after seeing **FDR** for the first time in a year, **Truman** said to a friend: "His hands were shaking and he talks with considerable difficulty... It doesn't seem to be any mental lapse of any kind but physically he's just going to pieces." **Truman** was called to the White House on April 12, 1945. Eleanor Roosevelt told him, "**Harry**, the President is dead." **Truman** responded, "Is there anything I can do for you?" Mrs. Roosevelt answered, "Is there anything we can do for you, **Harry**? For you are the one in trouble now." When he heard that **FDR** was gone, **LBJ** wept: "He was just like a daddy to me always." **George HW Bush** said: "His politics had drawn my dad's fire but the day **FDR** died we wept for our commander in chief. He was the symbol of our determination - good over evil." **Nixon** was a young navy officer stationed at the time in Philadelphia and was with his wife at dinner when he heard of **FDR's** death.

For many Americans who were alive at the time, the assassination of President **Kennedy** on November 22, 1963 by Lee Harvey Oswald a pro-communist American symbolizes a great gulf in American history. The historian Stephen Ambrose wrote in 1993: "There's a very strong sense that if he had not died, we would not have suffered the thirty years of nightmare that followed - the race riots, the white backlash, assassinations, Vietnam, Watergate, Iran-Contra."

When told of **Kennedy's** assassination, **Truman** by then 79, was reported to be too upset to make a statement. According to his daughter, he was "deeply grieved by President **Kennedy's** assassination. He felt that fate had cut him down before he had a chance to really master the intricacies of the presidency."

LBJ was with **JFK** at the hospital in Dallas in 1963 when **Kennedy** died. **Kennedy's** acting press secretary addressed **Johnson** as "Mr. President" and asked him if he could announce **Kennedy's** death. **Johnson** was startled by being addressed as President but agreed that an announcement should be made. Then: "No. Wait. We don't know whether it's a communist conspiracy or not. I'd better get out of here and back to the plane." Back in Washington DC that evening, **LBJ** wrote six-year old Caroline Kennedy the daughter of **JFK**: "Dearest Caroline - Your father's death has been a great tragedy for the Nation, as well as for you at this time. He was a wise and devoted man. You can always be proud of what he did for his country."

Nixon happened to be in Dallas Texas the day before **JFK** was shot there and he had urged the people of Dallas to give **Kennedy** "a courteous reception." His formal statement a few days later was: "President **Kennedy** yesterday wrote the finest and greatest chapter in his *Profiles in Courage*. The greatest tribute we can pay is to reduce the hatred which drives men to do such deeds." (The consensus of historians is that **JFK** did not write *Profiles in Courage* but that it was ghost-written.)

Ronald Reagan's daughter Patti Davis who as then 11 maintained that her parents showed no emotion at **JFK's** assassination and went to a convivial dinner party that had been planned.

Upon hearing that **JFK** was murdered, **George HW Bush** called the FBI to report hearsay that a certain individual in Houston had been heard talking about killing the President. This individual was cleared by the FBI. **Bill Clinton** heard about the assassination of **Kennedy** as a senior in a high school math class. He recalled a girl in the hallway making an insensitive remark that perhaps it was for the best and it angered him.

JFK's murder became the most complex and written about murder case in history. In 1967, at a difficult political time for President **Johnson**, William Manchester's book *The Death of a President* was published. Some read in it an argument that **LBJ** was partially responsible for the murder since **Kennedy** had decided that he needed to come to Dallas to resolve a political dispute within the state Democrat Party that **LBJ** should have been able to handle.

In 1975 **Reagan** served on the Rockefeller Commission appointed by **Ford** to investigate CIA activities. It went beyond its mandate to investigate whether the CIA was involved in the assassination of **JFK** and concluded that it was not.

When the Warren Commission issued its report in 1964 a national poll showed that a minority of Americans rejected its conclusion that the assassin Lee Harvey Oswald acted alone. This changed. By the early 2000s between 70 and eighty percent rejected the Warren Report's conclusions.

Here is what **John F. Kennedy** himself said on the morning of his death: "It would not be a very difficult job to shoot the president of the United States. All you'd have to do is get up in a high building with a high-powered rifle with a telescopic sight, and there's nothing anybody could do." On the day **Kennedy** died the major Dallas newspaper had this headline: "**Nixon** Predicts **JFK** May Drop **Johnson**." **Kennedy's** last words: "My God, I am hit." **JFK's** wife Jacqueline Kennedy lived another 31 years after his murder.

In November 2013 President **Obama** visited **JFK's** gravesite at Arlington. He spoke about it later that day: "This afternoon, Michelle and I were joined by President **Clinton** and Secretary Clinton to pay tribute to that proud legacy. We had a chance to lay a wreath at the gravesite at Arlington, where President **Kennedy** is surrounded by his wife and younger brothers, and where he will rest in peace for all time..."

When **Eisenhower** was in the hospital in 1968, **LBJ** sent him a movie screen, a projector, a projectionist and any White House film he wanted. By 1969 **Eisenhower** was near death. He was sedated but woke up and saw **Nixon** who had recently been elected to the presidency and said, "Oh, **Dick**, how are you? Good to see you! How is the administration going?" **Nixon** responded, "We're going to do all right." **Eisenhower** said: "You bet!" On the day he died in 1969 **Eisenhower** had his son and grandson in his hospital room and looked at his son and said: "I want to go; God take me." **Nixon** sobbed later that day when he heard that **Eisenhower** had died.

Upon **Truman's** death in 1972, **Nixon,** fresh off re-election, noted in an official proclamation: "President **Truman** had a deep respect for the office he held and for the people he served. He gave himself unstintingly to the duties of the Presidency while he held it, and in the years afterwards he honorably supported and wisely counseled each of his successors." **Lyndon Johnson's** death a month later left **Nixon** with no living predecessors. He called **LBJ** a "great American" and said that he had spoken with the former president the day before he died to tell him that the Vietnam War was ending.

In retirement **Nixon** would send **Clinton** long memos about world politics which according to staff **Clinton** read carefully. (And he appreciated that **Nixon** was circumspect, unlike **Carter** who in this time period would give advice to **Clinton** and then appear on television talking about it.) **Clinton** admired **Nixon** for opening the door to China, establishing the Environmental Protection Agency, the Legal Services Corporation, the Occupational Health and Safety Organization and supporting affirmative action. **Clinton** at **Nixon's** funeral in 1994: "May the day of judging President **Nixon** on anything less than his entire life and career come to a close."

In 2004 at **Reagan's** funeral, **George HW Bush** orated: "As his vice president for eight years, I learned more from **Ronald Reagan** than from anyone I encountered in all my years in public life. I learned kindness; we all did." President **George W Bush** said: "**Ronald Reagan** believed in the power of truth in the conduct of world affairs. When he saw evil camped across the horizon, he called that evil by its name. There were no doubters in the prisons and gulags where dissidents spread the news, tapping to each other what the American president had dared to say. There were no doubters in the shipyards and churches and secret labor meetings where brave men and women began to hear the creaking and rumbling of a collapsing empire. And there were no doubters among those who swung hammers at the hated wall that the first and hardest blow had been struck by President **Ronald Reagan**." In a reference to **Reagan's** suffering from Alzheimer's, **Bush** said: "In this last years he saw through a glass darkly; now he sees his savior face to face. And we look for that fine day when we will see him again, all weariness gone, clear of mind, strong and sure and smiling again, and the sorrow of this parting gone forever."

Presidents have expressed themselves about death – both of family members and their own. After the death of Abigail in 1818, **John Adams** wrote his son **John Quincy Adams**: "The separation cannot be so long as twenty separations heretofore. The pangs and anguish have not been so great as when you and I embarked for France in 1778." **Adams** also wrote his son that: "The bitterness of death is past. The grim spider so terrible to human nature has no sting left for me." **Jefferson** wrote **John Adams**: "God bless you and support you under your heavy affliction." **Adams** responded to him: "While you live, I seem to have a bank at Monticello on which I can draw for a letter of friendship and entertainment when I please." These must be some of the most personal notes between statesmen in the English language.

During the 1828 campaign, charges of adultery were raised against **Jackson** and bigamy against his wife because it was determined that she had not secured her divorce as she had thought before their marriage years before. When he heard of the issue, **William Henry Harrison** wrote his son who was associated with a Cincinnati editor to avoid any participation in the story. "If you have anything to do with the new paper for heaven sake do not mention **Jackson's** family affairs. It has done too much mischief already... I would not have one of my family concerned in such an affair." **Jackson** concealed from her the nature of the smear campaign directed against her. **Jackson's** wife died between the election and the inauguration after reading a pamphlet defending her against the charges. **Jackson** blamed **Adams** for this attack. **Adams**, finding this out, denied any responsibility. **Jackson's** rage may have been stoked by self-righteousness. During the same campaign he had heard a news story that the **Adamses** had had premarital sex but refused to exploit it saying: "I never war against females and it is only the base and cowardly that do."

During the Civil War **Lincoln's** young son died. **Pierce** had also lost a young son. The two presidents were adversaries. **Pierce** wrote

Lincoln in sympathy signing the letter: "I am truly your friend, **Franklin Pierce**." **Lincoln** didn't answer. We don't know why. **Lincoln** was a magnanimous character but he was in grief and possibly had an intense dislike of **Pierce** whom he had criticized severely in the past.

When **Wilson's** first wife died in 1914 he said, "God has stricken me almost beyond what I can bear." In 1924 **Coolidge's** son died at age 16 and he said, "The power and glory of the Presidency went with him." (**Coolidge**'s older son lived until the year 2000.) These other presidents lost children: **John Adams, John Quincy Adams, Jefferson, Monroe, William Henry Harrison, Taylor, Fillmore, Pierce, Lincoln, Hayes, Garfield, Arthur, McKinley, TR, FDR, Eisenhower, Kennedy**, and **George HW Bush**. At age 57 **Harrison** lost an adult son to typhoid fever. He described the death as "the most severe affliction I have ever experienced." He lost other adult sons in the last three years before he became president. (Another son lived to age 73 and was the father of **Benjamin Harrison**.) **Taylor** lost three children including his daughter who was the wife of Jefferson Davis the future president of the Confederacy. A year after he left the presidency, **Fillmore's** 22 year-old daughter who had often served as his official hostess died. **Cleveland's** daughter Ruth died at the age of 12 in 1904. The candy bar – Baby Ruth - was named for her about twenty years later.

Here are some of their own thoughts about their own deaths. **George Washington** in 1788: "[T]he great Searcher of human hearts is my witness, that I have no wish, which aspires beyond the humble and happy lot of living and dying a private citizen on my own farm." **John Adams'** top goal was to be remembered although he admitted to the idea being ridiculous because it would not matter after death. "For what folly it is. What is it to us what shall be said of us after we are dead? .... Yet the impulse is irresistible." As he aged **John Adams** had more difficulty writing. He noted to **John Quincy Adams**: "It is painful to the Vanity of an Old Man to acknowledge the decays of Nature but I have lost the habit of Writing...from weak Eyes and from a trembling hand to such a degree that a Pen is as terrible to me, as a Sword to a Coward, or a rod to a child." (He wrote this in 1795 and lived for thirty more years.)

Jefferson to **Adams** in 1812: "You and I have been wonderfully spared. Of the signers of the Declaration of Independence I see now living not more than half a dozen on your side of the Potomak, and, on this side, myself alone." In his letters to **Jefferson** late in life, **Adams** referred to senility as "dying at the top." He thought about the next life and said in 1816 that "if it should be revealed or demonstrated that there is no future state, my advice to every man, woman, and child would be...to take opium." **John Adams** to **James Madison** in 1817: "May you live to a greater age than mine, and be able to die with brighter prospects for your species than can fall to the lot of your friend." (**Adams** lived another nine years, **Madison** another nineteen.)

Jefferson may have realized that his presidential career did nothing to forestall a looming national crisis. His epitaph which he wrote himself mentions the Declaration of Independence (1776), the Virginia religious freedom law (1786) and the founding of the University of Virginia (1817) but nothing on the time period from the intervening 30 years.

Madison near the end of life: "Having outlived so many of my contemporaries, I ought not to forget that I may be thought to have outlived myself." In 1824, **John Quincy Adams** reflected at the graves of his ancestors in Quincy Massachusetts: "Pass another century and we shall all be moldering in the same dust or resolved into the same elements" and later, toward the end of life, he said he was "one of the relics of the past" and said: "The world will retire from me before I shall retire from the world."

In 1844 **John Quincy Adams** reflected that his late parents John and Abigail Adams had married eighty years previously. He wrote: "The recollection of the past is pleasing and melancholy; the prospect of the future - oh, how gloomy it is! Not a soul now living who was then in the bloom of life. Not a soul now living will be here in 1924. My own term - how soon will it close!" He fainted at age 80 in 1848 as he was about to give a speech in Congress and died two days later with these words: "This is the last of earth - I am composed." As he lay dying two years later, **Zachary Taylor** said: "I have always done my duty. I am ready to die. My only regret is for the friends I leave behind me."

Lincoln once told a friend he was not afraid to die, but for the fact "that he had not done anything to make any human being remember that he had lived." **Lincoln** was quoted by a New Salem friend: "It isn't a pleasant thing to think that when we die that is the last of us." **Grant** was writing his memoirs at the end of his life and it was a herculean effort. He knew that he had to finish the book to save his family from bankruptcy and to establish his written legacy. With every word, he wrote to his doctor, "I had been adding to my book and to my coffin." **McKinley** in 1899: "That's all a man can hope for during his lifetime - to set an example - and when he is dead, to be an inspiration for history." **McKinley** was shot in 1901. The crowd around him tackled the shooter. **McKinley** said: "Don't hurt him." He called him "some misguided fellow." He said to his chief aide: "My wife, be careful how you tell her - oh be careful." He died a week later whispering the words of the hymn "Nearer My God to Thee."

Theodore Roosevelt died at 60 in 1919. He wrote 1914: "I have already lived and enjoyed as much of life as any other nine men I know." He wrote another time: "I have no desire before my time has come to go out into the everlasting darkness." He hoped that there would be people "to whom it will be a pleasure to think well of us when we are gone." After **FDR's** election in 1932, **Coolidge** privately told a friend in December of that year: "We are in a new era to which I do not belong and it would be impossible for me to adjust it." He died within a month at 60. Late in retirement when he saw the plans drawn up for his own funeral **Truman** said, "Looks splendid; too bad I won't be able to enjoy it."

Eisenhower said to his wife about the presidency, "Hell, the job killed **Wilson**." After his 1955 heart attack **Ike** recalled **Wilson's** stroke and how the debilitating results were kept from the public. He ordered his press secretary to tell the public the whole truth. His first official visitor some days later was **Richard Nixon.** The President told him, "It hurt like hell, **Dick**." In his second term **Eisenhower** said to his doctor, "How in the hell can anyone carry the load of the presidency without permitting the tensions to affect his physical self?" **Eisenhower** lived for thirteen more years.

Billy Graham said of **LBJ**: "He was always a little bit scared of death."

A few weeks before **Nixon** died in 1994 **Ford** talked with him. He later said: "We had a nice chat. He was very grateful that Betty and I had been to Pat's (**Nixon's** wife) funeral and that I had gone to the twentieth anniversary of his first inauguration." **Carter** spoke at **Ford's** funeral in 2007. He began and ended his eulogy with the first sentence of his inauguration speech of 1977: "For myself and for my nation, I want to thank my predecessor for all he has done to heal our land." **Clinton** did not speak at **Ford's** funeral or any of the ceremonies because **Ford** wanted it that way.

What is the point of all this?

The presidency transforms the person and gives him both a type of institutional immortality and a sense of isolation driving him to his only peers. When they die their only peers are moved to comment. Before, during and after their presidencies, the presidents are typically in association with other presidents.

In the last four chapters we have seen that in most cases the loneliness of the position drives former foes like **John Adams/ Jefferson, Hayes/Arthur, Cleveland/TR, Taft/TR, and Hoover/ Truman** and others to closer relationships. As we have seen in the instance of **John Quincy Adams** at the death of **Jackson**, there are exceptions.

Chapter 5

Rivalry

Overall Context

James Monroe wrote **Jefferson** about **George Washington** before **Washington** took the presidency: "Having ...commenced again on the public theatre the course which (**Washington**) takes becomes not only highly interesting to him but likewise so to us: the human character is not perfect; and if he partakes of those qualities which we have too much reason to believe are almost inseparable from the frail nature of or being, the people of America will perhaps be lost."

During Aaron Burr's trial for treason in 1807 in Richmond Virginia, **Jackson** was reportedly present denouncing **Jefferson.** (Burr was acquitted following a strategy that in essence put the government on trial.)

In early 1828, Senator **Martin Van Buren** told a friend: "You may rest assured that the re-election of Mr. **Adams** is out of the question." He was correct as later that year, **Andrew Jackson** realigned American politics with a victory over the incumbent, **John Quincy Adams.** At a White House dinner, **Lincoln** once fed a cat with formal silverware. When his wife criticized him he said: "If the gold fork was good enough for **Buchanan** I think it is good enough for Tabby." In 1966 an out-of-office **Nixon** criticized an **LBJ** overture to North Vietnam that was called the Manila Statement. **LBJ** responded at a press conference by attacking **Nixon**, leading with: "I do not want to get into a debate on a foreign policy meeting in Manila with a chronic campaigner like Mr. **Nixon.**" **Nixon** responded carefully: "Let the record show that all over the world I have defended the administration's goal of no surrender to aggression. I have defended it in the capitals of the world and here at home against members of the president's own party." This exchange helped rehabilitate **Nixon's** image from political defeats in 1960 and 1962. During the 2000 campaign **George W Bush** told family members that **Clinton** "promised to have the most ethical administration in American history. He fell about forty-one presidents short."

When we discuss presidential rivalries, some work themselves out and some don't.

In 1837 **Martin Van Buren** and **Andrew Jackson** began the tradition of the incoming and outgoing presidents riding together to the inauguration. This tradition was important as a sign of stability and was an antidote to the decisions of both **Adamses** to boycott the inaugurations of their successors, **Thomas Jefferson** in 1801 and **Andrew Jackson** in 1829. But in 1869 **Grant** would not ride with **Andrew Johnson** to his inauguration. In 1933 **FDR** and **Hoover** drove to the former's inauguration in silence. Twenty years later **Eisenhower** refused to get out of his limousine when it came to pick up **Truman** on the way to **Ike's** inauguration.

There are other national symbols that have been the locus of disdain. In 1843 **John Quincy Adams** reacted negatively to Daniel Webster and **John Tyler** attending the dedication of the Bunker Hill Monument. He boycotted the ceremony and wrote: "What a name in the annals of mankind is Bunker Hill! What a day was the 17th of June 1775! And what a burlesque upon them by Daniel Webster, and a pilgrimage by **John Tyler** and his cabinet of slave drivers, to desecrate the solemnity by their presence!" (His mother had taken him to witness the battle as an eight-year old.) Forty years later **Hayes** was disgusted at **Arthur's** White House: "Nothing like it ever before in the Executive Mansion - liquor, snobbery and worse. Outbreaks of ill temper caused by drink no doubt were odd enough sometimes." In another eighty years, when **Eisenhower** heard that **JFK** had hosted a banquet at Mount Vernon in honor of Pakistan's Mohammed Ayub Khan who had taken power in a coup, he said, "What a desecration!"

In many cases the presidents have been political rivals over very high stakes. Take, for example the development of the United States

Constitution. In 1787 **Monroe** was disappointed at not being selected to be in the Virginia delegation to the Constitutional Convention and wrote **Jefferson** who was in Europe blaming **Madison.** After the Convention **Madison** pushed for ratification while **Monroe** thought it should not be ratified without amendments including a Bill of Rights. **Jefferson** and **John Adams** ran against each other for president twice as did **John Quincy Adams** and **Andrew Jackson** and **Grover Cleveland** and **Benjamin Harrison**. In 1948 **Truman's** path to a second term included worry about an **Eisenhower** surge in his own party. **Theodore Roosevelt**, **Taft** and **Wilson** all ran against each other. So did **JFK** and **Nixon**, **Ford** and **Reagan**, **Ford** and **Carter**, **Carter** and **Reagan** and **Clinton** and **George HW Bush** and others

Sometimes presidents have accused each other of power-seeking or too much ego, almost always a case of glass houses and stones. **Jefferson** on **Washington**: "His mind has been so long used to unlimited applause that it could not brook contradiction..." **Jefferson** came to believe that **Adams** had "been taken up by the monarchical federalists."

Sometimes this power is attributed to someone close to the president. **John Adams** in about 1800: "Hamilton, who ruled **Washington**, would still rule if he could." **Monroe** wrote **Jefferson** back in 1788 after the Virginia ratifying convention about **Washington**: "More is to be apprehended if he takes part in public councils again, as he advances in age, from the designs of those around him than from any disposition of his own." **Nixon** said that Nancy Reagan was a "bitch" and that she "runs **Ronald Reagan**." (**Nixon** made this comment through an intermediary to **Gerald Ford** as a piece of advice during a primary fight between **Ford** and **Reagan** in 1976.) In 1991 **Ford** said he thought Nancy Reagan influenced her husband's negative behavior particularly his reticence toward campaigning for **Ford** in 1976. "She had a tremendous impact on his decision. She was very bitter, and I think she had a checkrein on him."

Some criticisms are complaints about indecisiveness. In 1881 **Garfield** removed the Collector at the New York Custom House and nominated his own man angering New York Republican boss Roscoe Conkling, a **Grant** ally. **Grant** said that it proved that **Garfield** "lacked the backbone of an angle-worm." **Benjamin Harrison** thought **McKinley** lacked "a firm will." **TR** once said **McKinley** had "the backbone of a chocolate eclair." **Truman** said of **Eisenhower**; "He couldn't make a decision to save his soul in hell." In 1964 someone suggested to **Eisenhower** that the election that year would cause **LBJ** to have less of a backbone to stand up to a prominent labor leader. **Eisenhower** said of **LBJ's** backbone: "He never had any."

In the run-up to the Spanish-American War, Civil War veteran **William McKinley** said: "War should never be entered upon until every agency of peace has failed." **Theodore Roosevelt** was disdainful of what he saw as inaction and said about **McKinley**: "Do you know what that white-livered cur up there has done? He has prepared *two* messages, one for war and one for peace, and doesn't know which one to send in!" **McKinley's** response after **TR** made a speech urging military preparedness in 1897 was: "I suspect **Roosevelt** is right and the only difference between him and me is that mine is the greater responsibility." **McKinley** stopped seeing **TR**.

Presidents have also criticized one another while recognizing greatness.

Even the greatest are criticized by other Presidents. When **George Washington** was appointed commander of the army **John Adams** wrote Abigail that he was "one of the most important characters in the world" and that "the liberties of America depend on him." But **Adams** later called **Washington** a "muttonhead." After the Battle of Antietam **Lincoln** proceeded with his plans on the Emancipation Proclamation. When he issued it, Congressman-elect **James Garfield** in 1863 wrote a friend: "Strange phenomenon in the world's history when a second rate Illinois lawyer is the instrument to utter words which shall form an epoch memorable in all future ages." From the army **Hayes** was worried that he expected too much from the Emancipation Proclamation but was "glad it was issued." In 1864 **Arthur** within his own family circle was reputedly opposed to **Lincoln's** prosecution of the war. **Truman** succeeded the revered

FDR but said privately that the people closest to **Roosevelt** were "crackpots and the lunatic fringe."

Sometimes the criticism is intensely personal. **Andrew Johnson** was elected to the Senate in 1875, some six years after his presidency. He confided to a friend that he had two goals. One was to punish Southern leaders who had urged secession. The other was that he wanted to "make a speech against **Grant**, and I am going to make it this season." He made the speech and died three months later. The sinking *Lusitania* on May 7, 1915, led to President **Wilson** giving a speech that included this: "The example of America must be the example not merely of peace because it will not fight but peace because peace is the healing and elevating influence of the world and strife is not. There is such a thing as a man being too proud to fight. There is such a thing as a nation being so right that it does not need to convince others by force that it is right." **TR** was furious and wrote privately to a relative that **Wilson** was cowardly and "cordially supported by all the hyphenated Americans, by solid flubdub and (the) pacifist vote." Out of office, **Truman** said of **Nixon**: "All the time I've been in politics, there's only two people I hate and he's one." Sometimes it is not personal - just the reflection of a younger person. In Harvard law school in the early 1840s **Hayes** thought that Daniel Webster had damaged his reputation by staying in **Tyler's** cabinet as long as he did.

Sometimes presidents are flat wrong in their criticisms. In 2014, **Obama** decided to smear **Rutherford B Hayes**. According to President **Obama's** version, **Hayes**, when first shown a telephone, wondered if anyone would want one. **Obama** said: "That's why he's not on Mount Rushmore. He's explaining why we can't do something instead of why we can do something." Actually, **Hayes** was cutting-edge for his era. When he first saw a telephone during his 1877-1881 term he said: "That is wonderful." (A decade later, there still was only one phone number for the entire White House. After the clerical staff went home for the night, it was not out of the ordinary President **Cleveland** to answer the phone.)

Sometimes the criticism is light-hearted. **Eisenhower** liked to joke that one of his goals was to follow the example of **Andrew Jackson** and eliminate the national debt but added, "As **Jackson** was a Democrat, there must have been something fishy about it." When **Obama** first took office, someone in a press conference asked him if he had spoken with any former presidents in getting ready. He answered that he had talked with all the ex-presidents "that are living." But he added a comment making fun of the wife of the late **Ronald Reagan**: "I didn't want to get into a Nancy Reagan thing about doing any séances." This was inaccurate. Mrs. Reagan did not go for séances. She consulted an astrologer after **Reagan** was nearly assassinated in 1981. **Obama** quickly apologized. **Barack Obama** may have confused Mrs. Reagan with Hillary Clinton who, according to author Bob Woodward, consulted an adviser and held imaginary conversations with Eleanor Roosevelt during the **Clinton** administration.

James Buchanan who knew all the presidents from **Monroe** to **Lincoln** and who tried for the office several times before winning the 1856 election and who is often considered the worst of the US presidents said in 1851: "The wisest and most sagacious men become dunces when seized by a desire for the presidency." They certainly were critical of each other. Here are some examples.

Moving forward.

As noted, in 1776 **Monroe** was a young officer with **George Washington** in the evacuation of New York. He was with **Washington** at the crossing of the Delaware to take Trenton and was wounded. He was at Valley Forge. But **Washington** came to dislike **Monroe**. They first disagreed over the ratification of the Constitution. A decade later, **Monroe** was elected governor of Virginia and when the news reached **George Washington**, he reacted angrily, caught a cold and died.

In 1792 the Republicans knew they could not replace **Washington** so they concentrated on replacing **John Adams**. **Madison** and **Monroe** were active in coordinating the effort against **Adams**.

John Adams once said **Washington** could "not write a sentence without misspelling." He later added: "That he was too illiterate, unlearned, unread for his station is equally beyond dispute." **George Washington** became richer by marrying Martha Curtis, a widow. **Adams** later wondered: "Would **Washington** have ever been commander of the revolutionary army or president of the United States if he had not married the rich widow of Mr. Curtis?" **Adams'** problem was jealousy. He wrote to Benjamin Rush that people seemed to think that the country was started when "Dr. Franklin's electrical rod smote the earth and out sprung General **Washington**. That Franklin electrified him with his rod and thence forward these two conducted all policy, negotiation, legislation and war."

Jefferson in a letter to **Madison** about **Adams** in about 1784 wrote: "He hates Franklin, he hates Jay, he hates the French, he hates the English." (**Adams** did have strong dislikes. During the First Continental Congress he disliked fellow Congressman Benjamin Harrison who was the father of **William Henry Harrison** although he later said that Harrison's "many pleasantries" helped steady the Congress.)

As Vice President, **Jefferson** was leader of the opposition and met privately with the French charge d'affaires during a crisis with France urging the French, according to the diplomat's report, to stall in negotiations with American representatives in what came to be known as the XYZ affair. The report dated June 7, 1797 quoted **Jefferson**: "Mr. **Adams** is vain, irritable, stubborn, endowed with excessive self-love, and still suffering pique at the preference accorded Franklin over him in Paris."

In 1789 **Monroe** was pressured by Antifederalists to run for the first Congress against **Madison**. He wrote **Jefferson**: "Those to whom my conduct in public life had been acceptable, press'd me to come forward in this government on its commencement; and that I might not loose (*sic*) an opportunity of contributing my feeble efforts in forwarding an amendment of its defects, nor shrink from the station those who confided in me would wish to place me, I yielded." Amending the new Constitution was the key issue in the campaign. **Monroe's** backers without his knowledge spread rumors that **Madison** was opposed to amendments which he denied, saying that with ratification, now was the time to consider amendments. The two candidates toured together speaking at such places as court houses and churches. **Madison** won handily probably on the strength of the Baptist vote in appreciation for his stand on religious liberty.

During **Washington's** presidency **Jefferson** said that he had "got into one of those passions when he cannot command himself; ran on much on the personal abuse which has been bestowed on him." By 1796, **Jefferson** had been privately describing **Washington** as senile for years. In 1797 **Jefferson** wrote **Madison** that **Washington** was "fortunate to get off just as the bubble is bursting." He noted that **Washington** was "leaving others to hold the bag." **Jefferson** said that **Washington** "was first brought up to govern slaves(;) he then governed an army, then a nation." He wrote in 1814 about **Washington** that he had "neither copiousness of ideas nor fluency of words."

Jefferson wrote of **Jackson**: "When I was President of the Senate and he was a Senator, he could never speak on account of the rashness of his feelings. I have seen him attempt it repeatedly and as often choke with rage." He recalled **Jackson** as a "dangerous man." **Jefferson** and **Van Buren** worried about whether **Monroe** was leading the country in the wrong direction.

In the 1790s **Jefferson** had written a note about Thomas Paine's book *The Rights of Man* saying that it was the answer to "the political heresies that have sprung up among us." The **Adams'** family took it as an insult. A young **John Quincy Adams** wrote a series of articles in the defense of his father. They were anonymous and many assumed that **John Adams** was the author. **James Madison** perceived that it was the work of **John Quincy Adams** and observed that the younger **Adams'** style was more fluent than his father. (**John Adams** was not even the second-best writer in his family. There are about 1200 letters between him and Abigail. **John Adams** thought that Abigail was a better writer and most historians agree.) **John Quincy** made a sly reference to the word "heresy": "I am somewhat at a loss to determine what this very respectable gentleman means by political heresies. Does he consider this pamphlet of Mr. Paine's as a canonical book of political scripture? As containing the true doctrine of popular infallibility? From which it would be heretical to depart in one single point?" In the politicized atmosphere of New York, the articles were a sensation and helped push the two-party system forward. **Washington** wasn't happy to see this discord in his official family. **Jefferson** told **Washington** that this was caused by the "indiscretion of a printer" and he told **John Adams** that **John Quincy Adams** was the cause of the trouble. (I bet that went over well.)

While a Justice on the Tennessee Supreme Court during the crisis with France in 1798-1801 **Andrew Jackson** abhorred **John Adams'** curtailment of civil liberties. While a senator in the early 1800s, **John Quincy Adams** was chagrined over what he saw as **Jefferson's** tendency to embellish stories. It had to do with claims that while in Europe he could speak Spanish and claims about weather in France which **Adams** knew to be false.

Jefferson in 1823 worrying about his legacy wrote **Madison**: "Mr. **Adams'** papers and his biography will descend of course to his son, whose pen...is pointed, and his prejudices are not in our favor." He had reason to worry. **John Adams'** son carried on the family dislike of **Jefferson**. In 1831, after his own presidency, **John Quincy Adams** read the just-released letters of **Thomas Jefferson** (who had been dead for five years by then). He pointed out errors and omissions. "He tells nothing but what redounds to his own credit." He said that **Jefferson** had shown perfidy "worthy of Tiberius Caesar." He later added that **Jefferson's** letters exhibited "his craft and duplicity in very glaring colors. I incline to the opinion that he was not altogether conscious of his own insincerity, and deceived himself as well as others." (Two hundred years later, another presidential son defended his father. **George W Bush** said about his father's presidency: "When he was president, I was not a well-behaved person. I got really angry when people mischaracterized my dad.")

In 1804 while in the Senate **John Quincy Adams** corrected the grammar of one of **Jackson's** bills saying that it was "grossly and outrageously defective and blundering." But the two were not yet enemies and sometime later when Henry Clay criticized **Jackson** in a House speech, **John Quincy Adams** wrote, "His (Clay's) opposition to **Jackson** is now involuntary, and mere counteractive." But **Adams** and **Jackson** moved apart. In 1819 **Monroe, John Quincy Adams** and **Jackson** all agreed with the treaty with Spain that swapped a US claim on Texas for possession of Florida. **Jackson** later changed his mind and accused **Adams** of letting down the South by abandoning the claim on Texas. (**Jackson** recognized Texas independence on his last day in office.) **Adams** grew to hate **Jackson**. In the 1820s **Adams** wrote in his diary about President **Monroe** and his Secretary of the Treasury nearly coming to blows.

By this time, **Jefferson** had also come to distrust **Jackson.** In 1824 Daniel Webster came to Monticello. He quoted **Jefferson**: "I feel much alarmed at the prospect of seeing General **Jackson** President. He is one of the most unfit men I know for such a place. He has had very little respect for laws or constitutions. His passions are terrible." In the 1824 election, **Jackson** received more electoral votes than **John Quincy Adams**, but not a majority. As required by the Constitution, the election was then decided in the House of Representatives. (The outgoing President **James Monroe** favored **Adams** but stayed silent.) In the House vote, Henry Clay supported **Adams**, the ultimate winner. **Adams** subsequently selected Clay for the position of Secretary of State giving the outgoing President **Monroe** these reasons: "I consider it due to his talents and services and to the Western section of the Union, whence he comes, and to the confidence in me manifested by their delegations." **Monroe** didn't warn **Adams** of any negative consequences. **Jackson** partisans were outraged, or at least feigned outrage. We know this in history as the "Corrupt Bargain." Years later, **Adams** invoked Christianity to declare his innocence of any deal with Clay, declaring that when he died, "should those charges have found their way to the throne of Eternal Justice, I WILL, IN THE PRESENCE OF OMNIPOTENCE, PRONOUNCE THEM FALSE." – (During the House of Representatives phase of the 1824 presidential election, it was rumored that a young congressman **James Buchanan** approached Henry Clay to see if he would use his influence to swing the election to **Jackson** in return for an appointment to Secretary of State.)

As president, **John Quincy Adams** turned down a request from **William Henry Harrison** for reimbursement for services during the War of 1812. Also as president, **Adams** wrote in his diary: "**Van Buren** is now the great electioneering manager for General **Jackson** (and) has improved as much in the art of electioneering upon Burr as the state of New York has grown in relative strength and importance in the Union."

In the election of 1828 some of **Adams'** allies started a claim that **Monroe** deserved credit for the victory in the Battle of New Orleans since he had as Secretary of War given **Jackson** orders to move there from Mobile. **Jackson's** allies responded by claiming that **Monroe** had neglected to send sufficient supplies. **Monroe** assembled correspondence to rebut the charge but refrained from making it public for fear of becoming embroiled in politics. **Madison** and **Monroe** were then selected as electors for **Adams** in Virginia but they tried to withdraw from the role. **Madison** told **Monroe** that he was completely retired and thought that ex-presidents acting in politics would be viewed negatively by incumbents. **Monroe** was primarily worried about the success of his claims for financial reimbursements which were before Congress and did not want to make enemies. In **Monroe's** last years, animosity between him and **Jackson** complicated his efforts to get the government to make these payments. From the Senate **Tyler** tried to stay neutral but eventually opted for **Jackson**: "Turning to him I may at least indulge in hope; looking on **Adams** I must despair." **Adams** faced a political wave incarnated in **Andrew Jackson** who won handily.

Adams wrote in his diary after a visit by **Van Buren** early in **Andrew Jackson's** first term that **Van Buren** was the most able of the Jacksonians but driven by ambition. He wrote that **Van Buren** was "by far the ablest man of them all, but wasting most of his ability upon mere personal intrigues... His principles are all subordinate to his ambition..."

In **Jackson's** first term, a social dust-up in the administration involving the wife of the Secretary of War occurred. History knows it as the Peggy Eaton Affair. It had to do with wives of cabinet members refusing to meet socially with Mrs. Eaton on account of their views of her sexual behavior. It led to the Secretary challenging another cabinet member to a duel. **Jackson** was outraged at this division in his official family and probably protective of Mrs. Eaton in the memory of his own late wife. **Van Buren** a widower was able to side with the President without any domestic concerns. **John Quincy Adams** wrote in his diary that Vice President John C. Calhoun was of the "moral party" and **Martin Van Buren** led the "frail sisterhood." **Adams** wrote to his daughter-in-law: "It is the prevailing opinion... that Mr. **Van Buren** is about to scale the Presidency of the United States by mounting upon the shoulders of Mrs. Eaton." **Andrew Jackson** was shot at in 1835 by a house painter who apparently believed that **Jackson** had kept him from becoming King of England. **Jackson** who was then 67 clubbed his assailant with his cane. **Jackson** believed and spoke out that the assassination attempt was a plot of a US Senator with whom he was at odds. **John Quincy Adams** asked in his diary "if we were running into the manners of the Italian republics"

When **Tyler** who was a widower married a young woman **Adams** said that **Tyler** and his wife were the "laughing stock of the city." (**Buchanan** said that **Tyler** was lucky with both "a belle and a fortune to crown and close his Presidential career.")

As a member of Congress in 1833 in an era of developing parties **Fillmore** tried to recruit a justice of the Supreme Court to run for President in 1836 and thought he could take advantage of a split in the Democrat Party between those who favored and those who disfavored **Martin Van Buren**, the Vice President. As **Fillmore** put it: the "**Jackson** Anti-**Van Buren** people might be immediately induced to (support you)." His chosen candidate was uninterested and **Fillmore**, who did not want Henry Clay or Daniel Webster for the Whig nomination, moved by default to **William Henry Harrison**. In the general election **Fillmore** tried to find negative information on **Van Buren** dating back to 1812 and **Madison's** election. **Van**

Buren had supported **Madison's** opponent in 1812. In the 1836 election **Van Buren** beat **Harrison** but the latter won the rematch four years later.

Also in the election of 1836, **John Quincy Adams** thought that candidates **Martin Van Buren** and **William Henry Harrison** were "the golden calves of the people, and their dull sayings are repeated for wit, and their grave inanity is passed off for wisdom." In 1842 Congress created a committee to investigate whether **Tyler** should be impeached. This was the first time such an investigation had been called. **John Quincy Adams** was the chair. (Henry Clay assumed that **Tyler** would be impeached and said, "The Whig party bearded the old Lion (**Andrew Jackson**), amidst his loudest roars. Surely it will not give way, or suffer itself to be frightened by pranks of a monkey" (**John Tyler**). The committee held that **Tyler** had committed "offenses of the gravest character" and deserved to be impeached but it went nowhere. In Congress, as an ex-President **John Quincy Adams** frequently opposed **Polk** whom he said "has no wit, no literature, no point of argument, no gracefulness of delivery, no elegance of language, no philosophy, no pathos, no felicitous impromptus; nothing that can constitute an orator but confidence, fluency and labor."

Andrew Jackson turned against **Jefferson** for refusing to make him governor of Louisiana Territory. He said of **Jefferson** that he was "the best republican in theory and the worst in practice." **Jefferson** offered **Monroe** the governorship of Louisiana territory but he declined. The idea didn't immediately die. In the early years of the **Madison** administration **Jefferson** tried to reconcile **Madison** and **Monroe** who had temporarily fallen out by recruiting **Monroe** to the governorship of Louisiana. He was unsuccessful, reporting to **Madison**: "The sum of his answers was to accept of that office was incompatible with the respect he owed himself; that he would never act in any office where he should be subordinate to any but the President himself..."

Tyler in the Senate during **Jackson's** presidency: "There is already the spruce of monarchy on the presidential office." In 1834 **Tyler**

voted to censure **Jackson**. (Congressman **John Quincy Adams** opposed the censure.) In 1836 **Tyler** resigned from the Senate rather than obey to Virginia legislature's instructions to remove the censure. In 1841 when **Tyler** assumed the presidency, **Jackson** called him: "an imbecile in the Executive Chair."

William Henry Harrison during the 1840 campaign: "I am a true, simple Republican, aghast that the government under 'King Mat' (**Van Buren**) is now a practical monarchy." **Fillmore**, in 1840 supporting **William Henry Harrison** criticized the spoil systems under the Jacksonians and said that **Van Buren's** appointees were "mere brawling adherents" engaged in self-serving and "the most flagitious and culpable devices." In that campaign **Andrew Jackson** said that he "never admired **Gen. Harrison** as a military man, or considered him as possessing the qualities which constitute the commander of an army."

William Henry Harrison said **John Quincy Adams** was "a disgusting man to do business with - coarse, dirty, clowning in his address and stiff and abstracted in his opinions." But as a newly elected president, **Harrison** said that he considered **Adams** an old friend who "had been so unjustly put out." After **Harrison** died, **Adams** disdained **Tyler** and called him a "Virginia nullifier" although **Tyler** did not join Calhoun on that issue. In essence, **Tyler** believed that secession was constitutional but nullification was not.

As a legislator, **Franklin Pierce** was somewhat of an expert on government pensions and his actions put him at odds with at least two presidents. In 1840 **Pierce** met with President **Van Buren** trying unsuccessfully to get approval for a pension for his brother-in-law who had been wounded in the War of 1812. He wrote his brother-in-law telling him of his failure with **Van Buren** saying that it caused the meeting to "conclude without some warmth on my part." In 1841 in the Senate **Pierce** spoke against a bill to give twenty-five thousand dollars to the widow of the recently deceased **William Henry Harrison.**

In 1841 the Whig Party in New York experienced a general defeat. **Fillmore** publicly attributed the loss to the President, **John Tyler** whose "mental malady" drove him "on from folly to madness" and "insane hostility to his former friends." (He also blamed New York Governor, William Seward.) Years later, out of the presidency, **Fillmore** turned down an honorary degree at the University of Oxford saying that a person shouldn't receive a degree he couldn't read. He may have been thinking of **Jackson** receiving a degree at Harvard once shouting out phrases in Latin.

On the comeback trail, **Martin Van Buren** lost the support of **Andrew Jackson** and hence the nomination for the presidency in 1844 to **James Polk**. It was over the issue of admitting Texas into the Union as a state. **Jackson** feared British designs on Texas, then an independent country. **Van Buren** was equivocal on the issue whereas **Polk** was strong. **Van Buren** had had a majority of the delegates at the Democratic convention, but a two-thirds rule applied. **Polk** won the nomination on the ninth ballot and went on to win the election over Henry Clay becoming the first dark horse candidate in American history. The two-thirds rule for the Democrats stayed in effect until 1936. (In 1944, Southern Democrat politicians had two goals at the Democrat convention: dumping Vice President Henry Wallace from the ticket and restoring the two-thirds rule. They succeeded in the first, but not the second. Wallace was replaced by **Harry Truman**.)

Jackson was happy with the 1844 outcome but two other presidents were not. When **Polk** was elected **Fillmore** saw a "cloud of gloom" over America and said: "May God save the country; for it is evident the people will not..." **John Quincy Adams** was of a similar mind writing in his journal: "I mused over the prospects before me with the impression that they portend trials more severe than I yet have passed through."

Once in office, **Polk** quarreled with several past and future presidents. In 1845 **Van Buren** was upset at **Polk's** final cabinet selections and wrote: "It is an evil which neither civil words nor the disposition of patronage can repair & which, under the circumstances, nothing can justify." In early 1846 a **Polk** nominee to the Supreme Court failed confirmation and people saw this as an undermining of the

President by his Secretary of State, **James Buchanan** who by that time probably wanted the appointment himself. **Polk** wrote in his diary: "I cannot surrender the appointing power to anyone else, and if, because I will not do so, Mr. **B** chooses to retire from my Cabinet I shall not regret it." By 1847 Secretary of State **Buchanan's** treatment of **Polk** caused him to lose political standing. **Polk**, once an ally of Congressman **Andrew Johnson,** heard that **Johnson** reacted to his nomination with the word, "humbug." He later wrote in his diary that **Andrew Johnson** was "very vindictive and perverse in temper" and noted that "he has not appeared at the White House during the entire session." **Johnson's** relationship with President **Polk** frayed over patronage appointments. He said **Polk's** idea of politics was "to hang one friend in order to make two new ones." **Johnson** wrote a friend: "Take **Polk's** appointments all in all and they are the most *damnable* set that was ever made by any president...There is one thing I will say. *I never betrayed a friend or (was) guilty of the black sin of ingratitude.* I fear Mr. **Polk** cannot say as much." At one point in 1846, **Taylor** in command of an army in the Mexican-American War stationed in Texas, cut off communication with **Polk** in Washington. (**Polk** had complained that the battle of Buena Vista which **Taylor** won against a numerically superior foe was an unnecessary battle.) Later in the war **Polk** wrote of **Taylor**: "I have no prejudice against him but think he has acted with great weakness and folly." He thought **Taylor** had become "giddy with the idea of the presidency." In 1847 a Whig newspaper published a letter **Taylor** had written from the Southwest criticizing **Polk**. **Polk** thought **Taylor** should have been put on trial for the letter but his cabinet persuaded him to reduce it to his second reprimand. **Taylor** was unrepentant and said that his views were held by responsible statesmen.

Zachary Taylor also criticized other presidents. He evidently held a grudge against **Madison** for not intervening on his behalf when his rank was reduced in the demobilization back in

1815. **Taylor** archly noted that **Madison** was "perfectly callous & unacquainted with the noble feelings of a soldier..." In 1841 he wrote **William Henry Harrison** about the "corruption" of the **Jackson** administration and the "ineptness" of the **Van Buren** administration.

In 1856 **Buchanan** was the man whose nomination President **Pierce** most wanted to block. **Buchanan** was nominated and elected because he had been out of the country as ambassador to England while the Kansas-Nebraska Act was discussed and passed and, possibly, because former President **Millard Fillmore** helped split the opposition vote.

Abraham Lincoln was quite critical of **Franklin Pierce.** As the latter was about to leave office after failing to win renomination against **Buchanan**, **Lincoln** compared him to "a rejected lover, making merry at the wedding of his rival." In 1858 in the **Lincoln**-Douglas Debates **Lincoln** tried to tie Douglas to **Pierce**. In 1861 Secretary of State William Seward was worried that **Pierce's** travels in the North away from his New Hampshire home were disloyal to the Union cause. **Lincoln** was less alarmed: "I think it is well that **P** (**Pierce**) is away from the N.H. people. He will do less harm anywhere else; and *when* he had gone, his neighbors will understand him better." At one point, **Pierce** was called to account for his travels by the State Department to which he angrily replied and received the support of others including the aged **Martin Van Buren**.

Although **Lincoln** came to admire **Martin Van Buren** later, in the 1848 campaign when **Van Buren** had left the Democratic Party to head up the Free Soil Party he called him the "artful dodger." (Charles Dickens' *Oliver Twist* in which a boy named Oliver joins a group of juvenile pickpockets in London led by a boy nicknamed the Artful Dodger had been published ten years earlier.) **Lincoln** on **Polk**: "He is a bewildered, confounded and miserably perplexed man."

After **Pierce** was elected in 1852 **Andrew Johnson** thought his "transit had been too sudden." But he subsequently noted that **Pierce** kept his own counsel, "which is a very good trait in an executive officer." In 1858 while in the Senate **Andrew Johnson** wrote about President **James Buchanan**: "He is too timid to venture upon anything new or risk much upon anything old. To hear him talk, one would think he was quite bold and decided, but in practice he is timid and vacillating... I fear his administration will be a failure." He came to anticipate nothing from **Buchanan** but "grannyism."

As southern states seceded and before **Lincoln** took office, Ohio state Senator James **Garfield** wrote to a friend, "Just at this time (have you observed the fact?), we have no man who has power to ride upon the storm and direct it. The hour has come, but not the man."

During the time of the impeachment of **Andrew Johnson** in 1867-68, **Grant** was trying a balancing act. He was the commanding general in the Army and yet had already been approached about the Republican nomination for president and thus was trying to stay on good terms with the Republican opposition to **Johnson**. By the time of the Senate trial he was lobbying for conviction and the relationship between the seventeenth and eighteenth president was irretrievably broken. **Johnson** on **Grant** in 1868 after the election: "**Grant** has treated me badly; but he was the right man in the right place during the war, and no matter what his faults were or are, the whole world can never write him down - remember that."

Soon after his presidency **Andrew Johnson** ran for the Senate in Tennessee. In that era the legislature made the selection. **Grant** said his election would be "a personal insult." **Johnson** lost. Several years later he won a Senate seat.

In the Congress in 1877-78 **Garfield** opposed and **McKinley** supported the Bland-Allison bill that was passed over **Hayes'** veto. The bill was for the greater coinage of silver at a fixed rate and **Garfield** saw it as inflationary. After **Hayes** took office in 1877 **Garfield** who had done much to put him there became somewhat disillusioned. He wrote in his diary in 1878 about **Hayes**: "The impression is deepening that he is not large enough for the place he holds."

In 1880 the outgoing **Hayes** did not favor **Grant** for a third term. **Garfield** came to the 1880 Republican convention as **Polk** had come to the 1844 Democrat convention as a dark horse and he frustrated **Grant's** third term bid. He worked from both the conference room and the speakers' platform. In the former he acted as chair of the Rules Committee that successfully recommended disallowing the "unit rule" which would have given all of a state's delegates to the candidate who had the majority support in that delegation. This cost **Grant** about sixty crucial votes. Later, **Garfield** spoke after a massive pro-**Grant** demonstration. He was ostensibly speaking in favor of another candidate but may have been trying to preserve his own options. Knowing that the party was divided between pro and anti-**Grant** forces, he took the line of party unity. "Nothing touches my heart more quickly than a tribute of honor to a great and noble character; but as I sat in my seat and witnessed this demonstration, this assemblage seemed to me a human ocean in tempest." After the nomination of **Garfield**, **Hayes** said **Garfield** was "the ideal candidate." He hyberbolically said of **Garfield** that: "The truth is no man ever started so low that accomplished so much in all our history. Not Franklin or **Lincoln** even." **Hayes** regarded the nomination of **Arthur** for Vice President to be a "sop" to the pro-**Grant** forces. (Which it was.)

During the ensuing campaign **Garfield** requested that **Hayes** make certain patronage appointments in the interests of Republican unity. **Hayes** was reluctant to do this and told him: "You will of course be appealed to by all sorts of people and will be perfectly free to make known to me whatever you wish me to know. My purpose is to allow no danger to come through me." **Garfield** understood: "I want you to give me credit for many requests I do not make - or rather - for not making very many of those which I am asked to do." **Hayes** was disappointed in **Garfield's** campaign in 1880 for at least two reasons. He thought **Garfield** equivocated on the presidential power to appoint and on civil service reform. On the latter he did not approve of **Garfield's** attempts to reconcile with Roscoe Conkling of New York. In 1881, angry that **Garfield** would not reappoint one of his supporters, **Grant** wrote that he was "completely disgusted with **Garfield's** course." Their relationship fell apart. **Garfield** wrote in his journal that: "It is now evident (what I had not supposed) that **Grant** had his heart fully set on the nomination… and was deeply hurt at its failure."

Early in his term **Arthur** began to resent **Grant's** unsolicited advice. On constitutional arguments **Arthur** opposed a bill that would have given **Grant** the status and salary of an active general in order to improve **Grant's** difficult personal finances. **Arthur** believed that only the president could appoint generals. Ultimately he aided **Grant**. In 1884, Democratic leaders were trying to persuade **Cleveland** to run for president. He responded that he would run only if President **Arthur** or former Secretary of State James G Blaine were nominated by the GOP. At the Republican convention that year **TR** did not back **Arthur** and Blaine was given the nod.

When **Benjamin Harrison** rejected his recommendation to fire a postmaster for corruption, **TR** lamented, "It was a golden chance to take a good stand; and it had been lost." As **TR**, realized that **Harrison** was backing off from Civil Service reform, he spoke out: "Damn the President! He is a cold-blooded, narrow-minded, prejudiced, obstinate, timid old psalm-singing Indianapolis politician."

In 1892 **Benjamin Harrison**, running for re-election, was challenged before the nominating convention by his own former Secretary of State. This was in an era when convention delegates could be swayed and were an important factor. Some began to see **William McKinley** as an alternative. To forestall this, the **Harrison** forces got **McKinley** selected as convention chair thinking this would force him to avoid a draft by the convention. **Harrison** was renominated. However, the Ohio delegation voted for its governor **William McKinley**. In an effort toward party unity **McKinley** had cast his vote for **Harrison**. **Harrison** was not mollified and described **McKinley's** vote as "a clear pretense." "No mature man can believe that Ohio voted for him without his consent...nor that the Governor of Ohio and the head of the Ohio delegation could influence no single vote therein, save his own." **Harrison** did not forgive **McKinley**.

In the 1880s **Cleveland** vetoed a version of **Benjamin Harrison's** Dependent Pension Bill as he had hundreds of individual pensions with what **Harrison** called vetoes "tipped with poison arrows." In 1887 **Hayes** read **TR's** biography of Thomas Hart Benton and found it "vigorous, dogmatic and a little scattering."

TR criticized **Cleveland** for clumsy English. **TR** campaigned for **Benjamin Harrison** in 1888 but he later described him as the "little gray man in the White House." In 1889 **TR** campaigned for **McKinley's** rival for Speaker of the House but assured **McKinley** that he would one day vote for him for president. Yet, **TR** in a private letter in early 1896 said "it will be a great misfortune to have **McKinley** nominated.... If I could tell you all I have learned since his campaign has progressed, you would be as completely alarmed over the prospect of his presidential nomination as I am." In 1898 after his victory in Cuba **TR** and his fellow officers felt the soldiers had to be evacuated promptly to escape malaria. **TR** sent off a peremptory telegram to the press that outraged **McKinley** and the War Department. There was talk of a court-martial of **TR** that came to nothing but he was denied the Medal of Honor. It was awarded posthumously in 2001 by President **Bill Clinton** a week before he left office.

In the 1908 campaign **William Howard Taft** made a careless allusion to **Grant's** drinking that - even though **Grant** had been dead for twenty-three years - offended Civil War veterans. **Taft** on **Wilson** in 1911: "He is a good deal of a 'butter in.'" In 1912 **Taft** described **TR** as one of "the leaders of religious cults who promote things over their followers by any sort of physical manipulation and deception." **Taft** called **TR** a "fakir," a "juggler," a "green goods man," and a "gold brick man." He said that by manipulation and deceit, "he is seeking to make his followers Holy Rollers." **TR**, that same year began to regard **Wilson** as a credible rival, saying of him: "**Wilson** is a good man who has in no way shown that he possesses any fitness for the presidency. Until he was fifty years old, as a college professor and college president he advocated with skill, intelligence and good breeding the outworn doctrines which were responsible for four fifths of the political troubles of the United States.... Then he ran as Governor of New Jersey, and during the last eighteen months discovered that he could get nowhere advocating the doctrines he had advocated, and instantly turned an absolute somersault so far as at least half these doctrines were concerned...." **TR** added that at least **Wilson** would not "show **Taft's** muddleheaded inability."

In the Republican Party split of 1912 **Harding** sided with **Taft** and took on **TR.** He editorialized that **TR's** goal to return to office was a personal "lust for power." He called **TR** a "limelighter." He said **TR** was seduced by "malefactors of great wealth." He said **TR** was "an insufferable boss...intolerant...an unheeding dictator...His prototype in history was Aaron Burr, the same towering ambitions; the same ruthlessness in disregarding the ties of friendship, gratitude and reverence; the same tendency to bully and browbeat...the same type of egotism and greed for power." He also compared **TR** to Benedict Arnold saying that he was "utterly without conscience and truth, and the greatest faker of all time." **Harding** wrote: "If we do not skin **TR** here in Ohio, I'll feel like wishing the ship to sink." **Taft** beat **TR** in Ohio but **Wilson** beat them both with forty percent of the vote.

In 1916 **TR** called **Wilson**: a "damned Presbyterian hypocrite" and a "Byzantine logothete." During the part of World War I that preceded American involvement **TR** denounced **Wilson's** policies of neutrality. He derided **Wilson's** criticisms of Germany as **Wilson** first shaking "his fist and then his finger." He criticized **Wilson's** goal of peace without victory: "Peace without victory is the natural ideal of a man too proud to fight. It is spurned by all men of lofty soul, by all men fit to call themselves fellow-citizens of **Washington** and **Lincoln** or of the war-worn fighters who followed **Grant** and Lee." In the Spanish-American War **TR** left the position of Assistant Secretary of the Navy to go into combat. In World War I he criticized **FDR** his fifth cousin and also nephew-in-law for not doing the same thing. (In the 1940s, **Franklin Roosevelt** told Nelson Rockefeller that he had been prevented from enlisting in World War I by **Woodrow Wilson** who wanted him to remain as Assistant Secretary of the Navy.) In the 1912 campaign **TR** referred to the Democrat Champ Clark: "The nomination at Baltimore belonged to Mr. Clark, but the bosses handed it over to Mr. **Wilson**."

Wilson on **Chester Allan Arthur** who had served almost thirty years before him: "A nonentity with side whiskers." **Woodrow Wilson** defending **TR** in 1901: "He really determines an important part of the destinies of the world." He was "a very interesting and a very strong man." A few years later, **Wilson** had modified his views calling **TR** "the most dangerous man of the age." During the 1920 campaign **Wilson** told Navy Secretary Josephus Daniels that he was "deeply resentful" of **FDR's** ambition and doubtful loyalty. After **Wilson's** retirement **FDR** set up a foundation to support **Wilson's** liberal and internationalist principles but it may not have been meaningful to **Wilson** who said to FDR: "I shall try and be generous enough not to envy you."

The 1912 split between liberals like **TR** and conservatives like **Taft** also separated the three Republican presidents of the 1920s. In the **Harding-Coolidge** administrations **Hoover** was a

progressive. **Hoover** said **Harding** had a "bungalow mind." (This quote is also attributed to **Wilson**.) He didn't like **Harding's** oratory. **Harding** had his own concerns and said to **Hoover**: "Damn it, why don't you write the same English as I do?" **Coolidge** said that **Hoover** had given him "unsolicited advice for six years, all of it bad." **Coolidge**: "If you put a rose in **Hoover's** hand, it would wilt." **Coolidge** speculating about the 1928 election said: "They're going to elect that superman **Hoover**, and he's going to have some trouble." The Great Depression began seven months after **Coolidge** left office. **Hoover** did not seek his advice, further irritating **Coolidge**.

Truman managed to disparage three of his next four successors. In 1952, **Truman** thought that **Eisenhower**, a soldier, would be in over his head as president. In his memoirs he blamed the failure to take Berlin on **Eisenhower**. In 1960 **Truman** called a press conference. He listed about ten Democrats who would be acceptable to him as the nominee. He included **LBJ** but not **JFK**. He said to **JFK**: "Senator, are you certain you are quite ready for the country, or that the country is quite ready for you in the role of President in January 1961? May I suggest you be patient?" **JFK's** response was to focus on his fourteen years of public service. (six as a congressman; eight as a senator) and to subtly contrast that with **Truman's** experience in high elected office before he became president. **Truman** also said that the Democrat convention was "rigged" for **JFK**. Later in 1960 **Truman** came to support **Kennedy** with this statement: "I never liked **Kennedy**. I hate his father. **Kennedy** wasn't so great a Senator.... However, that no good son-of-a-bitch **Dick Nixon** called me a Communist and I'll do anything to beat him." **Truman**

in 1960: "If **Nixon** had to stick to the truth he'd have very little to stay." **Truman** said that anyone who voted for **Nixon** "ought to go to hell." **JFK** joked that he had written **Truman** and said that it was "important that our side try to refrain from raising the religious issue."

In 1934 **Eisenhower** was at a reunion with his brothers. The brothers argued about the New Deal and **Ike** was critical of **FDR**. **Eisenhower** put in his diary that the **FDR** victory in 1940 caused an election night party to "fall flat." As President-elect in 1953, **Eisenhower** wrote this about **FDR**: "Winston (Churchill) is trying to relive the days of World War II. In those days he had the enjoyable feeling that he and our president were sitting on some ... Olympian platform...and directing world affairs from that point of vantage. But many of us in various corners of the world had to work out solutions." (In 2009 President **Obama** noted to a European audience that a new financial order was being created by the world's top 20 financial powers, not by "just **Roosevelt** and Churchill sitting in a room with a brandy. ... But that's not the world we live in, and it shouldn't be the world that we live in." (President **Theodore Roosevelt** about a young Winston Churchill in a note to his ambassador in London: "I do not like Winston Churchill." On another occasion he said: "That young man Churchill is not a gentleman. He does not rise to his feet when a lady enters the room." **TR** was about 15 years older than Churchill. Winston Churchill once called **Herbert Hoover** who was in charge of food shipments throughout Europe during World War I an SOB.)

In 1951 **Herbert Hoover** called for an "American Gibraltar" which would be protected by atomic bombs and able to live in isolation from the rest of the world. **Eisenhower** wrote in his diary that while he had admired **Hoover** "extravagantly, I'm forced to believe he's getting senile."

In 1953 **Eisenhower** did not confer with Vice President **Richard Nixon** or **Herbert Hoover** in the selection of his cabinet or his White House staff. As President, **Eisenhower** mentioned to his personal secretary that **Nixon** had very few friends.

In 1957 **Eisenhower** heard from Republican leaders that **John Kennedy** was going to come out for Algerian independence from France and the Republicans were asking him how he would like them to respond. **Eisenhower** understood the practical problems associated with this nationalism but held some sympathy for it. In fact earlier he had told Senator Hubert Humphrey that through national independence people obtained "fierce pride and personal satisfaction," thinking of his experiences in the Philippines in the 1930s. To the Republican leaders he said: "Perhaps Republicans might best just chide Mr. **Kennedy** a bit for pretending to have all the answers."

Eisenhower had a difficult time relating with **Nixon**. His son later said: "He *made* himself like **Nixon**." In his speech before the 1960 Republican convention in Chicago which followed the Democrat convention that nominated **Kennedy** and **Johnson**, **Eisenhower** did not criticize **Kennedy** or **Johnson** or praise **Richard Nixon**. **Eisenhower** to a friend after the 1960 nomination of **Richard Nixon**: "...we nominated the wrong man." Late in the 1960 campaign **Eisenhower** was planning to campaign for **Nixon** but Mamie Eisenhower persuaded Pat Nixon to urge **Nixon** to ask **Eisenhower** not to campaign because she was worried about his health. **Nixon** did so but did not tell **Eisenhower** the reason. (Years later, Julie Nixon Eisenhower, **Nixon's** daughter – and the wife of **Ike's** grandson - said that Mamie Eisenhower disputed this account.) **Eisenhower** later blew up: "Goddammit, he looks like a loser to me." **Nixon** on **Eisenhower**: "He was a far more complex and devious man that most people realized." **Nixon** once observed that **Ike** said different things about extremist Senator Joe McCarthy in public than in the Oval Office. Speaking sarcastically, **Nixon** said he wished he had a recording device to "capture some of those warm, offhand, great-hearted things the man says, play 'em back, then get them press-released." (As president, of course, he put in such a "recording device.")

To summarize an interesting development in 1960: **JFK** had trouble getting **Truman's** support and **Nixon** had trouble getting **Eisenhower's**. Eventually both **Truman** and **Eisenhower** were driven to support their parties' candidate by their antipathy toward the opposite number.

JFK privately: "**Nixon** is a nice fellow in private and a very able man. I worked with him on the Hill for a long time, but it seems he has a split personality, and he is very bad in public, and nobody likes him." After **Nixon** conceded the 1960 election, **JFK** said: "He went out the way he came in...no class."

In 1959 **JFK** told *Look* magazine that **LBJ** "fluctuates and is not a heavyweight thinker." Arriving at the 1960 convention **LBJ** was asked if he would accept the vice presidential spot. He said that he might give it to **JFK**: "The vice presidency is a good place for a young man who needs experience." (Robert Kennedy said of **LBJ** after the 1960 Democrat convention: "I knew he hated **Jack**, but I didn't think he hated him that much.)

Johnson was ill-treated by **JFK's** staff including Robert Kennedy during his three years as Vice President. His animosity, kept under wraps while he served as president himself, came out occasionally. In the weeks after the assassination of **JFK**, **LBJ** told a **Kennedy** aide that **JFK's** death may have been "divine retribution" for his "participation" in assassination plots aimed at Cuban leader Fidel Castro. He stayed with this theme. In retirement, referring to plots to kill Fidel Castro, **LBJ** told a journalist that the Kennedys "had been operating a damn Murder, Inc. in the Caribbean."

After **Kennedy's** acceptance speech, actor **Ronald Reagan** wrote **Nixon**: "Under the tousled boyish haircut, it is still old Karl Marx."

After the 1960 election, at the request of **Kennedy's** father, **Hoover** suggested to **Richard Nixon** that he meet **JFK** to shake hands publicly. **Nixon** responded that that would be "a cheap publicity stunt." **Hoover** lost his temper with **Nixon**: "This is a generous gesture on his part and you ought to meet it with equal generosity."

In 1961 **JFK** got a cut in tax rates passed and signed it into law. **Eisenhower** and **Nixon** called the cuts reckless and said that they would add to the deficit.

Out of office, in 1962, **Nixon** ran for the governorship of California against the incumbent, Edmund G. Brown. **Truman** told Brown never to mention **Nixon's** name: "Let him go to hell on his own hook." **JFK** coached Brown on how he might debate **Nixon**. **Johnson** came to California to campaign for Brown. **Eisenhower** said at the time of **Nixon:** "I can personally vouch for his ability, his sense of duty, his sharpness of mind and his wealth in wisdom." **Nixon** lost that race. After **Nixon's** defeat, **JFK** said that he was "beyond saving." He said he was "sick."

LBJ was born poor on a farm but his father was in the state legislature and his mother had graduated from Baylor University. He bragged (inaccurately): "My ancestors were teachers and lawyers and college presidents and governors when the Kennedys in this country were still tending bar." In 1960 **LBJ** assessed **Kennedy's** victory over him in the Democrat primaries as follows: "They beat the hell out of us because they have superior educations." **JFK** said to **LBJ** in 1960 campaign: "I believe you're cracking up." In 1960 on election night **LBJ** called **JFK**: "I see *you* are losing Ohio, *I* am carrying Texas..." **JFK** on **LBJ**: "a very insecure, sensitive man with a huge ego."

As President, **Kennedy** said: "I cannot stand **Johnson's** damn long face. He just comes in, sits at the Cabinet meetings with his face all screwed up, never says anything. He looks so sad." Robert Kennedy once told his brother about **Lyndon Johnson's** failure to run the Committee on Equal Employment Opportunity. **John Kennedy** responded: "That man can't run this committee. Can you think of anything more deplorable than him trying to run the United States? That's why he can't ever be President of the United States." **LBJ** as Vice President told his staff, "Nothing and nobody is ever going to divide the president and me, and I'm not going to say anything to anybody, not even my wife, that might get back to the president and cause him a moment's concern." In the last month or so of **JFK's** life, **Johnson** expressed private concern that he would be dumped from the ticket.

Privately, Jacqueline Kennedy said during **LBJ's** presidency that **JFK** had told her, "Oh, God, can you ever imagine what would happen to the country if **Lyndon** was president?" She also said that **LBJ** had been drunk when he was asked to join **Kennedy** on the ticket in 1960.

As noted, **Ford** was an all-American football player at the University of Michigan in the 1930s. In the 1960s, President **Johnson** once said of **Ford** that "he played too much football with his helmet off." **LBJ** campaigned against **George HW Bush** in 1964 in the latter's race for the US Senate and helped wipe out his lead in the polls and defeat him. After the 1968 election **Lyndon Johnson** told an aide: "It's not enough for **Nixon** to win. He's going to have to put some people in jail." From the time he first met him in the 1940s, **LBJ** had considered **Nixon** too much a loner and a "chronic campaigner."

During his presidency **Nixon** hoped to find documents showing that **FDR** knew about Pearl Harbor in advance.

During the Watergate crisis **Richard Nixon** told an aide that Republican National Committee Chair **George HW Bush** was a "worrywart." **Bush** defended President **Nixon** throughout Watergate. So did **Reagan.** The conservative magazine *National Review* sent telegrams to well-known conservatives in the US asking for input on whether it should write an editorial advocating that **Nixon** resign as the Watergate crisis grew. Governor **Reagan's** response: "HELL NO." During his time as Vice President, **Ford** declared: "I can say from the bottom of my heart that the President of the United States is innocent!"

In 1973, calls made by both **Reagan** and **George HW Bush** to President **Nixon** after a speech the President made during the Watergate crisis were secretly recorded. **Reagan** said, "I just want you to know, we watched and my heart was with you. I know what this must have been and what this must have been in all these days and what you've been through." **Bush** called to say he had watched the speech with "great pride."

In August of 1974 **Nixon**, under a 8-0 order from the Supreme Court, released a taped conversation of a June 23, 1972 meeting he had had with an aide in which **Nixon** desired to get the CIA to stop the FBI investigation into Watergate. This recording contradicted **Nixon's** earlier denials and led to his resignation. **Bush** later said, "My temptation was to blast the president, blast the lie, and then I thought, why add to the personal tragedy and the personal grief? Events were moving so fast that it just didn't seem right to kind of 'pile on.'" On August 7, 1974 **Bush** sent **Nixon** a letter advising him to resign adding, "this letter is much more difficult because of the gratitude I will always feel toward you." In 1977 **Nixon** emerged from seclusion for interviews. **Bush** avoided comment: "I'm sparing myself. I've already lived through the agony of Watergate. I don't want to live through it anymore."

Nixon said in 1987 that **Reagan** was "somewhat fuzzy...far older, more tired and less vigorous than in public."

Gerald Ford said that **Nixon** was "so much more enamored with foreign policy" that he left congressional affairs to an "evil group" of aides. By the time he became president, **Ford** "had lost almost all respect" for **Nixon** because of **Nixon's** lies to him.

As **Carter** began to prepare to run for the presidency in 1973 he had very little name recognition. He began to highlight differences with **Nixon** saying that the President was "conspiring with major oil companies" to raise prices. **Carter** opened up his fall campaign in 1976 calling out the "**Nixon-Ford** administration." In a famous *Playboy* interview in 1976, **Jimmy Carter** lumped together **Richard Nixon** and **LBJ** in "lying, cheating and distorting the truth." He later backtracked on **LBJ**. **Carter** when asked in that campaign if it was fair to link **Ford** with **Nixon**: "It's not my fault if **Nixon** is unsavory." **Jimmy Carter** loathed **Nixon** and only invited him to a state dinner at the White House for Chinese leaders in 1979 at the insistence of the Chinese.

In the 1976 presidential primaries **Carter** made an awkward remark about preserving the "ethnic purity" of neighborhoods. He got a lot of criticism from Democrats. **Ford** also chimed in wondering "whether that remark will have any impact on the support he has heretofore gotten in the black communities of the various states." **Carter** responded: "I am happy to have aroused the interest and the opposition of the President... I guess now he's joined the 'Stop **Carter**' movement. But what he should know from me is that I am going to stop him in November."

In 1979 **Clinton** was in his first term as governor of Arkansas. He told **Carter** that people in his state had less of an understanding of who he (**Carter**) was than they did when he first ran three years earlier. In 1980 Fidel Castro unleashed one hundred thousand boat people on the US. Many were criminals or mentally ill. **Carter** dispatched about eighteen thousand of them to a fort in Arkansas where they rioted. **Clinton's** political opponents labeled him as a **Carter** puppet and he lost the next election and blamed **Carter.**

In 1978 **George W Bush** ran for Congress unsuccessfully from West Texas. **Reagan** supported his primary opponent angering **George HW Bush** forecasting their own intra-party rivalry in 1980. (**Ford** sent a check to the **George W Bush** campaign.) In early 1980 **Ford** said it would be "impossible" for **Reagan** to win the general election. In the 1980 Republican primaries **George HW Bush** labeled **Reagan's** tax proposals as "voodoo economics."

After being disadvantaged in a New Hampshire debate in the 1980 Republican primaries by a **Reagan**-supported change in the rules to allow more participants in what had been organized as a **Reagan-Bush** debate, **George HW Bush** wrote one of the other candidates: "I fear he used you to set me up. Governor **Reagan** had definitely not played fair with me." As the primaries went on George **HW Bush** fell farther and farther behind **Reagan**. He was angered by right wing attacks over his former membership in the Trilateral Commission, a group of business people and policy specialists and added: "And **Reagan** acquiesces - like he did when his people used it against my son **George**." However, **George HW Bush** came to regard **Reagan** "as a friend, a trusted and admired friend."

In 1980 **Jimmy Carter** faced off against **Ronald Reagan** and tried to label him as a right-winger: He went to Independence, Missouri the home of **Truman** and said: "**Reagan** is different from me in almost every basic element of commitment and experience and promise to the American people, and the Republican Party now is sharply different from what the Democratic Party is. And I might add parenthetically that the Republican Party is sharply different under **Reagan** from what it was under **Gerald Ford** and Presidents all the way back to **Eisenhower**." **Carter** was infuriated by this **Reagan** campaign joke: "I'm told I can't use the word depression. We'll, I'll tell you the definition. Recession is when your neighbor loses his job. Depression is when you lose your job. Recovery is when **Jimmy Carter** loses his." In a debate with about a week before the election watched by one hundred million people **Carter** accused **Reagan** of opposing Medicare. **Reagan** smiled and said, "There you go again." **Carter** said of **Reagan's** debate performance that he "memorized lines, and he pushes a button and they come out." By Election Day according to one poll nearly 40 percent of those polled indicated that they would vote for **Reagan** because he was not **Carter** instead of citing him as a conservative or a Republican.

At the 1992 Republican convention **George HW Bush** talked of our victory in Iraq and derided **Clinton** as "the leader of the Arkansas National Guard." Toward the end of the 1992 campaign, President **George HW Bush** called **Clinton** and his running mate "bozos." **Clinton** campaigned against **George HW Bush's** ties with the "butchers of Beijing" and said that continuing to extend "most favorite nation" status to China was "unconscionable." (After the 1992 election **George HW Bush** said he had been "outfoxed by a very shrewd politician, **Clinton**.") In **Clinton's** first term a minor scandal developed when White House officials were found to have FBI files of **George HW Bush** administration officials. **Clinton** accurately called this a "bureaucratic snafu" and **Bush** seemed to accept the explanation.

In 1993 **Nixon** conveyed to **Clinton** that if he wasn't respected he would publicly criticize **Clinton's** foreign policies. **Clinton** invited him to the White House. In 1994 **Carter** went to Haiti to try to negotiate with the military dictator to leave and return the government to civilian control before the US attempted to oust him. As a deadline approached, one account has it that **Clinton** called **Carter** and said: "You better get out because I'm sending in the troops." **Carter's** response: "You can send 'em but I ain't leaving."

In the 2000 Republican primary the rival John McCain campaign responded to an ad from the **George W Bush** campaign by putting out an ad of its own which stated: "His ad twists the truth like **Clinton**." **Bush** responded with an ad in which he said: "Politics is tough. But when John McCain compared me to **Bill Clinton** and said I was untrustworthy, that's over the line. Disagree with me, fine. But do not challenge my integrity." In 2000 **Clinton** did an impersonation of **George W Bush**: "My daddy was president. I own a baseball team. They like me down there." **George HW Bush** then said: "If he continues that, then I'm going to tell the nation what I think of him as a human being and a person."

Carter came to oppose the foreign policy of **George W. Bush** calling it the "worst in history." During his presidency, **George W Bush** was asked if he had consulted his father about his plans to invade Iraq. He answered that he had consulted his heavenly father.

As early as 2006 **Bill Clinton** saw **Barack Obama** as a threat to his wife's candidacy for the presidency. The Hillary Clinton-**Obama** race in 2008 was one of the iconic races in American history. **Clinton** worked assiduously for his wife and fought the **Obama** candidacy hard. He overreached more than once. One example was when he took **Obama's** comment that **Reagan** had been a "transformative figure" who could get conservative Democrat support and interpreted it as though **Obama** was asserting that **Reagan** had better ideas than Democrats. During the campaign **Obama** said of **Bill Clinton**: "You know the former President, who I think all of us have a lot of regard for, has taken his advocacy on behalf of his wife to a level that I think is pretty troubling." (At one point earlier, according to one report, **Obama** had said that if he were elected he would appoint **Bill Clinton** to a cabinet post "in a second." (He ended up appointing Hillary Clinton.)

President **Obama,** considering his vice president selection in 2008, told his advisors according to one insider account: "I still think

Hillary has a lot of what I am looking for in a VP. Smarts, discipline, steadfastness. I think **Bill** may be too big a complication. If I picked her, my concern is that there would be more than two of us in the relationship."

In 2008, **Obama** tried to tie his opponent John McCain to **George W Bush**. One comment of **Obama's** came in the context of defending his views toward more diplomacy: "If **George Bush** and John McCain have a problem with direct diplomacy led by the president of the United States, then they can explain why they have a problem with **John F. Kennedy**, because that's what he did with Khrushchev." (**JFK** met with Soviet premier Nikita Khrushchev in 1961 in what turned out to be a debacle. Minutes after the summit ended **Kennedy** told a reporter: "He just beat the hell out of me. I've got a terrible problem if he thinks I'm inexperienced and have no guts. Until we remove those ideas we won't get anywhere with him." Within two months Krushchev ordered the erection of the Berlin Wall which lasted until 1989.)

During the **Obama** presidency, **Jimmy Carter** was asked if Mr. **Obama** sought him out for advice. **Carter's** response: "Unfortunately, the answer is no." **Carter** noted that former presidents **Bill Clinton**, **George W. Bush** and **Ronald Reagan** asked for his help with diplomacy when dealing with "unsavory characters." He said that it is difficult to explain "with complete candor" why he and **Obama** did not have a closer relationship but added that his private diplomacy in the Middle East may be the source of the tension.

In 1993 **George W Bush** was deciding to run for governor of Texas while his brother was deciding to run in Florida. **George HW Bush** was enthusiastic about the brother's chances but did not think **George W Bush** could win. During the campaign, **George W Bush** said: "I am not running for governor because I am **George Bush's** son. I am running because I am Jenna and Barbara's father." (He appears to have appropriated this line from his brother.) But as the 1994 campaign heated up, **George HW Bush** said this about his eldest son: "He is good, this boy of ours. He is uptight at times, feisty at other times - He includes people. He has no sharp edges

170

on issues. He is no ideologue, no divider - All this talk about his wild youth days is pure nuts. His character will pass muster with flying colors."

It is of course very natural for fathers and sons to show both affinity and rivalry. This duality also is also a characteristic of many presidential relationships.

Both Affinity and Rivalry

Sometimes political alliances change. **Van Buren** supported Secretary of the Treasury William Crawford in for president 1824. This contributed to New York going for **John Quincy Adams** which potentially cost **Jackson** the election. Later **Van Buren** and **Jackson** became close allies. **Van Buren** served as **Jackson's** vice president and succeeded him.

Sometimes, of course, it is more complicated. **Polk** did not admire **Tyler** but they came to belong to the same "club." After his presidency **Tyler** answered a congressional subpoena to testify in an investigation of his Secretary of State Daniel Webster over a financial matter. (**Tyler** thought Webster was a careless administrator but honest and Webster ended up reimbursing the government about a thousand dollars.) He dropped in on **Polk** who expressed that **Tyler** had been subjected to "unjust annoyance."

Serving together in the post Civil War Congress **Garfield** wrote that **Hayes** was "the most patient listener in the Capitol." For his part, **Hayes** recorded this of **Garfield**: "a smooth, ready, pleasant man, not very strong." Sometimes relationships turn on the political issues of the day. At the 1876 Republican convention **Arthur** supported Roscoe Conkling the powerful senator from New York Republicans. After **Hayes** was nominated the *New York Times* reported of **Arthur**: "He fought hard for Conkling, but he is now willing to accept the situation and glad to do everything in his power for the next President, **Rutherford B Hayes**." Yet, their relationship was embittered during **Hayes'** term in office as **Hayes** attempted to dismiss **Arthur** from his post as head of the New York Custom House, setting off an inter-branch struggle within the federal government. As noted, when **Arthur** left office some affinity returned. **Hayes** visited **Arthur** shortly before he died and described him later as "thin and feeble." In another century **LBJ** and **Nixon** squared off politically many times but they recognized their common ground. In 1958 Vice President **Nixon's** party was attacked by a mob in Venezuela and for a while **Nixon** was in real danger. He comported himself courageously and returned to a hero's welcome in Washington DC at which Senate leader **Johnson** embraced him at the airport. **LBJ** had once referred to the Vice President as a "chicken shit." When asked by a reporter to reconcile this, **Johnson** said that "chicken shit can turn into chicken salad."

Sometimes there is real ambivalence. In 1993 **Ford** said of President **Clinton**: "This guy can sell three-day-old ice. He's that good." He also said: "I get confused by him. I don't know what's at his core. I don't know what's most important to him. But this guy is the best politician I've ever seen."

Here are other examples.

James Madison wrote to **Thomas Jefferson** in the late 1790s offering comparisons between **Washington** and **John Adams**: "There never was perhaps so great a contrast between two characters than between those of the present President & his predecessor, altho' it is the boast & prop of the present that he treads in the steps of his predecessor." But two decades passed. The bitter 1790s came to an end. Napoleon emerged and sunk. The Louisiana Purchase went forward. The US survived the War of 1812 although Washington DC was burned. **Jefferson** and **Madison** joined **John Adams** in retirement and **Madison** wrote **Adams**: "I have always been much gratified by the favorable opinion you have been pleased occasionally to express of the public course pursued while the Executive trust was in my hands, and I am very thankful for the kind wishes you have added to a repetition of it. I pray you to be assured of the sincerity with which I offer mine, that a life may be prolonged which continues to afford proofs of your capacity to enjoy and make it valuable."

Presidents who disdained each other occasionally have a good word. In 1842 England sent a pro-American minister, Lord Ashburton to Washington to try to work out a boundary issue between Maine and Canada. **Tyler** assisted by his daughter-in-law hosted a White House party for Ashburton. **John Quincy Adams** who attended wrote: "The courtesies of the President and Mrs. R. Tyler to their guests were all that the most accomplished European court could have displayed."

Some presidents dealt with antagonisms by working with close associates. **Eisenhower** had certain negative feelings toward his two predecessors but as president he was glad to work with the **Roosevelt** and **Truman** allies who led the Democratic Party in the Congress, Sam Rayburn and **Lyndon Johnson.** Other presidents who disagreed have been able to compose their relationships. In 1963 **Truman** wrote **Hoover:** "I didn't receive a single birthday telegram that I appreciated more than I did yours.... We understand each other."

Sometimes age and circumstances work the opposite effect. **Wilson** grew to hate **TR** but said in 1912: "He is a real, vivid person...I am a vague, conjectural personality, more made up of opinions and academic prepossessions than of human traits and red corpuscles."

We will look at several relationships that affected American history.

Adams-Jefferson

John Adams served with and sometimes for two men that people thought were greater: **Washington** and Benjamin Franklin. Over time he was hot and cold on both. But his most memorable public relationship was with **Jefferson**. This is the most famous and complex presidential relationship in US history.

Adams considered **Jefferson** his protégé in the Philadelphia of 1776 and **Jefferson** considered **Adams** a mentor. In the Continental Congress **Jefferson** described **Adams** as "our colossus on the floor." **Adams'** bravery may have made an impression on **Jefferson**.

In 1776 after the British drove the American army out of New York **Jefferson** left Philadelphia. **Adams**, who assessed the New York defeat succinctly - "in general, our generals were outgeneraled" - changed his own plans to leave. "The panic may seize whom it will, it will not seize me."

Jefferson and **Adams** worked together in the 1770's and 80's as Americans advocating independence from England and later as the chief diplomats from America in Europe. In 1786 they traveled together in the English countryside to Twickenham and to Stratford-on-Avon and to Birmingham. It was a six-day sojourn referred to by Abigail as: "their little journey into the country." **Jefferson** to **Madison** about **Adams** in 1787: "He is so amiable that I pronounce you will love him if ever you become acquainted with him."

During the Constitutional Convention of 1787 a newspaper in Philadelphia serialized **John Adams'** *Defense of the Constitutions of Government of the United States of America*. **Adams** was in London as the American ambassador. **James Madison** wrote to **Thomas Jefferson** who was also abroad on **Adams'** treatise: "Men of learning find nothing new in it, men of taste many things to criticize." **Jefferson** had once told **Madison** that he observed in **John Adams** a "want of taste" - apparently a reference to **Adams'** habit of occasionally chewing tobacco and drinking rum more or less straight.

In late 1787 **John Adams** got word that his resignation was accepted and he could return from his diplomatic post in London to America. From France **Jefferson** wrote him: "I learn with real pain the resolution you have taken in quitting Europe. Your presence on this side of the Atlantic gave me a confidence that if any difficulties should arise within my department, I should always have one to advise with on whose counsels I could rely. I now feel widowed."

The events of the 1790s pushed them apart. It may have started over protocol. As Vice President, **John Adams** argued that **Washington's** title should be "His Majesty" or "His Highness." The Senate rebuked this and went with "Mr. President." **Jefferson**, told of **Adams'** view, said it seemed to him "as the most superlative ridiculous thing I have ever heard."

But the relationship, though strained, was not yet severely damaged as they went into the 1796 election as competitors. **Jefferson** wrote **Madison** about **Adams** in the election saying that **Adams** deserved to win: "I am his junior in life, was his junior in Congress, his junior in the diplomatic line, his junior lately in the civil government." In 1796, the newspapers were reporting that four electoral votes from Vermont were invalid for a variety of technical reasons. **Adams** would lose the presidency if those votes were not counted since he only led **Jefferson** by three. **Adams** as Vice President had the constitutional responsibility to preside over the vote count. This was the first contested presidential election in American history. In a letter to **James Madison**, **Jefferson** wrote that "substance and not form should prevail." In other words, **Jefferson** was willing to overlook technical difficulties and let the will of the Vermont voters which was obviously pro-**Adams** be registered. However, the breach still widened. After the 1796 election **Jefferson** sent **Madison** the draft of a letter of congratulations he planned to send **John Adams**. **Madison** persuaded him not to send it.

During the **John Adams**' administration, **John Adams** wrote to **John Quincy Adams** about **Jefferson**: "However wise and scientific as a philosopher, as a politician he is a child and the dupe of party." In 1801 the lame-duck Federalist-dominated Congress passed the Judiciary Act. It established six new circuit courts and sixteen new judges and reduced the number of Supreme Court Justices from 6 to 5. **Adams** thereby was able to appoint sixteen Federalist judges and even to fill two vacancies on the Supreme Court before **Jefferson** was able to appoint.

After 1801, the two never met again. In 1804 **Jefferson** wrote Abigail Adams: "I can say with truth that one act of Mr. **Adams**' life, and one act only, ever gave me a moment's displeasure. I did consider his last appointments to office as personally unkind. They were among my most ardent political enemies, from whom no faithful cooperation could ever be expected..." Abigail Adams didn't buy it.

Yet, through the efforts of Benjamin Rush, **Adams** and **Jefferson** were reconciled. Rush elicited from **Adams** the comment, "I always loved **Jefferson** and still love him." **Jefferson** responded to Rush: "This is enough for me."

Adams and **Jefferson** then began a correspondence that lasted over a decade and forms an important installment of American literature. Some samples:

- **Adams** in an 1812 letter to **Jefferson**: "In the measures of administration I have neither agreed with you or **Mr. Madison**. Whether you or I were right posterity must judge."
- **Jefferson** to **Adams** to deflect a disagreement in 1813: "We are both too old to change opinions which are the result of a long life of inquiry and reflection."
- **Jefferson** in an 1814 letter to **Adams**: "...A letter from you calls up recollections very dear to my mind. It carries me back to the times when, beset with difficulties and dangers, we were fellow laborers in the same cause, struggling for what is most valuable to man, his right of self-government."
- **Adams** in an 1814 letter to **Jefferson**: "The result in time will be improvements; and I have no doubt that the horrors we have experienced in the last forty years will ultimately terminate in the advancement of civil and religious liberty, and amelioration in the condition of mankind. For I am a believer in the probable improvability and improvement, the ameliorability and amelioration in human affairs; though I never could understand the doctrine of the perfectibility of the human mind..."
- **Adams** in an 1816 letter to **Jefferson**: "Griefs upon griefs! Disappointments upon disappointments. What then? This is a gay, merry world notwithstanding."

Cleveland-TR

People today remember **Theodore Roosevelt** who died in 1919 far more than they remember **Grover Cleveland** who died in 1908. These two first interacted in the 1880s when **TR** was a state assemblyman and **Cleveland** was the governor of New York. Although **Cleveland** was a Democrat and **TR** a Republican, they had a solid working relationship.

During the 1883 New York state legislative session Governor **Grover Cleveland** said of Assemblyman **Theodore Roosevelt**, "There is a great sense in a lot of what he says but there is such a cocksureness about him that he stirs up doubt in me all the time." Looking back later **Cleveland** said of **TR** who was the minority leader in the Assembly: "It was clear to me even thus early, that he was looking to a public career, that he was studying political conditions with a care that I have never known any man to show, and that he was firmly convinced that he would someday reach prominence."

The relationship was complicated. As governor of New York **Grover Cleveland** vetoed a bill that **TR** supported which he viewed as unconstitutional. **TR** said the next day, "I have to say with shame that when I voted for this bill I did not act as I think I ought to have acted." **TR** eventually got a Civil Service Reform bill passed which was supported by **Cleveland** and which helped him get elected President in 1884.

But by then, **TR's** attitude had changed and **TR** saw the more accomplished and older **Cleveland** as a rival. In 1886 it came to light that when **Cleveland** was governor, in a veto of a bill sponsored by **TR, Cleveland** had said, "Of all the defective and shabby legislation that has been presented to me, this is the worst and the most inexcusable." While he was on the Civil Service Commission later in the 1880s, **TR** feuded with **Cleveland** and criticized **Cleveland's** "sheer hypocrisy." A decade later as he left the New York governorship for the vice presidency, **TR** said, "I think I have been the best governor of my time, better either than **Cleveland** or Tilden."

When **TR** went to the presidency after the murder of **McKinley**, **Cleveland** called him "the most perfectly equipped and effective politician thus far seen in the Presidency." **TR** was concerned that **Cleveland** might run against him in 1904. He circulated a letter from **Cleveland** that showed support for his labor policies. **Cleveland** wrote, "I am amazed at **Roosevelt**.... There are some people in this country that need lessons in decency and good manners." **TR** kept circulating the letter.

TR-Taft

Many presidential pairs have had rivalries and reconciliations. **Eisenhower** and **Nixon** may have pulled closer as did **Reagan** and **George HW Bush.** For **George HW Bush** and **George W Bush** it is less clear.

TR and **Taft** followed the **Adams-Jefferson** model. **Taft** reported to **TR** from positions as viceroy of the Philippines and Secretary of War. Answering to **TR** and knowing that **TR** could appoint him to the Supreme Court or even help him get the presidency, **Taft** may have kept silent about his disagreements with **TR's** views of the presidency and the Constitution. When he became president, **Taft** only slowly saw that he was **TR's** equal. Then, policy differences and the beginning of a century-long split within the Republican Party caused a breach. In retirement **TR** and **Taft** reconciled.

To elaborate:

They were initially very close. In 1906 **TR** helped mediate a dispute between France and Germany over Morocco. His role was behind-the-scenes. As he told his friend Senator Henry Cabot Lodge: "Do not let anyone except, of course, Nanny (Lodge's wife) know of this....I have told **Taft** ..." In 1908 **Taft** asked a wealthy contributor to reduce his proffered political contribution. He explained to **TR**: "I would like to have an ample fund to spread the light of Republicanism. But I am willing to undergo the disadvantage to make certain that in the future we shall reduce the power of money in politics for unworthy purposes." **TR** responded to **Taft**: "You blessed old trump, I have always said you would be the greatest president, bar only **Washington** and **Lincoln**, and I feel mighty inclined to strike out the exceptions. My affection and respect for you are increased by your attitude about contributions. But really I think you are oversensitive." When **Roosevelt** made **Taft** Secretary of War, he made him, in effect, assistant president. **Roosevelt**, joking about **Taft's** weight, said that he felt free to leave Washington with **Taft** "sitting on the lid."

TR practically handed the presidency to **Taft**. He had announced on election night in 1904 that he would not run for a third term and in 1908 said about the Republican leaders: "They'll take **Taft** or they'll get me." By then **TR** was probably having regrets. (He was only 50.) Shortly before the inauguration of **Taft**, **TR** said: "He's all right. He means well and he'll do his best. But he's weak." Their relationship was about to fall apart.

By late 1909 **Taft** was caught in a bind. He owed his presidency to **TR** but he did not believe in **TR's** policies. Between 1909 and 1912 **TR** became critical of his successor over issues and matters like conservation, style, appointments and Republican politics. He declared that he would run again and the party split. When **Taft** was accused of straying from **Roosevelt's** legacy and called a reactionary he said: "We have a government of limited power under the Constitution, and we have got to work out our problems on the basis of law. Now, if that is reactionary then I am a reactionary." In the 1912 campaign **Taft** said of **TR** that he was "obsessed with his love of war and the glory of it..." (**TR** himself had said in one of his last annual messages to Congress, "a just war is in the long run far better for a man's soul than the most prosperous peace.") At the same time, **Taft** said that **TR** wanted to make himself a "czar." Further: "Mr. **Roosevelt** and his followers in their tendency would do away completely with the Constitution formed by the Fathers of the Republic. They would wholly destroy all constitutional limitations and restrictions, and replace them with the unchecked will and emotions of a bare majority of the people.... That would be a monstrous form of despotism that quickly would utterly destroy our liberties and lead to the establishment of a monarchy - probably by a referendum of the people themselves."

TR called **Taft** "one of the best haters" he ever knew. **Taft** in 1912: "Whether I win or lose is not the important thing. But I am in this fight to perform a great public duty - the duty of keeping **Theodore Roosevelt** out of the White House." **Taft** admitted to close associates that **TR's** third party effort meant probable defeat. "But I can stand defeat if we retain the regular Republican Party as a nucleus for future conservative action." When **TR** was shot in 1912 **Taft** sent a telegram: "I am shocked to hear of the outrageous and deplorable assault made upon you, and I earnestly hope and pray that your recovery may be speedy and without suffering." **TR's** response: "I appreciate your sympathetic inquiry and wish to thank you for it. **Theodore Roosevelt**."

At about that time **Taft** said of his predecessor: "the truth is, he believes in war and wishes to be a Napoleon and to die on the battle field."

Finally they reconciled. In 1918 **William Howard Taft** and **Theodore Roosevelt** met by chance and shook hands in a Chicago hotel restaurant to the cheers of other patrons. **TR** wrote: "I never felt happier over anything in my life." In 1919 **Taft** wept at **TR's** funeral.

Hoover-FDR

One of the myths of the twentieth century presidential history is that in 1932 **FDR** defeated the arch-conservative **Hoover**. But **Hoover** actually was a progressive who took **TR's** part in the 1912 Republican split and was admired by **Wilson** and around the world. **FDR**, before running against him, called him a "wonder" and said "I wish we could make him president....There couldn't be a better one."

Moreover, **FDR** saw **Hoover** as a big government type and criticized him for it during the 1928 campaign: "Mr. **Hoover** has always showed a most disquieting desire to investigate everything and to appoint commissions and send out statistical inquiries on every conceivable subject under Heaven. He has also shown in his own Department a most alarming desire to issue regulations and to tell businessmen generally how to conduct their affairs...." **Taft** who was by that time Chief Justice agreed. He wrote in his diary that President-elect **Hoover** was a "dreamer" with "some rather grandiose ideas" about the roles of government and the presidency in setting the national agenda. Even in the 1932 campaign **FDR** accused **Hoover** of overseeing the "greatest spending administration on peacetime in all of history." His running mate (John "Cactus Jack" Garner) accused **Hoover** of "leading the country down the path to socialism." For his part, Hoover said that **FDR** stood for "the same philosophy of government which has poisoned all Europe....the fumes of the witch's cauldron which boiled in Europe."

In the 1932 election the Democrats required a villain and they assigned **Hoover** to that role. For the next generation the Democratic Party's criticism of **Herbert Hoover** was a staple. In 1942 **FDR** passed on to his director of postwar relief a letter linking **Hoover** to the 1917 execution of a British nurse on spy charges even though this accusation against **Hoover** had been repudiated by its author in court years earlier. The bitterness between **Roosevelt** and **Hoover** lasted for the rest of their lives. **Herbert Hoover** was correct but unemotional at **FDR's** death issuing this formal statement: "The nation sorrows at the passing of its president. Whatever differences there may have been, they end in the regrets of death."

A final note: In 1940 as **FDR** sought rearmament, **Hoover** broke with his hatred for **Roosevelt** and said: "The President is right. There can be no partisanship upon the principle of national defense... We must be thoughtfully and scientifically armed."

Truman-Eisenhower

Truman and **Eisenhower** forged a foreign policy that contained the USSR and kept the US in the role of world leadership. Their personal relationship was close at first and then withered.

In 1945 **Eisenhower** returned to Washington DC from Europe. **Truman** wrote his wife: "He's a nice fellow and a good man. He's done a whale of a job." As to talk of **Eisenhower** running for President, **Truman** wrote: "I'd turn it over to him now if I could." In 1945 in Germany **Truman** said to **Eisenhower**: "General, there is nothing you may want that I won't try to help you get. That definitely and specifically includes the presidency in 1948." **Eisenhower** according to a witness General Omar Bradley looked flabbergasted and said: "Mr. President, I don't know who will be your opponent for the presidency, but it will not be I."

In 1947, according to **Eisenhower**, **Truman** offered to run as Vice President with **Eisenhower** heading the ticket but a year later he sent emissaries to **Eisenhower** to see if **Ike** would repudiate any interest in the Democratic nomination for president. **Eisenhower** refused. He finally wrote Claude Pepper a refusal when Pepper announced that he would place **Eisenhower's** name before the convention. He declined as he didn't want to be part of the Democratic Party. **Truman's** upset of Thomas Dewey derailed **Eisenhower's** retirement plans. He wrote **Truman** praising his "stark courage and fighting heart." "It seems almost needless for me to reaffirm my loyalty to you as President." As late as 1951 **Truman** wrote privately about **Eisenhower**: "My faith in him has never wavered nor ever will."

The 1952 campaign ruined the **Eisenhower-Truman** relationship. Initially **Truman** was angry because **Ike** indicated that that he would not accept a draft by the Democratic Party but would consider one from the Republicans. Other issues included **Truman's** resentment over Republican charges of corruption in Washington, **Eisenhower's** criticism of **Truman's** foreign policy and **Truman's** anger that **Eisenhower** did not stand up for Secretary of State George Marshall in the presence of Senator Joseph McCarthy's attacks. At one point **Truman** said **Eisenhower** didn't know as much about politics "as a pig does about Sunday."

In the election **Eisenhower** promised to go to Korea "and put an end to the fighting." **Truman** sarcastically asked if he had a solution why he hadn't given it when he was his military advisor and added: "Let's save a lot of lives and not wait - not do a lot of demagoguery and say that he can do it after he is elected. If he can do it after he is elected, we can do it now."

Eisenhower as President-elect went to Korea. **Truman** called the trip a "piece of demagoguery." During this time, **Truman** made a point of telling **Eisenhower** that he (**Ike**) had not attended **Truman's** own inauguration in 1949 because he was not invited. Out of office, **Truman** refused to attend a White House dinner in honor of Winston Churchill for whom he had high regard out of anger toward **Eisenhower.**

Truman and **Ike** reconciled at the funeral of **John F. Kennedy** in 1963. They worked together one more time in 1967 as antiwar protests were spreading. In response, **Eisenhower** and **Truman** joined a group to support the war in Vietnam. The group announced: "Voices of dissent have received attention far out of proportion to their actual numbers."

Ford-Reagan

In 1968 **Ronald Reagan**, Governor of California for less than two years, made his first try for the Republican nomination for the presidency on the eve of the Republican convention. In that era, a stampeded convention was still considered a possibility and **Reagan** gave **Richard Nixon's** team considerable concerns, especially among southern delegations. Nelson Rockefeller was also considered a possibility. One delegate asked **Reagan** if he would endorse **Nixon** if the race became a **Nixon**-Rockefeller contest. **Reagan's** response was a deliberate ambiguity: "It is inconceivable to me that anyone who could support **Dick** or me could support Nelson Rockefeller." In the end **Nixon** prevailed.

By 1975 **Reagan** was ready again but he faced the obstacle of an incumbent but unelected president from his own party, **Gerald Ford.** That year **Ford** was asked in a press conference if he was worried about **Reagan** challenging him and replied that he was not. (**Reagan** had not yet announced.) **Ford** told his close advisors that he thought **Reagan** was a lightweight. That year **Ford** sent messengers to **Reagan** suggesting him as a running mate and **Ford** also offered him a cabinet post.

As **Reagan** came closer to committing he told a close advisor: "… I just don't think **Jerry** can do it and if I don't do it, I'm going to be the player who's always been on the bench who never got into the game."

When **Reagan** got ready to announce his candidacy he called **Ford**:

Reagan: "Well, Mr. President, I am going to make an announcement and I want to tell you about it ahead of time. I am going to run for President. I trust we can have a good contest, and I hope it won't be divisive."

Ford: "I'm sorry you're getting into this. I believe I've done a good job, and that I can be elected. Regardless of your good intentions, your bid is bound to be divisive."

Reagan: "I don't think it will harm the party."

Ford: "Well, I think it will."

Ford then hung up.

Ford painted **Reagan** as an extremist who would lead the party to defeat. His team labeled **Reagan** as a tax raiser in tax-phobic New Hampshire during the primary.

During the race **Reagan** defended himself against a charge of extremism coming from the **Ford** camp with this: "I'm a little surprised by this statement about my so-called extremism. It does come rather strange because [**Ford**] tried on two different occasions to persuade me to accept any of several cabinet positions in his administration, and he did appoint me subsequently to his CIA investigating commission."

Reagan also leveled criticism: "Despite Mr. **Ford's** evident decency, honor, and patriotism, he has shown neither the vision nor leadership necessary to halt and reverse the diplomatic and military decline of the United States."

The race for delegates was close. **Ford** won most of the early contests with **Reagan** finishing fast. **Reagan** beat **Ford** in Texas by about 66-33.It was the worst ever election loss of a sitting US president.

184

As the 1976 Republican Convention neared and he was looking for unity, **Ford** said that his earlier statements that **Reagan** was not qualified to be president were to be understood as "political license." **Ford** compromised with **Reagan** on some platform issues. **Ford** said later: "We felt that if we fought on the platform and lost, it would give to the **Reagan** people an added arrow in their quiver."

The wives of the two men found it harder to paper over differences as memorialized in dueling interviews: Betty Ford on **Reagan**: "He's a good speaker, he comes across well on TV – after all, that was his trade… **Jerry Ford** is not fluff; he knows the meat and potatoes part." Betty Ford on Nancy Reagan: "I just think that when Nancy met **Ronnie**, that was it as far as her own life was concerned. She just fell apart at the seams." Nancy Reagan on the loss to **Ford**: "It was just **Ron** and a handful of staff against the tremendous power of the other side. I've never known the White House to be used by either party the way it was in this campaign. The White House stands for something. I don't think it should be concerned about uncommitted delegates."

Late in the night or early the morning after **Ford** clinched the nomination **Ford** and **Reagan** met. **Reagan's** camp had stipulated in advance that he didn't want to be asked to run as Vice President. **Ford** did not ask him. In 1982, **Reagan** told his chief of staff Jim Baker who had been in a **Ford** aide in 1976 that he would have run if **Ford** had asked him.

Ford believed **Reagan** cost him the election to **Carter**.

In the years ahead, the **Ford-Reagan** relationship was correct but not close. **Ford** considered entering the presidential primaries in 1980 because he said that **Reagan** could not win but backed out.

In a biography based on three decades of interviews entitled *Write It When I'm Gone* which was published in 2007 after **Ford's** death, **Ford's** disdain of **Reagan** comes through. However any animosity melted when **Reagan** announced to the world that he had Alzheimer's disease in 1994. **Ford** said at that time: "The day of the terrible announcement, we called and both of us talked to Nancy. That's sad. Betty has talked to Nancy several times since and the report is not encouraging. In a 2000 interview **Ford** said: "I went to see **Reagan** in Los Angeles eighteen months ago, in Century City. He didn't recognize me at all."

What is the point of all this?

The forty-three people who have been presidents of the US lived and live in a political and human context. As this section and a preceding section have shown they could be both affable and contentious with each other, often in the extreme. The bitterness is best exemplified by **John Quincy Adams** who in 1835 put **Jackson** on a list with Henry Clay, John C. Calhoun, Daniel Webster and nine others who had "conspired together (and) used up all their faculties in base and dirty tricks to thwart my progress in life." (This strange man could be hard on himself too: **Adams** wrote in 1819 that he was a "man of reserved, cold, austere and forbidding manners; my political adversaries say a gloomy misanthropist, and my personal enemies an unsocial savage.")

Sometimes the criticism seems based on little more than personal resentments. We can put in that category **John Quincy Adams'** comments about **William Henry Harrison** or some of his observations of **Martin Van Buren**. But in other instances, the presidents' negative interactions illuminate American history. **John Quincy Adams'** hatred of **Jackson** speaks of the widening franchise. His disdain of **Tyler** highlights the growing breach over slavery in the US as well as constitutional issues. His criticism of **Polk** reflected his view of the Mexican-American War. **Truman's** and **Eisenhower's** disdain for each other was real but subordinate to their joint drive to position the US well in the Cold War. During **Carter's** presidency **Ford** credited **Carter** with settling the Panama Canal negotiations, finishing the SALT II negotiations and other aspects of his foreign policy but added: "I think on economics, the **Carter** administration has been a disaster." This was at a time when inflation was running in double digits.

Often either in the name of patriotism or loyalty to another who holds the office, criticism is muted. **Truman** commented to reporters that he disapproved of deficit spending in **JFK's** budgets but at the request of the White House he muted his criticisms. **Ford** disagreed with **George W Bush's** decision to go to war in Iraq but at his (**Ford's**) request that was announced only after his death in 2006.

Chapter 6

The Icons

In 2011 Richard Norton Smith writing in *Time* magazine listed these presidents as "The Transformers. The visionaries who reshaped the Republic."

- **Thomas Jefferson**: "In the early days of the Republic, he curtailed the growing clout of federalism."
- **Andrew Jackson**: "Converted the Founders' Republic to a democracy (of sorts)."
- **Abraham Lincoln**: "Faced with a house divided, **Lincoln** freed the slaves and kept the Union intact."
- **Theodore Roosevelt**: "Revived a muscular central government to police a reckless marketplace."
- **Franklin Roosevelt**: "With millions out of work, he pushed Congress to create a social safety net."
- **Ronald Reagan**: "Restored confidence in free markets at the expense of government."

Presidents like both **Roosevelts** and **Reagan** have near-iconic status in American history. So do those two figures of the American Enlightenment, **Jefferson** and **Madison** holding that status if, for nothing more, their connections respectively with the Declaration and the Constitution. **Lincoln** said of the third president: "**Jefferson** was, is and...will continue to be the most distinguished politician in our history." **Jefferson's** decision-making approach was the drafting and re-writing of texts. This left a paper trail that made his process available to historians. His use of language was unmatched by any subsequent president except for **Lincoln**. But in looking at the administrations of **Jefferson** and **Madison** and their dealing with

188

Pitt, Napoleon and the Spanish it's easy to form the view that they were out of their league. But they were protected by the Atlantic Ocean and they number in the near-great.

George W Bush on **Reagan**: "I watched him a lot. Yeah, I did. I admired his leadership style. I think he was a great president, I do. Look, obviously I love my dad, but...I do think **Ronald Reagan** was one of the great presidents, and for a lot of reasons. One is his - he was able to change the mood of the country." **Bush** was asked if he thought **Reagan** really knew him. "No. I never had the feeling - it was hard for me to tell whether or not he was interested or not interested. ..." **Bush** was asked who was the last great president before **Reagan**. "I'd say **Franklin Roosevelt**. He was a president able to be a mood setter and a changer of philosophy." **Lincoln** had great respect for **Jefferson** but allied as he was with the industrial power of the North he did not see him as a strong president but one from the southern culture that in his time he fought. (**Thomas Jefferson**'s grandson died fighting for the Confederacy.)

FDR honored **Jefferson** in various ways. He started the **Jefferson** Memorial. He put **Jefferson's** image on the first class postage stamp. But there is irony here or possibly revisionist history. Alexander Hamilton, not **Thomas Jefferson**, favored an expansive national government. Moreover, Hamilton had been a good friend of **FDR's** paternal great-grandfather. This man named one of his sons Hamilton.

Of course, two presidents standout above all the rest. They are **Washington** and **Lincoln**. They were and are constantly cited even by other presidents. In 1881, after **James Garfield** was mortally wounded, the public hoped for weeks that he would survive and his popularity soared. His predecessor, **Rutherford B Hayes** wrote: "**Garfield** will now have a hold on the hearts of the people like that of **Washington** and **Lincoln**. He can do any righteous and necessary work."

Their greatness adds luster to all the rest, even in backhanded ways. **LBJ** took comfort in the fact that **Washington** was called a tyrant and **Lincoln** a baboon. So did **George W Bush**: "...and if they were calling **Abraham Lincoln** a baboon, they certainly could call me worse, because he was a great president." When his poll numbers slumped in 2011 **Obama** said this in a slightly different way: "**Lincoln**--they used to talk about him almost as bad as they talk about me."

Moving Forward

Washington

Only Benjamin Franklin could rival **George Washington** as the greatest of Americans during the Revolutionary era and Franklin was a generation older. Yet even Franklin looked up to **George Washington.** During his time as ambassador in France, he had a full length portrait of the general in his office. In 1790 shortly before his death Benjamin Franklin willed **Washington** his walking stick as a "sceptre."

Washington's greatness derives from this:

- He held his armies and the colonies together at a time of maximum crisis.
- He unified the country, putting off schism for another sixty years.
- He kept America neutral.
- He set a two-term tradition; he voluntarily left office unlike peers such as Napoleon or Simon Bolivar.

At six feet, 1 and 1/2 inches he was a physically imposing man in that era (although **Jefferson** was slightly taller). **John Adams** once claimed that the reason **Washington** was chosen for leadership positions was that he was the tallest person present. **Jefferson** called **Washington** "the best horseman of his age and the most graceful figure that could ever be seen on horseback." In 1783 when hostilities were over **Washington's** army was camped in Newburg, New York. The soldiers were edging toward mutiny due to pay issues stemming from the weakness of the Congress. **Washington** refused to lead an uprising and the crisis passed. **Thomas Jefferson** later said: "The moderation and virtue of one man probably prevented this Revolution from being closed by a subversion of the liberty it was intended to establish."

Washington was the chair and said very little at the Constitutional Convention of 1787. But as **Monroe** wrote **Jefferson** in 1788 about **Washington's** influence at the Virginia ratifying convention which supported the new Constitution by an 89-79 vote: "Be assured, his influence carried this government." The US Constitution probably kept the American experiment from an early death. It came into being because a small group of elites hatched a plan to draft and ratify it. History-minded critics of the Constitution have pointed out that the convention was extralegal because its charter was to revise – not replace - the Articles of Confederation, sessions were held in secrecy, the 55 delegates were not representative, southerners used the process to protect slavery and the rules for ratification did not require unanimous agreement as did the Articles. There is truth to all of these charges but the Constitution steadied the new country and as much as military victory in the Revolutionary War secures **George Washington** in world history. As an ambassador to France in the 1780s **Jefferson** contacted the sculptor Jean-Antoine Houdon to make the statue of **George Washington** for the Virginia state capitol in Richmond. He wrote **Washington** that Houdon would come to America "for the purpose of forming your bust from the life."

Washington died in 1799. In 1814 **Jefferson** said of him: "[H] is was the singular destiny and merit, of leading the armies of his country successfully through an arduous war, for the establishment of its independence; of conducting its councils through the birth of a government, new in its forms and principles, until it had settled down into a quiet and orderly train; and of scrupulously obeying the laws through the whole of his career, civil and military, of which the history of the world furnishes no other example." He also said: "His person, you know, was fine, his stature exactly what one would wish, his deportment easy, erect and noble." He further said: "Perhaps the strongest feature in his character was prudence, never acting until every circumstance, every consideration, was maturely weighed;

refraining if he saw a doubt, but, when once decided, going through with his purpose, whatever obstacles opposed." **John Adams** said of **Washington** that he was "the central stone in the geometrical arch. There you have the revelation of the whole mystery."

Andrew Jackson kept a set of pistols that Lafayette had given **Washington** which

Washington's family passed on to him. **Washington** was Robert E. Lee's idol.

Former President **John Tyler** was with President **Zachary Taylor** in Richmond on February 22, 1850 - **Washington's** Birthday - observing the festivities. Thousands of cheering people were present. **Tyler** later wrote his son: "General **Taylor**...mistook all the demonstrations of popular feeling as evidences of his popularity, in...which he was in great error." In 1855 **Pierce** appointed his 1852 rival Winfield Scott lieutenant-general by brevet on **Washington's** Birthday. The rank of lieutenant-general had not existed since **Washington**. (Scott later appealed to the government for back pay.) **Andrew Johnson** used the occasion of **Washington's** Birthday in 1866 to deliver an impromptu speech against the Radical Republicans which led to an open breach between him and them. (At the time, **Hayes** wrote his uncle: "Many of our good men still hope that we may retain the President but it is a very faint hope...The general impression is...the Rebel influences are now ruling the White House and the sooner **Johnson** is clear over, the better for us.")

Lincoln's hero was **Washington** because he left a life of comfort to fight against the British Empire for American independence. In 1838 **Lincoln** said: "**Washington** is the mightiest name of earth - *long since* mightiest in the cause of civil liberty; *still* mightiest in moral reformation." **Lincoln** had attended the dedication of the **Washington** Monument in 1850 but when he arrived in Washington DC in 1861 it was unfinished. When he left for his inauguration in 1861, **Lincoln** acknowledged to his Springfield neighbors that he faced a crisis as big as any since **Washington**.

As a college student in the 1850s **Garfield** read Washington Irving's *Life of Washington*. He wrote his future wife: "Hard-hearted as I am, I cried more than a dozen times while reading the last 50 pages of the first volume." In 1864 as **Grant** took command of all Union armies, the northern public placed its hopes on him. The *New York Times* editorialized: "**WASHINGTON** is completing his second cycle. He was with **JACKSON** in 1832, when he suppressed treason... He has been with **ABRAHAM LINCOLN**, and has gone with us through the war, teaching us to bear reverses patiently. He was with **GRANT** at the taking of Vickburg (*sic*), and will go with him to Richmond."

As a boy, **Hayes'** hero was **George Washington**. As president in 1880 **Hayes** traveled to the West Coast in a trip stressing national unity. In Oregon he referred to **Washington's** tour in his term of office saying that it seemed "altogether fitting and proper that I should follow the example of the most illustrious president of the republic..." He regarded the **Washington** Monument's uncompleted form as "a reproach to the nation" and he helped move it toward completion during his time in office. In retirement **Hayes** accepted an invitation from President **Chester Alan Arthur** to come to the unveiling in 1885 although he was reluctant to travel: "Seeing the prominent place in the program given to ex-Presidents, and in view of my active interest in the monument, and thinking what is due the Father of his Country, I am not sure but I ought to come."

Truman during the 1945 Christmas season: "It is well in this solemn hour that we bow to **Washington**, **Jefferson**, **Jackson**, and **Lincoln** as we face our destiny with its hopes and fears..."

In high school **Eisenhower** had **Washington** as a hero. "I conceived almost a violent hatred of Conway and his cabal" for trying to relieve **Washington** of his command. (Thomas Conway was a rival within the American army and long forgotten.) In 1957 Henry Wallace wrote **Eisenhower** comparing him to **George Washington**. **Ike** wrote back: "I've often felt the deep wish that the Good Lord had endowed me with his clarity of vision in big things and his genuine greatness of mind and spirit."

In 1968 **Lyndon Johnson** tried unsuccessfully to elevate Justice Abe Fortas to the Chief Justice of the United States. In the confirmation hearings, the Senate questioned Fortas' ties to **Johnson** as compromising the independence of the Court. **Johnson** cited other such ties including between **George Washington** and John Jay.

On the two hundred seventy-fifth anniversary of **Washington's** birth in 2007, **George W Bush** said, "President **Washington** believed that the success of our democracy would also depend on the virtue of our citizens. In his farewell address to the American people, he said, 'Morality is a necessary spring of popular government.' Over the centuries, America has succeeded because we have always tried to maintain the decency and the honor of our first President. His example guided us in his time; it guides us in our time, and it will guide us for all time." **Bill Clinton** at the 2012 Democratic convention supporting President **Obama** said: "People have predicted our demise ever since **George Washington** was criticized for being a mediocre surveyor with a bad set of wooden false teeth. And so far, every single person that's bet against America has lost money because we always come back." (**Clinton** was improvising and ignoring his teleprompter while talking well past his allotted time. If people in the 1700s said that **George Washington** was a mediocre surveyor, that is lost to history. It was his first profession and he surveyed hundreds of tracts of land.)

Lincoln

There have been more books written about **Abraham Lincoln** than any other American but he was not always seen as an icon. Although **Hayes** supported him for president in 1860 he acknowledged to his uncle that "a wholesome contempt for (**Lincoln's** opponent Stephen) Douglas on account of his recent demagoguery is the chief feeling I have." **Hayes** voted like many Americans do in presidential elections to keep the other guy out although he described **Lincoln** as "shrewd, able, and possess(ing) strength in reserve." From his unit during the Civil War in 1861 **Hayes** wrote his wife not "to give up (on) President **Lincoln**." He acknowledged that **Lincoln** was "not all that we could wish" but was "honest, patriotic, cool-headed, and safe."

Henry Adams wrote of his first impression in 1861 that **Lincoln** was "a long, awkward figure; a plain, ploughed face; a mind, absent in part, and in part worried by white kid gloves; features that expressed neither self-satisfaction nor any other familiar Americanism, but rather the same painful sense of becoming educated and of needed education that tormented a private secretary, above all a lack of apparent force." His father Charles Francis Adams wrote of **Lincoln** at the same time: "The man is not equal to the hour." Henry Adams wrote of his experiences in London during the American Civil War: "London was altogether beside itself on one point, in especial: it created a nightmare of its own, and gave it the shape of **Abraham Lincoln**..... English society seemed demented. Defense was useless; explanation was vain; one could only let the passion exhaust itself;" The British talked about **Lincoln's** "brutality." Henry Adams noted that in 1800 European intellectuals also loathed **Jefferson**.

Prince Napoleon, cousin to Napoleon III, met with President **Lincoln** and reported: "What a difference between this sad representative of the great republic and its early founders! He's a poor specimen of a president, and they tell me here that he is the commonest they have had thus far."

Grant personally reported the surrender at Appomattox to **Lincoln** and his cabinet on April 14, 1865 and then declined the President's invitation to attend the theater with him. **Abraham Lincoln** was assassinated at the theater later that night - which was Good Friday. **Grant** got the news of the assassination at a train stop in Philadelphia and returned to Washington DC. **Grant**: "He was incontestably the greatest man I have ever known." By Sunday ministers were connecting **Lincoln** to Jesus. One quoted the Apostle Paul: "Without the shedding of blood is no remission." In his *Memoirs* **Grant** wrote of **Lincoln**: "He always showed a generous and kindly spirit toward the Southern people, and I never heard him abuse an enemy.... Never in my presence did he evince a revengeful disposition - and I saw a great deal of him at City Point, for he seemed glad to get away from the cares and anxieties of the capital." For the rest of his life **Grant** regretted his absence at the theater that fateful night believing that he would have heard John Wilkes Booth sneaking into the box and would have prevented the murder of **Abraham Lincoln**.

Secretary of State and one-time **Lincoln** rival William Seward, two days after the 1864 election: "Henceforth, all men will come to see him, as you and I have seen him....**Abraham Lincoln** will take his place with **Washington** and Franklin, and **Jefferson**, and **Adams**, and **Jackson**, among the benefactors of the country and of the human race." **Grant** appealed to the "better angels" of the voters in the 1872 election which was a paraphrase of **Lincoln's** first inaugural.

Hayes' reaction a day or so later to **Lincoln's** assassination: "As to Mr. **Lincoln's** name and fame and memory, - all is safe. His firmness, moderation, goodness of heart; his quaint humor, his perfect honesty and directness of purpose; his logic, his modesty, his sound judgment and great wisdom; the contrast between his obscure beginnings and the greatness of his subsequent position and achievements; his tragic death, giving him the crown of martyrdom, elevate him to a place in history second to none other of ancient or modern times. His success in his great office, his hold upon the confidence and affections of his countrymen, we shall all *say* are only second to **Washington's;** we shall probably *feel* and *think* that they are not *second* even to his." A year after **Lincoln's** death **Hayes** recorded: "The truth is, if it were not sacrilege, I should say **Lincoln** is overshadowing **Washington**. **Washington** is formal, statue-like, a figure for exhibition" but **Lincoln** was "the highest character." Then: "Neither could have done the other's work, and without the work of both we should have had a different history." **Hayes** exalted the Declaration of Independence and the Constitution with its Reconstruction amendments. He often quoted **Lincoln** that everyone should "have a fair start and an equal chance in the race of life." **Lincoln's** secretary John Hay became Secretary of State under **William McKinley.** When opponents of the administration criticized Hay, **McKinley** told his staff that they should respond: "Yes, he was trained under **Abraham Lincoln**." In Abilene, Kansas **Eisenhower** went to the **Lincoln** elementary school in the 1890s.

TR said that "so far as one who is not a great man can model himself upon one who was" he tried to emulate **Lincoln**. **TR** hung a portrait of **Lincoln** in his office. When he was dealing with a problem: "I look up to that picture, and I do as I believe **Lincoln** would have done." **TR** wrote: "(Our) greatest national asset is that ...we have produced the greatest examples that the world has ever seen in **Washington** and **Lincoln**." As president **Theodore Roosevelt** said: "I have had a most vivid realization of what it must have meant to **Abraham Lincoln**, in the midst of the heartbreaking anxieties of the Civil War, to have to take up his time in trying to satisfy the candidates for postmaster in Chicago." **Roosevelt** also said: "In social and economic, as in political reforms, the violent revolutionary extremist is the worst friend of liberty, just as the arrogant and intense reactionary is the worst friend or order. It was **Lincoln**, and not Wendell Phillips and the fanatical abolitionists, who was the effective champion of union and freedom." He said that **Lincoln** "was that statesman who in this absolutely democratic republic succeeded best, was the very man who actually combined the two sets of qualities which the historian the supports in antithesis."

After his defeat in 1912, **TR** said: "The official leaders of the Republican Party today are the spiritual heirs of the men who warred against **Lincoln**."

During World War I, **Wilson** opposed some aspect of congressional oversight and offered a comparison saying that during the Civil War Congress had "rendered Mr. **Lincoln's** tasks all but impossible."

FDR called on the Democrats to claim **Lincoln** as "one of our own." In his court appointments **FDR** said that he hoped for "youthful **Lincolns** from Manhattan and the Bronx." He wanted them to be "liberal from belief and not by lip service... They must know what life in a tenement means."

Truman wrote that if **Lincoln** had failed, "we would have been divided into half a dozen countries." After his party suffered defeats in the 1946 elections **Truman** wrote, "To be president of the United States is to be lonely, very lonely at times of great decisions. **Lincoln**

had fits of melancholy. Melancholy goes with the job." **LBJ** in 1960: "The principal difference for the Republicans between 1860 and 1960 is **Lincoln**." **LBJ** in 1964: "And if **Lincoln** abolished slavery, let us abolish poverty." The 1966 elections went badly for **Johnson.** His social programs, commonly known as the Great Society, were severely criticized and his credibility in the handling of the Vietnam War was destroyed. He then sought to curtail spending. In his State of the Union address in January of 1967 **LBJ** quoted **Lincoln**: "We must ask 'where we are and whither we are tending.'" In March of 1968 at a time when Martin Luther King was planning a huge demonstration in Washington DC that people feared would turn violent, **LBJ** said: "If our country is to survive, **Lincoln** said, we must realize that 'there is no grievance that is a fit object of redress by mob law.'"

In college, **Richard Nixon** read John Nicolay and John Hay's ten-volume life of **Lincoln.** In a speech in 1952, **Nixon** said: "Remember **Abraham Lincoln** - you remember what he said, 'God must have loved the common people - he made so many of them.'" In 1973 after **Nixon** appointed him Vice President, **Ford** quipped: "I'm a Ford, not a Lincoln." At the 1976 Republican convention **Ford** was nominated and paraphrased the matchless conclusion of **Lincoln's** second inaugural address in his acceptance speech: "As we go forward together I promise you once more what I promised before: to uphold the Constitution, to do what is right as God gives me to see the right and to do the very best I can for America." In 1985 **Reagan** visited Bergen-Belsen the Nazi concentration camp: "We're all witnesses; we share the glistening hope that rests in every human soul. Hope leads us, if we're prepared to trust it, toward what our President **Lincoln** called the better angels of our nature. And then, rising above all this cruelty, out of this tragic and nightmarish time, beyond the anguish, the pain and the suffering for all time, we can and must pledge: Never again"

After he left office, **Clinton** said, "I love **Lincoln** – for all his problems, he grows larger with history." During his presidency **George W Bush** read 14 biographies of **Lincoln.**

The Forty-Three Presidents

In 2007 **Barack Obama** announced his candidacy at the Old State Capitol in Springfield Illinois where **Abraham Lincoln** gave his "House Divided" speech in 1858 and he stated, "**Lincoln** basically pulled in all the people who had been running against him into his Cabinet because whatever personal feelings there were, the issue was: How can we get the country through this time of crisis?"

What is the point of all This?

Alone and in captivity, Napoleon uttered a truth learned too late, "They wanted me to be a **Washington**." Toward the end of his presidency **Andrew Johnson** regarded **Lincoln** as "the greatest American that ever lived." He elaborated: "I doubt whether there will ever be another **Washington** or another **Lincoln**."

Leo Tolstoy wrote in 1909: "The greatness of Napoleon, Caesar or **Washington** is only moonlight by the sun of **Lincoln**. His example is universal and will last thousands of years." Was Tolstoy's ranking of our two greatest presidents accurate? This is an argument we don't need to have. They are both icons of world history.

Chapter 7

Constitutional

Overall Context

In 1787 delegates to what became known as the Constitutional Convention wrote the United States Constitution. It was ratified over the next year and in 1789 the first government was formed. It is one of the great stories of western civilization. British Prime Minister William Gladstone (1809 – 1898) called it the "most wonderful work ever struck off at a given time by the brain and purpose of man." How did it happen?

Seventy-four delegates to the Constitutional Convention of 1787 were appointed. Only 55 showed up. No more than 30 attended the full four months. **Thomas Jefferson** and **John Adams** were out of the country. **Jefferson** described the delegates to the Constitutional Convention of 1787 to **Adams** as "an assembly of demigods."

The Constitution was recognized by the presidents to be an epoch-making event. **John Quincy Adams** wrote about **Madison** that it was his good luck to be "sent into life at a time when the greatest lawgivers of antiquity would have wished to live. How few of the human race have ever enjoyed an opportunity of making an election of government - more than air, soil or climate - for themselves and their children." **Madison's** role was crucial indeed. It may have been a gathering of elites, but two were key: **Madison** and the man he teamed up with, **George Washington**. Their partnership started a couple of years before the Convention as seen in some of these comments **Washington** wrote to his younger colleague:

- In 1785: "We are either a united people or we are not. If the former, let us, in all matters of general concern, act as a nation.... If we are not, let us no longer act a farce by pretending to it."

- In 1786: "No morn ever dawned more favorable than ours did; and no day was ever more clouded than the present! Wisdom, and good examples are necessary at this time to rescue the political machine from the impending storm."
- In 1786: The states were acting like "thirteen sovereignties pulling against each other."
- In 1786: "We are fast verging to anarchy and confusion."'

Madison recruited **Washington** to chair the Constitutional Convention. **Madison** wrote of **Washington's** decision to attend the Convention that he (**Washington**) had decided "to forsake the honorable retreat to which he had retired and risk the reputation he had so deservedly acquired." **Madison** was coy about seeking office under the new Constitution writing **Washington** in 1788 about his "extreme distaste" of "any step which may seem to denote a solicitude" for office. He got over it and beat **Monroe** for a congressional seat.

Later, from his position in the new House of Representatives, he wrote the address welcoming **Washington** to the Presidency, drafted **Washington's** response and wrote the Bill of Rights. **Madison** told **Washington** that the amendments were a "blemish, but in the least Offensive form."

Washington and **Madison**, then, started off on good terms. **Washington** sought out **Madison** and confided in him. In 1792 **Washington** wrote **Madison** that although the country might be "diversified in local & smaller matters" that he thought the public good "is the same in all the great & essential concerns of the Nation." **George** and Martha **Washington** arranged the marriage of **James** and Dolley **Madison**. (Dolley Madison was a Quaker and since **James Madison** was not, the Quakers expelled her.)

As president **Washington** was conscious of setting precedent. He consulted with **Madison** on many aspects of his duties. But in 1796 they ultimately fell out over the Jay Treaty with England. **Madison** tried to persuade the House of Representatives to not fund the Treaty. **George Washington** viewed this as unconstitutional since foreign policy was described in the Constitution as belonging to the President and the Senate. **Madison** backed a House demand for **Washington** to send the record of how the treaty was negotiated hoping to show some corrupt influence. **Washington** had the official notes for safekeeping from the Constitutional Convention. He released them and they showed that the intention of the Convention clearly gave the role of treaty approval to the Senate and that **Madison** had approved such a move. **Madison** called the release of the notes "improper and indelicate." Their relationship was at an end. Eventually the House passed the appropriations. **John Adams** said that **Madison** appeared "pale, withered, haggard."

Over the past two hundred years, presidents have offered to each other commentary on the US Constitution. The day after the Constitutional Convention ended in Philadelphia in 1787, **George Washington** sent a copy of it to **Thomas Jefferson** in Paris. **Adams** read a copy in England and wrote **Jefferson** that is "seems to be admirably calculated to preserve the Union, to increase affection, and to bring us all to the same mode of thinking." **Jefferson** wrote **Adams** after reading the proposed constitution that the presidency was "a bad edition of a Polish king." **Jefferson** worried that the new Constitution would lead to presidents getting re-elected routinely for life. **John Adams'** response: "So much the better it seems to me."

In the debates of 1788, **Jefferson** wanted a world where government had disappeared. **Madison** was promoting a Constitution giving the federal government authority. **Jefferson** emphasized the Bill of Rights and came across as somewhat of a dreamer. In 1789 he wrote **Madison**: "But with respect to future debt; would it not be wise and just for that nation to declare in the constitution they are forming that neither the legislature, nor the nation itself can validly contract more debt, than they may pay within their own age, or within the term of 19 years."

Jefferson looked for the Constitution to limit federal power. He wrote in 1791 in the debate over whether to establish the Bank of the United States about the Congress: "They are not to do anything they please to provide for the general welfare, but only to lay taxes for that purpose. To consider the latter phrase not as describing the purpose of the first, but as giving a distinct and independent power to do any act they please which may be good for the Union, would render all the preceding and subsequent enumerations of power completely useless. It would reduce the whole instrument to a single phrase, that of instituting a Congress with power to do whatever would be for the good of the United States; and as they would be the sole judges of the good or evil, it would be also a power to do whatever evil they please.... Certainly no such universal power was meant to be given them. It was intended to lace them up straightly within the enumerated powers and those without which, as means, these powers could not be carried into effect." **Madison** wrote at about the same time: "If Congress can do whatever in their discretion can be done by money, and will promote the General Welfare, the Government is no longer a limited one, possessing enumerated powers, but an indefinite one, subject to particular exceptions." **Washington** disagreed and certainly the changes of the next two centuries went against **Jefferson's** and **Madison's** viewpoints.

Jefferson and **Madison** authored the Virginia and Kentucky Resolutions in 1798 which held for the rights of states to nullify federal laws within their borders. At the time, **Jefferson** said to **Madison** that if the federal government could not be restrained the best course for states might be "to sever ourselves from the union we so much value rather than give up the rights of self-government." (A half a century later, this view got a back-handed compliment from **Abraham Lincoln.** In a speech in Congress in1847 about Texas separating from Mexico he said: "Any people anywhere, being so inclined and having the power, have the right to rise up and shake off the existing government and form a new one that suits them better. This is a most valuable - a most sacred right - a right, which we hope and believe, is to liberate the world. Nor is this right confined to cases in which the whole people of an existing government, may chose to exercise it. Any portion of such people that can, may revolutionize, and make their own, of so much of their territory as they inhabit.")

One of the first constitutional tests was the Louisiana Purchase which more than doubled the size of the US. In 1803 to his closest colleagues and in his private letters **Thomas Jefferson** recognized that this transaction lay beyond the government's constitutional authority and he toyed with the idea of a constitutional amendment. But he thought the purchase a good thing and he wrote a friend that the country would realize that it was in the national interest and that Congress should move toward it "casting behind them metaphysical subtleties." When he heard that Napoleon was having second thoughts he wrote **Madison**, "the less we say about constitutional difficulties respecting Louisiana the better." He added: "what is necessary for surmounting them must be done *sub silentio*." In 1821 **John Quincy Adams** wrote that the Louisiana Purchase was "an assumption of implied power" greater than in the combined years of the **Washington** and **Adams** administration." Yet **John Quincy Adams** had supported the Purchase. So did **John Adams.** He wrote: "The Union appears to me to be the rock of our salvation, and every reasonable measure for its preservation is expedient. Upon this principle, I own, I was pleased with the purchase of Louisiana, because without it, we could never have secured and commanded the navigation of the Mississippi. The western country would infallibly have revolted from the Union." **Andrew Jackson** on news of the Louisiana Purchase: "Every face here's a smile and every heart leaps with joy." Henry Adams later wrote: "...the Louisiana treaty gave a fatal wound to 'strict construction,' and the Jeffersonian theories never again received general support."

In 1813 as Secretary of State **Monroe** advised **Madison** not to permit the Secretary of War who was a cabinet rival to move his office to the field to oversee the military during the war with England. **Monroe** argued that this would separate the military from civilian control in a way that was at odds with the Constitution. Later that year with **Madison** seriously ill **Monroe,** angry at the Senate for not approving diplomatic nominations, wrote **Jefferson** that the Senate hoped for the death of **Madison** and wanted to usurp executive power.

In 1826 **James Madison** wrote **Martin Van Buren** to analyze possible constitutional amendments to allow for federal support of roads and canals. His worry: "But whilst the term 'common defense & general welfare,' remain in the Constitution unguarded against the construction which has been contended for, a fund of power, inexhaustible & wholly subversive of the equilibrium between the General and the State Governments is within the reach of the former. Why then, not precede all other amendments by one, expunging the phrase which is not required for any harmless meaning; or making it harmless by annexing to it the terms, 'in the cases required by this Constitution.'..." This is an important letter. It shows the primary author of the Constitution believing that the expansion of federal power was dangerous and unconstitutional. Democrat presidents hewed to this line for the rest of the century as seen in these two vetoes:

- **Pierce** in 1854 was considering a bill for which the reformer Dorthea Dix had lobbied. It involved granting public lands to the states to be sold to set up a fund to care for the mentally ill. After a meeting with **Pierce**, Dix talked to the previous president, **Millard Fillmore,** about concerns on whether **Pierce** would veto the bill. **Fillmore** told her: "My inference is that he is really and truly sympathetic with the object but he has not fully satisfied himself that as President he can constitutionally approve the measure." **Pierce** vetoed it on exactly those constitutional grounds: "I cannot find any authority in the Constitution for public charity. [To approve this measure] would be contrary to the letter and spirit of the Constitution and subversive to the whole theory upon which the Union of these States is founded."
- **Cleveland** in 1887 vetoing a bill that would have provided $10,000 for drought relief in Texas: "I can find no warrant for such an appropriation [for charity relief] in the Constitution, and I do not believe that the power and duty of the General Government ought to be extended to the relief of individual suffering which is in no manner properly related to the public service or benefit."

Presidents are often skeptical of presidential power – both of others and even their own. When **Jackson** fought the Bank of the United States in 1833, **Tyler**, even though he opposed the Bank, opposed

Jackson's move to remove all federal funds from it. "Concede to President the power to dispose of the public money as he pleases, and it is vain to talk of check(s) and balances. The presidential office swallows up all power, and the president becomes every inch a king." (This was the issue that led to **Tyler's** vote to censure **Jackson**.) After the election of **Lincoln, Buchanan** denied the right of southern states to secede but also any constitutional authority for federal to coerce them to remain in the Union. In 1861 **Lincoln** suspended *habeas corpus*. Thousands were arrested and jailed. **Lincoln** was at odds with Chief Justice Roger Taney. **Pierce** wrote Taney supporting him and forecasting "a reign of terror...ruinous to the victors as well as the vanquished." Republican Senators in 1862 who thought that Secretary of State William Seward had too much influence with **Lincoln**, noted with approval that **John Quincy Adams** adhered to the majority vote of his cabinet even when he disagreed.

Presidents often find the Supreme Court objectionable. **TR** appointed Oliver Wendell Holmes Jr., to the Supreme Court. However, he came to dislike Holmes' strict constructionalism as seen in a dissent refusing to rewrite the Sherman Anti-Trust Act and said of him: "I could carve a better judge out of a banana." **Obama** criticized the Supreme Court in his 2010 State of the Union address. In 2012, while the High Court was considering the constitutionality of the Affordable Care Act, he said: "I'm confident that the Supreme Court will not take what would be an unprecedented, extraordinary step of overturning a law that was passed by a strong majority of a democratically elected Congress." **Jefferson** frequently criticized the judiciary. **Truman** called the appointment of Justice Tom Clark "my biggest mistake." **Truman** who made four appointments said: "Packing the Supreme Court simply can't be done. I've tried it, and it won't work." **Eisenhower** reportedly said his two biggest mistakes as president were the appointments to the Supreme Court of William Brennan and Earl Warren.

Moving Forward

The Constitution of the US addresses such themes as: Democracy, the Presidency, National Unity, Presidential terms, the Veto, the

Pardon, the Free Press/Speech, Elections, and the Vice Presidency. We will look at how the forty-three presidents have interacted on these.

Democracy

In 1784 **Jefferson** wrote **Washington**: "The foundation on which all [constitutions] are built is the natural equality of man, the denial of every preeminence but that annexed to legal office, and particularly the denial of a preeminence by birth." But the Constitutional Convention restrained democratic impulses by such features as bicameralism, long Senate terms, rotation of Senate terms, separation of powers, checks and balances, super majorities for overriding vetoes and a court system.

Adams wrote **Jefferson** a few months after the Convention: "Elections, my dear sir, I look at with terror." This echoed a comment **Madison** wrote to **Monroe** at the same time: "There is no maxim in my opinion which is more liable to be misapplied, and which therefore needs elucidation than the current one that the interest of the majority is the political standard of right and wrong.... In fact it is only reestablishing under another name and a more specious form, force as the measure of right...." **Madison** overcame these reservations in his support of a House of Representatives. **Jefferson's** insight was to expand the democracy. In his first inaugural he said: "The will of the majority is in all cases to prevail."

But this was a long-running debate. **Adams** in his retirement wrote **Jefferson**: "Checks and Balances, **Jefferson**, however you and your party may have ridiculed them are our only Security." He wrote **James Madison** in 1817: "The questions concerning universal suffrage, and those concerning the necessary limitations of the power of suffrage, are among the most difficult. It is hard to say that every man has not an equal right; but admit this equal right and equal power, and immediate revolution would ensue."

John Adams in a letter in retirement to Benjamin Rush: "Absolute power in a majority is as drunk as it is in one." He wrote John Taylor in 1814: "Remember democracy never lasts long. It soon wastes, exhausts, and murders itself. There never was a democracy yet that did not commit suicide." **Madison** expressed the same thought in Federalist 10 in 1787: "[D]emocracies have ever been spectacles of turbulence and contention; have ever been found incompatible with personal security, or the rights of property; and have, in general, been as short in their lives as they have been violent in their deaths."

Jefferson saw democracy within the context of an orderly society. In 1825 he wrote to **John Adams** upon the election of **John Quincy Adams**: "So deeply are the principles of order, and of obedience to law impressed on the minds of our citizens generally that I am persuaded that there will be as immediate an acquiescence in the will of the majority as if Mr. **Adams** had been the choice of every minute."

By 1828 presidential elections were moving from a system where typically state legislatures chose electors to popular votes and thus a broader electorate. **John Quincy Adams** had missed the significance of this trend; as he saw his defeat coming by the hands of **Jackson** he wrote that he would "await my allotted time. My own career is closed." (It wasn't.) Prefiguring a debate that would resonate as late as the **Bush**-Gore 2000 election, **Polk** in 1826 gave his first speech as a Member of Congress in favor of direct election by the people for the presidency. **Jackson** read the speech and wrote him: "Your speech...I have read with much pleasure and I can assure you is well received by all your constituents, and gives you a strong claim to their future confidence."

In 1853 **Andrew Johnson's** inaugural speech as governor of Tennessee was a much-mocked paean to common people and asserted: "I hold that the Democrat party proper, of the world, and especially of the United States, has undertaken the political redemption of man, and sooner or later the great work will be accomplished. In the political world it corresponds to that of Christianity in the moral. They are going along, not in divergents, not in parallels but in converging lines; the one purifying and elevating man religiously, the other politically. At what period of time they will have finished the work...is not for me to determine; but, when finished, these two lines will have approximated each other... (and) the Divinity of Man having now fully developed, it may be confidently and exultingly asserted *that the voice of the people is the voice of God."*

Other presidents took a more realistic view. **Theodore Roosevelt** once said that vox *populi* was "the voice of the devil, or what is still worse, the voice of a fool." Later in the twentieth century, **Eisenhower** told a friend: "Even though we agree with the old proverb, 'The voice of the people is the voice of God,' it is not always easy to determine just what that voice is saying." **Bill Clinton** after the election in November 2000 led to a lengthy court battle over the outcome between **George W Bush** and Albert Gore said: "The American people have now spoken, but it's going to take a little while to determine exactly what they said."

The Presidency

Washington's death and Napoleon's seizure of power within about 5 weeks of each other in late 1799 symbolized the end of an era. The American Founders were about to experience a changed world. **Madison** wrote to **Jefferson** at the time: "The late defection of France has left America the only theater on which true liberty can have a fair trial." In the election crisis of 1800-01 **John Adams** compared Aaron Burr to Napoleon. As ambassador, **Monroe** attended the coronation of Napoleon. **Jefferson** called Napoleon "the first and chiefest apostle of the desolation of men and morals." Later he called Napoleon "the Attila of the age." In 1805 **Jefferson** wrote **Madison**: "Considering the character of Bonaparte, I think it material at once to let him see that we are not of the Powers who will receive his orders." **John Quincy Adams** was in Moscow when its inhabitants burned it as Napoleon's armies drew near. The defeat of Napoleon by 1814 was celebrated by **Thomas Jefferson** but it freed up Britain to concentrate on America and turned the War of 1812 into a war for survival.

The role of the presidency began to evolve in this era. **Monroe** had a viewpoint that went to a strong presidency. In the Virginia ratifying convention of 1788 he had criticized the Electoral College holding that the president should be directly elected and that the Electoral College would be susceptible to bribery or manipulation or even foreign influence. As president, **Monroe** was summoned by Congressman John Cocke a supporter of **Jackson** to answer questions to Congress. **Adams** recorded in his diary that **Monroe** "desired that the person who brought him the message to tell Cocke that he was a scoundrel, and that was the only answer he would give him."

Together **Polk** and his Secretary of State **James Buchanan** worked to greatly expand the geographical size of the US but they didn't like each other. **Polk** wrote in his diary that **Buchanan** "had shown a willingness to carry out my views instead of his own" but added that **Buchanan** was "brooding, in a bad mood, not pleasant in his intercourse with me." Other presidents have had difficulties with the top position in the cabinet. In 1861 when **Lincoln** appointed William Seward Secretary of State, and Seward tried to dictate other cabinet choices, **Lincoln** demurred. As he put it to others, "I cannot afford to let Seward take the first trick." In 1981 **Reagan** gave **George HW Bush** more foreign policy work partly to curb his Secretary of State Alexander Haig. When Haig resigned in 1982, he said it was over disagreements on foreign policy. **Reagan** wrote in his diary: "Actually, the only disagreement was over whether I made policy or the Sec of State did." (As **Truman** said the buck stops here.)

Cleveland in accepting the Democrat Party's nomination in 1884 said: "It should be remembered that the office of the President is essentially executive in its nature. The laws enacted by the legislative branch of the government, the Chief Executive is bound faithfully to enforce." In his first term, **Cleveland** kept the government out of what we would call social spending. He saw himself as the constitutional chief executive, a referee making sure that no individual or group was denied rights or given special favors. He said: "Though the people support the government, the government should not support the people."

TR on the other hand thought a president could do anything the Constitution did not forbid. He said he was of the "**Lincoln-Jackson**

school" of presidential power. **TR** on **Jackson** in 1903 when he was considering action in Panama: "*There* was an executive who realized not only the responsibilities, but the opportunities of the office." **TR**: "I took the Isthmus, started the canal and then left Congress - not to debate the canal, but to debate me. But while the debate goes on, the canal does too."

Taft swung back toward **Cleveland**. He thought a president needed to stay within the bounds of the Constitution. When **Taft** left the presidency in 1913, he went to teach law. He hoped to teach about the Constitution noting that it needed protection from "a class of fanatical enthusiasts seeking short cuts to economic perfection." In 1916 he wrote that **TR's** idea that there was "an undefined residuum of power to the President" was "an unsafe doctrine that...might lead under emergencies to results of an arbitrary character, doing irremediable injustice to private right."

A teen-age **FDR** wrote about his cousin **TR** that: "His tendency to make the executive power stronger than the Houses of Congress is bound to be a bad thing, especially when a man of weaker personality succeeds him in office." Even then, however, **FDR** didn't intend to be that weaker person. When he was fifteen, **FDR** spent a summer at **TR's** house in Oyster Bay, New York. From that point forward, he modeled his career on "Cousin **Theodore**." Much later, when confronted with constitutional challenges to the New Deal from a businessman, **FDR** quoted **Cleveland**: "We are faced with a condition and not a theory." **FDR** added: "I wish you would give me a solution."

In an era of hereditary leadership, the US was probably lucky in that only one of the first five presidents had sons. That one, **John Adams**, had a son who ascended to the presidency. Only one other son made it that far, **George W Bush**. A grandson, **Benjamin Harrison,** made it to the presidency. (**Benjamin Harrison** was born at his grandfather's - **William Henry Harrison** - house.) The presidency evolved therefore as a remarkable institution with a fresh election like clockwork every four years.

National Unity

In 2010, after his first year in office, when his legislative agenda had been stalled, President **Obama** said: "Let's start thinking of each other as Americans first....Nothing human beings do will be perfect. But we shouldn't assume that the other side is either heartless or doesn't care about sick people, or is some socialist/communist who's trying to take over the health care system. We start getting into these caricatures."

Presidents have stood as a unifying symbol throughout the last two-hundred years. National unity was not taken for granted in the era before Gettysburg: It would have been normal for the constitutional system to fail. South American states that federated at that time split up more than once in the next generation with political jurisdictions intended to be larger countries becoming smaller countries like Colombia, Venezuela, Ecuador, and Panama. The twentieth century saw the USSR become 15 countries and Europe go from 23 to 50. The office of the presidency and the character of some who held it may have prevented a similar outcome in the US.

Even prior to the US Constitution, those who would become the first five American presidents grappled with the meaning of national unity. During the Confederation period John Jay negotiated with Spain. Jay's instructions were to not give up American rights on the Mississippi River. Jay subsequently requested to be relieved of this requirement. The northern states would have agreed to swap access to the Mississippi for trade concessions. The southern states would not. The underlying issue was whether national or sectional interests would be advanced. **Monroe** favored the West and nationalism. The North talked of forming a confederation. The dispute within the Congress became bitter. **Monroe** proposed transferring the negotiations to Madrid to be put under the oversight of **Thomas Jefferson** and **John Adams** who were in Europe. **Madison** did not think this was a good alternative since he thought it would lead to further concessions. **Monroe** also tried to involve **George Washington** who stayed out of the issue.

Jay gave in and negotiated a treaty with Spain that guaranteed Spain's exclusive right to the Mississippi River for 30 years in return for Spain opening its ports in Europe and the Americas to US shipping. However the treaty was never ratified by Congress. As he was leaving the last Congress under the Confederation, **Monroe** 28 wrote **Jefferson** 44: "It has been a year of excessive labor & fatigue & unprofitably so." He did not realize his contribution in blocking the plan to trade away navigational rights on the Mississippi.

At the end of the Constitutional Convention, **George Washington** suggested that the new federal government might not last twenty years. The politics of the 1790s were affected by concerns over a monarchy. In the 1790s the Federalists did not see themselves as a party but as the government trying to ward off people allied with revolutionary France. The Republicans saw themselves as at most a temporary party trying to prevent a British-backed monarchy. The US came as close to civil war as it would come until 1861. More than anyone, **Washington** held the country together. To promote unity, **Washington** supported roads, canals and the post office. He told a confidant that if the US broke up he would join the North. In 1792, tired of ongoing crises in the government and in the country, **George Washington** longed for retirement. **Jefferson** urged **Washington** to accept re-election because "North and South will hang together if they have you to hang on." On May 5, 1792 **Madison** met with **Washington** and also urged him to serve another term as President. He said that if **Washington** retired it would "surprise and shock the public mind."

Abigail Adams, the wife of **John Adams**, opined that the union of states would break apart. **Thomas Jefferson** referred to Virginia as "my country." Patrick Henry had suggested that Virginia and North Carolina would make a good country. Alexander Hamilton had proposed a scheme to incent Revolutionary War veterans to New York State to protect the state against Vermont. **Jefferson** in 1804 said about the lands acquired in the Louisiana Purchase: "Those of the western confederacy will be as much our children & descendants as those of the eastern." **John Quincy Adams** wrote during the **Monroe** administration that Henry Clay, Speaker of the House, foresaw the US breaking into three confederacies.

George Washington was a symbol of the opposite tendency. At his Farewell Address in 1796 he told the public: "Citizens by birth or choice of a common country, that country has a right to concentrate your affections. The name of American, which belongs to you, in your national capacity, must always exalt the just pride of Patriotism, more than any appellation derived from local discriminations."

In **John Adams'** term in office **Jefferson** and **Madison** agreed that the Federalists wanted to change the political system into a monarchy. **Jefferson** came to believe that **Adams** had "been taken up by the monarchical federalists." That was the influence behind their Virginia and Kentucky Resolutions. **John Quincy Adams** claimed he told **Jefferson** in 1807 that some in Massachusetts were plotting with the governor of Nova Scotia to take New England out of the Union. **Jefferson**, however, was much more concerned with Aaron Burr's secessionist activities in the Southwest.

Upon learning of the Hartford Convention, **Adams** supported **Madison** although both may have viewed it more darkly than it warranted. Just a week before the Convention, Congressman Daniel Webster had argued that states might have the right to find some "measures thus unconstitutional and illegal" and therefore could protect citizens of their state from "arbitrary power." The convention was called by the state legislatures in New England in language that echoed **Jefferson's** and **Madison's** Virginia and Kentucky Resolutions. When it concluded, the Convention just proposed several constitutional amendments. One would have abolished the three-fifth rule by allowing that only free persons would be counted for representation and direct taxes. This was a move to limit the South's power which was based on the constitutional formula that gave Whites extra votes equal to three-fifths of the Blacks living in those states. (Blacks of course could not vote).

Nevertheless, the stigma of the Hartford Convention remained. Several years after the War of 1812, **Andrew Jackson** wrote

James Monroe about it that "these kinds of men although called Federalists, are really monarchists, and traitors to the constituted government." This from **Jackson** who in 1806 had sold Aaron Burr boats during a western expedition of Burr's for which he (Burr) was later tried for treason.

Madison, writing in 1829, predicted that the American Republic would last for another hundred years. However, the "Nullification" crisis of the 1830s rocked the federal system and was a predictor of the Civil War of another generation. It posited that states could abrogate or nullify federal laws. Here is some background.

In **Jackson's** first term, Congressman and former President **John Quincy Adams** worked with him to revise the 1828 Tariff - the "Tariff of Abominations." However, this did not resolve matters and the Nullification crisis resulted when South Carolina threatened to cancel the federal tariff. **Jackson** wrote that the state approached treason and "the power to amend a law of the United States, assumed by one state, is *incompatible with the existence of the Union*." **Adams** supported **Jackson** and said that his message in response to the crisis "contained much sound constitutional doctrine, more indeed than properly belonged to the source whence it originated." **Adams** called nullification a "hallucination" in a July 4 speech that concluded with "Independence and Union forever."

James Madison argued that Nullification was neither constitutional nor within the spirit of the Virginia and Kentucky Resolutions. **Madison** said: "The nullifiers who make the name of Mr. **Jefferson** the pedestal for their colossal heresy shut their eyes and their lips whenever his authority is ever so clearly and emphatically against them." **Jefferson** had been dead for several years by then and **Madison's** view on how he would have felt about Nullification does not seem correct. In fact, **John Quincy Adams** wrote, "**Jefferson** was the father of South Carolina Nullification which points directly to the dissolution of the Union. **Madison** shrunk from his conclusions, but I think admitted rather to many of his premises." **Adams** believed that **Madison** "moderated some of [**Jefferson's**] excesses" and was "in truth a greater and a far more estimable man."

Jackson saw preserving the union as his mission. At a **Jefferson** Day dinner in 1830 he traded toasts with his Vice President, John C. Calhoun:

- **Jackson** - "Our Union. It must be preserved."
- Calhoun - "The Union, next to our liberty, most dear."

(Calhoun who was Vice President under **John Quincy Adams** and **Jackson** was one of two people who served in that post under different Presidents. The other was George Clinton who served under **Jefferson** and **Madison**. Thomas Hendricks, Democrat of Indiana, ran for Vice President in 1876 and lost, declined the nomination in 1880 and won under **Cleveland** in 1884.)

Jackson told **Van Buren** that he would "nullify the nullifiers." During the Nullification crisis, **Tyler** had been working behind the scenes in the Senate to resolve the issues. His position was based on strict constructionist principles that the Constitution did not allow nullification but did allow secession. When **Tyler** learned that **Jackson** was going to ask Congress for authorization to use force against South Carolina – the "Force Bill" - he turned against **Jackson**: "His Proclamation has swept away all the barriers of the Constitution, and given us, in place of the Federal government ... a consolidated military despotism....I tremble for South Carolina." **Tyler** added that it was a "Bloody Bill." **William Henry Harrison** supported it: "I hope to Heaven that the President will adhere to his Proclamation...altho we disapproved of some of his former acts..."

In the interests of Union, **Jackson** opposed British, Spanish, Indians, nullifiers and abolitionists. Many years later, **Theodore Roosevelt** wrote that **Jackson** "had many faults but he was devotedly attached to the Union, and he had no thought of fear when it came to defending his country." **Truman** said **Jackson** "helped once again to make it clear...that we were becoming a stronger and stronger country and wouldn't always be a weak, upstart little nation that had to kowtow to the big European powers."

John Tyler went further than anyone in criticizing another president's policies on national unity. He joined the enemy. **Tyler** was elected to the Confederate Congress in 1861. He died before serving. The North regarded him as a traitor. The US Congress did not erect a memorial on his grave until 1915. During the Civil War **Pierce** was a "Peace Democrat" suggesting that he was soft on the South's right to leave the Union. At times he was regarded with suspicion and probably came close to being arrested.

In December of 1860 a group of New York businessmen met with **Fillmore** over the sectional crisis. The group asked **Fillmore** to go to South Carolina to urge that state to stay in the union. **Fillmore** declined saying South Carolina wanted assurances from the victorious Republicans. In the 1860-61 crisis when **Buchanan** did not take quick action to prevent South Carolina secession **Fillmore** called it a "mistake." He added: "That the general government is sovereign...admits of no doubt in my mind." When the Confederates fired on Fort Sumter, **Fillmore** addressed a large crowd in Buffalo and said: "Civil War has been inaugurated, and we must meet it. Our government calls for aid, and we must give it."

Lincoln embodied two aspects of **Andrew Jackson**: a desire to hold the union together and a tendency to expand presidential power. In a letter that years later was shown to **Lincoln**, **Jackson** said – in an Old Testament reference - that rebels starting civil wars "should be sent to Haman's Gallows." When, urged at the outset to make peace with the rebels, **Lincoln** said, "There's no **Washington** in that - no **Jackson** in that." **Abraham Lincoln** at the end of 1860 wrote: "The right of a state to secede is not an open or debatable question. It was fully discussed in **Jackson's** time, and denied...by him...It is the duty of a President to execute the laws and maintain the existing government." During the war, **Lincoln** cited **Jackson's** action in New Orleans in 1814 in suspending *habeas corpus* as justification for more widespread action of his own.

Lincoln's views followed those of his hero Daniel Webster. **Lincoln** thought Webster's *Reply to Hayne* in 1830 was the greatest American speech. Webster argued that Americans had constituted themselves as one people in 1776, and in the Articles of Confederation which formed "a perpetual union." **Lincoln** developed these thoughts in his first inaugural and in the Gettysburg Address in which he:

- Gave the Declaration a new perspective as a matter of founding law ("four score and seven years ago").
- Put its central proposition, equality, as a principle of the Constitution ("of the people, by the people, for the people").

On December 18 and 19, 1860 **Andrew Johnson** spoke in the Senate against secession. It was a time of high tension with the question of whether states could secede unanswered. Liberals of the time like Horace Greeley of the *New York Tribune* felt that the South should be allowed to separate. As he wrote: "Let the erring sisters go." Abolitionists generally agreed.

Johnson quoted **Washington**, **Jefferson**, **Madison**, and **Monroe** to make his case. He made reference to **Madison** to say that if a state could secede a group of states could possibly expel another state. He said of **Lincoln**, that he (**Johnson**) would stay in the Senate and "put down Mr. **Lincoln** and drive back his advances upon Southern institutions, if he designs to make any. Have we not got the power? We have." He went on that **Lincoln** would have to work with the Senate and that "I voted against him; I spent my money to defeat him; but still I love my country; I love the Constitution; I intend to insist upon its guarantees. There, and there alone, I intend to plant myself."

During this time, states were seceding. President **James Buchanan** said he was powerless to prevent it. Former presidents were ambivalent on secession. Most important army positions were held by Southerners. There were rumors that the inauguration of **Lincoln** would be disrupted or even prevented. A ship attempting to re-provision Fort Sumter in South Carolina was turned away by gun fire. **Johnson's** most consistent opponent in the Senate in December 1860-March 1861 was a northerner, Joseph Lane of Oregon. During the period between the election of **Lincoln** and the inauguration - about four months - **Johnson** kept the Union hopes alive and even inspired these hopes by speaking for the Union as a southern man.

In 1861 **Andrew Johnson** was the only senator from a seceding state to stay loyal to the Union. He was also a co-author of the Crittenden-**Johnson** Resolution that passed Congress in the summer of 1861 asserting that the objective of the war was the restoration of the Union not the interference with any state's institution.

Presidential Terms

The Founders were concerned that the office of the presidency would transform to that of a monarchy. **Jefferson** worried about the president being re-elected continually and wished for a single term limitation. Even though terms were not limited, a two-term tradition emerged. Although **Jefferson** once expected that **Washington** might be president for life, in early 1796 **Madison** wrote to **Monroe** in Paris: "It is pretty certain that the President will not serve beyond his present term." **Thomas Jefferson** said in 1805: "Gen'l **Washington** set the example of voluntary retirement after 8 years. I shall follow it." He added "indulgence and attachments will keep a man in the chair after he becomes it dotard." In 1822 rumors started that **Monroe** would seek a third term and that he even would use the military to remain in power. He did not. **William Henry Harrison** running in 1840 pledged to serve only one term. His death one-month into that term mooted the issue. **Polk** as noted pledged to serve only one term, honored that pledge and died shortly after leaving office. **Pierce** running in 1852 also pledged to serve one term. In his acceptance letter for the nomination in 1876 **Hayes** promised not to seek another term. **Grant** who was finishing his second term and had considered a third term, and would again - saw this as implied criticism of him.

In the mid-1930s, possibly laying the foundation for his own run for a third term, **FDR** said that if John Wilkes Booth had not killed **Lincoln, Lincoln** would have had a "duty" to run for a third term to complete Reconstruction.

Only **FDR** has been elected more than twice and it was controversial. In 1940 when Joseph Kennedy returned from England to visit **FDR**, he backed off his opposition to a third term. Kennedy later said that he and **FDR** had made a deal: Joseph Kennedy would support **FDR** in return for **FDR** backing Kennedy's son Joe for governor of Massachusetts in 1942. **JFK** later said that **FDR** had suggested that his father could be natural successor to **FDR** in 1944. Yet another version is that **FDR** warned Joseph Kennedy that if he did not support him it would ruin his sons' careers.

Also in 1940 **Truman** ran for re-election to the Senate and opposed a third term for **FDR**. He ended up supporting him of course. **Truman** wrote to his wife: "While the President is unreliable the things he's stood for are, in my opinion, best for the country..."

In 1947 **Truman** established the "Commission on Organization of the Executive Branch of the Government," dubbed the "**Hoover** Commission" because **Truman** appointed **Hoover** to chair it. One of the **Hoover** Commission's recommendations was to amend the Constitution to limit presidents to two terms. The Twenty-Second Amendment was ratified in 1951 which vindicated **Jefferson's** view of 150 years earlier. The Twenty-Second Amendment did not apply to **Truman**, the sitting President. But **Truman** agreed with it. He wrote to himself: "In my opinion, eight years as President is enough and sometimes too much for any man to serve in that capacity. There is a lure to power. It can get into a man's blood just as gambling and lust for money have been known to do."

As noted, **FDR** was not the first president who tried for a third term. As the 1800 election approached, some Federalists pushed to draft **Washington** for a third (nonconsecutive) term. This effort was stopped only by **Washington's** death. **Grant** and **Cleveland** were considered for nonconsecutive third terms by leaders in their parties. For the 1880 election, **Grant** made a serious effort. Another former president **Andrew Johnson** denounced him for doing so as did **Garfield** more discretely.

On election night 1904 **TR** honoring the memory of **George Washington** said that he would not seek another term. In 1912

TR tried for a third, non-consecutive term. A would-be assassin of **TR** that year was opposed to a third term. He styled himself, **McKinley's** "avenger." By 1919 **TR's** nomination as the Republican candidate was likely but like **Washington** over one hundred years earlier, death came first. Seriously deluded, **Wilson** hoped to be renominated in 1920. Even more deluded, he hoped to be called out of retirement in 1924. **Coolidge** ascended to the presidency in 1923 upon the death of **Harding** and was re-elected in 1924. In 1927 while very popular he announced that he would not run for another term. He privately explained: "If I take another term I will be in the White House till 1933... Ten years in Washington is longer than any other man has had it - too long."

Lyndon Johnson apparently hoped to be drafted by the 1968 Democrat convention after dropping out of the race earlier in the year. In 1960 **Eisenhower** could probably have been elected to a third term if he had wanted and if the Constitution had permitted. **JFK** thought that he would have been unbeatable. But **JFK** defeated **Nixon** that year with a subtle reproach of **Eisenhower** with the slogan: "Let's get America moving again."

There are other one-term presidents who tried for non-consecutive second terms, an effort that would be perfectly constitutional. (At this writing both **George HW Bush** and **Carter** are eligible to run for president.) As noted, **Van Buren** tried a comeback in 1844 and as the nominee of the Free Soil Party in 1848 he got about ten percent of the popular vote. As the American Party candidate in 1856 **Fillmore** got more than twenty percent of popular vote. After the presidency **Tyler** hoped for the Democrat nomination for the presidency in 1856 and even more so in 1860. In 1856 **Pierce** hoped for re-nomination although he had pledged to one term. In 1860 some Democrats began to favor **Pierce** for another term as someone who could hold the union together. But **Pierce** was unwilling and thought Jefferson Davis should run. Some friends wanted the Democrats to nominate **Pierce** in 1864. He showed no interest except to say that he hoped **Lincoln** would be defeated. **Hoover** who was defeated by **FDR** in 1932 hoped to get renominated both in 1936 and 1940. (In 1944 he supported Douglas MacArthur's unofficial campaign for the

Republican nomination for the presidency.) **Ford** who lost to **Carter** in 1976 considered entering the Republican primaries in 1980 to run against **Reagan**.

At least three one-term presidents were denied an additional term due to inflation. Between 1898 and 1910 prices went up about 30 percent. The president at the end of that period, **Taft**, was replaced after one term. **Ford** dealt with inflation between 1974 and 1977. It remained high and he was replaced after completing **Nixon's** term. **Carter** dealt with inflation between 1977 and 1981 when prices went up over forty percent. He was replaced after one term.

Veto and Pardon

Under the US Constitution, presidents have a unique ability to veto laws and issue pardons.

Vetoes

Jefferson vetoed nothing in two full terms. Other than **Jefferson**, **George W Bush** served the longest without any vetoes. His first one was in 2007 after the Democrats took the Congress and it was over stem cell research funding. **Cleveland** used the veto 584 times second only to **FDR's** 635.

Polk and **Van Buren** helped draft an important veto message in 1830 for **Jackson**, known as the Maysville Road veto after a road in Kentucky. It made a fuzzy distinction between local projects which **Jackson** vetoed and national projects which he approved giving **Jackson** flexibility to challenge Henry Clay's American System of federal money for local works. The veto was issued for reasons of policy, not constitutionality and thereby seemed to increase presidential power. **John Quincy Adams** said: "These are remarkable events.... The presidential veto has hitherto been exercised with great reserve. Not more than four or five Acts of Congress have been thus arrested by six Presidents, and in forty years. He has rejected four in three days. The overseer ascendancy is complete." In other words, **Adams** was objecting to what he saw as an over-reaching presidency although he apparently saw that the federal government had authority for projects. In response to Maysville Road veto he wrote that "the constitution is but one great organized engine of improvement - Physical, moral, political." (In the Senate **Tyler** had opposed the Maysville Road bill in the name of states rights.)

Jackson then used the veto more than all six predecessors and for broader reasons- not just on constitutional grounds. **Jackson's** 1832 veto of the Bank of the United States held that it was unnecessary and improper: a challenge to a previous Supreme Court decision.

The Whigs took a more restrained view toward the veto. **William Henry Harrison** in his inaugural in 1841 noted that it should be used only very occasionally. "It is preposterous to suppose that the President....could better understand the wants and wishes of the people than their own immediate representatives." As a candidate in 1848 **Taylor** echoed this, writing that the veto power should only be used in "cases of clear violation of the Constitution, or manifest haste or want of due consideration by the Congress..."

In 1855 **Pierce** vetoed a bill that would have set aside five million dollars for US citizens for claims against France for shipping losses in the quasi-war of the 1790s. **Pierce** regarded this bill as a boondoggle. He cited an 1803 treaty with France that set aside money for this purpose. He said that no "new facts, not known or not accessible during the Administration of Mr. **Jefferson**, Mr. **Madison**, or Mr. **Monroe**" had emerged. As this example shows, presidential vetoes often exhibit a unity of purpose between presidents across time. So does the next example.

The first debate on an interpretation of the Constitution was over whether the advice and consent requirement of the Senate on presidential appointments also applied to removals. **Madison** successfully argued no. The Senate deadlocked with Vice President **Adams** casting the deciding vote agreeing with **Madison's** stance. This prefigured the Tenure of Office act in the Civil War era that led to the impeachment of **Andrew Johnson**. In 1867 Congress attached a rider to a military appropriations bill requiring that all orders must be routed through the commanding general who was **Grant**. It also passed the Tenure of Office Act to restrict the President's ability to fire advisors without the Senate's consent. This act attached criminal penalties to those who broke it. **Johnson** vetoed the bill but his veto was overridden. In 1868 after **Johnson** fired his Secretary of War Edwin Stanton in defiance of the act, **Garfield** supported impeachment (as did **Hayes** from the Ohio governorship) even though he was afraid that it would elevate Ben Wade of Ohio to the presidency.

In 1869 **Grant** requested repeal of the Tenure of Office Act but Congress refused (although it did modify the act to allow a president to suspend if Congress was not in session).

As a member of Congress, **Garfield** defied **Grant** and voted against repeal of the Tenure of Office Act in 1869. He felt it was wrong to set aside the law that had been the basis of the impeachment of **Johnson**. However, he came to change his mind. In 1876 future president **Garfield** wrote in opposition to the Tenure of Office Act as did future president **Wilson** in 1885. In 1886 **Cleveland** opposed the Tenure of Office Act in a message to Congress. In 1887 it was repealed

In 1924 during the Teapot Dome scandal, **Calvin Coolidge** had to react to a Senate vote to remove his Secretary of the Navy. **Coolidge** was advised by Senator William Borah to resist. **Coolidge** then gave a statement citing **James Madison** and **Grover Cleveland** on separation of powers. He said: "The President is responsible to the people for his conduct relative to the retention or dismissal of public officials. I assume that responsibility...." The supposed prerogative of the Senate to approve the removal of certain non-Cabinet officials was declared unconstitutional by the US Supreme Court in 1926 in a decision written by Chief Justice **William Howard Taft**.

In 1874 **Grant** vetoed a bill that would have injected greenbacks bills (more printed money) into the economy to raise the money supply to bring relief to small businessmen and farmers. The bill had passed both houses of Congress by wide margins but offended hard money interests and was clearly inflationary. **Garfield** was tremendously pleased: "For twenty years no president has had an opportunity to do the country so much service by a veto message as **Grant** has, and he has met the issue manfully." This was an important veto and put the Republican Party on a pro-capitalist path.

In 1972 in a memo to his National Security Advisor Henry Kissinger, **Nixon** who had ordered the mining of the harbors of North Vietnam asserted: "We have the power. The only question is whether we have the will to use that power. What distinguishes me from **Johnson** is that I have the will in spades. If we now fail it will be because of the bureaucrats and the bureaucracy and particularly those in the Defense Department..." In 1973 Congress passed over **Nixon's** veto the War Powers Act. Every president since **Nixon** regarded it as unconstitutional.

Pardons

Presidents responded to early rebellions early in US history in a very compassionate way, by historical standards. In 1794 the anti-tax Whiskey Rebellion broke out in Pennsylvania. The rebels made mock guillotines and extolled Maximilien Robespierre of France's Reign of Terror in which the estimates of those guillotined in Paris alone range from 18,000 - 40,000 the higher figure being the more likely. (Ultimately the French sent Robespierre himself to the guillotine where he was executed face-up and then thrown in a common grave) **Washington** proclaimed the situation in Pennsylvania an "open rebellion," the only other such occasion in US history has been the Civil War. **James Madison** wrote **James Monroe** who was in France about it. He worried about the government using the occasion to stifle rights. **Washington** put on a show of force that was bloodless and eventually pardoned the leaders. **Adams** dealt with a tax revolt known as Fries' Rebellion in 1799. The leaders were sentenced to hang but **Adams** pardoned them.

Madison pardoned the pirate Jean Lafitte in 1815 for his service in the Battle of New Orleans alongside **Jackson**.

In 1858 **Buchanan** pardoned Brigham Young for his role in the "Mormon War." After receiving the pardon, Young approved a sarcastic editorial in the *Deseret News* that noted: "We tender our thanks to President **Buchanan** for pardoning acts committed in holding the risk to a hand grasping a weapon to destroy our lives, and that too for no breach of law on our part, for we emphatically affirm that all allegations of our disobedience to the Constitution and laws of the United States are untrue."

In 1865 **Andrew Johnson** consulted **Grant** as to whether Robert E. Lee should be arrested and charged with treason. **Grant** disagreed and Lee was not disturbed but he did not receive a pardon for his rebellion as other Confederates did. **Grant** in his *Memoirs* about Robert E. Lee at Appomattox: "I felt like anything but rejoicing at the downfall of a foe who had fought so long and valiantly, and had suffered so much for a cause, though that cause was, I believe, one of the worst for which a people ever fought." **TR** also said that Lee "was without any exception the very greatest of all the great captains that the English-speaking peoples have brought forth." In 1975 **Ford** pardoned Lee posthumously.

In 1865 **Andrew Johnson** refused to pardon Mary Surratt convicted in the conspiracy trial after **Lincoln's** assassination and she became the first woman ever executed by the federal government. On Christmas Day of 1868 **Johnson** unconditionally pardoned Jefferson Davis and others involved in the rebellion. In 1923 **Coolidge** pardoned those who had been convicted under the Sedition Act during the **Wilson** administration. He also pardoned Black nationalist Marcus Garvey who had been convicted of mail fraud who was then deported. In 1942 **FDR** commuted the prison term of Earl Browder the Communist Party Secretary. Browder had been jailed for passport fraud.

In 1950 two Puerto Rican nationalists attempted to shoot their way into the Blair House in Washington DC where President **Truman** was staying. A police officer was killed as was one of the Puerto Ricans. The other, Oscar Collazo, was sentenced to the electric chair. In 1952 **Truman** commuted the sentence to life in prison. In

1979 President **Carter** pardoned him. (**Truman** had thought about the dangers of the job and had imagined that he would handle a would-be assassin much as **Jackson** had in 1835.)

In 1953 **Eisenhower** refused to pardon Julius and Ethel Rosenberg convicted of espionage for sharing information about the atomic bomb with the Soviet Union.

Ford pardoned **Nixon** in 1974. In so doing he paraphrased **Lincoln**: "I do believe that right makes might, and that if I am wrong, ten angels swearing I was right would make no difference." (Some versions of this quote have **Lincoln** saying ten "thousand" angels.) **Reagan** supported the pardon.

Running for Congress that year, **Clinton** criticized **Ford** for pardoning **Nixon**. "If President **Ford** wants to pardon anybody, he ought to pardon the administration's economic advisors." **George HW Bush** on the **Nixon** pardon: the US was better off "with this behind us." He added: **Nixon** "has paid a big price already." In considering the **Nixon** pardon, **Ford** relied on a Supreme Court decision that accepting a pardon was an admission of guilt. In 1976 **Jimmy Carter** said: "Had I been president, I would not have pardoned **Richard Nixon** until after the trial had been completed in order to let all the facts relating to his crimes be known." By 2000 **Clinton** had changed his mind on the **Nixon** pardon. He then believed that **Ford** did the right but unpopular thing. In 2001 **Ford** received a "Profiles in Courage" award from the **John F. Kennedy** Foundation for the 1974 pardon of **Nixon**. **Ford** spoke of **JFK** upon receiving the award: "To know **Jack Kennedy**, as I did, was to understand the true meaning of the word [courage]. Physical pain was an inseparable part of his life, but he never surrendered to it - any more than he yielded to freedom's enemies during the most dangerous moments of the nuclear age."

In 1974 domestic terrorists kidnapped heiress Patty Hearst. She was brutalized, kept in a closet for weeks and eventually seemed to side with her captors even participating in a bank robbery. In 1975 surviving members of the terrorist group were captured along with Hearst. She stood trial asserting that she had been brainwashed but was convicted and sent to prison. Her sentence was later commuted by **Carter** and she received a full pardon some twenty years later by **Clinton** who was urged to do so by both **Ford** and **Carter**.

George W. Bush's formal meeting with President **Clinton** at the White House on Inauguration Day in 2001 was delayed as **Clinton** was still in his office signing pardons. He granted 140 pardons and 36 commutations of sentences that day. One pardon was of his brother Roger Clinton the first presidential family member ever to receive a presidential pardon. Other last-day pardons or commutations included:

- Carlos Vignali, a drug dealer had his prison sentence commuted to time served.
- Susan McDougal a former business partner of **Clinton** who had been convicted for misusing a federal loan and who had gone to jail for refusing to give testimony under oath about the Clintons.
- Marc Rich a tax fugitive whose ex-wife had often visited the White House often and was supportive of her former husband.

Hugh Rodham the President's' brother-in-law got $200,000 from the Vignali family for lobbying the president. Tony Rodham the President's' other brother-in-law successfully sought pardons for a couple who were paying him consulting fees. According to witnesses, Roger Clinton was paid to try to get pardons for people but the President did not grant them. Marc Rich or his former wife had given at least $1.5 million to causes related to the Clintons. His ex-wife even gave $7,000 in furniture to the Clintons for their homes after the White House.

When some of these pardons and commutations became controversial **Clinton** wrote an opinion piece. He put his actions in the context of these presidential pardons and commutations:

- **Washington's** pardon of the leaders of the Whiskey Rebellion.
- **Harding's** commutation of socialist Eugene Debs' prison sentence. (Note: his Vice President **Calvin Coolidge** opposed the commutation.)

- **Nixon's** commutation of labor leader Jimmy Hoffa's prison sentence.
- **Ford's** pardon of **Nixon**.
- **Carter's** pardon of Vietnam War resisters.
- **George HW Bush's** pardon of Defense Secretary Caspar Weinberger and other figures associated with a **Reagan**-era scandal.

Jimmy Carter didn't buy it. He said: "I think President **Clinton** made one of his most serious mistakes in the way he handled the pardon situation the last few hours he was in office." On the pardon of Marc Rich, **Carter** said: "I don't think there is any doubt that some of the factors in his pardon were attributable to his large gifts. In my opinion, that was disgraceful."

Gerald Ford later weighed in similarly: "There was a lot of skulduggery, a lot of it. I think the Marc Rich action was unconscionable."

Free Press/Speech

Presidents have had ambiguous relationships with the press.

In 1789 **Jefferson** had drafted a Charter of Rights for France. In it he wrote that French printers would be liable for printing false facts. Yet, in 1792 he wrote **George Washington** that "No government ought to be without censors & where the press is free, no one ever will." **Washington** responding to criticism over the Jay Treaty in 1795 wrote that "infamous scribblers" were criticizing him in "such exaggerated and indecent terms as could scarcely be applied to a Nero." In 1796 **Washington** complained to **Jefferson** about the press, saying that his administration was subject to the "grossest and most insidious representations." **Jefferson** thought that **Washington** took public attacks to heart "more than any person I ever yet met with."

In 1800 James Callender was arrested and charged in Virginia under the Sedition Act for a book he had written against **John Adams**. **Jefferson** wrote Virginia Governor **Monroe** to urge the raising of financial support for Callender's defense: "I think it is essentially just and necessary that Callender should be substantially defended." As he was about to leave office in 1809, **Thomas Jefferson** told **John Quincy Adams** that he was looking forward to never having to look at a newspaper again. (I guess **George Washington** wasn't the only one sensitive to public criticism.)

When he entered office in 1829 **Jackson** replaced many government workers with his own supporters, a political ally said "to the victor belong the spoils of the enemy" forever associating **Jackson** with what came to be called the "spoils system." **Jackson** was also the first president to appoint journalists to top positions. **John Quincy Adams** wrote: "The appointments are exclusively of violent partisans and every editor of a scurrilous and slanderous newspaper is provided for." **Tyler** was in the Senate and considered an independent Democrat. He opposed **Jackson's** appointments of some friendly newspaper editors on grounds that the free press should not be compromised. Many years later **Tyler** admitted that this opposition had probably been a "too Utopian." **Tyler**, however, was pretty solid on the issue of free expression. In 1841 a mob of about thirty people besieged the White House and burned him in effigy after he vetoed the national bank bill. When the rioters where prosecuted **Tyler** sent the court a letter stating that their action "was one of those outbreaks of popular feeling incident, in some degree, to our form of government, and entirely evanescent and harmless in character." Charges were dropped and the rioters apologized.

Taft said in 1913 as he left office: "I wish to keep as far in the background as I can. I have grown fully used to reading the papers without my name in them, and it is not an unpleasant change." During the **Coolidge** administration, **Hoover** once complained to **Coolidge** about an attack in the media. **Coolidge** responded, "Do you mean to say that a man who has been in public life as long as you have bothers about attacks in the papers?" "Don't you?" replied **Hoover**. He cited an article critical of **Coolidge** in a magazine called *American Mercury*. "You mean that one in the magazine with the green cover?" **Coolidge** said. "I started to read it but it was against me, so I didn't finish it." **Coolidge** frequently spoke off the record preventing direct quotations other than to a "White House spokesman." His rationale:

"The words of the president have an enormous weight and ought not to be used indiscriminately. It would be exceedingly easy to set the country all by the ears and foment hatreds and jealousies, which, by destroying faith and confidence, would help nobody and harm everybody." Whatever the downside to this approach, it encouraged candor. **Coolidge** met more regularly with the press than any other president before or since. After the presidency, **Coolidge** reverted to a natural privacy, writing Chief Justice **Taft**: "I am trying to avoid making speeches or attending public gatherings."

In the 1950s **JFK** defended **Nixon** to another guest at a dinner party: "You have no idea what he has been through. **Dick Nixon** is the victim of the worst press that ever hit a politician in this country. What they did to him in the Helen Gahagan Douglas race was disgusting." (**Nixon** won against Helen Gahagan Douglas in a senate race in California in 1950 that is remembered for its low tactics. **Nixon** kept painting Douglas as ultra-left. She referred to him as a "fascist." Neither **Truman** nor **JFK** gave Ms. Douglas much help. Democrat and famous actor **Ronald Reagan** went for **Nixon**. Ms. Douglas was the mistress of Senator **Lyndon Johnson** although that was not known to the general public.)

In 1967 **Lyndon Johnson**, under attack from the press, noted: "The things said about (**Franklin**) **Roosevelt** were more vicious." **Johnson** often joked that if he ever was able to walk on water, reporters would say he couldn't swim. When he left the presidency **Lyndon Johnson** told his staff to keep the media away. "I've served my time with that bunch and I give up on them. There's no objectivity left anymore."

In 2008 **Bill Clinton** said during the campaign between his wife and **Obama**: "It is wrong that Senator **Obama** got to go through 15 debates trumpeting his superior judgment and how he had been against the war (in Iraq) in every year, enumerating the years, and never got asked one time -- not once -- 'Well, how could you say that when you said in 2004 you didn't know how you would have voted on the resolution? You said in 2004 there was no difference between you and **George Bush** on the war. . . .' Give me a break. This whole thing is the biggest fairy tale I've ever seen. . . . [T]he idea that one of these campaigns is positive and the other is negative when I know the reverse is true and I have seen it and I have been blistered by it for months is a little tough to take. Just because of the sanitizing coverage that's in the media doesn't mean the facts aren't out there."

Presidents of course have tried to use the press. During his Senate impeachment trial **Andrew Johnson** gave newspaper interviews to get his side of the story out - to the chagrin of his attorneys. **Taft** said that **TR** "talked with correspondents a great deal. His heart was generally on his sleeve. I find myself unable to do so." **Truman** on **TR**: He "loved press coverage more than anything on earth."

Others have ignored the media. In 2009 President **George W Bush**, out of office, said that attacks in the media never bothered him although his father used to get upset: "He'd read the editorial pages, he'd watch the nightly news, and I didn't. I mean, why watch the nightly news when you *are* the nightly news?"

Elections of 1800, 1876, 1960, 2000

Three presidential elections stand out as too-close-to-call and mired in controversy: those of 1800, 1876 and 2000. The election of 1960 represents a special case.

1800

In 1800 **Thomas Jefferson** and Aaron Burr ran on the ticket of the new Republican Party for president and vice president. In the spring of the year elections in New York appeared to commit that state to **Jefferson** and thereby make his election nationally very likely. He and **Adams** then met in Philadelphia still the nation's capital. **Adams**: "Well, I understand that you are to beat me in this contest. **Jefferson** said, "This is no personal contest between you and me. Two systems of principles on the subject of government divide our fellow citizens into two parties. With one of these you concur, and I with the other... Were we both to die today, tomorrow two other names would be in place of ours." They

232

parted cordially. But **Jefferson** did not win outright. He and Burr tied in the Electoral College in December due to the Constitution's lack of differentiation between electoral votes for president and vice president.

The Constitution provided that the tie would be broken in the House of Representatives which was a lame duck Congress controlled by members of the opposing political party, the Federalists. **Jefferson** wrote to **James Madison** that the tie had "produced great dismay and gloom on the part of the republican gentlemen here, and equal exultation on the federalists." A crisis emerged and was not resolved until right before the inauguration in March of 1801 in an atmosphere of great political tension.

During the votes in the House in the standoff, the Federalists abstained which had the effect of denying the election to **Jefferson.** He wrote **Madison**: "We consider this therefore as a declaration of war on the part of this band." **Monroe**, of course, was anything but aloof. He was governor of Virginia and threatened that his state would secede if **Jefferson**'s election was thwarted. He set up a type of pony express system to cover the one hundred mile distance between Richmond and Washington DC to keep informed. **Jefferson** wrote **Monroe** again: "Four days of balloting have produced not a single change of vote." He later wrote **Monroe** that his party had told the Federalists that they would not stand for a usurpation but that the "middle states would *arm*, & that no such usurpation, even for a single day, should be submitted to." **Tyler's** father was one of **Monroe's** advisors in Virginia during the election crisis.

Some in the Republican Party called for a new Constitutional Convention. **Jefferson** wrote **Monroe** that due to the "present democratic spirit of America" the Federalists opposed this. He said that the word *convention* suggested to them the violence of the French Revolution and that they also were afraid of losing their "favorite morsels of the constitution." **Jefferson** wrote **Madison** that the Federalists were trying to "reverse what has been understood to have been the wishes of the people." He added: "This opens upon us an abyss, at which every sincere patriot must shudder."

Adams played a passive aggressive role although he considered Burr "a much more dangerous Man than Mr. **Jefferson**." Notably, it was also at a time when **Adams** was grieving the death of a son. In turn **Madison** wrote **Jefferson** that **Adams** had "infinitely sunk in the estimation of all parties." **Adams** and **Jefferson** met on a street in unfinished Washington DC. **Jefferson** expressed concern over Federalist support of Aaron Burr for president, that this would have "incalculable consequences." **Adams** told him that if he made certain concessions to the Federalists he would gain Federalist support. **Jefferson** responded, "I will not come into the government by capitulation. I will not enter on it, but in perfect freedom to follow the dictates of my own judgment." **Adams** said, "Then, things must take their course." This was one of their last face-to-face meetings. (**Jefferson** later may have made certain concessions.)

Ultimately, Federalist Congressman James Bayard of Delaware broke with the Federalist caucus to announce his support for **Thomas Jefferson**. He later wrote that he did so because "...it was admitted on all hands that we must risk the Constitution and a civil war or take Mr. **Jefferson**." He also told **John Adams** that Delaware depended on the Constitution for its "political existence."

1876

When the Republican convention nominated **Rutherford B Hayes** in 1876 **Grant** telegraphed him that he had "the greatest assurance that you will occupy my present position from the fourth of March next." He was right, but just barely.

The election of 1876 could have led to another civil war - between parties, not regions. The suppression of civil liberties and the violence would have been significant. The Southern Democrats however wanted peace and home rule more than they wanted to win the White House. The candidates were the Republican **Rutherford B Hayes** and the Democrat Samuel Tilden. Historians generally regard this election as a case of Republican election fraud but that is an oversimplification. There was also a racial angle. On November 8,

1876 when he thought he had lost the election **Rutherford B Hayes** said: "I do not care for myself; but I do care for the poor colored man in the South."

The election turned on four states. By some analysis the Republicans would have won fair elections in South Carolina and Louisiana but not Florida and they did carry Oregon. A total of 20 electoral votes was at issue and **Hayes** needed all 19 from the three southern states and a disputed electoral vote in Oregon to win.

Grant had at least privately expressed doubt as to whether **Hayes** had carried Louisiana. **Garfield** who was sent to monitor the post-election fiasco gave **Hayes** assurances that he carried that state. On December 12, 1876 **Garfield** wrote to **Hayes** about the South: "Several of our more thoughtful Republicans there have said to me during the last three days that they believed it possible to make an inroad into the Democratic camp, which should at least divide them on their policy of violence and resistance.... Just what sort of assurances the South wants is not quite so clear, for they are a little vague in their expressions, but I have no doubt it would be possible to adopt a line of conduct which would be of great help to them... It would be a great help if in some discreet way these Southern men, who are dissatisfied with Tilden and his violent followers, could know that the South is going to be treated by kind consideration by you." **Hayes** following an approach that another century would call plausible deniability replied: "Your views are so nearly the same as mine that I need not say a word."

Garfield's strategy was to have the Senate which was Republican-controlled count the electoral votes. This proved unacceptable to the Democrats and an Electoral Commission was considered. **Grant** supported the Electoral Commission, **Hayes** privately opposed it and **Garfield** called it an unconstitutional "surrender of a certainty for an uncertainty." Nevertheless, the Electoral Commission was established to resolve the deadlock.

Garfield was chosen by the House to serve on the Commission. The Election Commission consisted of:

- From the Democrat-controlled House of Representatives - 3 Democrats, 2 Republicans.
- From the Republican-controlled Senate - 3 Republicans, 2 Democrats
- From the US Supreme Court - 2 Republicans, 2 Democrats and these four were to pick a fifth member. It was reputed that they would pick Justice David Davis who had been appointed to the High Court by **Lincoln** but he was selected by the Illinois legislature to the US Senate and left the Court. The justices then picked their colleague Joseph P. Bradley who had been appointed to the Court by **Grant**.

The Commission then had eight Republicans and seven Democrats. In the deliberations of the Commission, the Southern Democrats bargained for home rule. The Republicans had the President, the army and the veterans behind them. By 8-7 counts **Hayes** got all 20 votes to win. The congressional Southern Democrats agreed to break up a threatened filibuster in the Democrat-controlled House. Here is what the South got in the disputed election of 1876:

- Although he was too cautious to put anything in writing **Hayes** was committed to withdrawing federal troops from South Carolina, Louisiana and Florida.
- By not going behind the canvassing boards, the Republicans tacitly acknowledged states' rights.

Garfield played a key role - if not the key role - in resolving a crisis and making **Hayes** President. As Collector at the New York Custom House **Chester Alan Arthur** helped raise money for the 1876-77 **Hayes** post-election challenge.

1960

Six men who either had been or would be presidents participated in the 1960 election. **Herbert Hoover** and **Harry Truman** made speeches for **Richard Nixon** and **John F. Kennedy**. **Dwight Eisenhower** was the incumbent. **Lyndon Johnson** was the Democrat nominee for Vice President.

On election night Vice President **Nixon** conceded to **Kennedy** and from that moment until his inauguration, **JFK** was recognized as the President-elect. However, as was later shown, President **Eisenhower** wanted the Justice Department to investigate allegations of fraud in the vote count. What was this all about?

Consider:

1. **JFK** beat **Nixon** in the Electoral College by an apparently large margin: 303 - 219. But that is deceptive. **Kennedy** won Illinois and Texas by very slim margins. If **Nixon** had won those states, he would have won the election.

2. The tallies in Illinois and Texas were controversial because Richard J. Daley, the Mayor of Chicago, and **Lyndon Johnson** of Texas both had track records of abetting voter fraud. The *New York Herald-Tribune* documented dozens of examples of possible fraud in the 1960 election. (**JFK** was reported to say about Daley and **Johnson**: "Thank God for a few honest crooks.")

The voting in these two states was what concerned **Eisenhower**. However, in the interests of national stability **Nixon** was against the challenges and **Eisenhower** let the matter drop.

But there is an interesting historical question: who won the popular vote that year?

Consider:

1. In Alabama, where there were 11 electoral votes, **Kennedy's** name was not on the ballot. Alabama voters chose between **Richard Nixon** and a slate of "unpledged Democrat electors." Earlier in the year a statewide Democrat primary had selected five electors who were committed to **JFK** and six who were free to vote for anyone. This Democrat slate beat **Nixon**, 324,050 - 237,981.

2. At the Electoral College, the six unpledged electors voted for Harry Byrd of Virginia, and the five pledged to **Kennedy** stuck with him.

3. However: When the Associated Press at the time counted up the popular vote from all 50 states it tallied all the Democratic votes, whether or not they were for electors pledged to **Kennedy** in the **Kennedy** column. Since 1960, counts have always given all of Alabama's Democrat votes to **Kennedy**. But those Democrat voters were not voting for **Kennedy**. They were voting for a slate, of which only 5/11 was pledged to him and indeed ended up voting for him. If in Alabama, **Kennedy** was only assigned 5/11 of the Democratic vote, **Nixon** would have won in Alabama (but not the Electoral College) and **Nixon** would have had about fifty-eight thousand more popular votes that **JFK** nation-wide.

All of this was set aside in historical memory for two reasons:

- **Nixon's** selfless concession.
- **JFK's** assassination.

2000

The disputed election of 2000 between **George W Bush** and Albert Gore turned on the Florida recount and was not decided until about 36 days after the election.

The total vote count in Florida in 2000 was about 5.8 million. Here is what developed:

- On election night 2000 most of the networks called Florida for Gore by 8:02PM Eastern Standard Time. The 24 states where polls closed after that saw a voter participation decline from 1960-2000 averages. The 26 other states and Washington DC showed a voter participation gain. In each case the change was 2-3%. This probably cost **Bush** New Mexico and Oregon and clearly affected the popular vote. In short, the media was a participant in the 2000 election.

- On November 8, the day after the election, **Bush** led in Florida by 1784 votes.
- On November 15 after a statewide machine recount **Bush** led by 327.
- Also on November 15 Florida Secretary of State Katherine Harris announced that she would not accept further hand recounts and asked the Florida Supreme Court to halt them. Four counties were still engaged in hand recounts. She based that decision on her reading of Florida law which held that county totals needed to be submitted to her office within seven days of the election. In 2000 that was November 14. Circuit Court judge Terry Lewis had upheld Harris' refusal to extend. The Associated Press estimated that the count of undervotes had reduced **Bush's** lead to 286. (Undervotes were ballots that contained no recorded vote for one or more offices but may have had some designation on them.)
- The Florida Supreme Court blocked Harris from certifying vote totals until the Court could decide on the Democrats' request to allow the manual recounts. **Carter**, when asked if the hand counts should be allowed to proceed, replied, "Well, I think so. And if that is not acceptable, when the courts make a ruling, then I think the final determination -- which should be as a fall back only -- that the hand counting should be conducted in every county in Florida."
- On November 18 military and overseas ballots pushed **Bush's** lead to 930. The Gore team was able to invalidate about fourteen hundred military and oversea ballots disproportionately in counties that **Bush** carried.
- On November 21 the Florida Supreme Court ruled 7-0 that Gore-requested manual hand counts should continue giving the four counties five additional days.
- On November 26 Secretary of State Harris certified the Florida results after the Florida Supreme Court deadline expired. **Bush** had a 537-vote lead.
- On December 4 Leon County Judge Sanders Saul rejected Gore's contest of the Florida results.
- Also on December 4 the US Supreme Court by a 9-0 vote asked the Florida Supreme Court to explain why it had

extended the manual recounts past the state's statutory limits.

- On December 6 the Gore legal team moved to throw out twenty-five thousand absentee votes in two other counties which had Republican majorities: Seminole and Martin.
- On December 8 the Florida Supreme Court in a 4-3 vote ordered a manual recount of all undervotes in the state. The Court also ordered a recount of all votes in Miami-Dade and added to Gore's total 215 votes from Palm Beach County and 168 from Miami-Dade.
- On December 9 the US Supreme Court accepted **Bush's** appeal of the Florida Supreme Court decision of the day before.
- On December 12 the US Supreme Court ruled. Seven justices held that the Florida Supreme Court had violated the Equal Protection Clause of the Fourteenth Amendment because it allowed Florida's varying counting standards. Five Justices held that because the Florida Supreme Court had asserted repeatedly that the legislature wanted the electors appointed no later than December 12, that was the deadline and therefore no further recount was permissible under Florida law. (Gore's lawyer in his arguments before the Florida Supreme Court in the case that led to the extension to November 26 had also said that December 12 was the deadline for electors to be appointed.)

The sitting president and two of his predecessors weighed in during this period.

A week after the election **Clinton** said: "I want to congratulate both Vice President Gore and Governor **Bush** for a vigorous and hard-fought campaign. Once again, the world has seen democracy in action. The events unfolding in Florida are not a sign of the division of our nation, but of the vitality of our debate, which will be resolved through the vibrancy of our Constitution and laws. Regardless of the outcome, we will come together as a nation, as we always do." Later, **Clinton** took a partisan approach telling the media that the only way **George W Bush** could win "was to stop the vote count in Florida."

Late in November, **George HW Bush** said his family had been on an "emotional roller-coaster" since the election but he believed his son would prevail over Al Gore's challenges.

Clinton later wrote in his autobiography: "If Gore had been ahead in the vote count and **Bush** behind, there's not a doubt in my mind that the same Supreme Court would have voted 9 to 0 to [re]count the vote and I would have supported the decision... *Bush* v. *Gore* will go down in history as one of the worst decisions the Supreme Court ever made, along with the *Dred Scott* case."

Carter said four years later that election officials working for Florida's governor Jeb Bush, the brother of **George W Bush**, were "highly partisan."

Vice Presidency

The Constitution of 1787 held that the vice president would be the runner up in the Electoral College. After 1800, the Constitution was amended with the result that vice presidential candidates were then picked by party bigwigs to achieve some type of balance for the ticket. This is how it happened:

The original constitutional vision was that the Electoral College would act as a sort of screening committee and refer to Congress the "best" candidates as finalists and that Congress would designate two for the highest two positions in the executive branch of the federal government. The system produced top-notch people to serve as vice president like **John Adams** (1788 and 1792) and **Thomas Jefferson** (1796). One unanticipated consequence of that approach was divided government in the executive branch. This did not manifest during **George Washington's** presidency but it did in the **Adams** administration with **Jefferson**, the Vice President, leading the opposition.

After the disputed election of 1800 the next Congress passed and the states ratified the Twelfth Amendment to the Constitution requiring members of the Electoral College to vote separately for the offices of president and vice president. This has been reported by most historians as the correction of a constitutional flaw. But the correction also had some unanticipated consequences. The trend toward political parties, antithetical to **George Washington's** vision and previously labeled as factionalism, was encouraged by this amendment. The selecting of vice presidential candidates for reasons other than their qualifications to be president was also encouraged.

After the Twelfth Amendment, presidential candidates were incented to pick a running mate for political appeal, often regional balance. This was abetted by the Constitutional requirement that a president and a vice president come from different states. A succession of nonentities resulted. (**Woodrow Wilson** once said that there was nothing to say about the vice presidency and after you have said that, there was nothing more to say.) Sometimes these men elevated to the presidency itself. The Electoral College in its original vision may well have picked **William Henry Harrison**, **Zachary Taylor**, **Abraham Lincoln** and **James Garfield** in 1840, 1852, 1860 and 1880 but it seems unlikely that it would have found the second "best" man to be **John Tyler**, **Millard Fillmore**, **Andrew Johnson** or **Chester Alan Arthur** in those years. In 1968 would it have picked Spiro Agnew who had to resign in disgrace at a critical time in 1973 or someone like **Ronald Reagan** or Hubert Humphrey?

Fourteen of the forty-three presidents previously served as vice president. Two of them, **Truman** and **Ford**, considered running for vice president again after being president. In 1947 **Truman** suggested to **Eisenhower** that he would be **Eisenhower's** running mate - with **Eisenhower** on the top of the ticket. This came out in **Eisenhower's** memoirs. **Truman** denied it but it was confirmed by a passage in **Truman's** diary discovered in 2003. **Ford** and **Reagan** discussed the possibility in 1980. (Additionally, allies of **John Quincy Adams** urged former President **Monroe** as a vice president running mate in 1828. **Monroe** declined.)

Of the twenty-one individuals who held the office of vice president in the nineteenth century just **Martin Van Buren** was later elected president. Four others elevated to the presidency because the incumbent died, and none of those four accidental presidents subsequently won election in his own right. But in the twentieth century these elevated vice presidents were later elected president: **TR** (1904), **Calvin Coolidge** (1924), **Harry Truman** (1948) and **LBJ** (1964). **Richard Nixon** (1968 and 1972) and **George HW Bush** (1988) were two other vice presidents who went to the presidency upon election. Hubert Humphrey (1968) and Al Gore (2000) came close. Walter Mondale (1984) won a total of one state and Washington DC. Others made attempts but could not get their party's nomination: John Nance Garner (1940), Alben Barkley (1952) and Dan Quayle (2000). Henry Wallace ran as a minor party candidate in 1948 coming in fourth behind **Truman**, Thomas Dewey and Strom Thurmond.

Consider the office of the vice presidency. Its role was unclear. In office, **George Washington** began to distance himself from **Adams**, causing, perhaps, the permanent reduction of that office. **John Adams** while vice president: "I am nothing, but I may be everything." About two hundred years later **LBJ** echoed him: "Every time I came into **John Kennedy's** presence, I felt like a goddamn raven hovering over his shoulder." After he went to the presidency, **Johnson** said: "I always felt sorry for **Harry Truman** and the way he got the presidency but at least his man wasn't murdered." Years later **LBJ** told a young Doris Kearns, now Doris Kearns Goodwin: "I took the oath. I became president. But for millions of Americans I was still illegitimate, a naked man with no presidential covering, a pretender to the throne, an illegal usurper. And then there was Texas, my home, the home of both the murder and the murderer. And then there were the bigots and the dividers and the Eastern intellectuals, who were waiting to knock me down before I could even begin to stand up. The whole thing was almost unbearable."

Although he also described the support he gave **Washington** as vice president as "which is and shall be the pride and boast of my life," **John Adams** wrote to **John Quincy Adams** about the office that it was "a kind of Duty, which, if I do not flatter myself too much, is not quite adapted to my Character." **Adams** spoke of his relationship with **Jefferson** during the time when he was president and **Jefferson** vice president: "We consulted very little together." **Tyler** supported Henry Clay over **William Henry Harrison** at the 1839 Whig nominating convention and was extremely disappointed in Clay's defeat. This may have gotten him the vice presidential nomination. From that undistinguished post he stepped into history.

Whether or not the Founders intended for the vice president to assume the office of the presidency upon the death or disability of the president was very much in doubt in 1841, the time when the question was first tested. In *The Federalist* No. 68, Alexander Hamilton had written, "The Vice-President may occasionally become a substitute for the President." It was probably assumed by the Founders that the vice president would be a stopgap for a period of time until a president could be elected. **Tyler** was a Democrat who had been added to the Whig ticket in 1840 for Southern votes. After the election **Tyler** was neither asked nor volunteered advice on cabinet members as President-elect **William Henry Harrison** consulted with Henry Clay and Daniel Webster. **Harrison** fell ill at his inauguration and died within a month. (In one of history's coincidences, fifty years before that, the father of **William Henry Harrison** died and the father of **John Tyler** succeeded him in the Virginia legislature.) While **Harrison** was sick, Secretary of State Daniel Webster apparently decided that **Tyler** would become president largely as a figurehead whom the cabinet would control. He was given the oath, not by the Chief Justice, but by the chief of the Circuit Court of the District of Columbia. **John Quincy Adams** wrote in his diary that **Tyler's** assumption of the presidency "violated" the Constitution. He referred to **Tyler** as "His accidency." He saw him as "a nullifier" and a man devoid of ideas. He said **Tyler** was a man for whom he had "utter distrust."

Tyler was an anomaly. He had broken with **Jackson** in the Nullification crisis of 1832-33 and eventually left the Democratic Party in time to be nominated for vice president under the Whig **Harrison** and then elevated to the presidency. Some thought **Tyler** had broken promises he made at the Whig convention which he denied and his denial had some basis as the Whigs had no party platform that year given their diversified interests. **Tyler** later said: "I have no recollection of having opened my lips in that body (the nominating convention) on any subject whatever. In short, I do state, resting upon my memory, which is not apt to deceive me, that I was perfectly and entirely silent in that Convention. I was ...wholly unquestioned about my opinions..." As president he became a man without a party. **Millard Fillmore** said at the time: "I have heard of but two **Tyler** men in this city (Buffalo) and none in the country, and I need not add that both of these are applicants for office." **Adams** thought that **Harrison's** death brought to the presidency "a man never thought for it by anybody." Questions about **Tyler's** assumption of the presidency persisted. As late as 1848 when **Buchanan** was Secretary of State, the State Department addressed correspondence to **Tyler** as "ex-vice-president."

Andrew Johnson disagreed. In a congressional speech during the **Polk** administration defending the power of the veto, **Johnson** mentioned "**John Tyler**, called by some, but not be me, in derision, 'the Accidency President.'" History proved **Johnson** right. **Tyler** set the course followed much later by powerful presidents such as **Theodore Roosevelt**, **Calvin Coolidge**, **Harry Truman** and **Lyndon Johnson**. The **Tyler** precedent was finally put into the Constitution in 1967 as the Twenty-Fifth Amendment.

In 1844 **Fillmore** sought and failed to get the vice presidential nomination of the Whig Party to run on the ticket with Henry Clay. He lost out to Theodore Frelinghuysen of New Jersey and that ticket lost to **Polk** probably because the anti-slavery Liberty Party took 15,000 votes in New York. (The Whig slogan - "Hurray, Hurray the Country's Risin; Vote for Clay and Frelinghuysen" - was limp compared to the Democrats' "Fifty-four Forty or Fight!" The latter became one of the most famous slogans in American history and referred to a boundary dispute with England in the Northwest which was settled in subsequent years south of that latitude.)

In 1848 **Taylor's** handlers' first choice for vice president was Abbott Lawrence of the textile fortune in Massachusetts whose wealth at half a million dollars made his family one of the ten richest in the

US. He was disqualified as a "Cotton Whig" meaning that he was allied with the South. The convention went with **Fillmore** (whom **Taylor** had never met) who helped the Whigs carry New York which turned out to be crucial. In patronage disputes in New York in 1849, Vice President **Fillmore** appealed to **Taylor** who remained neutral and then sided with **Fillmore's** New York adversaries. **Fillmore** met with **Taylor** and asked if in the future he "was to be treated as friend or foe." A few days before **Taylor** died **Fillmore** visited him again and said that if called upon as vice president to break a tie in the Senate he would probably vote against **Taylor's** preferences and for the legislation that became the Compromise of 1850 because he "deemed it for the interest of the country." As president, **Fillmore** helped usher in the Compromise.

Arthur was briefly considered for the vice presidential nomination at the 1876 Republican convention. He got it in 1880 but he was actually the second choice. **Arthur** had come to the convention supporting **Grant** and the offer was a gesture to the **Grant** forces at the convention known as Stalwarts. As **Garfield** and **Arthur** greeted well-wishers **Arthur** was still wearing a **Grant** button. However, **Arthur** successfully ran **Garfield's** campaign to an upset win. In 1881 in a patronage dispute, Vice President **Arthur** like **Fillmore** three decades earlier appeared to openly side against the president (**Garfield**) leading some to question his fitness for the vice presidency. **Arthur** also lobbied the New York legislature to reappoint Roscoe Conkling who had resigned from the Senate to embarrass **Garfield**. **Arthur** told a reporter: "**Garfield** has not been square, nor honorable, nor truthful with Conkling." However, when **Garfield** was assassinated in 1881 and **Arthur** promoted to the presidency he realized that the shooting changed everything. He broke with Conkling and moved away from earlier positions to embrace civil service reform, a great issue of the day that he had earlier opposed.

Picking the vice president has been pretty hit-and-miss. In 1832 **Jackson** made **Van Buren** the vice president to spite the Senate that had rejected him as Ambassador to England. (**Tyler** had voted to confirm **Van Buren**. He voted this way not because "he liked the man over much" but he didn't want to be identified with the opposition National Republicans.) In 1864 **Andrew Johnson** was **Lincoln's** second choice to be vice president. General Ben Butler of Massachusetts was his first and he declined. Butler did not believe that **Lincoln** would be re-elected. **Lincoln** told a confidant: "The British and the French don't know that the number two position in our government is not all that important. **Johnson** is from the South and his selection proves that this is not a sectional fight but a fight about slavery." **Arthur** later claimed to have supported **Andrew Johnson** for vice president at the convention.

Harding was nominated for president in 1920. He was asked whom he wanted for a running mate and responded, "search me." **Coolidge** was not the first choice for **Harding's** running mate by the Republican bosses. Senator Irvine Lenroot of Wisconsin was. A delegate from Oregon acting alone shouted out to push for **Coolidge** after Lenroot was nominated and the delegates then voted decisively for **Coolidge**. During the campaign, **Harding** said of **Coolidge** that he would not be a "mere substitute in waiting" and that he would attend cabinet meetings. No vice president had ever done so. **Coolidge** purportedly considered **Hoover** for vice president in 1924.

Former Justice of the Supreme and **FDR**-ally Jimmy Byrnes expected to be nominated as vice president to run with **FDR** in 1944. **FDR** played a game with the nomination. In a transcribed conversation with Byrnes he said, "After all, Jimmy, you are close to me personally and Henry (Wallace, the current vice president) is close to me. I hardly know **Truman**. (Supreme Court Justice William O.) Douglas is a poker partner. He is good in a poker game and tells good stories." Jimmy Byrnes would probably have been selected as **FDR's** running mate except for the opposition of labor leader Sidney Hillman. At a secret meeting in his train car with a few advisors, **FDR** seems to have consented to Byrnes but told them as they were leaving, "Clear it with Sidney." At a meeting with Hillman, the **Roosevelt** advisors were told that Byrnes was not acceptable to labor. When **Truman** was told that he was **FDR's** choice, his response was: "Tell him to go to hell. I'm for Byrnes." When then told that **Truman** was reluctant to accept the vice presidential nomination **FDR** said: "You tell him, if he wants to break up the Democratic Party in the middle of the war, that's his responsibility." As vice president, **Truman** identified **Roosevelt** as "the Boss." (As president, **Truman** called his wife "the Boss.")

Upon receiving word that **Eisenhower** had chosen him as a running mate, **Nixon** went into **Eisenhower's** hotel suite at the 1952 Republican Convention saying, "Congratulations, Chief." **Eisenhower** bristled at the informality. There would be more "informality." When **Eisenhower** remained silent in the opening stages of a slush fund scandal that engulfed **Nixon** during the campaign, **Nixon** said to him over the phone, "There comes a time on matters like these when you've either got to shit or get off the pot." After **Truman** ordered the attorney general to start a criminal investigation of the fund. **Nixon** prepared a nation-wide address to answer the scandal. His speech came to be known as the "Checkers Speech" in reference to **Nixon's** dog which he cited as a gift that he would not give up. **Eisenhower** had sent word to **Nixon** that he wanted him to offer his resignation at the end of the speech. This would have left **Eisenhower** free to accept or reject it. **Nixon** ignored **Eisenhower's** directive, which saved his career because the speech gained great public approval. **Eisenhower** then contacted him to tell him, "You're my boy." This was a wound in the relationship of the men who would become our thirty-fourth and thirty-seventh presidents that would take fifteen years to heal. Of note: **Hoover** spoke up for **Nixon** to the **Eisenhower** camp as did Minnesota Republican Convention delegate Warren Burger and Congressman **Gerald Ford**. Two decades later, **Nixon** appointed to Burger to Chief Justice of the United States and **Ford** to the vice presidency.

Nixon's time as vice president may not have been a happy one. According to Nelson Rockefeller who had been a special assistant to **Ike**, **Nixon** "had his feet cut right off" by **Eisenhower's** close associates.

In 1956 **LBJ** sent word to nominee Adlai Stevenson that he wanted the vice presidential nomination. Stevenson was noncommittal and

LBJ withdrew the request. Stevenson threw it open to the convention where **John Kennedy** competed for the nomination, losing on the second ballot to Estes Kefauver which was the last time a major convention went past the first ballot in selecting the president or vice president nominees.

In May of 1960 in an effort to jump-start **Nixon's** campaign **Eisenhower** leaked a list of possible running mates to a friendly journalist. The list included **Gerald Ford** and Prescott Bush who was the father and grandfather of presidents.

Clark Clifford said that **JFK** wanted to pick Stuart Symington as his running mate in 1960. Clifford quoted **JFK** shortly before **LBJ** was announced: "I must do something that I've never done before. I made a serious deal and now I've got to go back on it. I have no alternative." Hyman Raskin who was in charge of **JFK's** communication room at the 1960 convention claimed that **JFK** told him: "You know we had never considered **Lyndon**, but I was left with no choice. He and Sam Rayburn made it damn clear to me that **Lyndon** had to be the candidate. Those bastards were trying to frame me. They threatened me with problems and I don't need more problems. I'm going to have enough problems with **Nixon**."

However, Hugh Sidey of *Time* recalled that before the convention **JFK** said: "If I had my choice I would have **Lyndon Johnson** as my running mate. And I'm going to offer it to him, but he isn't going to take it." After the nominating convention, **LBJ** suggested having **JFK's** staff read and approve his speeches in advance. **JFK** demurred: "You know what to say as well as I do, **Lyndon**." **JFK** might not have won without **LBJ** on the ticket in 1960 because of his strength in the South.

After winning the election, things soured. **JFK** told an aide: "I can't afford to have my vice president, who knows every reporter in Washington, going around saying we're all screwed up." The **Kennedy-Johnson** relationship did not improve. Many factors widened this breach – personal styles, the hatred of Robert Kennedy for the Vice President, a lessening of reliance on the Solid South by **Kennedy** for the 1964 election. As the distance between the two men grew more apparent, rumors that **JFK** would drop **LBJ** from the ticket in 1964 emerged. What **Kennedy** would have done is, of course, not to be known. The evidence is mixed:

- As late as 1963, **JFK** had told a confidant that the idea of dumping **Johnson** was "preposterous on the face of it. We've got to carry Texas in '64, and maybe Georgia."
- In 1964 Robert Kennedy said that there had never been a plan to drop **Johnson.**
- In 1968 President **Kennedy's** secretary wrote that **Kennedy** was intending to drop **Johnson** in 1964. Robert Kennedy also disputed this.

Nixon considered **George HW Bush** for the vice presidency in 1968. **Nixon** was "profoundly impressed by his fighting competitiveness." Vice President Spiro Agnew resigned in 1973. Under the Twenty-fifth Amendment **Nixon** had to designate a vice president. **Ford** told him that if he remained as vice president he would not run for President in 1976. **Ford** later acknowledged that he viewed the vice presidency as the worst job he ever had. In 1974, also under the Twenty-fifth Amendment, **Ford** had to designate a vice president. **George HW Bush** was a close runner-up to Nelson Rockefeller. There was history to all this. Rockefeller had turned down the opportunity to run as vice president on a **Nixon** ticket in 1960 and even, in 1968, had privately rebuffed feelers from Democrat Hubert Humphrey to run with him. In 1973 he had been on **Nixon's** short list when Spiro Agnew resigned. This was his fourth opportunity but it too was no sure thing. In his last hours as president, **Nixon** told his Secretary of State Henry Kissinger who had worked for Rockefeller: "Tell your friend not to get mixed up with this **Ford** administration. The worst mistake I made in my life was appointing this man vice president." Yet, in the first week or so after his resignation, **Nixon** told his son-in-law, **"Ford's** got to make Rockefeller the vice president." **Ford** did, although Rockefeller proved unhappy in the job saying later: "Every vice president goes through hell - let's face it. He's an able man and he's sitting there and he can't do anything; can't express himself; he's got to follow the line. And it's a very frustrating experience."

A year later **Ford** nominated **George HW Bush** for the Director of the CIA in 1975 at a time when Rockefeller was becoming a political liability for **Ford**. **Bush** was asked by some of the senators during the confirmation process to pull out of any consideration for the vice presidential nomination in 1976. **Ford** called **Bush** and told him that to ensure his confirmation he would have to be removed from consideration for the 1976 Republican ticket.

At the 1980 Republican convention **Reagan** first offered the vice presidency to **Ford** who seemed to blow his chances in a television interview in which he did not object to the term "co-presidency." **Ford** had been attractive to **Reagan** mainly because he wanted to avoid **George HW Bush**. Ultimately, talks between the **Ford-Reagan** parties broke off and **Reagan** contacted **Bush** and said: "**George** it seems to me that the fellow who came the closest and got the next most votes for president ought to be the logical choice for vice president. Will you take it?" **Reagan** only asked that **Bush** support his pro-life position on abortion. He then went to the convention hall to quell any rumor that he would pick **Ford**: "He and I have come to the conclusion, and he believes deeply, that he can be of more value as the former president campaigning his heart out, as he has promised to do, and not as a member of the ticket." He quickly added that he had chosen "a man we all know and a man who was a candidate, a man who has great experience in government, and a man who has told me that he can enthusiastically support the platform across the board." **George HW Bush** then came onto the stage: "If anyone wants to know why **Ronald Reagan** is a winner, you can refer him to me. I'm an expert on the subject. He's a winner because he's our leader, because he has traveled the country and understands its people. His message is clear. His message is understood." In 1991 **Ford** said that he had not been interested in the vice presidential nomination in 1980 and that he favored **George HW Bush**: "**George Bush** was always my candidate for vice president. In fact, Betty and I went to Detroit with the hope that we could be helpful to him. But **Reagan** screwed it all up by getting me involved.")

As Vice President **George HW Bush** explained to **Nixon** his loyalty to **Reagan**: "I don't believe a president should have to be looking over his shoulder wondering if the vice president was out there carving him up or undermining his programs in one way or another."

Section 4 of the Twenty-Fifth Amendment reads in part: *Whenever the Vice President and a majority of either the principal officers of the executive departments or of such other body as Congress may by law provide, transmit to the President pro tempore of the Senate and the Speaker of the House of Representatives their written declaration that the President is unable to discharge the powers and duties of his office, the Vice President shall immediately assume the powers and duties of the office as Acting President.*

In 1981, **Reagan** was shot and rushed into emergency surgery. Some cabinet members tried to persuade **George HW Bush** to assume the role of Acting President but he refused.

Section 3 of the Twenty-Fifth Amendment reads: *Whenever the President transmits to the President pro tempore of the Senate and the Speaker of the House of Representatives his written declaration that he is unable to discharge the powers and duties of his office, and until he transmits to them a written declaration to the contrary, such powers and duties shall be discharged by the Vice President as Acting President.*

In 1985 when **Reagan** had surgery the third section of the Twenty-Fifth Amendment was invoked for the first time. It provides for the vice president to temporarily assume the powers of the presidency when a president "is unable to discharge the powers and duties of his office." When **Bush** visited **Reagan** in the hospital, **Reagan** said, "What the hell are *you* doing here? (After **Reagan** returned to the White House a few days later, Vice President **Bush** visited again. As described years later by **George W Bush**, **Reagan** was lying on a couch with his eyes closed and a flower in his mouth. "As **Dad** tried to process the scene, the President jumped off the couch, and they both roared with laughter.")

In 1992 **Ford** wanted **George HW Bush** to remove Vice President Dan Quayle from the ticket as **Bush** prepared to run for re-election.

He told an interviewer: "So I called the president and told him exactly what I told you before: '**George**, the campaign is dead in the water. The one thing that I think would change the atmosphere politically would be to have Dan Quayle himself, on his own initiative, walk into the Oval Office and offer to step aside."

There are some in American history who seems to have missed the chance at the presidency because they did not take the take or keep the vice presidency. Daniel Webster turned down the vice presidential nomination twice in instances which had he accepted he would have been elevated to the presidency. He could have run with **William Henry Harrison** in 1840 and **Zachary Taylor** in 1848. Hannibal Hamlin who was vice president in **Lincoln's** first term was dumped by him in favor of **Andrew Johnson** in 1864. In 1944, **FDR** dumped his vice president, Henry Wallace in favor of **Truman**.

It was reported that Hillary Clinton was offered the vice presidential nomination in 2008. Her answer to her pollster: "I've already done that job." (She referred to her role as a powerful First Lady during her husband's presidency.)

What is the point of all this?

The Constitution describes the presidents; the reverse is also true. Two presidents – **Washington** and **Madison** - were directly involved in its formation. All have commented on it by words or actions. The most candid may have been **Theodore Roosevelt.** As president he once said he wished he always had a great constitutional lawyer nearby. He was reminded that he had Secretary of State Elihu Root and **Taft.** He responded: "Yes, but they don't always agree with me."

Chapter 8

Policy

Overall context

The Civil War is arguably the hinge point of American history. By 1864 the military situation in the East was basically unchanged since 1861. The South only had to fight defense and wear down the Union resolve. **Lincoln** brought **Grant** from the West where his victories had made him an American hero, promoted him and bet his presidency on his success. This was also the first time the two had met. **Lincoln** said that **Grant** "doesn't worry and bother me. He isn't shrieking for reinforcements all the time. He takes what troops we can safely give him...and does the best he can with what he has got." Here as in many other instances in our history, the presidents have interacted on the setting of policy. At times of course policy prescriptions are ignored. In 1961 as vice president, **Lyndon Johnson** counseled **JFK** to make it clear to South Vietnamese President Diem that unless there was a massive invasion we would not send combat troops there. Under **Johnson** our troop commitment got to half a million. Sometimes policy input is never sought. **FDR** never discussed the development of the atom bomb with his vice president **Harry Truman** who shortly became the only person in history to authorize its military use. Sometimes it comes to nothing at all. In 1970 **Nixon** persuaded Congressman **Ford** to put together a House committee to look into the impeachment of Justice William O. Douglas. In 1975 **Carter** supported **Ford's** request of Congress for last-minute aid to South Vietnam.

Moving Forward

After Lexington and Concord, **Adams** wrote privately: "Powder and artillery are the most efficacious, sure and infallible conciliatory measures we can adopt." Operating as a *de facto* Secretary of Defense in the early stages of the Revolutionary War, **John Adams** persuaded **Washington** to require smallpox inoculation of the troops of the Continental Army. In 1782 **Adams** negotiated recognition and a loan from Holland. To Abigail: "Some folks will think your husband a negotiator, but it is not to be, it is General **Washington** at Yorktown who did the substance of the work. The form only belongs to me."

In 1780 **Adams** wrote the Congress that no European power wanted America to "rise very fast to power." He wrote: "Let us treat them with gratitude, but with dignity. Let us remember what is due to ourselves and our posterity as well as to them. Let us above all things avoid as much as possible entangling ourselves with their wars and politics.....America has been the sport of European wars and politics long enough." In Europe **John Adams** and **Jefferson** had to negotiate trade treaties with **Adams** as the senior partner. **Jefferson** wanted free trade anticipating globalization. He wrote **Adams**: "I think all the world would gain by setting commerce at perfect liberty." **Adams** disagreed: "We must not, my Friend, be the Bubbles of our own liberal sentiments. If we cannot obtain reciprocal Liberality, we must adopt reciprocal Prohibitions."

They also dealt with Muslim pirates from North Africa and with the governments of those countries who were demanding protection payments. **Jefferson** and **Adams** wrote the American Congress that they had asked the ambassador from Tripoli for justification for this piracy. "The ambassador answered us that it was founded on the Laws of the Prophet, that it was written in their Koran, that all nations who should not have acknowledged their authority were sinners, that it was their right and duty to make war upon them wherever they could be found, and to make slaves of all they could take as Prisoners." **Jefferson** wanted to align with European countries to fight, anticipating NATO of more than a century later. **Adams** was more cautious: "We ought not to fight them at all unless we determine to fight them forever." **Jefferson**: "You make the result differently from what I do. It is of no consequence, as I have nothing to say in the decision."

This problem was initially addressed by bargaining and bribes and eventfully by warfare.

John Adams in 1797 attempted some type of reconciliation with the Muslims through a treaty with Ottoman Tripolitania, a region in what is now Libya. The Treaty of Tripoli contained this remarkable language: "*As the government of the United States of America is not in any sense founded on the Christian religion* as it has in itself no character of enmity against the laws, religion or tranquility of the Musselmen (Muslims) and as said States have never entered into any war or act of hostility against any Mahometan nation, it is declared by the parties that no pretext arising from religious opinions shall ever produce an interruption of the harmony existing between the two countries." (Emphasis added).

Under **Jefferson**, however, in the early 1800s US Marines attacked Tripoli to free American sailors giving rise to the famous phrase in the Marine Hymn. (In the 2000s, **George W Bush** who made special efforts to assure people that Islam was a religion of peace while sending American troops to fight Middle East terrorism had to deal with Islamic sensitivities over western media or history. He once said in exasperation, "If it's not the Crusades, it's the cartoons" referring to Muslim fundamentalists rioting over cartoons depicting the prophet Muhammad.)

In 1786 New England farmers, agitated over foreclosures, broke out in an uprising. It is known in history as "Shay's Rebellion." It was put down. The varying reactions of **George Washington** and **Thomas Jefferson** are of interest. **Washington** to **Madison**: "What stronger evidence can be given of the want of energy in our government than these disorders?" In 1787 **Jefferson's** response was his famous statement that "the tree of liberty must be refreshed from time to time with the blood of patriots and tyrants; it is its natural manure." He noted that it was the only American rebellion in the previous eleven years. Shay's Rebellion caused the first rift between **Adams** and **Jefferson** and Abigail Adams and **Jefferson**. (**Jefferson** wrote her: "The spirit of resistance to government is so valuable on certain occasions, that I wish it to be always kept alive. It will often be

256

exercised when wrong, but better so than not to be exercised at all. I like a little rebellion now and then. It is like a storm in the atmosphere.") What followed were the Constitutional Convention and then the presidency of **George Washington.**

When **John Adams** left Europe in 1788 **Jefferson** was effectively in charge. **Adams** worried about **Jefferson's** competence in dealing with Dutch bankers who held loans to the American government. He warned **Jefferson** of "the immeasurable avarice of Amsterdam." He added: "I pity you, in your situation, dunned and teased you will be, all your philosophy will be wanting to support you. But be not discouraged... Depend upon it, the Amsterdammers love Money too well to execute their threats."

Jefferson when he saw war clouds in Europe in 1790: "Our object is to feed, and theirs is to fight." Also: "War is not the best engine for us to resort to; nature has given us one in our commerce, which if properly managed, will be a better instrument for obliging the interested nations of Europe to treat us with justice." **Jefferson** once told **Washington**: "One loves to possess arms, though they hope never to have occasion for them."

The French Revolution was a shock to the US as it was to the rest of the world. On July 14, 1789 a mob freed the (seven) prisoners - none of them political - from the Bastille. The mob beat the commander to death and decapitated him, carrying his head through Paris on a pike. An official was hanged from a lamp post, another cut to pieces. **John Adams** in 1792 saw it as "a complication of tragedy, Comedy and Farce" and as an alarm bell. He hoped for its success and understood the ideals but predicted that a single legislative assembly would mean "great and lasting calamities." **Adams** commented: "It appears to me that most of the events in the annals of the world are childish tales compared to it." After reading a sermon that was positive about the French Revolution **Adams** wrote that such principles had been "from the year 1760 to this hour, the whole scope of my life." But he couldn't accept enshrining reason as a religion: "I know not what to make of a republic of thirty million atheists." **Adams** saw most clearly of anyone in the US government the chaos, horror and tyranny that lay ahead. **Adams** to Samuel Adams: "Will the struggle in Europe be anything other than a change in impostors?"

Jefferson as a past envoy to France had underestimated the coming violence of the French Revolution. He wrote in 1793: "The liberty of the whole earth was depending on the issue of the contest and was ever such a prize won with so little blood?....Were there but an Adam and an Eve left in every country, and left free, it would be better than it is now." This is the voice of either a very sophomoric dilettante or a Pol Pot. In 1793 **Jefferson** reluctantly agreed with **Washington** on neutrality in the wars between England and France writing **Madison** that neutrality was "a disagreeable pill, though necessary to keep out of the calamities of war."

This neutrality was tested. Edmond-Charles Genet was born in Versailles in 1763. The revolutionary government of France sent him to the US in the early 1790s to build support for France in its wars with England and Spain. Genet's approach was to appeal directly to American crowds rather than to **George Washington** who was steering a neutral course. For a while, Genet enjoyed great popularity and built up an American following. **Washington** was vilified. **Adams** described the time as "when ten thousand people in the streets of Philadelphia, day after day, threatened to drag **Washington** out of his house and effect a revolution."

Jefferson's supporters toasted France and had models of the guillotine at their festivities. Genet lectured **George Washington** that he was misusing executive power, outfitted a privateer in Philadelphia and embarrassed **Jefferson**. **Washington** demanded his recall. **Jefferson** acquiesced in the recall of Citizen Genet, confiding to **Madison** that he saw the "necessity of quitting a wreck which could not but sink all who cling to it." Practicing what politicos would later call "damage control," **Monroe** and **Madison** worked together to contain the problems of the Genet crisis and in so doing learned more of party politics and public appeals. They got a slow start. A letter from **Jefferson** in Philadelphia that reached them both at **Monroe's** farm near Charlottesville Virginia was partly in cipher and **Madison** had left his key in Fredericksburg. (The distance is about

70 miles.) In an only-in-America story, Genet avoided execution by staying in the US where he married the daughter of New York Governor George Clinton and lived out his life in the Hudson Valley. He was one lucky man. His pestiferous approach would have earned him sure death in most countries.

In a generation, **Jefferson** came around to **John Adams'** view on the French Revolution writing him in 1816: "Your prophecies... proved truer than mine and yet fell short of the fact, for instead of a million, the destruction of 8 or 10 millions of human beings has probably been the effects of the convulsions. I did not, in 89 believe they would have lasted so long, nor have cost so much blood." He also agreed that **Adams'** prediction that England would eventually win out over France was accurate. **Adams'** response: "I know not what to say of your Letter but that it is one of the most consolatory I have ever received."

In 1794 **Jefferson** called the army led by **Washington** against tax rebels in Pennsylvania an "armament against people at their ploughs." Also that year, after **George Washington** criticized political clubs known as "Democratic-Republican societies for their sympathy with the French Revolution, **Jefferson** wrote **Madison** sarcastically: "It is wonderful indeed that the President should have permitted himself to be the organ of such an attack on the freedom of discussion, the freedom of writing, printing and publishing."

In 1794 Senator **Monroe** was worried by rumors that **Washington** would send Alexander Hamilton to England to negotiate a treaty. He wrote the President objecting to Hamilton and offering to meet with him to explain his position in more detail. **Washington** answered: "In reply to your letter of yesterday, I can assure you, with the utmost truth, that I have no object in nominating men to offices than to fill them with such characters as in my judgment...are best qualified to answer the purposes of their appointment." He went on to emphasize that "I *alone* am responsible for a proper nomination..." **Monroe** replied with a letter making among other points that the nomination of Hamilton would alienate France. **Washington** had already eliminated Hamilton and did not reply. Subsequently he appointed John Jay.

Jefferson and **Madison** opposed the Jay Treaty. From France **Monroe** wrote to **Madison**: "If it is to be ratified, it may be deemed one of the most afflicting events that ever befell or country. Our connection here will certainly be weakened by it... The opinion which is gone forth to the world...is that we are reduced by it to the condition of British colonies - an opinion undoubtedly untrue, abhorrent as the treaty is, but yet that is the state of things..." **Washington's** house in Philadelphia was surrounded by an anti-treaty mob. **Washington** signed it because of the US vulnerability to England although he said he was "not favorable to it."

In 1796 the Federalist Party asked Congress to praise **George Washington** and his Farewell Address, considered one of the greater state papers in American history. Some of his contemporaries did not agree. Congressman **Andrew Jackson** voted no. He was angry over the Jay Treaty. From France **Monroe** criticized it because he thought was a disavowal of France. He wrote to **Madison** on January 1, 1797: "Most of the monarchs of the earth practice ingratitude in their transactions with other powers...but Mr. **Washington** has the merit of transcending, not the great men of the antient republicks, but the little monarchs of the present day in preaching it as a publick virtue. God only knows, but such a collection of vain, superficial blunderers, to say no worse of them, were never...before placed at the head of ant respectable state." Seventeen years later, however, **Monroe** attacked Federalists opposing the build-up to the War of 1812 by quoting sections of **Washington's** Farewell Address pertaining to factionalism. (From the vantage point of one hundred years, **TR** credited **George Washington** for supporting the Jay Treaty.) **Washington** stayed his neutral course because he believed it was in the young country's best interest.

During the administration of **John Adams** the US drifted toward war with France. He sent negotiators to Paris. **John Quincy Adams** wrote **John Adams** from Europe that the French felt invincible under Napoleon's army. He felt that the world situation was "in the hands of a Corsican stripling whose name two years ago might have been hidden under a dog's ear on the role of fame, but which at the moment disdains comparison with less than Caesar or Alexander."

In 1803 in discussing the negotiations with Napoleonic France that led to the Louisiana Purchase, President **Thomas Jefferson** wrote Secretary of State **James Madison** about the importance of tact and diplomacy in dealing with the French. "An American contending by stratagem against those exercised in it from their cradle would undoubtedly be outwitted by them." He ultimately sent **Monroe** to France to close the deal. **Jefferson** asked **Monroe** for "a temporary sacrifice to prevent the greatest of all evils in the present prosperous tide of our affairs." He also explained to **Monroe** that he needed to neutralize the issue to prevent Federalists from aligning with Westerners.

During their presidencies, **Jefferson**, **Madison** and **Monroe** all subtly encouraged filibustering into Spanish territories that we now know of as the states of Florida and Texas - although in 1805 **Jefferson** declined **Monroe's** advice to occupy Texas as far as the Rio Grande. From outside the government, former Vice President Aaron Burr had similar ambitions. In 1805 Burr made a trip through the then West that raised suspicion that he would try to separate the western territories and states. He met separately with **Andrew Jackson** and **William Henry Harrison** who was governor of Indiana territory. In 1807 **Andrew Jackson** thought the trial of Aaron Burr was political persecution and that **Jefferson** had been duped. In 1812 **Jefferson** wrote **Monroe** that he had never trusted Aaron Burr's accuser General James Wilkinson except in the instance that Wilkinson had accused Burr of treason. **John Quincy Adams** opposed Aaron Burr during Burr's treason trial of 1807.

Jefferson's pacifistic foreign policy was based on peaceful coercion through embargoes. In 1807 Senator **John Quincy Adams** supported **Jefferson's** trade restrictions against England because he was told it would strengthen the administration's bargaining position with England. In executive sessions **Adams** urged his colleagues: "The President has recommended the measure on his high responsibility.

I would not consider. I would not deliberate. I would act." **Adams** acted on principle because he disliked **Jefferson** and had no faith in the embargo. This was later used against him in Massachusetts by his Federalist colleagues. In 1808 the Massachusetts legislature voted to recall **Adams** from the Senate. (In that era, state legislatures selected the US Senators.) The legislature was upset at him for his support for the embargo and of the presidential candidacy of **James Madison**. In 1809 **James Madison** appointed him to be minister to Russia as a tacit reward.

In **Jefferson**'s second term his trade embargo became increasingly unpopular and **James Monroe** advised Jeffersonians not "to bury ourselves in the same tomb with it."

Jefferson's policy toward the Indians in what was then considered the Northwest was to claim the lands of nearly-extinct tribes. He encouraged an approach of indebting chiefs as a prelude to buying the tribes' lands. As a territorial governor, **William Henry Harrison** worked with Indian tribes in Indiana and reported the abuses against them to the federal government. **Harrison** wrote the Secretary of War: "Whether something ought not to be done to prevent the reproach which will attach to the American Character by the extermination of so many human beings I beg leave most respectfully to submit to the consideration of the President. That this extirpation will happen no one can doubt." **Jefferson** responded by advocating that the Indians turn to agriculture. **Harrison** told an assembly of chiefs in 1802: "Your father, the President, wishes you to assemble your scattered warriors and to form towns and villages in situations best adapted to cultivation; he will cause you to be furnished with horses, cattle, hogs, and implements of husbandry, and will...instruct you in management."

Jefferson worried about the international situation as Spain gave Louisiana to France. He thought the French army in New Orleans might be seen by the Indians as an ally. He wrote to **Harrison** that such an alliance might "immediately stiffen" the Indians against giving up more land. He elaborated: "Live in perpetual peace with the Indians...cultivate an affectionate attachment from them... The

262

decrease of game rendering their subsistence by hunting insufficient we wish to draw them to agriculture, to spinning and weaving... When they withdraw themselves to a small piece of land, they will perceive how useless to them are their extensive forests and will be willing to pare them off ...in exchange for necessities... We shall push our trading houses and be glad to see the good and influential individuals among them run into debt... When these debts get beyond what the individuals can pay, they become willing to lop them off...by cession of lands..."

Finally **Jefferson** added to **Harrison**: "I must repeat that this letter is to be considered as private. You will also perceive how sacredly it must be kept within your own breast...how improper to be understood by the Indians..." In 1805 **Harrison** settled a treaty with the Wyandots, Ottowas and other Indian tribes which gained lands in the present Ohio. He said to the territorial legislature about the Indians: "A miserable remnant is all that remains to mark the names and situation of many numerous and warlike tribes.... Is it then to be admitted, as a political axiom, that the neighborhood of a civilized nation is incompatible with the existence of savages? Are the blessings of our republican government only to be felt by ourselves?"

In 1812 after General William Hull surrendered Detroit to the British, **Monroe** raged to **Jefferson**: "We must efface the pain before we make peace and that may give us Canada." **Jefferson** wrote **Madison**: "Hull will of course be shot for cowardice and treachery..." In 1813 **Madison** ordered a court-martial of Hull and the trial took place the following year. **Martin Van Buren** was assigned the role of chief prosecutor representing the government. Hull was found guilty of cowardice, neglect of duty, unofficer-like conduct and sentenced to death, the only American general ever so-sentenced by an American court-martial. **Madison** later remitted this sentence. In 1891 Henry Adams wrote that Hull was a scapegoat.

John Quincy Adams while he was serving as US Ambassador to Russia quickly accepted the Tsar's offer to mediate between England and the US. **Madison** also accepted. England refused.

However it led to delegations meeting at Ghent. The Americans were led by **Adams**.

As a young lawyer **Buchanan** in 1815 was a Federalist who criticized **Madison's** leadership during the War of 1812. He accused **Madison's** "democratic administration" with "wild and wicked projects." And: "They had deprived us of the means of defense, by destroying our navy and disbanding our army; after they had taken away from us the power of re-creating them, by refusing the Bank of the United States."

During the **Jefferson** and **Madison** administrations foreign affairs were usually directed by interests of the southern states rather than the North. The difference was most acute with relation to the acquisition of Florida. In 1814 Secretary of State **James Monroe** twice sent instructions to **Andrew Jackson** to not disturb the Spanish in West Florida. But given the communication systems of that era **Jackson** had taken Pensacola when the first letter was in transit. The second may have been diplomatic cover.

During **Monroe's** presidency England offered to mediate between the US and Spain over possession of Florida. Secretary of State **Adams** would have accepted but **Monroe** rejected and the issue remained. In 1818 **Jackson** received an assignment to pursue the Seminoles but not to go into Florida. Shortly before getting that assignment he had written **Monroe** that the US could take Florida as compensation for Spanish outrages. "This can be done without implicating the government." He got no response. **Monroe** didn't have a secretary at the time and was ill and didn't read the letter until a year later when Congress was investigating **Jackson's** actions.

In 1818 both **Monroe** and **John Quincy Adams** covertly or openly supported **Jackson's** incursions into Spanish Florida. On the basis of this diplomatically oblique letter from President **James Monroe** to **Andrew Jackson** dated December 28, 1817, **Jackson** seized Spanish Florida: "This is not a time for you to think of repose. Great interests are at issue, and until our course is carried through triumphantly...you ought not to withdraw your active support from it."

Monroe influenced Congress not to censure **Jackson** for his actions in Florida in 1818. Secretary of State **John Quincy Adams** also defended the action. He wrote the Spanish government and released to the press that "the President will neither inflict punishment, nor pass a censure on General **Jackson**." He added that this was because his actions were "founded in the purest patriotism...as well as the first law of nature - self-defense."

Two Members of Congress who would run on the same national ticket a generation later participated in the debate. **William Henry Harrison** supported a censure for at least one of **Jackson's** acts during the operation, an execution of a foreign agent in the area. **Tyler** supported resolutions condemning **Jackson's** conduct but said that the resolutions should not be considered as censures because "censure implies bad motives and bad acts." He accepted that **Jackson** had good motives and even referred to him as "this gallant hero." He said: "We do nothing here but combat the opinions and actions of the General, and if gentleman will have it so, of the Executive" (**Monroe**). His primary point: "However great may have been the services of General **Jackson,** I cannot consent to weigh those services against the Constitution of the land." And: "Your liberties cannot be preserved by the fame of any man." (This was a courageous stand about a national hero.) The controversy over **Monroe's** role in this persisted until the end of his life. In 1830 **Jackson** claimed that **Monroe** had actually given him permission to take Florida which **Monroe** denied.

In 1821 President **Monroe** appointed **Jackson** governor of Florida, in part because due to budget cuts he needed to reduce the number of generals in the army. He wrote him: "Past experience shows that neither of us are without enemies. If you still have any, as may be presumed, they will watch your movements, hoping to find some inadvertent circumstance to turn against you. Be therefore on your guard."

The President might as well have saved his breath. **Jackson** embarrassed **Monroe** when he arrested the outgoing Spanish governor violating his immunity. **Monroe** defended him telling an aide: "From the view which I have of his conduct I entirely approve it...however I should be glad to receive Mr. (**John Quincy) Adams'** opinion." **Adams** defended **Jackson** who resigned anyway blaming **Monroe**. **Monroe** was shocked and responded: "I have been much hurt to find in your late letters that I had not done you justice."

Monroe was far more interested in military preparedness than his two Republican predecessors. This difference carried over into his post-presidential years. In 1830 **Monroe** suggested military training for the students at the University of Virginia where he and **Madison** were on the Board of Directors to help quell discipline problems. This idea was shelved by **Madison.**

As Secretary of State, **John Quincy Adams** authored the **Monroe** Doctrine in 1823. Here is some background.

To thrive the US had to unite and then expand into the land between the Allegheny Mountains and the Rocky Mountains. It bought that territory in the Louisiana Purchase of 1803 but because commerce depended on controlling the mouth of the Mississippi River it was not secured until two developments: the Battle of New Orleans in 1814 and Texas independence won at the Battle of San Jacinto in 1836. North America and South America are essentially separate islands connected by the Isthmus of Panama. South America is divided north to south by impassable land preventing unification. The **Monroe** Doctrine was to discourage European naval bases in this difficult-to-settle area

Monroe consulted **Madison** and **Jefferson** in developing the Doctrine. Both **Jefferson** and **Madison** wanted to accept an offer from Great Britain for a joint declaration of neutrality although **Jefferson** wanted to modify it by taking Cuba and **Monroe** initially agreed. **John Quincy Adams**, however, argued successfully that the US should act alone, overcoming the objections of these three Founding Fathers and the entire **Monroe** Cabinet, finally convincing the President. As **Jefferson** then came to support **Monroe**, he said: "I have ever deemed it fundamental for the United States, never to take an active part in the quarrels of Europe. Their political interests are entirely distinct from ours." A young **Zachary Taylor** praised **Monroe** for the **Monroe** Doctrine in 1824. President **John Tyler** extended the protections of the **Monroe** Doctrine to Hawaii in the 1840s. **Fillmore** protected Hawaii's independence against the French in the early 1850s through firm diplomacy.

Benjamin Harrison tried to annex Hawaii and pushed the US toward the world stage - a position it would take in 1898. **TR** wrote in 1897 that in the future Japan could have designs on Hawaii. In retirement **Benjamin Harrison** became dissatisfied with America acquiring territories such as the Philippines in the **McKinley** presidency. He thought this would transgress the **Monroe** Doctrine which he interpreted as that the US should "leave the rest of the world alone." **Theodore Roosevelt** applied the Corollary to the **Monroe** Doctrine in 1904 which asserted the right of the US to intervene in states in the Caribbean and Central America if they were unable to pay their international debts. In his 1909 message to Congress **Taft** seemed to walk back from the **Monroe** Doctrine. In regard to unstable governments in Latin America he said: "The apprehension which gave rise to the **Monroe** Doctrine may be said to have nearly disappeared, and neither the doctrine as it exists nor any other doctrine of American policy should be permitted to operate for the perpetuation of irresponsible government, the escape of just obligations, or the insidious allegation of dominating ambitions on the part of the United States." **Hoover's** administration clarified that the **Monroe** Doctrine was "a declaration of the US versus Europe - not of the US versus Latin America and appeared to in part repudiate the **Roosevelt** corollary. This was favorably received in Latin America. Later **FDR** said that "old **Hoover's** foreign policy has been pretty good."

In his 1825 State of the Union **John Quincy Adams** proposed that the US attend a pan-American conference of the newly independent Latin American states to be held in Panama. In the Senate, **William Henry Harrison** supported US participation in the conference. **Jackson** and **Van Buren** opposed it. **Jackson**: "The moment we engage in confederation or alliances with any nation we may from that time date the downfall of our republic." **Adams** wanted to send former President **Monroe** to the conference but **Monroe** declined out of a reluctance to offend **Jackson** allies in the Congress who as noted were considering financial reimbursement claims he had made for his earlier service abroad.

In 1832 during the Bank crisis **Andrew Jackson** said to **Martin Van Buren**, "The Bank, Mr. **Van Buren**, is trying to kill me. *But I will kill it.*" He vetoed a bill that would have rechartered the bank. As a Member of Congress **Polk** helped **Jackson** with the destruction of the Bank and **Jackson** wrote him in 1832: "An investigation kills it and its supporters dead. Let this be had." In the Bank fight **Jackson** got **Polk** appointed Chair of the Ways and Means committee. Afterward, he said, "**Polk** for the hard service done in the cause deserves a Medal from the American people." As a Jacksonian in the 1830s **Buchanan** opposed the rechartering of the Bank of the US. In 1837 Whig Congressman **Fillmore** opposed **Van Buren's** response to the Panic of 1837. He saw the administration's efforts as a continuation of **Jackson's** war on the Bank of the United States. Looking forward to the 1840 presidential election the Bank ill-disposed **Fillmore** toward Henry Clay. He saw the bank fight as "really a war of the State banks against the United States bank got up by artful politicians." In vetoing a bank bill in 1841 **Tyler** called the veto "the great conservative principle in our system" echoing **Jackson's** veto of the second BUS in 1832.

In 1834-36 a diplomatic crisis emerged over the French reneging on a treaty obligating them to pay an indemnity to the US for French damages to US shipping during the Napoleonic era. **John Quincy Adams** stood by **Jackson** in this crisis. He argued against reopening negotiations with France: "Do it, and soon you will find your flag insulted, dishonored, and trodden in the dust by the pygmy States of Asia and Africa - by the very banditti of the earth." **Adams** disappointed his party by supporting **Jackson**.

In 1835 **Andrew Johnson** was mayor of Greenville Tennessee. He ran for the state legislature against a Whig. At a joint appearance the Whig made a pitch for the Whig platform: internal improvements – such as roads and canals built at federal expense - a high tariff to protect American industry and a national banking system. **Johnson** started by giving a tribute to **Andrew Jackson** for thwarting Nullification. He also opposed the tariff. **Abraham Lincoln** in the 1830s was on the other side: "My politics can be simply stated. I am in favor of the internal improvement system and a high protective tariff." **Lincoln** was a Whig following the party line.

In 1838, **John Quincy Adams** visited President **Martin Van Buren** who assured him that the grant that led to the Smithsonian would be appropriately used. In Congress **Andrew Johnson** opposed funding the Smithsonian. He wanted it turned into an industrial school.

In 1842 **Fillmore** as Chair of the Ways and Means Committee aided by Congressman **John Quincy Adams** used the issue of tariff revisions to pressure President **Tyler**. Also during the **Tyler** administration Member of Congress **Andrew Johnson** supported him in opposing the National Bank and supporting the annexation of Texas.

Tyler a Democrat had been elected vice president in 1840 with a Whig **William Henry Harrison** at the top of the ticket. When **Harrison** died and **Tyler** elevated, he opposed most Whig programs and became a man without a party. In 1844 **Tyler** dropped out of the race to endorse **Polk** in order to help him defeat Henry Clay, the Whig. **Polk** consulted **Jackson** who agreed that **Tyler** would be helpful. **Tyler** and **Polk** agreed on Texas.

As a foreign diplomat **John Quincy Adams** had begun to formulate his ideas about the US focusing on independence and union and what a slightly later period would call "Manifest Destiny." As he wrote his father: "The whole continent of North America appears to be destined by Divine Providence to be peopled by one nation, speaking one language, professing one general system of religious and political principles, and accustomed to one general tenor of social usages and customs. For the common happiness of them all, for their peace and prosperity, I believe it indispensable that they should be associated in one federal union." **John Quincy Adams,** then, like **Polk,** was a continentalist. **Adams** supported

Polk's aggressive stand against England over Oregon. In the Senate in the 1830s and 1840s **Buchanan** also stood for Manifest Destiny. In 1837-38 tensions between the US and England flared over the boundary between Maine and New Brunswick, Nova Scotia. The Treaty of Paris ending the Revolutionary War had left the boundary unclear. Mediation including one attempt by the King of the Netherlands who offered a compromise acceptable to England but not to the US had failed. **Buchanan**: "If war must come, it will find the country unanimous....The only alternative is war or national dishonor; and between these two, what American can hesitate?" **Van Buren**, however, arranged a truce. The issue was carried over to the **Tyler** administration where it was resolved in 1842 by the Webster-Ashburton Treaty. **Buchanan** attacked the treaty in the Senate for "needlessly and shamefully" giving too much territory to England.

In the **Polk** administration Secretary of State **James Buchanan** negotiated the Canadian border with England. By treaty the US and England jointly occupied the Oregon territory and were trying through diplomacy to settle any pertinent issues. But in 1845 tensions escalated. **Polk** made a claim to the territory in his inaugural address raising threats in the British parliament which in turn outraged certain American commentators. **Jackson** wrote **Polk** in this environment: "This is the rattling of British drums to alarm...the timid, & give strength to the traitors in our country, against our best interests & growing prosperity." **Jackson** added that during the campaign "I gave a thousand pledges for your energy & firmness, both in war & peace, to carry on the administration of our government." He urged **Polk**: "No temporizing with Britain on this subject now..." **Polk** assured him that British statements had "not disturbed my nerves." Then, he worked with his Secretary of State **James Buchanan** toward a compromise. But it was not easy. When **Polk** heard rumors that **Buchanan** was covertly recommending a compromise with England to Members of Congress out of line with **Polk's** position he wrote in his diary: "The truth is, Mr. **Buchanan** has from the beginning been, as I think, too timid and too fearful of War on the Oregon question."

In the last days of the **Tyler** administration, Congress had passed a memorial annexing Texas. New Secretary of State **James**

Buchanan guaranteed Texas three thousand troops. **Polk** ordered General **Zachary Taylor** to the Rio Grande. **Grant** as a young officer saw **Tyler's** and **Polk's** efforts to incorporate Texas into the Union as an attempt to extend slavery and as a threat to regional balance. The Mexican-American War of 1846-48 that followed divided more presidents.

In the diplomacy of 1845 before the Mexican-American War Secretary of State **Buchanan** worried about a war with England over the question of Oregon and Mexico over Texas. He was a voice of restraint challenging **Polk** in the cabinet. He wanted to avoid a stern diplomatic letter to England that **Polk** wanted to send over the boundary issue in Oregon territory or at least wait to see how the Mexico issue developed. **Polk**: "We should do our duty to both Mexico and Great Britain and firmly maintain our rights and leave the rest to God and country. **Buchanan** responded: "God won't have much to do in justifying us in a war for country north of 49 degrees." **Buchanan** wanted **Polk** to authorize him to pledge to England and France that the US would not seize California. **Polk** disagreed: "Before I would make a pledge like that I would meet the war with England or France or all the powers of Christendom ... And that I would stand and fight until the last man." Out of office **Fillmore** opposed the Mexican-American War as did **Abraham Lincoln** and **John Quincy Adams** from the Congress. (When **Polk's** request for a declaration of war with Mexico passed a House vote overwhelmingly in 1846 **Adams** shouted "No" as loudly as he could.)

Lincoln in 1847 as part of the antiwar Whigs said **Polk** was trying "to avoid scrutiny of his own conduct...by fixing the public eye on military glory - that rainbow that rises in showers of blood - that serpent's eye that charms but to destroy." He said that **Polk** "talked like an insane man." He added: "His mind, taxed beyond its power, is running hither and thither, like an ant on a hot stove." He added that "as to the end, he himself has (not) even an imaginary conception." In 1847 **Polk** did not fully comply with a congressional demand to turn over correspondence pertaining to allowing Santa Ana back in Mexico through naval blockades earlier. **John Quincy Adams**: "This House ought to assert, in the strongest manner, this right to call for information; and especially in those cases where questions of war and peace are depending." **John Quincy Adams** died before armistice during the Mexican-American War, collapsing on the floor of the House. In 1846 General **Zachary Taylor's** forces were in an exposed and dangerous situation in northern Mexico. In his war message to Congress **Polk** noted that he had authorized **Taylor** to get reinforcements in Texas. As a young lawyer in Ohio in 1846 **Hayes** called the Mexican-American War "one of **Polk's** blunders." But he saw **Taylor** as "a first rate leader" who had "flogged the Mexicans." In a similar vein, in 1848 **Lincoln** wrote that the nomination of **Taylor** would allow the Whigs to blame the Democrats for the Mexican-American War but still get credit for its success.

Taylor's liberal terms to the defeated Mexicans at Monterrey in 1846 have been compared by historians to **Grant's** at Appomattox in 1865. **Polk** was angered at the terms. He declared "I am now satisfied that he is a narrow-minded, bigoted partisan, without resources and wholly unqualified for the command he holds." When **Grant** issued his similar terms he knew he would have critics but said, "Mr. **Lincoln** is certain to be on my side." Within days of **Lincoln's** assassination **Grant** met with the new President **Andrew Johnson** who complained about these terms. **Grant** later said, "I felt that reconstruction had been set back, no telling how far." (In the 1950s Winston Churchill said to **Richard Nixon** of **Grant's** actions at Appomattox: "In the squalor of life and war, what a magnificent act.")

As a young veteran in 1848 back from the Mexican-American war **Grant** told people in his hometown that the invasion of Mexico was "unjust and unholy." **Grant** later said "We were sent to commence a fight, but it was essential that Mexico should commence it." He wrote in his *Memoirs*: "The Southern rebellion was largely the outgrowth of the Mexican war." **Grant** as president wrote: "I would not fire a gun to annex territory. I consider it too great a privilege to belong to the United States for us to go around gunning for new territories." **Grant's** view toward the Mexican-American war has greatly influenced historians. However, it must be remembered that Texas had been recognized by England and France and that Mexico had tried to get England and France into an anti-American alliance.

Further, there were claims that the US had against Mexico for the imprisoning and even killing of American citizens that a neutral umpire had awarded to the US which Mexico had refused to pay. Mexico exercised nominal control over California and none over Texas. Further still:

1. Texas had won its independence and claimed the Rio Grande as its boundary.
2. Mexico made no effort to reclaim that disputed land.
3. The US had a right to negotiate treaties with Texas.
4. Mexico's response to annexation of Texas was to declare it an act of war.
5. Mexico fired the first shots in the disputed territory.
6. Mexico had abused American citizens. France had actually attacked Mexico to get redress for abuses against its citizens and England had accomplished that goal by threatening to attack.
7. Mexico was dysfunctional, unable to control the lands in its domain.
8. The US was an expanding population. It was creating a new kind of country, democratic, expanding, and linked by railroads.
9. There was an antiwar party but it was rejected by the voters. It included Henry Clay, **Martin Van Buren,** and **Abraham Lincoln**.
10. Mexican claim to the territory only dated from 1820 when it wrested it from Spain.

In short, the views of **Polk** won out over those of two generations of presidents: **John Quincy Adams**, **Van Buren, Lincoln, Grant** and **Hayes**.

In 1862 **Grant** was the military commander in the "Department of Tennessee" which consisted of Kentucky, Mississippi and Tennessee. He barred "the Jews, as a class." He was reacting to some Jews who among others were illegally speculating in cotton. **Lincoln** revoked the order. **Grant** apologized publicly and privately and later assured people "that I have no prejudice against sect or race but want each individual to be judged by his own merit." This evidence of anti-Semitism did not hurt **Grant's** reputation.

In the Congress in 1864 **Garfield** voted against a proposal to extend the provision to pay for draft substitutes which was a program that **Cleveland** used. In 1865 **Lincoln** reached out to Confederate peace overtures at Hampton Roads. **Garfield** who disagreed said: "Our odd President is doing that odd thing."

In 1865 **Grant** urged **Andrew Johnson** to take action against Maximilian in Mexico saying that "nonintervention on Mexican affairs will lead to an expensive and bloody war hereafter or a yielding of territory now possessed by us." Also: "To let the Empire of Maximilian be established on our frontier is to permit an enemy to establish himself who will require a longstanding army to watch." **Grant** may have felt guilt about the Mexican-American War.

Grant advised **Andrew Johnson** not to fire Edwin Stanton, the event that precipitated impeachment. Toward the end of his presidency **Andrew Johnson** said of **Grant**: "**Grant** was untrue. He meant well the first two years, and much that I did that was denounced was through his advice. He was the strongest of all in support of my advice.... But **Grant** saw the radical handwriting on the wall, and heeded it. I did not see it, or, if seeing it, did not heed it. **Grant** did the proper thing to save **Grant**, but it nearly ruined me. I might have done the same thing under the circumstances. At any rate, most men would."

In 1873 **Garfield** dissuaded **Grant** from a public works program to alleviate a depression: "We had something of a struggle to keep him from drifting into that foolish notion that it was necessary to make large appropriations on public works to give employment to laborers."

A political battle touching six presidents, five of them Republicans, in the late 1870s and early 1880s led to Civil Service reform. **Hayes** wanted to remove **Chester Alan Arthur** from his job as head of the Custom House in New York, a position to which he had been appointed by **Grant**. **Hayes** first offered him the consulship in Paris.

Arthur declined. In 1878 **Hayes** dismissed **Arthur** and appointed **Theodore Roosevelt's** father to the position. This was a slap at **Grant** ally Senator Roscoe Conkling from New York who wanted **Arthur** retained. The Senate contested the dismissal based on the Tenure of Office Act that had led to the impeachment of **Andrew Johnson** and eventually rejected the older Roosevelt who died prematurely, purportedly from the strain of a rough and unsuccessful confirmation hearing. Historians cite this as a factor in making **TR** an anti-machine politician, later part of the reform-minded Progressive movement. The investigation and political issues dragged on for nearly two years. When **Hayes** finally prevailed in getting the confirmation of a new Collector he wrote him: "Let no man be put out merely because he is Mr. **Arthur's** friend, and no man put in merely because he is our friend."

Hayes won with mostly Democrat support. Republican **Garfield** privately thought that **Hayes** wasted political capital in the intra-party fight. In an irony, **Arthur** was nominated for vice president in 1880 to balance the ticket with **Garfield** and when he succeeded to the presidency upon the murder of **Garfield**, he pushed through Civil Service reform. The firing of **Arthur** also helped put down the Tenure of Office Act and solidified the role of the president to make appointments.

One of the long-running issues over which presidents have interacted is that of the tariff. Its roots trace to Alexander Hamilton who was impressed by the British system and advocated protective tariffs. For fifty years, the manufacturers were a weak minority and generally unsuccessful in getting the tariffs they wanted. Agrarians and planters carried the day. Natural advantages however favored certain industries. **Madison** went against his earlier beliefs and favored some degree of tariff after the War of 1812, a sure sign that the Jeffersonian Republicans were taking up Federalist priorities. In 1828 the Tariff of Abominations was passed. By 1833 a compromise was reached calling for the gradual elimination of that tariff by 1842.

The Whig Party came into being as pro-tariff. **Fillmore** was an early supporter. Republican presidents starting with **Lincoln** supported tariffs for the rest of the century. During the Civil War, Congress had greatly increased import tariffs and internal duties to meet military expenses. Although taxes had been lowered somewhat after the war, for several years following that, the government had collected a surplus of revenue, often far beyond current expenditures. **Garfield's** position on tariffs was somewhat ponderously articulated: "I hold that a properly adjusted competition between home and foreign products is the best gauge to regulate international trade. Duties should be so high that our manufacturers can fairly compete with the foreign product, but not so high as to enable them to drive out the foreign article, enjoy a monopoly of the trade and regulate the price as they please. If Congress pursues this line of policy steadily, we shall, year by year, approach more nearly to the basis of free trade, because we shall be more nearly able to compete with other nations on equal terms. I am for a protection that leads to ultimate free trade. I am for that free trade which can only be achieved through a reasonable protection."

Rather than risking the success of American industries by lowering tariffs in the 1880s, Senator **Benjamin Harrison** wanted to spend the revenue on such matters as pension bills for soldiers and federal aid to education. In 1884 **Grover Cleveland** ran on a platform of a limited tariff to protect infant industries, the rights of workers to unionize, and restriction of Chinese immigration. The Republicans also favored a tariff and restrictions on Chinese.

One of the principal problems confronting the nation in **Benjamin Harrison's** time was the federal government's collection of excess revenue, which withdrew money from the private economy. At the 1888 Republican convention Congressman **William McKinley** drafted a high tariff protectionist platform in direct opposition to the Democrats led by **Grover Cleveland** who had began to move away from protectionism. In 1890 Congressman **McKinley** put forth a tariff bill revising rates and he paraphrased **Benjamin Harrison's** goals asserting that he and his cohorts "have not looked alone to a reduction, but have kept steadily in view the interests of our producing classes." In 1912 **Taft** ran as a protectionist. The coming of income tax in 1913 caused the tariff to recede somewhat as an issue. But in the 1920s in a symbolic move, the **Coolidge** administration put the image of Hamilton on the ten dollar bill. **Coolidge's** policies - high tariffs and promoting the interests of business were Hamiltonian. In 1993, the issue was revived in modern form when **George HW Bush**, **Carter** and **Ford** supported **Clinton** in the debate over the North American Free Trade Agreement (NAFTA) lowering trade barriers with Mexico and Canada.

In the run-up to World War I, **Warren Harding** criticized **Wilson's** preparedness as insufficient. **Theodore Roosevelt** sent a letter to **Harding** that read in part: "... I am certain that what you said is exactly true! We have invited war by our feeble, timid, shuffling course!" As war was declared and as **Wilson** said it was to "make the world safe for democracy," **Harding** said this in a Senate speech: "I want to say...that I am not voting for war in the name of democracy. I want to emphasize that fact for a moment, because much has been said upon that subject on the floor. It is my deliberate judgment that it is none of her business what type of government any nation on earth may choose to have;" He said he was supporting the war to protect American rights.

Wilson supported **Coolidge** in the Boston police strike in which Coolidge issued his famous statement to Samuel Gompers by telegram: "There is no right to strike against the public safety by anybody, anywhere, any time." **Wilson** characterized the strike as "a crime against civilization." Later that year, **Coolidge** was re-elected governor against an opponent who promised to reinstate the police. **Woodrow Wilson**: "I congratulate you upon your election as a victory for law and order. When that is the issue, all Americans must stand together." In the 1912 campaign **TR** said: "We cannot get better working conditions, shorter hours, the minimum wage for women, or general enforcement of employers' liability if we are to put into effect the vague ideas of Mr. **Wilson**. As to **Taft**, he is even less definite and offers not the shadow of a solution to the industrial problem." That same year **TR** read this from one of **Woodrow Wilson's** speeches of 1905: "The objection I have to labor unions is that they drag the highest man to the level of the lowest." In January of 1921 **Wilson** refused to pardon socialist Eugene Debs who had opposed US entry into World War I calling him "a traitor to his country." **Harding** commuted Debs' sentence in December of 1921. In 1925 **Taft** recommended to **Coolidge** to nominate Harlan Stone to the Supreme Court. He was an outstanding Justice and **FDR** elevated him to Chief Justice. Both **FDR** and **Truman** supported and were supported by the labor unions of their era but they did not always get along with their leaders. **Roosevelt** battled famously with United Mine Worker chief, John L Lewis. **Truman** privately referred to Lewis as a "son of a bitch." In 1947 **LBJ** voted for the Taft-Hartley Act and to override **Truman's** veto. **Truman** called the decision to go to war in Korea "the toughest decision I had to make as President." **LBJ**, then a senator, called **Truman's** decision to go to war as "inspired act of leadership [which] will be remembered as the finest moment of American maturity." In 1951 **Truman** fired General Douglas MacArthur commanding general of American forces in the Korean War for publicly questioning **Truman's** strategy. **Truman** reflected amidst the ensuing controversy that **Lincoln** had fired General George McClellan during the Civil war. By 1950 Senator Joseph McCarthy was a force in American politics recklessly attacking the **Truman** administration and even some Republicans for alleged communist sympathies. Some commentators think that **Truman** did not speak out sufficiently against McCarthy and **Truman** himself believed that **Eisenhower** was too reticent. **LBJ** believed that **Truman** was right to hold off, reasoning that McCarthy would eventually self-destruct. **Nixon**, for his part, told a press conference in 1950 that only the Communist Party was benefitting from McCarthy's unsubstantiated claims. By 1954 the United States Senate voted to condemn McCarthy with **JFK** the only Senator not voting due to a hospitalization. (He never revealed how he would have voted. His brother Robert had served on McCarthy's staff.)

During his time in office, **JFK's** people had talked about giving China a seat in the United Nations. **Richard Nixon** said that would "irreparably weaken" the rest of Asia, and **Eisenhower** warned that if any rapprochement began he would come out of retirement to oppose it. In 1971 **Nixon** appointed former Texas Governor John Connally to Secretary of the Treasury over the objections of Connally's in-state rival **George HW Bush.**

In 1976 **Carter** and **Ford** debated on live television, only the second time presidential debates took place - the first were the iconic **Kennedy-Nixon** debates of 1960. It was at a time of great US concern over the USSR and its military. In response to a question, **Ford** improbably said, "There is no Soviet domination of Eastern Europe and there never will be under a **Ford** administration." **Carter** went for the throat: "I would like to see Mr. **Ford** convince the Polish-Americans and the Czech-Americans and the Hungarian-Americans in this country that those countries don't live under the domination and supervision of the Soviet Union behind the Iron Curtain."

Truman had proposed health care for the aged as president. In 1965 as **Lyndon Johnson** proposed Medicare to make this a reality. **LBJ** signed the Medicare bill in the **Truman** library in Independence Missouri. **Truman** told him, "You have made me a very, very happy man." At the time, **Reagan** said that Medicare would "invade every area of freedom in this country." **Richard Nixon** said as president: "Comprehensive health insurance is an idea whose time has come in America. There has long been a need to assure every American financial access to high quality health care... Now, for the first time, we have not just the need but the will to get this job done. There is widespread support in the Congress and in the nation for some form of comprehensive health insurance." In 2009, **Barack Obama** enlisted **Theodore Roosevelt** in his campaign for increased governmental control of health care, claiming that **TR** "first called for reform nearly a century ago." In 2010 **Clinton** supported **Obama's** health care reform package.

In 1985, there was a significant controversy as **Reagan** was planning to visit a German cemetery that contained buried Nazis: The five year-old daughter of Arkansas Governor **Bill Clinton** wrote him: "I have seen the *Sound of Music*. The Nazis don't look like nice people. Please don't go to the cemetery."

As a candidate for president **Barack Obama** said that he opposed same-sex marriage for religious reasons although earlier in his career, while a churchgoing Christian and a state legislative candidate, he endorsed the right of gays and lesbians to marry. As he put it in an August 2008 presidential candidates' forum, "I believe that marriage is the union between a man and a woman. Now, for me as a Christian ... it is also a sacred union. God's in the mix." **Clinton** signed the Defense of Marriage Act as president but said in 2009 that he favored marriage rights for gays and lesbians. "I realized that I was over 60 years old, I grew up at a different time, and I was hung up about the word 'marriage' ...I was wrong.... If gay couples want to call their union marriage and a state agrees ... I don't think the rest of us should get in the way." In 2010 **Obama** said his "attitudes are evolving" toward gay marriage. In 2011 he came to support gay marriage.

We will cover the role of the military as a related separate area of presidential policy-making

The Role of the Military

Presidents have rallied the nation at times of war or crisis: In 1865 in his second inaugural **Lincoln** said of the Civil War then near an end: "Both parties deprecated war, but one of them would *make* war rather than let the nation survive, and the other would *accept* war rather than let it perish, and the war came." Here's **Wilson** in 1917: "...the right is more precious than peace, and we shall fight for the things which we have always carried nearest our hearts... God helping her, she can do no other." Here's **FDR** at the start of World War II in 1941: "With confidence in our armed forces - with the unbounding determination of our people - we will gain the inevitable triumph - so help us God." In 1948 the USSR cut-off West Berlin from the rest of Germany causing an East-West crisis. Americans were in West Berlin. **Truman's** staff presented him with recommendations that we could not counter the Soviets and with options for withdrawal. His response on June 28, 1948: "We stay in Berlin. Period." The Berlin Airlift resulted. Here's **Kennedy** at the Cuban Missile crisis in 1962: "Any hostile move anywhere in the world against the safety and freedom of peoples to whom we are committed-including in particular the brave people of West Berlin-will be met by whatever action is needed..... Our goal is not the victory of might but the vindication of right-not peace at the expense of freedom, but both peace and freedom, here in this hemisphere and, we hope, around the world. God willing, that goal will be achieved." The **Carter** Doctrine which the President announced in the wake of the 1979 Soviet invasion of Afghanistan held that any attempt by an external power to take control of the Persian Gulf Region would be seen as an attack on the vital interests of the US. Here is **George HW Bush** in 1991 at the beginning of the Iraq War: "This won't be another Vietnam."

As Commander in Chief, all of the Presidents have had to consider the role of the military. Many also offered thoughts on it before and after their presidencies.

In 1794 Senator **James Monroe** was disappointed by the failure of the US to confront England. He wrote **Jefferson**: "Thus you find nothing has been carried agnst. that nation, but on the contrary the most submissive measures adopted that cod. be devised, to court her favor and degrade our character."

In 1796 **Washington** said: "Twenty years peace combined with "our remote situation" would "enable us in a just cause, to bid defiance to any power on earth." **Adams** was anxious to avoid war while also building a Navy. In 1809 **Jefferson** updated **George Washington's** neutrality in a letter to **Monroe**: "If we can keep at peace eight years longer, our income will be adequate to any war...and our position, increasing strength put us *hors d"insulte* from any nation." **Jefferson:** "Whatever enables us to go to war, secures our peace." That same year the third President told his successor, **James Madison,** that he thought war with England could be avoided but also advised **Madison** in 1809 that "war however may become a less losing business than unresisted depredation."

(Two centuries later **Reagan** said that no war in his lifetime ever started because the US was too strong.)

Early in the War of 1812 state militias experienced serious losses on the battlefield to England's professional army. **Madison** wrote to **Monroe**: "Proofs multiply daily of the difficulty of obtaining regulars, and of the fluctuating resources in the militia. High bounties and short enlistments, however objectionable, will alone fill the ranks, and then too in a moderate number." **Monroe** initially opposed a draft. He informed **Madison** that the Secretary of War was lobbying for military conscription contrary to the President's policies. General **William Henry Harrison** sided with the President. In fact at a public dinner he had offered a toast to "THE MILITIA OF THE UNITED STATES." **Harrison** also said: "We must become a nation of warriors, or a nation of Quakers... No instance can be produced of a free people preserving their liberties who suffered the military spirit to decline amongst them."

As late as 1814 after the burning of Washington, **Jefferson** still held for militias instead of a regular army. He wrote Secretary of War **Monroe**: "We must prepare for interminable war. To this end we should put our house in order by providing men and money to an indefinite extent. The former may be done by classing our militia, and assigning each class to the description of duties for which it is fit. It is nonsense to talk of regulars. They are not to be had among a people so easy and happy at home as ours. We might as well rely on calling down an army of angels from heaven." **Monroe** ignored this advice and sought a significant increase in the regular army and even came to recommend a draft. He did so in late 1814 realizing that England was freed up to concentrate on an invasion of America by the defeat of Napoleon. He used the broad-construction reasoning that Alexander Hamilton once used in justifying a National Bank. **Monroe** argued that the constitutional power to raise armies was broad enough to encompass a draft. The war ended before a draft was instituted.

Due to the slowness of early nineteenth century communications, the Battle of New Orleans in early 1815 took place two-weeks after the war-ending Treaty of Ghent. However it had a great deal to do with how the Treaty was interpreted. England along with most countries did not recognize the Louisiana Purchase since by treaty France was obligated to offer to return the territory to Spain before selling it which it did not do. **Monroe** told **Madison** that if **Jackson** had lost the battle, England would have been tempted to offer to

Spain to return the land of the Purchase. The Battle also sealed the fate of the Indians in the region. By the Treaty of Fort Jackson in 1814 which **Jackson** imposed on Creek chiefs the US acquired 23 million acres - most of present-day Alabama and about 20 percent of Mississippi. By the Treaty of Ghent the US agreed to restore lands taken from the Indians during the war. Under pressure from England the **Madison** administration conveyed to **Jackson** in the South: "The President...is confident that you will...conciliate the Indians upon the principles of our agreement with Great Britain." **Jackson** ignored this directive and with the British gone and the US government unwilling, there was no force to make him do so.

Arthur began to add to a decimated Navy although his program was narrow compared to **TR's** later approach. As Assistant Secretary of the Navy in the 1890s, **TR** scorned **Jefferson** for not building a strong navy that might have prevented the War of 1812 but instead relying on defensive gunboats. He favorably quoted **George Washington** that "to be prepared for war is the most effectual means to promote peace." He wrote a history of the US Navy and advocated more ships, quoting Presidents **Washington**, **Jackson**, **Lincoln** and **Grant**.

TR on May 5, 1910 gave a postponed Nobel Lecture for his 1906 prize: "Peace is generally good in itself, but it is never the highest good unless it comes as the handmaiden of righteousness; and it becomes a very evil thing if it serves merely as a mask for cowardness and sloth, or as an instrument to further the end of despotism or anarchy." Andrew Carnegie who had hoped that as an ex-president and world figure **Roosevelt** would be an advocate for peace gave up on **TR** in disgust after that speech. Mark Twain said about **TR** that he was "clearly insane...and insanest upon war and its supreme glories."

In 1918 **Wilson** called for the congressional elections to be seen as a vote of confidence for his leadership particularly in finishing the war and shaping the postwar world. The voters however turned both houses of Congress to the Republicans the week before armistice. **Theodore Roosevelt** then wrote French premier

Georges Clemenceau and British foreign secretary Arthur Balfour: "He demanded a vote of confidence. The people voted a want of confidence." He added that the Republicans were in favor of "the unconditional surrender of Germany and for absolute loyalty to France and England in the peace negotiations." In 1919 when **Wilson** returned from Europe with the treaty calling for the League of Nations he landed to enthusiastic crowds in Boston. **Calvin Coolidge** said that he was "feeling sure the people would back the President." **Harding** opposed **Wilson** on the League of Nations: "My own judgment is that President **Wilson** is such a bullhead that he will have no hesitancy in risking ruin of this country to carry his points in Paris." **Hoover** favored ratification of the Versailles treaty including establishment of the League of Nations. By the 1920 election, however, **Hoover** implausibly said that voting for **Harding** was to support the League and that the **Wilson** administration was "in the main reactionary." **Wilson** said **Hoover** was "no friend." By then **Wilson** had come to distrust **Hoover**: "I have the feeling that he would rather see a good cause fail than succeed if he were not the head of it."

Taft also supported **Wilson's** proposal for the League of Nations although **TR** had opposed it. **Taft** however urged **Wilson** to make certain amendments to the proposed charter. **Taft** favored international arbitration more than **TR** did. In 1923 **Coolidge** favored US entrance into the World Court as had **Harding** and **Taft. Coolidge's** recommendation had an anti-League reservation. **TR** resented **Wilson** for apologizing for our role in Panama and in getting Congress to provide compensation.

In 1937 **FDR** asked Member of Congress **LBJ** to join the House Naval Affairs Committee where he advocated for money for a two-ocean Navy. In 1941 **Roosevelt** got **Johnson** to run for the Senate as a war-preparedness candidate. Although he lost, people remembered his campaign statement, "It is later than you think." When **FDR** instituted the draft in 1940 he said that if **Lincoln** had started the draft earlier, the Civil War would have been done by 1862. **Hoover** supported the isolationist America First Committee which formed in September, 1940 after France fell. **JFK** sent a $100 check to the Committee and **Ford** who was then a college student supported it and signed a statement that he would never go to war. **Reagan** was also a pacifist in college.

FDR had worked with Winston Churchill in launching the Manhattan Project leading to the development of the atomic bomb. In 1945 after V-E Day, **Eisenhower** recommended to **Truman** against using it against Japan. However, **Truman's** ultimate decision was noncontroversial at the time. It was largely motivated by the desire to spare American soldiers. **Hoover** had cautioned **Truman** that an invasion of Japan could result in the loss of between half a million and a million American lives. (Of note, however, **Hoover** wrote in a book only published in 2011 about "...**Truman's** immoral order to drop the atomic bomb on the Japanese. Not only had Japan been repeatedly suing for peace, but it was the act of unparalleled brutality in all American history. It will forever weigh heavily on the American conscience.")

In 1947 as Army Chief of Staff **Eisenhower** felt **Truman's** commitment to Greece was too open-ended. He urged that support for threatened countries should be more social and economic and less military. **Eisenhower** was a supporter of the Marshall Plan. In December 1951 **Truman** sent a handwritten note to **Eisenhower** in Paris at NATO that he would like to retire but that he wanted to keep the isolationists out of the presidency and he wanted to know **Eisenhower's** intentions. **Eisenhower's** reply took two weeks to reply and was noncommittal.

In 1956 the Soviets brutally put down a revolt in Hungary and refugees streamed into Austria. **Nixon** visited them and sought council from **Herbert Hoover**, renowned for his relief efforts in World War I. **Hoover** suggested sending agricultural surpluses. **Nixon** even with the support of **Eisenhower** could not win congressional approval.

Decrying the arms race in 1953, President **Dwight Eisenhower** said, "This is no way of life at all...Under the cloud of threatening war, it is humanity hanging from a cross of iron." Of note: in 1955 **Eisenhower** was asked at a press conference whether he would consider the use of atomic weapons in a far eastern war. His response: "Yes, of course they would be used." On March 16, 1955, President **Eisenhower** was asked at a press conference, "Would the United States use tactical nuclear weapons in a general war in Asia? **Ike** answered: "I see no reason why they shouldn't be used just exactly as you would use a bullet or anything else." The context was his desire to protect Taiwan from the Communist Chinese and in his memoirs years later said that he wanted to exhibit to the Chinese "the strength of our determination." Moreover, at the same press conference he added: "I believe the great question about these things comes when you begin to get into those areas where you cannot make sure you are operating merely against military targets." At a planning meeting in 1958 in the context of military budget requests that he thought were too high, **Eisenhower** said: "How many times do we need to calculate that we need to destroy the Soviet Union?"

In the late 1950s **LBJ** who as Senate Majority Leader was generally supportive of **Eisenhower** focused on failure in the space program and pushed for the creation of the National Aeronautics and Space Administration or NASA. **Johnson** had concern for the military race against the USSR.

By 1959 **Eisenhower** thought the defense industry created an artificial demand for missiles and bombers. At that time he had also been lobbied by Congressman **Gerald Ford** for a contract for a Michigan firm which was in the missile business. **Eisenhower** later recommended to **Kennedy** to withdraw troops from Europe and let Europeans take responsibility for their defense.

In 1959 Vice President **Richard Nixon** engaged in an impromptu "kitchen debate" with Soviet premier Nikita Khrushchev in Moscow. **Ronald Reagan** wrote **Nixon** that **Nixon** had told the Soviets "truths seldom if ever uttered in diplomatic exchanges." **JFK** criticized both **Eisenhower** and **Nixon** as soft on communism.

In the 1960 Campaign, **JFK** appeared to have knowledge of the planning for the invasion of Cuba. He pushed hard for help to the Cuban exiles in the campaign. **Nixon** was forced to protect the secrecy of the planning and in the debate said that **Kennedy's** proposal was "probably the most dangerously irresponsible recommendation that he's made during the course of this campaign." He said such an approach would violate treaties. **Nixon** received praise from the liberal press. **JFK** could have received his information from the CIA. In his post-presidential memoir *RN* **Nixon** wrote that **JFK's** statements on Cuba "jeopardized the project, which could succeed only if it were supported and implemented secretly...I had no choice but to take a completely opposite stand and attack **Kennedy's** advocacy of open intervention in Cuba."

In 1961 **JFK** said at the UN: "Every nation today should know; be he friend or foe, that the United States has both the will and the weapons to join free men in standing up to their responsibilities."

Eisenhower tried to distance himself from responsibility for **JFK's** actions at the Bay of Pigs in 1961 but he advised **Kennedy** after the disaster. Others have noted that there were four interrelated events in the first year of **JFK's** administration:

- US humiliation at the Bay of Pigs.
- Khrushchev's bullying of **JFK** in Austria six weeks later.
- Building of the Berlin Wall.
- **JFK** sending Green Berets to Vietnam explaining privately that "we have a problem making our power credible, and Vietnam looks like the place."

The Cuban Missile Crisis of 1962 was one of the most tense stand-offs of the Cold War. A US Air Force U-2 plane obtained photographic proof that Soviet engineers were installing missile bases in Cuba. During the crisis, Vice President **Lyndon Johnson** urged military attacks on Cuba. **JFK** ended up following his brother Robert Kennedy's advice and forced the Soviets to remove the bases through diplomacy and a naval blockade. As the crisis defused after a tense two-week period, **JFK** called the three living ex-presidents - **Hoover**, **Truman** and **Eisenhower** – all of whom congratulated him.

After South Viet Nam President Ngo Dinh Diem was assassinated in 1963 following a coup, there was speculation that the CIA was involved. **Eisenhower** wrote **Nixon**: "I rather suspect the Diem affair will be shrouded in mystery for a long time to come. No matter how much the administration may have differed with him, I cannot believe any American would have approved the cold-blooded killing of a man who had, after all, shown great courage when he undertook the task some years ago of defeating Communist's attempts to take over his country." Later, as president, **Lyndon Johnson** said that this coup was sanctioned by **Kennedy** and was the greatest mistake the US made in the entire Vietnam War. **Nixon** also believed that **JFK** had played a crucial role in the overthrow and assassination of Diem and that that had been a point after which more US involvement was required.

Nixon however cited **JFK** for his own Vietnam policy, saying in a 1969 speech: "In 1963, President **Kennedy**, with his characteristic eloquence and clarity, said: 'We want to see a stable government there, carrying on a struggle to maintain its national independence. We believe strongly in that. We are not going to withdraw from that effort. In my opinion, for us to withdraw from that effort would mean a collapse not only of South Vietnam, but Southeast Asia. So we are going to stay there.'"

Eisenhower privately thought that **JFK's** challenge to the USSR to race to the Moon was a mistake thinking it put American prestige on the line and elevated a single effort at the expense of a coherent space program and added costs. He saw it as a knee-jerk reaction to the Bay of Pigs disaster. **Eisenhower** was disgusted that **JFK** did not react forcibly to the building of the Berlin Wall. In April 1963 **Nixon** criticized **JFK** for limiting Cuban exile raids against Cuba: "The United States cannot tolerate the continued existence of a Soviet military and subversive base 90 miles from our shores."

In 1963, **JFK** stood at the Berlin wall and said: "*Ich bin ein Berliner.*" In 1987, **Reagan** said, "Mr. Gorbachev, Tear down this wall." It fell in 1989. In 2008 **Barack Obama** as a candidate stood at the Berlin Wall and said of 1989, "A wall came down, a continent came together, and history proved that there is no challenge too great for a world that stands as one." In 2009 **Obama** spurned German chancellor

Angela Merkel's invitation to attend to twentieth anniversary of the fall of the wall.

In 1964 **LBJ** asked **Eisenhower** for support for military appropriations. **Eisenhower** called Congressman **Gerald Ford** and said: "I can remember **LBJ** whimpering and crying that Senator George was defeated because of his support for Mutual Security and he was afraid he would be too when I asked his support." In the 1964 election, through spies set up by future Watergate figure E. Howard Hunt, **LBJ** learned that Republican nominee Barry Goldwater's team was considering a promise to send **Eisenhower** to Vietnam to try for peace if Goldwater won the election in an echo of **Ike's** similar promise with regard to Korea when he ran for president in 1952. **LBJ** called **Eisenhower**: "You don't have to wait for Senator Goldwater to get elected in order to go to Vietnam. I've got a Boeing 707 all warmed up and waiting at Andrews Air Base and I'll send a helicopter after you any time you care to go." **Ike** did know what **LBJ** was talking about as the Goldwater camp had not contacted him.

In the Congress in 1965 **Ford** expressed concern about **LBJ's** build-up in Vietnam but ultimately went along with it to the point that he called for a declaration of war. In this **Ford** was opposed by out-of-office **Richard Nixon** who thought it might increase the likelihood of USSR and Chinese intervention. As a member of Congress elected in 1966, **George HW Bush** supported **LBJ's** commitment in Vietnam. In 1967 **Lyndon Johnson** sought a tax increase due to the costs of the Vietnam War and he was opposed in the House of Representatives by the Republicans. **Johnson** complained: "**Jerry Ford** and his group ...are not going to lose any sleep if we have a $40 billion deficit."

According to **LBJ** writing in 1971: **Ike** told him in 1964, "We could not let the Indochina peninsula fall." In mid-1965 **LBJ** was considering insertion of more troops into South Vietnam. **Ike** advised him: "When you go into a place to hold sections or enclaves you are paying the price and not winning. When you once appeal to force in an international situation involving military help for a nation, you have to go all out! This is war, and as long as [the North Vietnamese] are putting them down there, my advice is 'do what you have to do!'" In 1966 two **LBJ** officials, Secretary of Defense Robert McNamara and his deputy Cyrus Vance visited **Eisenhower** at the hospital where the former president was recovering from a heart attack. **Ike** said: "Why don't you declare war? Take Hanoi." They didn't know what to say. **Eisenhower's** son recalled that "Those two turned blue and got out of there."

In 1967 **Lyndon Johnson** told **Gerald Ford** that an October 21 anti-war march on the Pentagon was "basically organized by international Communism." **Ford** announced this in Congress and asked **Johnson** to provide supporting evidence. **Johnson** demurred. He allowed his Secretary of State to tell a news magazine that he was concerned about causing a new "wave of McCarthyism."

In 1972 **Nixon** made an historic trip to China. Chinese Premier Chou En-lai told him that **Truman** provoked Chinese involvement in the Korean War. **Nixon** later told congressional leaders that if **Truman** had met with the Chinese twenty-five years earlier the Korean War might have been averted.

As president, **Carter** opined that **Eisenhower** had had a "passive" foreign policy.

In 1982 **Reagan** talked with his staff on nuclear weapons and how to approach the Soviets: "It's too bad we cannot do ...what **Ike** proposed on all nuclear weapons. First, we need to restore the balance." **Reagan** was alluding to a UN speech by **Eisenhower** on December 8, 1953 where he called for the abolishment of all nuclear weapons. **Reagan** in 1983: "A nuclear war cannot be won and must never be fought."

On the anniversary of **JFK's** murder in 1982, **Reagan** said: "[T]he 1970s were marked by neglect of our defenses... Too many forgot **John Kennedy's** warning that only when our arms are certain beyond doubt can we be certain beyond doubt they will never be used." At about that same time **Reagan** commented on **JFK's** 1940 book, *Why England Slept*: "Even after war broke out in Asia and in Europe, our own country was slow to take the steps necessary to defend itself. Warning us of the impending crisis, a young Harvard student, **John Fitzgerald Kennedy**, wrote a book titled *Why England Slept*. His thoughtful study holds as true now, forty-two years later, as when it was first published."

In 1947 President **Harry S. Truman** told a joint session of Congress that it was "the policy of the United States to support free people who are resisting attempted subjugation by armed minorities or by outside pressures." Congressmen **John Fitzgerald Kennedy** (age 30), **Lyndon Baines Johnson** (age 39) and **Richard Milhous Nixon** (age 34) were in the audience. This came to be called the **Truman** Doctrine and it held that the US would contain communism. Later the **Nixon** Doctrine was to support friendly countries to help them from going communist. Still later, the **Reagan** Doctrine involved military and other support for people trying to throw off communism. Its examples were Poland, Afghanistan, and Angola.

In 1983 **Reagan** made a speech in which he famously called the USSR the "evil empire." **Richard Nixon** disagreed and said off-the-record: "You don't humiliate your opponent in public like that." Yet when he took office in 1989 **George HW Bush** was concerned that **Reagan** had tilted *too far* in favor of Soviet Premier Mikhail Gorbachev the last head of state of the Soviet Union until its collapse. However, after an uprising in China led to a government crackdown there in Tiananmen Square, **Bush** reached out more to Gorbachev. Events then outpaced both men. With the fall of the Berlin Wall in 1989, **Bush** quietly stood for German reunification against the caution of Mikhail Gorbachev and British Prime Minister Margaret Thatcher. He told **Nixon** that his preparation for the first summit with Gorbachev in Malta was to "brief, brief, brief." At one point in 1990 **Nixon** said that **George HW Bush** was repeating **Reagan's** mistake of believing that Mikhail Gorbachev's political survival in the USSR was linked to US interests.

The fall of Communism, tracing from the presidency of **Ronald Reagan** was a tumultuous time. In 1991, **Nixon** summed it up: "**Ronald Reagan** has been justified by what has happened. History has justified his leadership."

In 1990 under Saddam Hussein, Iraq invaded neighboring Kuwait. The US Congress approved **George HW Bush's** proposal to go to war to reverse the occupation. However, **Carter** was opposed to the use of force. He wrote a letter to the heads of state of members of the United Nations Security Council and several other governments urging them to oppose the American request for UN authorization of military action. **Clinton** was then governor of Arkansas. Later as a candidate for president he was asked how he would have voted if he had been in Congress. His response: "I guess I would have voted with the majority if it was a close vote. But I agree with the arguments the minority made."

In 1991 after the air war against Iraq had started, Mikhail Gorbachev asked **George HW Bush** to suspend bombing to allow for diplomacy. **Bush** recalling that **LBJ's** bombing pauses in the Vietnam War allowed the Communists to regroup declined.

The International Atomic Energy Agency (IAEA) discovered in 1992-93 that communist North Korea was not complying with its regulations. North Korea responded by announcing that it would withdraw from the Nuclear Non-proliferation Treaty (NPT) in 1993. The **Clinton** administration was faced with a very difficult issue. It was reluctant to impose sanctions because North Korea said it would regard those as an act of war. But **Clinton** said: "North Korea cannot be allowed to develop a nuclear bomb." In 1994 North Korea began threatening to build nuclear weapons. **Jimmy Carter** by then out of office nearly fifteen years went to North Korea to negotiate "with the approval of President **Bill Clinton**." However, even though **Clinton** asserted that all options were on the table including a military response, **Carter** unilaterally promised that even economic sanctions would not be forthcoming. When asked about this discrepancy, **Clinton** told reporters, "None of us have talked directly with President **Carter**. We don't know what he said." For his part, **Carter** found the shops in North Korea's capital to be similar to the "Wal-Mart in Americus, Georgia" and the neon lights reminded him of Times Square. He said the people were "friendly and open" and the government reflected the popular will, which he imagined to be "homogeneous."

Carter negotiated what became the 1994 Agreed Framework. In that agreement the US helped North Korea finance two light-water nuclear reactors and agreed to deliver fuel to them. In return, the North Koreans were to stay in the NPT, freeze and eventually dismantle its nuclear program, allow inspections and fully account for its weapons.

Carter called his accomplishment of the Agreed Framework a "miracle." But questions about his involvement and effectiveness surfaced. Historian Douglas Brinkley, a **Carter** admirer, claimed that one **Clinton** Cabinet member called him a "treasonous prick." In 1995 in a private interview **Ford** said that **Clinton** was angry that **Carter** had put himself into the negotiations in North Korea. He added: "I think he injected himself in the North Korea negotiations unwisely. The White House was very upset, I can tell you that." **Carter's** Agreed Framework was a failure and a dangerous one. In October, 2002, the North Koreans admitted to a uranium enrichment program and in 2006 North Korea tested a nuclear device. **Carter** later claimed that North Korea build nuclear weapons because **George W Bush** labeled it as part of the "Axis of Evil."

In the immediate aftermath of the 9/11 attacks, **Clinton** urged his wife, Senator Hillary Clinton, to make a bold statement. The next day in the Senate she said that any country that chose to harbor terrorists and "in any way aid or comfort them whatsoever will now face the wrath of our country." **Bush** admired this rhetoric and used a close variation before Congress several days later. In 2002-03 **Bill Clinton** was his wife's main counsel on the Iraq war vote in which she supported **Bush's** position.

In 2009 **Obama** quoted **Eisenhower** on "the need to maintain balance in and among national programs" as he announced a troop escalation in Afghanistan. That same year **Obama** won the Nobel Peace Price. This is from his speech in Oslo on December 10, 2009:

"We must begin by acknowledging the hard truth that we will not eradicate violent conflict in our lifetimes. There will be times when nations -- acting individually or in concert -- will find the use of force not only necessary but morally justified.

"I make this statement mindful of what Martin Luther King said in this same ceremony years ago: 'Violence never brings permanent peace. It solves no social problem: it merely creates new and more complicated ones.' As someone who stands here as a direct consequence of Dr. King's life's work, I am living testimony to the moral force of nonviolence. I know there is nothing weak -- nothing passive -- nothing naive -- in the creed and lives of Gandhi and King. But as a head of state sworn to protect and defend my nation, I cannot be guided by their examples alone. I face the world as it is, and cannot stand idle in the face of threats to the American people. For make no mistake: Evil does exist in the world. A nonviolent movement could not have halted Hitler's armies. Negotiations cannot convince al Qaeda's leaders to lay down their arms. To say that force is sometimes necessary is not a call to cynicism -- it is a recognition of history; the imperfections of man and the limits of reason."

In 2013 war with was Syria a possibility. Former President **George W. Bush** said that **Obama** had "a tough choice to make. And if he decides to use our military he'll have the greatest military ever backing him up."

The United States has the closest relationship of any country to Israel and this relationship has military ramifications. The presidents have interacted with each other on this matter as well. The Blackstone Memorial – a petition in favor of Jewish national home in Palestine - was signed by **William McKinley** and about 400 others and sent to **Benjamin Harrison** in 1891. This began a path that led to **Truman's** recognition of Israel in 1948.

President **George W Bush** said of Palestinian leader Yasser Arafat in 2002 or 2003 when he realized that Arafat had personally lied about a shipment of explosives from Iran: "You can't make a peace deal with that guy. He screwed President **Clinton**." **Carter** disagreed. In retirement he wrote: "When I met with Yasser Arafat in 1990, he stated 'the PLO has never advocated the annihilation of Israel. The Zionists started the "drive the Jews into the sea" slogan and attributed it to the PLO.'" **Carter** quoted this statement without qualification as though it should be taken as the simple truth. In fact, of course, the covenant of the Palestine Liberation Organization views Israel as illegitimate. Specifically, Article 19 holds that "The partitioning of Palestine in 1947 and the establishment of Israel are fundamentally null and void." **Carter** said Arafat was a "misunderstood" figure.

What is the point of all this?

The presidency is an institution. Decisions live on. For example,

Jackson's decision to reverse the Indian policies of **Monroe** and **John Quincy Adams** and forcibly remove the Cherokee tribe from the State of Georgia set Indian policy for the future. **Polk's** decision to rebut British claims to the Columbia River forever shaped the American Northwest. **Truman's** decisions to drop atom bombs on Japan, then decline to use atomic weapons in Korea and to recognize Israel have all helped shape other presidencies. By 2010 **Obama** who promoted to the presidency mostly by his criticism of **George W Bush's** handling of the Iraq War was fighting in Afghanistan using **Bush's** Secretary of Defense and **Bush's** key general and **Bush's** strategy.

Presidents by the design of our system frequently take over projects begun by other Presidents and respond to some of the same issues in turn affecting future presidents. In 1852 **Millard Fillmore** sent Commodore Matthew Perry to Japan to open trade relations and wrote a letter to the emperor carefully wrapped for delivery. The mission was completed under **Franklin Pierce**. As Assistant Secretary of the Navy in 1898, **TR** wrote his superior about a "flying machine" he had witnessed along the Potomac River near Washington DC. He recommended further study for military purposes. "The machine worked. It seems to me worth while for this government to try whether it will not work on a large enough scale to be of use in the event of war." **JFK** committed to landing an American on the moon in the 1960s which we did in 1969. In 2004 when **George W Bush** proposed to phase out the space shuttle, phase down the space station, establish a moon base, and then eventually go on to Mars, he was met with ridicule. In 2010 President **Obama** on NASA and the future: "We'll start by sending astronauts to as asteroid for the first time in history. By the mid-2030s, I believe we can send humans to orbit Mars and return them safely to Earth. And a landing on Mars will follow. And I expect to be around to see it."

Certainly presidents get credit for things that other presidents started. **Thomas Jefferson** is known throughout the world as the author of the Declaration of Independence. **John Adams** saw the beginning of this and gave this counter-view: "Was there ever a Coup de Theatre that had so great an effect as **Jefferson**'s Penmanship of the Declaration of Independence?" It would be fair to say that **Adams** had a hand in the project – just as **Truman** finished the Second World War and **Nixon** got us to the moon even though history mostly credits **Franklin Roosevelt** and **Kennedy** with those accomplishments.

Here is a final example of an issue of presidents carrying forth the policies of other presidents: the Panama Canal.

Jefferson may have discussed the idea of an isthmus canal with a traveler in 1804 and had shown an interest in it when he was a minister to France. As steam ships came into being in **Fillmore's** time, Americans looked for more convenient travel from the east coast to the Pacific. The Clayton-Bulwer Treaty with England guaranteed a neutral canal with the American hope that the British would evacuate San Juan Island, an island on the Atlantic side of the Canal that the British had taken recently, supposedly to protect the Mosquito Indians. **Fillmore** said, "It is to be hoped that the guarantees which (the treaty offered would be) sufficient to secure the completion of the work..." The British, however, didn't leave and thus digging didn't start. Ultimately **Fillmore's** patient diplomacy composed matters with England but Nicaraguan revolutionaries quashed the canal plan.

Both **Grant** and **Garfield** expressed interest in building an isthmus canal. At the end of his term **Arthur** concluded a treaty with Nicaragua for a canal. In 1891 **Benjamin Harrison** was willing to devote federal money for a canal across Central America which he thought of "transcendent importance to the commerce of this country, and, indeed, to the commercial interests of the world" but Congress did not act. After **Theodore Roosevelt** helped foment revolution in the area of the canal leading to American construction of it, **Taft** went to Panama five times as **TR's** Secretary of War to assess the construction and to resolve certain issues with the new Republic of Panama such as postal rates and tariffs for Panamanian goods brought into the Canal Zone. In 1964 when riots broke out in Panama over US control in the Canal Zone, a friend advised **LBJ** that somebody has "got to play the part of ole **Andrew Jackson**." In the 1976 presidential primaries **Ford** said **Reagan's** position against the Panama Canal negotiations could eventually cause "guerilla war." In 1977 **Carter** concluded the treaties with Panama ceding control of the canal to that country after 1999. In 1989 **George HW Bush** invaded Panama to depose the president who spent the next twenty years in an American prison for drug trafficking and other crimes. In 1999 under President **Clinton** the US turned control of the Canal over to Panama.

There is another issue far greater than the Panama Canal, tariffs or even war in the American experience. In the next chapter we will see how the forty-three presidents have interacted on religion.

Chapter 9

Religion

Overall context

Most if not all of our presidents have believed in God or some sort of Destiny. When faced with challenges to the New Deal in 1936 **FDR** had an aide provide him with this **Lincoln** quote: "I do the very best I know – the very best I can; and I mean to keep on doing so until the end. If the end brings me out all right, what is said against me won't amount to anything. If the end brings me out wrong, 10,000 angels swearing I was right would make no difference."

John Adams to **John Quincy Adams** on the eve of the 1796 election: "I look upon the Event as the throw of a Die, a mere Chance, a miserable, meager tryumph to either Party." **Grant**, traveling in Germany after his presidency, received praise for saving the Union during the war and responded: "There are many men who would have done far better than I did under the circumstances in which I found myself during the war. If I had never held command; If I had fallen; If all our generals had fallen, there were ten thousand behind us who would have done our work just as well..." In 1920 after he was nominated to run for vice president, **Coolidge** was told by a friend, "All the country is talking about you today, **Calvin.**" **Coolidge** responded, "Are they? Well, by tomorrow they'll have found something else to talk about." Later, **Coolidge** as president said: "I am in the clutch of forces that are greater than I am." **Truman:** "I am just an ordinary American citizen but I am also President of the United States. There may be a million other Americans who could hold this office as well as I, but I am holding it and I intend to fill it to the best of my capacity." **Eisenhower** had a saying that he had taken from his mother: "The Lord deals the cards. You play them." **Barack Obama** told a Catholic priest in Chicago in 2005: "I really believe that my plan in life is to be president of United States, and that God has called me to go now."

The forty-three presidents have for the most part been men of religious temperament. In some instances there is evidence of deep reflection: **Jefferson:** "I have sometimes asked myself whether my country is the better for my having lived at all? I do not know that it is. I have been the instrument of doing the following things; but they would have been done by others; some of them, perhaps, a little better." **Lincoln**, according to his wife believed "what is to be will be, and no prayers of our can reverse the decree." Sometimes their thoughts were more casual. During **Lincoln's** time many Americans were fascinated by Spiritualism, a notion that humans could contact the dead. While **Lincoln** was in office Robert Dale Owen a famous spiritualist once read a paper at the White House. **Lincoln** was later asked about the presentation and gave this classic response: "Well, for those who like that sort of thing, I should think it is just about the sort of thing they would like." (When his wife tried to communicate to their dead son through a medium **Lincoln** did not prevent the séances and may even have attended.)

Polk did not join a church until late in life. **Taylor**, **Andrew Johnson**, **Lincoln** and **Hayes** never did. **Fillmore** and **Taft** were Unitarians. **Jefferson** was a figure of the Enlightenment. **Polk, Pierce** and **Grant** were baptized after the presidency. **Eisenhower** was baptized as he began the presidency as he said "to set an example." **Reagan** didn't go to church as president but drew great support from evangelical Christians.

So what have our presidents believed? A few have been evangelicals. More stood for some form of Christian monotheism, hoped for an afterlife and made concrete policies for religious liberty.

Moving forward

In 1830 **Madison** assessed **Washington's** religious attitudes saying that he didn't think **Washington** had opinions on the arguments for Christianity or the different systems of religion. "But he took things as he found them existing, and was constant in his observations of worship according to the received forms of the Episcopal Church in which he was brought up."

George Washington often referred to God in philosophical terms. He called God, the "great Searcher of human hearts." In his inaugural address, he described God as "that Almighty Being who rules over the universe, who presides in the councils of nations, and whose providential aids can supply every human defect." Later he employed the terms the "Great Arbiter of the Universe" and "the Supreme Ruler of Nations." One rare mention of Jesus was along this line as he called him "the Divine Author of our blessed Religion." He had an idea about sin, however. In a letter to John Jay in 1786 **Washington** wrote; "We must take human nature as we find it, perfection falls not to the share of mortals."

John Adams saw the Christianity of his young-adult period in the 1760s as burdened with "the whole cartloads of trumpery, that we find Religion encumbered with in these Days."

In the election of 1800 **Thomas Jefferson** was excoriated by his political enemies for supposed unorthodox religious views. His party responded that **Jefferson** was a champion of religious liberty. He was portrayed as standing for "the equal brotherhood of the Moravian, the Mennonist, and the Dunker." His supporters said that he "does not think that a Catholic should be banished for believing in transubstantiation or a Jew from believing in the God of Abraham, Isaac and Jacob." **John Adams** was reportedly also distressed by the attacks on **Jefferson** and was quoted as saying: "What does that have to do with the public?"

Jefferson believed in a Creator but wrote in 1790 that he trusted in "the sufficiency of human wisdom for the care of human affairs." **Jefferson** wrote to the famous physician Benjamin Rush that "I am a Christian in the only sense that (Jesus) wished any one to be; sincerely attached to his doctrines, in preference to all others; ascribing to himself every *human* excellence; and believing he never claimed any other." (Italics in the original)

When they resumed their relationship through letters in the last decade of their lives, **John Adams** and **Jefferson** ruminated frequently on religion. **Jefferson** had no patience with the theological arguments and the violence attending them. He wrote to **Adams**: "It is too late in the day for men of sincerity to pretend they believe in the Platonic mysticisms that three are one, and one is three; and yet that the one is not three, and the three are not one....But this constitutes the craft, the power, and the profit of the priests." **Adams,** who was more or less in agreement, once wrote to **Jefferson** about a pamphlet that he had heard about from Virginia that predicted the apocalypse for June of 1812. **Adams** wondered at the continuing popularity of doomsday predictors despite the "continual refutation of all their prognostications by time and experience."

The second and third Presidents' view of Christianity was quite simple, anticipating the doctrines of liberal Christianity that came to the forefront later in the nineteenth century. In 1816 **Adams** wrote **Jefferson** that "The Ten Commandments and the Sermon on the Mount contain my religion." Almost ten years later **Adams** closed a letter to **Jefferson** on the subject of free inquiry by this: "The substance and essence of Christianity, as I understand it, is eternal and unchangeable, and will bear examination forever, but it has been mixed with extraneous ingredients, which I think will not bear examination, and they ought to be separated. Adieu." On this they were very much on the same page. **Jefferson**, while president, researched the gospels to try to identify only the sayings that Jesus could have said, which he described in an 1813 letter to **Adams** "as distinguishable as diamonds in a dunghill." **Jefferson** told a nephew: "Question with boldness even the existence of God; because, if there be one, he must more approve the homage of reason, than that of blindfolded fear." As an ambassador to France in the later 1780s **Jefferson** had collected about sixty paintings. Many of these had religious themes. Some were: "Prodigal Son", "St. Peter Weeping", Magdalen Penitent", "Herodias Bearing the Head of John the Baptist."

In an uninspiring war message in 1812 **James Madison** called on Congress to "commit a just cause into the hands of the Almighty

Disposer of events." **Madison**, in a lukewarm call for prayer during the war, called God, the "Sovereign of the Universe" and the "Benefactor of Mankind."

As a Senator, **John Quincy Adams** was quite composed at the time of a recall vote having his confidence in God, whom he called "the Disposer of Events." **Madison** then sent **Adams** abroad as a diplomat. He wrote a number of exhorting religious letters from Russia to his eldest son. These letters were published thirty-five years later. He said he was a Christian and believed in life after death. "If the existence of man were limited to this life, it would be impossible for me to believe the universe made any moral sense." As seen above, his father felt the same way and **Jefferson** also looked forward to another life or said he did. **John Quincy Adams** was also content, with respect to evil people to be patient with "the delays of divine justice." (Apparently so was **Herbert Hoover** a century or so later. When **Hoover** was President in 1929 his wife was criticized in the southern press and elsewhere for inviting a black woman to an official White House function. The woman was the wife of a congressman. **Hoover** told his wife that one of the advantages of being an orthodox Christian was "that it included a hot hell" adding that her critics would find "special facilities in the world to come.")

In about 1815, **John Adams** tried to debate infallibility of the Bible by letter with **John Quincy Adams** the US Ambassador in London. The younger **Adams** protested that he had not thoroughly studied scripture and replied that he preferred to rely on faith: "I am not called upon to be its judge." However, his father drew him in and **John Quincy Adams** wrote that he cautiously supported Calvinism and Trinitarians but "I do not approve of their intolerance." He said he opposed Unitarianism whose leaders ranked Socrates with Jesus. **John Quincy Adams** said that was like comparing "a farthing candle with the sun." He joked to **John Adams** that "I hope you will not think me in danger of perishing everlastingly, for believing too much."

In 1816 **Jefferson** wrote to **Adams**: "It is a good world on the whole." But with age they began to think about a life after this one. **Jefferson** wrote **Adams** that after death the "essence" of the individual will "ascend to an ecstatic meeting with the friends we have loved and lost and shall love and never lose again." In 1823 **Jefferson** wrote **John Adams** questioning such Christian doctrines as the Virgin Birth of Jesus: ".... the day will come when the mystical generation of Jesus, by the supreme being as his father in the womb of a virgin will be classed with the fable of the generation of Minerva in the brain of Jupiter." This was standard stuff for the third President. Yet, in the same letter the he assured **John Adams** of an afterlife: "May we meet there again, in Congress, with our ancient Colleagues, and receive with them the seal of approbation `Well done, good and faithful servants.'" **Adams** took an agnostic but hopeful view writing to **Jefferson** in 1825 (a year from death): "...while I breath I shall be your friend. We shall meet again, so wishes and so believes your friend, but if we are disappointed we shall never know it."

A young **James Madison** in 1773 wrote a friend that perhaps they should initially pursue other careers and, then, later in life publicly become outspoken Christian advocates. He said they would then act as a "cloud of witnesses" alluding to Hebrews 12:1. In 1825 **Madison** wrote another friend: "The belief in a God All Powerful wise and good, is so essential to the moral order of the world and to the happiness of man, that arguments which enforce it cannot be drawn from too many sources nor adapted with too much solicitude to the different characters and capacities impressed with it." In 1803 as ambassador to England **Monroe** had an audience with King George III who asked him about the French: "They have no religion, have they?" **Monroe** cautiously answered that he thought there were many in France who had none.

After the death of his young daughter while he was serving as US Ambassador to Russia in 1812 **John Quincy Adams** turned more to religion, studying the Bible and Christian theology. He wrote in his journal: "Religious sentiments become from day to day more constantly habitual to my mind. They are perhaps too often seen in this journal." In his studies he began to come closer to his father's broader religious views. As Secretary of State, **Adams** accepted the presidency of the American Bible Society. He took the position because of his concern for two trends in American religious life: Unitarianism and Evangelicalism. He opposed the Unitarian approach which appealed to "the liberal class who consider religion as merely a system of morals." He also opposed what he saw as intolerance among evangelicals. In the 1828 election he was asked about his "ideas of the Trinity." **Adams** said that he was not a Trinitarian or a Unitarian. He said he "believed the nature of Jesus Christ was superhuman: but whether he was God, or only the first of created beings, was not clearly revealed to me in the Scriptures." **Adams** preferred the moral beauty of Christ's teachings downplaying doctrine "It is enough for us to know that God hath made foolish the wisdom of this world." He confided to his diary late in life that he could not believe that Christ died for man's sins: "It is not true. It is hateful. But how shall I contradict St. Paul?" **Adams** went on to say, "I reverence God as my creator. As creator of the world. I reverence him with holy fear. I venerate Jesus Christ as my redeemer; and, as far as I can understand, the redeemer of the world. But this belief is dark and dubious." He wrote that it was "the doom of the Christian church to be always distracted with controversy." Late in life, **Adams** studied the life of the early American religious leader, Roger Williams. He called Williams a "polemical porcupine." He said that Williams deserved expulsion from the Plymouth colony. But he also said: "Yet his inflexible and finally triumphant principle of universal toleration makes him a name and praise for all future time."

Andrew Jackson in 1833 in New York Harbor: "What a country God has given us! How thankful we ought to be that God has given us such a country to live in." In old age **Andrew Jackson** was impressed with Jesus' physical courage in his suffering on the cross.

Van Buren didn't pay close attention to sermons. "I am accustomed, when men are preaching, to occupy my mind with political thoughts."

In the campaign of 1840 **William Henry Harrison** met with a delegation at his home on a Sunday that wanted to discuss politics. He demurred: "I have too much respect for the religion of my wife to encourage the violation of the Sabbath." **Harrison** read the Bible most evenings for the last twenty years of his life. "At first...a matter of duty...it has now become a pleasure." In Washington in 1841 he bought a new Bible and announced that he would join St. John's Episcopal Church.

John Tyler grew up in Virginia under the influence of Jeffersonianism. It was refected in this comment in 1843: "No religious establishment *by law* (last two words emphasized in the original) exists among us. The conscience is left free from all restraint to worship his Maker after his own judgment.... The Mohammedan, if he were to come among us, would have the privilege guaranteed to him by the constitution to worship according to the Koran; and the East Indian might erect a shrine to Brahma if it so pleased him." As he grew older **Tyler** became more oriented toward Christianity accepting that there was a personal God and that there was meaning behind suffering. According to a minister he had a "bright faith in the Christian religion."

As a young officer, **Zachary Taylor** reflected religious pluralism, writing in 1824 calling for noninterference in European affairs. He asserted that although Americans wanted every country to be free that "it to be very immaterial, as regards the interest of this country, whether the Crescent or Cross prevails." Although he never joined a church, future president **Taylor** urged his children to read a chapter of the Bible each night.

In the Mexican-American War, **Polk** appointed at **Zachary Taylor's** request two Roman Catholic chaplains. This was at a time of rising anti-Catholicism in the US. The factors that contributed to it included:

- Ethnic tensions within the Catholic Church.
- Rapid growth of the church.
- Immigration.
- Protestant efforts at solidarity in the face of inter-sectarian discord.
- The Puritan heritage back to Queen Elizabeth.
- Conflicts with certain Catholic countries.
- The Enlightenment influence.

As a state legislator, **Fillmore** sponsored a law - which did not get passed - to eliminate a test oath that witnesses in New York courts had to give attesting to their belief in God and an afterlife. **Fillmore** a Unitarian called it an "absurd" law and said that "the narrow feeling of prejudice and bigotry" in it should give "way to more enlightened and liberal views."

As an attorney in New Hampshire in 1848-49 **Pierce** defended the Shakers from discriminatory laws before the legislature. The Shakers were accused of breaking up families and child abuse and other charges. **Pierce**: "They hold to the same teachings of Christian love which Christ held and communicated to his disciples more than eighteen centuries ago.... They are in a church which they believe a true church...." In 1850-1 **Pierce** worked unsuccessfully to try to get a provision barring Roman Catholics from public office eliminated. Of the forty-three presidents who have taken the Oath of Office, only **Pierce** in 1853 decided to "affirm" – not to "swear" - noting the New Testament prohibition against swearing an oath. **Pierce** was also the first president not to kiss the Bible after his inauguration – that tradition had been started by **George Washington**. (But, **Pierce** was the first to have a Christmas tree in the White House.) In 1865 **Pierce** was baptized. He wrote a friend: "I have turned, I hope, with submission of spirit to Him who is 'the resurrection & the life.'" He died in four years.

In 1856 the American Party under **Millard Fillmore** used anti-Catholic messages against the Democrats (as Whigs had against Democrats back to **Van Buren**) and also John C. Fremont of the Republicans. The Republicans in turn publicized that **Fillmore** was a Unitarian. They advertised that he had rejected "the American Protestant faith that Jesus Christ is the Son of God." **Fillmore** responded by distancing himself: "In my view, Church and State should be separate, not only in form, but fact - religion and politics should not be mingled."

Lincoln was a great religious thinker. In 1846 **Lincoln** was running for Congress against a preacher who accused him of not being a Christian. He responded in a handbill: "That I am not a member of any Christian Church is true: but I have never denied the truth of the Scriptures; and I have never spoken with intentional disrespect of religion in general, or of any denomination of Christians in particular." **Lincoln** was frequently asked why he didn't join a church. The clearest answer recorded: "When any church will inscribe over its alter as its sole qualification for membership the Savior's condensed statement of the substance of both the law and the Gospel, 'Thou shall love the Lord thy God will all thy heart, and with all thy soul, and with all thy mind, and thy neighbor as thyself' - that Church will I join with all my heart and soul."

A clergyman once asked **Lincoln**, "Do you love Jesus?" His answer: "When I left Springfield I asked the people to pray for me. I was not a Christian. When I buried my son, the severest trial of my life, I was not a Christian. But when I went to Gettysburg and saw the graves of thousands of our soldiers, I then and there consecrated myself to Christ. Yes, I love Jesus." (One of those graves was for **Richard Nixon's** great-grandfather who had taken the place of a wealthy man in the army and perished at Cemetery Ridge. **Obama's** 3G Grandfather also fought for the North in the Civil War.)

Lincoln read the King James Bible for the cadence. According to his wife **Lincoln** said shortly before he was shot that "there was no city on earth he so much desired to see as Jerusalem." In 1862 John Hay, **Lincoln's** secretary found a private note **Lincoln** had written: "The will of God prevails. In great contests each party claims to act in accordance with the will of God. Both may be, and one must be wrong. God cannot be for, and against, the same thing at the same time. In the present civil war it is quite possible that God's purpose is something different from the purpose of either party." Union victory in the Battle of Antietam in 1862 led to **Lincoln's** decision to proceed with the Emancipation Proclamation. He told his cabinet: "I said nothing to anyone; but I made the promise to myself, and, (hesitating a little according to Treasury Salmon P. Secretary Chase) to my Maker."

Lincoln's religious faith may have deepened during his presidency. But he still held: "these are not ... the days of miracles. I must study the plain physical facts of the case, ascertain what is possible and learn what appears to be wise and right." He put "In God We Trust" on coins in 1864 but his religion is hard to classify. He echoed

Jefferson and **Adams** in his evocation of simple Christianity. He read the Bible. He identified as a Christian but was skeptic and tolerant. He perceived a reality larger than himself guiding life.

Andrew Johnson was never a church member. In the 1830s in the Tennessee legislature **Johnson** opposed opening the sessions with prayer as a violation of the Constitution. He said there were nearby churches where legislators could get guidance from God. Running for re-election as governor of Tennessee in 1855 **Johnson** was confronted by the Know-Nothing party officially known as the American Party. Defending Catholics, **Johnson** derided the American Party's anti-Catholicism based on the Catholic Church's "foreign origin." He said that rule would allow only Mormonism. He also criticized certain Protestant preachers: "Instead of preaching Christ crucified, they preach crucify the Catholics." At the time, young **Rutherford Hayes** wrote, "How people do hate Catholics, and what happiness it was to thousands to have a chance to show it in what seemed like a lawful and patriotic manner (by voting Know-Nothing.)" This helped destroy the northern Whigs.

Andrew Johnson was a reader of the Bible. When asked about his religion he responded that his creed was: "the doctrines of the Bible, as taught and practiced by Jesus Christ." In 1862 **Johnson** as military governor of Tennessee withstood a Confederate siege of Nashville. He prayed one night with a local evangelist after which he said he felt confident the city would not be taken. Then to the evangelist: "I don't want you to think that I have become religious because I asked you to pray. But... there is one thing I do believe: I believe in Almighty God; and I also believe in the Bible: and I say, *I'll be dammed if Nashville shall be surrendered.*" **Johnson** in 1866 defending his policy toward the South: "The Son of God, when he descended and found men condemned under the law, instead of executing the law, put himself in their stead and died for them. If I have erred in pardoning, I trust in God I have erred on the right side." (A century later **Ford** used similar logic when pardoning **Nixon**: "I do believe with all my heart and mind and spirit that I, not as President, but as a humble servant of God, will receive justice without mercy if I fail to show mercy.")

The three Republican presidents who followed **Lincoln** were nonorthodox in their religious beliefs.

As a boy **Grant** was not baptized or forced to go to church although his siblings were. During the Civil War as his armies took Confederate areas, his staff discovered that local ministers were still offering prayers in church services for Jefferson Davis and required that the clergymen cease immediately and begin offering prayers for **Lincoln**. **Grant** demurred. The orders were changed to omit any treasonable prayers but to not require any others. As president, **Grant** opposed both financial aid for Catholic parochial schools and the intrusion of religion – primarily the forced reading of the Protestant Bible - into the public schools. **Grant** was baptized a few months before he died at the request of the women in his family. He was barely conscious. Famous preacher Henry Ward Beecher said to his church that **Grant** was going to heaven. **Grant's** son later said he was "a pure agnostic."

In the area of religion, one of the most interesting US presidents was **Rutherford B Hayes. Hayes** was somewhat of an agnostic and did not belong to any church although his mother was devout. As a young man he read a chapter a day of the New Testament in German to improve his language skills. Throughout his life – from youth, to college, to frontier society in the 1850s, to the Civil War, to politics and to old age - **Hayes** remained outside the orthodox fold.

In 1839 as a student at Kenyon College **Hayes** was in a minority of students who did not convert during a religious revival. He referred to those who did convert as "gone." (As a student at Whittier College in California about nine decades later, **Richard Nixon** who joined many campus clubs did not join one of the most popular, a religious society.) As a young man in the 1850s in Cincinnati **Hayes** read a biography of William Ellery Channing the Unitarian minister. He wrote his fiancé: "If ever I am made a Christian, it will be under the influence of views like his. He says the test of Christianity is the state of the heart and affections, not the state of a man's intellectual belief.... The half of the orthodox creeds, I don't understand and can't fully believe." To his diary he was blunter: "Most of the notions which orthodox people have of the divinity of the Bible, I disbelieve. I am so nearly infidel in all my views, that...in *spite* of my wishes... none but the most liberal doctrines can command my assent." (In this he was much like the older **John Quincy Adams**.) He wrote at about that time "Providence interferes no more in the greatest affairs of men than in the smallest and... Neither individuals nor nations are any more the objects of special interposition of the Divine Ruler than the inanimate things of the world." He heard and met with Ralph Waldo Emerson. He liked Emerson but thought he was self-centered and did not carry his ideas to their logical conclusions. He said that the Transcendentalists thought "that the hearty, earnest, sincere benevolence in the world is centered in themselves; that all others...'Have too little *pluck* to avow'" the truth. **Hayes** wrote that Emerson's "misty notion(s) on religion" which emphasized that all people possessed some sort of "magnetism or divinity" was unsatisfying because it "*intimates* or walks around about what he *would* say but *don't* say."

Death did not change **Hayes'** views:

- His response to the death of a beloved cousin: "The mystery of our existence - I have no faith in any attempted explanation of it. It is all a dark, unfathomed profound."
- His response in 1856 when his sister died and he was consoled by a religious friend that she was in Heaven: "If there are any Mansions of the blessed, she I know is there and I shall again be with her. But the agonizing doubt or disbelief leaves me with a 'rooted sorrow' which will remain."

His attitude on churchgoing was not unlike **Van Buren's**. He once told his son: "I hope that you will be benefited by your churchgoing. Where the habit does not christianize it generally civilizes." **Hayes** wrote in his diary during the Civil War: "But will I not take refuge in the faith of my fathers at last? Are we not all impelled to this? The great abyss, the unknown future - are we not happier if we give ourselves up to some settled faith? Am I not more and more carried along, drifted, toward surrendering to the best religion that the world has yet produced? It seems so." This sentiment passed. His attitude toward ministers prefigured those of **Truman's** toward Billy Graham (see below). Once in camp during the Civil War he wrote, "The chaplain returned today - not an agreeable or useful person. I wish he had not returned."

In late 1861 from his army camp **Hayes** wrote in his diary wondering what happens after "we fret our little hour, are happy and pass away." He called himself "an unbeliever" but thought he would go toward Christianity in his "closing years on the down-hill side of life." But he added: "My belief in this war is as deep as any faith can be." At one point in 1863 when ordered into action **Hayes** wrote his family: "Dear boys, darling Lucy, and all, good-bye! We are all in the hands of Providence and need only be solicitous to do our duty here and leave the future to the Great Disposer."

He attended the Methodist church with his wife. **Hayes'** wife knew that he read the Bible "as he did Shakespeare, for illustration and language, for its true pictures of man and woman nature, for its early historical record." **Hayes** called his wife Lucy "the Golden Rule incarnate." After she died in 1889 **Hayes** acknowledged that although he longed for a life after death he did not think that "the conscious person ...will meet you in the world beyond." He thought that "we believe, or disbelieve, or are in doubt according to our own make-up - to accidents, to education, to environment."

This seems the final word: Late in life after hearing "a fair sermon" **Hayes** said: "I am a Christian according to my conscience...not of course by the orthodox standard. But I am content, and have a feeling of trust and safety."

Garfield was a serious Disciples of Christ preacher, although never ordained. His first sermon in 1853 or 1854 compared Jesus Christ to Napoleon. His two years at Williams College in Massachusetts broadened his horizons from his orthodox background. In 1856 he wrote his future wife: "It is always disagreeable to talk about money in connection with the Gospel, and yet I must and will say that I do not intend to abandon our earthly support to the tender mercies of our Brotherhood... I think that I shall not become a preacher now, if

I ever do." After graduation from Williams in 1856 **Garfield** taught and was a college administrator back in Ohio. He also did itinerant preaching in his Campellite denomination. One colleague noted later: "For full five years he preached somewhere nearly every Sunday.... his sermons live only in the hearts of those who heard them. They were strong in the ethical rather than in the evangelical element.... His stricter brethren found much fault with him because he was not more denominational, but the people, wherever he went, would turn out to hear **Garfield** preach." Another commentator on **Garfield's** sermons of the late 1850s said: "His meetings were always well attended and were even more popular with the sinners of the world than the saints of the church. There was a lack of spirituality about him that grieved the latter...but the sinners liked to hear his short, sparkling, logical discourses."

In 1862 **Garfield** was trying to leave the military to run for Congress. One of his local Campellite rivals said: "**Garfield** has an interest everywhere...but in the Kingdom of Heaven."

A key aspect of **Garfield's** career both in the military and politics stemmed from his college training as an evangelist. But **Garfield** said, "I would rather be defeated than make capital out of my religion." In 1874 **Garfield** looked back at his 1851-54 diary with its devout statements about religion and noted: "I am amazed at the gush and slush of those days. I was a very pulpy boy till I was at least twenty-two years old. But... I was dead in earnest and working by the best light I had. In looking over it now I am not ashamed of the most of it." **Arthur,** far less experienced in Christianity than **Garfield**, was still of the same point of view: "I may be President of the United States, but my private life is nobody's damned business."

In 1864 **Benjamin Harrison** joined William Sherman's assault on Atlanta and wrote his wife that if he should die; "let your grief be tempered by the consolation that I died for my Country & in Christ." **Harrison** had considered going into the ministry and was an active churchman. **Harrison's** cabinet was entirely Presbyterian. **Harrison** was a great grandfather of evangelist Pat Robertson who ran for the Republican nomination in 1988.

When **Cleveland's** mother died shortly before he was elected governor of New York in 1882, he wrote his brother: "Do you know that if Mother were alive I should feel so much safer? I have always thought her prayers had much to do with my success."

In 1884 a Protestant minister may have cost the Republicans the election when he labeled the Democrats the party of "Rum, Romanism and Rebellion." Upon his election that year **Grover Cleveland** who had endured accusations from political enemies including a clergyman named Reverend George Ball wrote a friend: "I intend to cultivate the Christian virtue of charity toward all men except the dirty class that defiled themselves with filthy scandal and Ballism. I don't believe God will ever forgive them and I am determined never to do so."

McKinley: "The more profoundly we study [the Bible], and the more closely we observe its divine precepts, the better citizens we will become and the higher will be our destiny as a nation." **TR** called Tom Paine that "filthy little atheist." **TR** approved the deletion of **Lincoln's** "In God We Trust" on a new issuance of pennies and ten and twenty-dollar gold pieces in 1905. There was a public outcry and Congress restored it. **Roosevelt** did not talk a lot about God – he referred to "unseen and unknown powers" - but he had a sense of reverence for nature. In 1903 upon seeing the Grand Canyon for the first time he said: "Leave it as it is; the ages have been at work on it, and man can only mar it." (**Jimmy Carter**, echoed this sense of awe in 1980 flying over Mount St. Helens in Washington State after a volcanic explosion when he commented that it made the Moon look like a golf course.) **TR** was more interested in the teachings of Christ than his atonement for sins, saying once: "I have always believed in the truth of the statement that 'He who seeks his life shall lose it.'" A definitive formulation of his religion was one he offered at the end of the 1912 campaign: "The doctrines we preach reach back to the Golden Rule and the Sermon on the Mount. They reach back to the commandments delivered at Sinai. All that we are doing is to apply those doctrines in the shape necessary to make them available for meeting the living issues of our own day."

In the 1908 election, **Taft's** Unitarianism was attacked by his opponent William Jennings Bryan: "Think of the United States with a President who does not believe that Jesus Christ was the Son of God, but looks upon our immaculate savior as a ...low cunning imposter." **TR** counseled **Taft** that "the same attack was made upon **Lincoln** as being a non-orthodox Christian as upon you, and far severer attacks upon **Jefferson**." **Taft** wrote that he did not believe "in the divinity of Christ." As president, **Taft's** tolerant attitude toward liquor, his Unitarian faith and the fact that he was known to play cards on Sundays alienated some Protestants. During World War I, as a former president, **Taft** said that "Germany has mistaken the Devil for God"

Wilson in his diary: "I used to wonder vaguely that I did not have the same deep-reaching spiritual difficulties that I read of other men having. I saw the intellectual difficulties, but I was not troubled by them: they seemed to have no connection with my faith in the essentials of the religion I had been taught... I am capable, it would seem, of being satisfied spiritually without being satisfied intellectually." It seems though that he got carried away, even by the standards of the time. In 1905 he said, "There is a mighty task before us and it welds us together. It is to make the United States a mighty Christian Nation, and to Christianize the world." At Versailles after World War I he informed the other statesmen: "Why has Jesus Christ so far not succeeded in inducing the world to follow His teachings in these matters? It is because He taught the ideal without devising any practical means of attaining it. That is why I am proposing a practical scheme to carry out His aims." This attitude was pretty grating. French Prime Minister Clemenceau called **Wilson** a "Protestant Priest." He added that **Wilson** "talked like Jesus Christ but acted like (Prime Minister) Lloyd George." Mexican revolutionary Pancho Villa said of **Wilson** in 1916 after the US had recognized Villa's rival, Venustiano Carranza's government in the Mexican Revolution that he was "an evangelical professor of philosophy...."

Coolidge avoided the anti-Darwinism and fundamentalism of the 1920s. His religion was closer to the Social Gospel without the liberal outlook. In 1926 he said: "It would be difficult for me to conceive of anyone being able to administer the duties of a great office like the presidency without a belief in the guidance of divine providence." Although he was not known as a philosophical man, **Coolidge** said, "The things of the spirit come first. Unless we cling to that, all our material prosperity, overwhelming though it may appear, will turn to a barren scepter in our grasp." In his autobiography **Coolidge** said of one of his professors at Amherst: "His course was a demonstration of the existence of a personal God, of our power to know him, of the Divine immanence, and of the complete dependence of all the universe on Him as the Creator and Father 'in whom we live and move and have our being.' Every reaction in the universe is a manifestation of His presence.... No doubt there are those who think they can demonstrate that this teaching is not correct. With them I have no argument. I know that in experience it has worked." **Coolidge** once said: "Of the books of the Bible, I have found the writings of Saint Paul the most interesting to me." Privately, and by then an ex-president, **Coolidge** despaired during the Depression, not seeing any solutions. He said: "But there is still religion, which is the same as yesterday, today, and forever."

Sounding a little like **Van Buren** one hundred years earlier, **Hoover** once said: "I came of Quaker stock. I never worked very hard at it." **Hoover** as Secretary of Commerce in 1921-29 oversaw commercial radio in its infancy. Leaders from a religious sect applied to build a radio station to warn people about the end of the world. Sounding as light-hearted as **Lincoln** could be, **Hoover** advised them that if the world's end was imminent, it would be a wiser investment to buy time at existing stations.

President **Franklin Roosevelt** occasionally alluded to scripture. In 1942 he was asked to place former president **Herbert Hoover** into a responsible position dealing with manpower shortages on the home front as the US had entered World War II. **Hoover** was a marginal figure by that time in American public life. **FDR** declined, saying, "Well, I'm not Jesus Christ, I'm not going to raise him from the dead." **FDR** was not known as a deep religious thinker. When Eleanor Roosevelt asked him if he believed in the basics of the Episcopalian faith in which he had been raised, **FDR** said, "I really never thought about it. I think it is just as well not to think about things like that too much." When asked about his creed, **FDR** said: "I am a Christian and a Democrat - that's all." **FDR** liked to talk of his own "lucky star."

But there are countervailing signs. **Roosevelt** once told Francis Perkins, the Secretary of Labor in his administration, that when he was in despair after his affliction with polio he thought God had abandoned him. And, on D-Day **FDR** did not give a speech, just a prayer that he wrote. Here are the closing lines:

> *"And, O Lord, give us faith. Give us faith in Thee; faith in our sons; faith in each other; faith in our united crusade. Let not the keenness of our spirit ever be dulled. Let not the impacts of temporary events, of temporal matters of but fleeting moment — let not these deter us in our unconquerable purpose.*

> *"With Thy blessing, we shall prevail over the unholy forces of our enemy. Help us to conquer the apostles of greed and racial arrogances. Lead us to the saving of our country, and with our sister nations into a world unity that will spell a sure peace — a peace invulnerable to the schemings of unworthy men. And a peace that will let all of men live in freedom, reaping the just rewards of their honest toil.*

> *"Thy will be done, Almighty God.*

> *Amen."*

By the time he was 12 **Truman** had read the Bible twice. "I spent a lot of time on the 20th chapter of Exodus (where the Ten Commandments are contained) and the 5th, 6th and 7th chapters of Mathew's Gospel (the Sermon on the Mount)." In 1949 **Truman** told a group of Anglican Church leaders that the Sermon on the Mount was "what America was living by." **Truman** believed that "God has created (the United States) and brought us to our present position of power and strength" in order to defend "spiritual values - the moral code - against the vast forces of evil that seek to destroy them."

A dialog between President **Truman** and a young Billy Graham in 1950 went off-track. Graham asked **Truman** about his faith. **Truman** answered, "Well, I try to live by the Sermon on the Mount and the Golden Rule." Graham replied, "I just don't think that's enough." Graham then asked **Truman** if he wanted to pray with him. **Truman's** response: "Couldn't do any harm." After he left office, **Truman** said of Graham: "He claims he's a friend of all the presidents, but he was never a friend of mine when I was President. I just don't go for people like that."

During the 1960 Democratic convention, **Truman** did not initially back **JFK** but said it wasn't over **JFK's** Catholicism. Apparently, he did not like **Kennedy's** father: "I'm not against the Pope, I'm against the Pop."

Dwight Eisenhower was named after the great American evangelist, Dwight L Moody. **Eisenhower** described himself as "the most intensely religious man I know." **Eisenhower** in 1955: "Application of Christianity to everyday affairs is the only practical hope of the world." **Truman's** and **Eisenhower's** religious outlooks were that democracy was based on Biblical values and each individual was worthy in the eyes of God. The signs of this belief were: prayer, high view of the Bible, a positive view toward life after death, belief that God directs history, belief that the US has a religious base.

JFK in 1960: "I am not the Catholic candidate for President. I am the Democratic candidate for President who happens to be Catholic." **JFK** did not bring Catholic intellectual tradition to the Presidency. (His ambition was to put a man on the Moon.) But he symbolized a more tolerant America. He once said, "**Johnson** had to prove that a Southerner could win in the North, just as I had to prove a Catholic could win in heavily Protestant states. Can you imagine me, having entered no primaries, trying to tell the leaders that being a Catholic was no handicap? When **Lyndon** said he could win in the North, but could offer no concrete evidence, his claims couldn't be taken seriously." **JFK**, the first (and so far only) Roman Catholic President (the current Vice President Joseph Biden is also Catholic) wore his religion lightly. A writer once told one of **JFK's** sisters that he wanted to write a book about **JFK's** personal religion. Her reply: "That will be a very short book." However, he had some thoughts on the matter. President-elect **Kennedy** asked Billy Graham, "Billy do you believe in the Second Coming of Jesus Christ?" Also: in the middle of the Cuban missile crisis, President **Kennedy** prayed at St. Matthew's Cathedral. Finally, **JFK's** spiritual side may have come out in comments such as these at a dinner for the America's Cup Crews on September 14 1962: "I really don't know why it is that all of us are so committed to the sea, except I think it's because in addition to the fact that the sea changes, and the light changes, and ships change, it's because we all came from the sea. And it is an interesting biological fact that all of us have in our veins the exact same percentage of salt in our blood that exists in the ocean, and, therefore, we have salt in our blood, in our sweat, in our tears. We are tied to the ocean. And when we go back to the sea - whether it is to sail or to watch it - we are going back from whence we came."

In announcing his candidacy for president in 1960, **LBJ** called himself a Baptist American in contrast to **JFK** a Catholic American. (He said the Americans for Democratic Action didn't want "any Catholic Americans or Baptist Americans" to become president.) President **Lyndon Johnson** repeatedly called for national days of prayer and reportedly prayed a dozen times a day.

After he left the presidency **LBJ** asked Billy Graham if he would preach at his funeral: "I want you to look in those cameras and tell 'em what Christianity is all about. Tell 'em how they can be sure they are going to heaven. I want you to preach the gospel. But somewhere in there, you tell 'em a few things I did for this country."

Richard Nixon's acceptance speech at the 1960 Republican convention was well-received by the media including the generally anti-**Nixon** *New Republic*. Theodore Sorensen, **JFK's** speechwriter said the speech was "brilliant." In it **Nixon** said: "**Abraham Lincoln** was asked during the dark days of the tragic War between the States whether he thought God was on his side. His answer was, 'my concern is not whether God is on our side, but whether we are on God's side.' My fellow Americans, may that ever be our prayer for our country."

Nixon was a complex figure. **Hoover** saw **Nixon** as a preacher pretending to be a politician. In the Cold War **Nixon** still said: "I'm not necessarily a respecter of the status quo in foreign affairs. I'm a chance taker in foreign affairs; I would take chances for peace. The Quakers have a passion for peace, you know." Late in life **Nixon** said that in 1974 after his resignation he had felt as **FDR** did when afflicted with polio that God had abandoned him.

When **Nixon** released edited transcripts of the taped conversations from the Oval Office under court pressure and political pressure in 1974, there was widespread revulsion at the profanities and moral turpitude revealed. In a reaction, Governor **Jimmy Carter** told the Southern Baptist convention that: "There has never been an adequate role played by Christians in this nation...in shaping the standards and quality of public life."

During the1976 presidential primaries **Carter's** evangelical religion was an issue. He defused some criticism through modesty saying: "I don't think I'm ordained by God to be President." He went on that the "only prayer that I've ever had concerning the election is that I do the right thing. And if I win or lose, my religious faith won't be shaken." A news commentator asked **Carter** if he had any doubt about God or himself or about life. **Carter** responded: "I can't think of any." At a later stage in the campaign **Carter** alluded to Jesus' statement in the Sermon on the Mount to the effect that anyone who lusts for a woman has in effect committed adultery and said: "I've looked upon a lot of women with lust. I've committed adultery in my heart many times. This is something that God recognizes I will do - and I have done it - and God forgives me for it. But that doesn't mean that I condemn someone who not only looks on a woman with lust but who leaves his wife and shacks up with somebody out of wedlock." **Carter** went on to urge tolerance and not to be proud of being relatively less sinful - a theologically sound point.

Ford struck a more reserved note saying later about the 1976 campaign: "Throughout the campaign, **Carter** had talked about his religious convictions in a way I found discomfiting. I have always felt a closeness to God and have looked to a higher being for guidance and support, but I didn't think it was appropriate to advertise my religious beliefs." In this he sounded like the mature **Garfield**.

Ford reportedly "accepted Christ" in 1971. Earlier he had reacted to *Engle v. Vitale*, the US Supreme Court decision striking down school prayer, with this: "Already we have gone too far in establishing a religion of secularism in the United States. While many still do profess to believe in God, they act as if He did not exist...."

After the presidency, **Carter** said: "There's no doubt that during my time as president, I prayed more intensely and more fervently for God's guidance than at any other time in my life. ... The problems were so complex that I sought counsel." Billy Graham in 1976: "I would say there wouldn't be a hairs difference between what **Jimmy Carter**, **Gerald Ford** and **Reagan** believe religiously." In 1978 in introducing Menachem Begin and Anwar Sadat to the US Congress after the negotiations of a peace treaty between Israel and Egypt known as the Camp David Accords, **Carter** quoted from the Sermon on the Mount: "Blessed are the peacemakers." (Camp David is a presidential retreat site in Maryland named for **Eisenhower's** grandson David Eisenhower.)

Reagan's father was Catholic. His mother was a deeply religious Protestant who had far greater influence on him. Her favorite saying was: "The Lord will provide." In 1983 **Reagan** said: "We must never forget that no government schemes are going to perfect man. We know that living in this world means dealing with what philosophers call the phenomenology of evil, or, as theologians would put it, the doctrine of sin. There is sin and evil in the world, and we're enjoined by Scripture and the Lord Jesus to oppose it with all our might." At age 80 he said: "My optimism comes not just from my strong faith in God but from my strong and enduring faith in man."

As vice president, **George HW Bush** became slowly more acquainted with evangelical Christians and came to defend them. He wrote a friend: "Why do you feel a threat from the Religious right and not the left?" He asked why it was acceptable for liberal Christian ministers "to urge defiance on Vietnam, tolerance on (Iranian leader)

Khomeini, or advocate 'gay marriages' but it's not okay for the Right to get together to work against abortion or for prayer in schools?" He added in a cultural signal: "We must understand that that in our post-Vietnam post-Watergate guilt, we have condoned things we should have condemned." He gradually moved more into that camp but still lacked the vocabulary at times. Asked if he were a born again Christian, he responded that "I'm clear-cut affirmative to that."

Bill Clinton and **George W Bush** were very comfortable with modern evangelical beliefs with a stress on accepting Jesus Christ as personal savior. In this they were far different than **Jefferson** or the **Adamses** or for that matter **Hayes, Garfield, Theodore Roosevelt,** the older **Bush** and most presidents other than **Carter.**

Clinton wrote in his memoirs about his childhood conversion: "In 1955, I had absorbed enough of my church's teachings to know that I was a sinner and to want Jesus to save me..." In the 1990s Bible-toting **Bill Clinton** said, "I assure you that no president makes decisions like (an agreement with Haiti) without deep thought and prayer." He noted that "the First Amendment...does not convert our schools into religion-free zones." The Reverend Jesse Jackson said this about President **Clinton** in 1998: "He knows even in a biblical sense the perils and treasures of leadership...He has a great sense of biblical journeys of leaders."

George W Bush was known for a short temper. His family worried that he would erupt under partisan attacks against his family in his 1994 run for governor. But he kept control of himself citing Proverbs 13:3: "He who guards his lips guards his life. But he who speaks rashly will come to ruin." In a Republican candidates debate in 2000 **George W Bush** was asked to name a "favorite philosopher." He answered: "Christ, because he changed my heart." The moderator asked him how. **Bush** replied: "Well, if they don't know, it's going to be hard to explain. When you turn your heart and your life over to Christ, when you accept Christ as the savior, it changes your heart. It changes your life. And that's what happened to me." **Bill Clinton** once said about his successor: "I believe President **Bush** is a good Christian. I believe that his faith in Jesus gave him new purpose and direction to his life but that doesn't mean that he doesn't see through a glass darkly." **Clinton** was a fluent speaker and had a good working knowledge of scriptures – in this instance quoting from I Corinthians 13.

But **George W Bush** was not a strict fundamentalist. He was once asked if he had a Bible in the Oval Office. He said he did but that he only read it in the private residence. "I'm strengthened by people who pray for me, not by specific verses. This is not a Christian country. The strength of our country is that we can all worship freely..." This position was echoed in 2009 by **Barack Obama** is a state trip to Turkey: "We do not consider ourselves a Christian nation or a Jewish nation or a Muslim nation. We consider ourselves a nation of citizens who are bound by ideals and a set of values."

Obama converted to Christianity as a young man in Chicago. As a candidate in 2008 defending his position on civil unions for gays **Obama** said: "If people find that controversial then I would just refer them to the Sermon on the Mount, which I think is, in my mind, for my faith, more central than an obscure passage in (the New Testament book of) Romans."

In 2010 **Obama** became the twelfth president, dating back to **Harry Truman**, to meet with Billy Graham who said, "I am pleased to have had President **Obama** in my home this afternoon." Graham gave **Obama** with two Bibles, one for him and one for the First Lady. Then they prayed together.

What is the point of all this?

The religion of this country may be religious freedom. Our first president issued a statement remarkable for its time. In 1790, **George Washington** went to Rhode Island and wrote to a Jewish congregation in Newport. He said: "It is now no more that toleration is spoken of as if it was by the indulgence of one class of people, that another enjoyed the exercise of their inherent natural rights. For happily the government of the United States which gives bigotry no sanction, to persecution no assistance, requires only that they who live under its protection should demean themselves as good citizens..." (Thomas Paine echoed him the next year writing *in Rights of Man*: "Toleration is not the opposite on intoleration, but is the counterfeit of it. Both are despotisms. The one assumes to itself the right of withholding liberty of conscience, and the other of granting it." Some modern diversity consultants must think they are on the cutting edge in stressing that mere "tolerance" is not enough when they are just echoing American statesmen of two hundred years ago.) In America religious liberty is a strength. In regard to religion, **Jefferson** made the point this way: "Divided we stand, united we fall." It was a point **Eisenhower** made in his own way in 1954 and **Clinton** in 1995:

- **Eisenhower:** "Our government makes no sense unless it is founded on a deeply felt religious faith - and I don't care what it is."
- **Clinton:** "Don't you believe that if every kid in every difficult neighborhood in America were in a religious institution on weekends -- a synagogue on Saturday, a Church on Sunday, a mosque on Friday -- don't you really believe that the drug rate, the crime rate, the violence rate, the sense of self destruction would go way down and the quality and character of this country would go way up?"

A perspective on the development of religious liberty in the US can be seen in the Presidents' reactions to the Mormon Church. The Mormons began as a small sect among other sects now long forgotten in upstate New York in the 1830s and evolved to a powerful and respected institution.

Mormon leader Joseph Smith came to see **Van Buren** to seek redress for persecutions in Missouri in 1839, **Van Buren** told him, "I can do nothing for you. If I do anything, I shall come in contact with the whole state of Missouri." Smith came to refer to the issue of states' rights as "a stink in the nostrils of the Almighty." Smith said of **Van Buren**: "He is not as fit as my dog for the chair of state for my dog will make an effort to protect his abused and insulted master, while the present chief magistrate will not so much as lift his finger to help citizens of the United States."

After Joseph Smith's murder in 1844 Brigham Young skillfully played on President **Polk's** anxieties about British and Mexican designs in the West to get assistance. He set some distance, writing to **Polk** in 1846: "While we appreciate the Constitution of the United States as the most precious among the nations, we feel that we would rather retreat to the deserts, Islands or mountain caves than consent to be ruled by governors and judges whose hands are drenched in the blood of innocence and virtue, who delight in injustice and oppression." **Polk** was faced with war with Mexico. He wrote in his diary on June 3, 1846: "It was with the view to prevent this singular sect from becoming hostile to the US that I held the conference with (Young's agent)." This led to the creation of the Mormon Battalion, a military unit serving the US. **Polk** dealt with critics who were cautious about having Mormon troops be the first to reach California saying: "If I could interfere with the Mormons, I could with the Baptists or any other religious sect."

The next administration fell into conflicts with the Mormons and when **Taylor** died in 1850, Brigham Young said of him: "Dead and in hell, and I am glad of it." Or, on another occasion: "I know **Zachary Taylor**, he is dead and damned, and I cannot help it." **Taylor's** successor was **Millard Fillmore** whose Unitarian religious convictions may have softened him toward the Mormons. In 1850 he appointed Brigham Young territorial governor of Utah. The Mormons responded by establishing a town named **Fillmore** with seventeen families in 1851. They named the surrounding county **Millard.**

In the next administration, **Franklin Pierce** tried to appoint a replacement for Brigham Young as territorial governor of Utah but in the face of Young's opposition it was difficult to find a suitable successor who would accept. Young: "President **Pierce** and all hell could not remove me from office."

The Mormons soon became a type of side show to the great issue of the time. The Kansas-Nebraska Act of 1854 called for popular sovereignty over the question of slavery. That is, the citizens of states in the new territories should decide the question. The Democrat platform supported this. The platform of the new Republican Party in

1856 called for Congress to prohibit in the territories the "twin relics of barbarism, polygamy and slavery." Mormonism was ridiculed during the campaign with, for example, parades featuring a Brigham Young look-alike with multiple wives each with a baby. In 1857 Senator Jefferson Davis who had been Secretary of War under **Franklin Pierce** proposed a bill that would have increased regiments in the army to put down the Mormons in Utah territory. **Andrew Johnson** opposed this bill and it was defeated. "A standing army is an incubus, a canker, a fungus on the body politic. I want no rabble here on one hand, and I want no aristocracy on the other. Lop off the aristocracy at one end, and the rabble at the other, and all will be well with the republic."

In 1857 **Buchanan** submitted evidence to Congress against the Mormons and the Congress declared Utah Territory to be in a state of insurrection. A military crisis was averted mostly with diplomacy and subsequent pardons. Later Brigham Young predicted the dissolution of the United States in the sectional crisis during the **Buchanan-Lincoln** transition. He added: "South Carolina has committed treason, and if Prest. **Buchanan** had been a smart man he would hang up the first men who rebelled in South Carolina." He also said: "There is no more a United States....if a state has the right to secede, so has a Territory, and a town from a county, and a family from a neighborhood, and you will have perfect anarchy.... What will King **Abraham** do? I do not know, neither do I care." He said the government was in trouble because they had killed Joseph Smith and would have to pay just as the Jews did for killing Jesus. Utah was mostly ignored during the Civil War. The Mormons sent an emissary named TBH Stenhouse to **Lincoln**. **Lincoln** said: "Stenhouse, when I was a boy on the farm in Illinois there was a great deal of timber on the farm which we had to clear away. Occasionally we would come to a log which had fallen down. It was too hard to split, to wet to burn, and too heavy to move, so we plowed around it. You go back and tell Brigham Young that if he will let me alone I will let him alone."

Grant visited Brigham Young in 1875 in Salt Lake City. **Grant** who had opposed the Mormons said that he had been deceived about them. **Hayes** visited Salt Lake in 1880. He disapproved of polygamy and Mormon political power and in his 1880 State of the Union he urged Congress to roll-back local self government in Utah. In 1907 **TR** supported the seating in the Senate of Reed Smoot who was under suspicion of polygamy. In 1911 the Mormon Tabernacle Choir sang at the White House at the invitation of **Taft**. Utah was one of only two states carried by **Taft** in 1912.

Besides religious liberty, the religion of this country also may be one of monotheism. The writer John O'Sullivan noted the reactions of three giants of the late twentieth century to assassination attempts. Pope John Paul II attributed his survival to God, specifically Our Lady of Fatima. British Prime Minister Margaret Thatcher, when asked if God had saved her, answered, "No." When **Reagan** was shot by a would-be assassin in 1981 he lost half the blood in his body and he nearly died. He prayed. "But I realized that I couldn't ask for God's help while at the same time I felt hatred for the mixed-up young man who had shot me. Isn't that the meaning of the lost sheep? We are all God's children and therefore equally loved by Him. I began to pray for his soul and that he would find his way into the fold." A few weeks later he wrote in his journal, "Whatever happens now, I owe my life to God and will try to serve him in every way I can." To the American public he reprised this as: "Whatever time I have left belongs to the Big Fella Upstairs."

Reagan's homespun monotheism spoke for many other Americans. That monotheism and the religious liberty caused by the First Amendment are the characteristics of American Christianity.

Chapter 10

Political Parties

Overall Context

Presidents are creatures of their parties and are not reluctant to attack the other party.

Speaking in support of **Hayes** in 1876 **Benjamin Harrison** defended the rhetoric blaming the Democrats for the Civil War, the tactic known as "waving the bloody shirt." He said: "I prefer the old gray army shirt, stained with but a single drop of a dead comrade's blood, to the black flag of treason or the white flag of cowardice." (He was defeated in a re-election bid for governor ofIndiana that year.)

The **Roosevelts** were of different parties. Between 1900 and 1944 there were twelve national elections. A **Roosevelt** was on the ticket in eight of those elections although they never faced each other. In a non-**Roosevelt** election in 1916 **Woodrow Wilson** and most of the country went to bed thinking that he had been defeated. Late returns from the western states, however, put **Wilson** over the top. The next day **FDR** who loved puns jested with a play on the title of one of **TR's** books: "It is rumored that a certain distinguished cousin of mine is now engaged in revising an edition of his most noted historical work, *The Winning of the West.*"

In the election of 1952 **Truman** said that the Republican Party led by **Eisenhower** was the "the Party of the Generals." He went on: "The Republicans have General Motors and General Electric and General Foods and General MacArthur and General Wedemeyer. And then they have their own five-star General who is running for President... I want to say to you that every general I know is on this list except general welfare, and general welfare is in with the corporals and the privates in the Democratic Party." President **Obama** in 2010 about the Republicans: "They don't have a single idea that is different from **George Bush's.**"

However, they have not always been loyal to party.

JFK told a friend in late 1959 that if he didn't win the Democrat nomination he would vote for **Nixon**. (Robert Kennedy had voted for **Eisenhower** over the Democrat Adlai Stevenson in 1956.) Once **JFK** said: "Sometimes party loyalty asks too much." An earlier example of that: in the Senate in the late 1850s **Andrew Johnson** opposed expenditures for a railroad to the Pacific Coast demanded by the California senators. When told that he was opposing the Democratic Party platform **Johnson** said: "I am no party man, bound by no party platform, and will vote as I please."

Moving forward

The Founders did not easily move toward political parties. One can find favorable comment about them only from Alexander Hamilton who wrote in Federalist No. 70: "In the legislature, promptitude of decision is oftener an evil than a benefit. The differences of opinion, and the jarrings of parties in that department of the government, though they may sometimes obstruct salutary plans, yet often promote deliberation and circumspection, and serve to check excesses in the majority."

But most disagreed, hoping for some type of national consensus.

Thomas Jefferson once said "If I could not go to heaven but with a party, I would not go at all." **John Adams** in 1780: "There is nothing which I dread so much as a division of the republic into two great parties, each arranged under its leader, and concerting measures in opposition to each other." As a sign that their wartime alliance was long past, **John Adams** said to Abigail during **George Washington's** administration: "I am really astonished at the blind spirit of party which has seized on the whole soul of this **Jefferson**." **Adams** also remarked to his wife: "**Jefferson** went off yesterday, and a good riddance of bad ware. He has talents I know, and integrity I believe; but his mind is now poisoned with passion, prejudice, and faction."

The American Revolution overthrew a government and yet did not lead to chaos and blood. However, its leaders discovered that they had contradictory ideas of how to proceed: the individual liberty of **Jefferson** versus the nationhood of Hamilton. In the 1790s during the unifying effects of **Washington**, these interests were placed into incipient political parties.

The Federalist Party grouped around Alexander Hamilton. It is one of the ancestors of the modern Republican Party. The Republican Party adhered to **Jefferson** and **Madison** and eventually became the Democratic Party of **Jackson**.

The French Revolution was a further cause for party development in the US which lay beyond even **Washington's** powers to reconcile. In 1794 as a new ambassador **James Monroe** gave an address to the National Convention in France. It was a full-throated commitment of the US to France. It contained phrases like:

- "Republics should approach near to each other... This is more especially the case with the American and French Republics: their governments are similar; they both cherish the same principles and rest on the same basis, the equal and unalienable rights of men. The recollection too of common dangers and difficulties will increases their harmony, and cement their Union."
- "America had her day of oppression, difficulty and war but her sons were virtuous and brave and the storm which long clouded her political horizon has passed and left them in the enjoyment of peace, liberty and independence. France ...has now embarked in the same noble career..."

It was not until **George Washington** read this address that he realized how wide the split between the Federalists and the Republicans was. A couple of years later when **Monroe** was considering quitting France **Jefferson** urged him to stay, saying that the ambassadorship was a "post which the public good requires to be filled by a Republican."

Jefferson's opposition to the Jay Treaty led him back into politics. On constitutional questions, **Jefferson** thought that House of Representatives could vote on the treaty. **Madison** held that the House could block it because certain sections needed to be funded. The consensus of historians is that the treaty avoided war with England at a time when peace was necessary and that **Jefferson's** and **Madison's** role in opposition was an early signal of a two-party system in the US.

After **Washington's** State of the Union address which touched on the Whiskey Rebellion of 1794, **Jefferson** said that whereas **Washington** had been "the head of a nation," now he was "the head of a party." In 1795 **Jefferson** wrote **Madison** that the Republican Party represented the "Southern interest." (In similar tones **Ford** said about two hundred years later, "...we must stake out our positions independent of any preplanning with the southern Democratic leadership also to correct the frequently distorted image of a Republican-southern Democratic coalition.")

In May of 1796 as **Washington's** time in the presidency was ending, **Madison** like other observers saw the election that year as the first real presidential election in US history: "**Jefferson** would probably be the object on one side (and) **Adams** apparently on the other." **John Adams** won a close one and as he came into office William Patterson, an Associate Justice of the Supreme Court, noted favorably that **Adams** and **Jefferson** had taken rooms in the same house in Philadelphia (the capital of the US at the time): "The thing looks well....it carries conciliation and healing with it, and may have a happy effect on the parties....I hope that in a short time, we shall have no interest or views but what are purely American."

John Adams seems to have tried to maintain this approach. He offered **Jefferson** cabinet-level authority and through him he offered **Madison** the ambassadorship to France. **Jefferson's** early response seemed favorable. He wrote **Adams** that the political culture was tense and he hoped to recover the time "when we were working together for our independence." But the attempt at a bipartisan presidency failed on party lines. **Adams'** Federalists were opposed and **Madison** told **Jefferson** that bipartisanship was not in the interests of the Republican Party which he needed to lead. Soon **John Adams** wrote **John Quincy Adams** about **Jefferson**: "You can witness for me how loath I have been to give him up. It is with much reluctance that I am obliged to look upon him as a man whose mind is warped with prejudice...as to be unfit for the office he holds."

In essence, during **John Adams'** presidency, the hope for politics above party was defeated by two factors: majority rule and the French Revolution. Majorities require some sort of coalitions which are most efficiently organized into parties. The French Revolution was almost like a Rorschach test for the statesmen and politicians of the early American Republic: Federalists abhorred it; Republicans drew inspiration from it. However the modern idea of a legitimate organized opposition to the elected government did not yet exist. It was considered a "faction."

In the two years after he returned from France in 1797 **Monroe** worked with **Madison** and **Jefferson** in developing and managing the Republican Party. He declined their recommendation that he run for the Congress since he felt it would be futile or worse with the Federalists in the majority. Instead, in 1799 he was elected governor of Virginia.

Monroe worked as a party leader in resolving some nettlesome political issues. In 1800 he helped manage the response to the Callender issue. He quietly prevented public demonstrations in favor of Callender but arranged for his defense. After Callender left prison **Monroe** advised **Jefferson** and **Madison** that Callender felt he had been deserted by the administration and that he should be handled carefully. (**Monroe** was in full damage-control mode, much like **George HW Bush** dealing with the Watergate crisis on behalf of **Richard Nixon** in the twentieth century.) **Monroe** also carefully managed separate receptions in Richmond for **Jefferson** and newly-appointed Secretary of State John Marshall, also a Virginian but a Federalist.

John Adams has been called by one biographer a party of one. During **Adams'** presidency between 1797-1801, **Jefferson** was both his Vice President and the leader of the opposing party. **Jefferson** wrote to an ally who flirted with the idea that Virginia and North Carolina might secede that "in every free and deliberating society there must, from the nature of man, be opposite parties, and violent dissensions and discords; and one of these, for the most part, must prevail over the other for a longer or shorter time.... But if on a temporary superiority of the one party, the other is to resort to a scission of the Union, no federal government can ever exist....A little patience, and we will see the reign of witches pass over, their spells dissolve, and the people, recovering their true sight, restore their government to its true principles." So he saw the time of **Adams** and the Federalist Party as the "reign of witches." (A similar exchange occurred over sixty years later which shows the difficulty of assessing a political context. As **Abraham Lincoln's** re-election campaign gained momentum in 1864, former President **Franklin Pierce** a Democrat wrote **Millard Fillmore**, a Whig: "What have we to do but observe the march of events thus far beyond the control of human wisdom and wait for returning wisdom and patriotism?" *Another* similar comment was made by **Ford** in 1974 after **Nixon's** resignation in the wake of Watergate: "My fellow Americans, our long national nightmare is over.")

The **Jefferson** victory of 1800-01 brought about first real governmental transition - from the Federalist Party to the Republican Party with its small-government principles. **Monroe** warned the incoming **Jefferson** to continue to oppose the Federalists: "There is no political error more to be avoided, than a step which gives cause to suspect an accommodation with that party... Such a step would shake the republican ranks, and prove the foundation of a growing interest to its antagonist. The royalist faction has lost deservedly the public confidence. It will sink under its own weight if we leave it to itself." **Jefferson** wrote back that he agreed.

Jefferson's re-election in 1804 was overwhelming. But **Jefferson** may have moved close to the Federalists than they to him. Like presidents after him **Jefferson** faced the need to adjust his beliefs to real-world events including the Barbary pirates of Morocco, Algiers, Tunis and Tripoli which required US military attention. Henry Adams wrote that **Jefferson** "stretched out his hand to seize the powers he had denounced." The Louisiana Purchase was accomplished on Federalist principles. The Bank of the US was preserved. The national debt was larger. The Navy was maintained. The powers of the federal government were greater. So, the Federalist Party died off but its principles guided **Jefferson's** Republicans, Moreover, the failure to convict Justice Samuel Chase in the impeachment trial in 1805 was a blow to the Republican Party from which it never wholly recovered because it preserved judicial independence and kept Chief Justice John Marshall a Federalist secure. By 1805 **Jefferson**, with the responsibility for the territory of the Louisiana Purchase, looked forward to internal improvements to "begin upon canals, roads, colleges, etc." Henry Adams: "Except in his aversion to military measures and to formal etiquette, he stood nearly where President **Washington** had stood ten years before."

In 1805 after failing in negotiations with Spain to define the boundaries of the Louisiana Purchase **Monroe** proposed, as noted, that the US seize the Floridas and occupy the territory beyond the Colorado to the Rio Grande. When **Jefferson** and **Madison** did not follow the advice a wedge developed between them and **Monroe** and he was courted by John Randolph and John Taylor of the "Old Republicans." This was a faction of the party that believed that **Madison** had led **Jefferson** astray from true Republican principles. **Jefferson** wrote **Monroe** calling these political opponents "mischief-makers" motivated by "the rancor of party spirit among us." (Nearly one hundred fifty years later another president also blamed interveners for his strained relationship with a future president. **Truman** said to **Eisenhower** after **Eisenhower** won the Republican nomination in 1952 and was moving to accommodate some of the Republican leaders who had opposed **Truman's** foreign policies: "Politics should stop at the United States. I am extremely sorry that you have allowed a bunch of screwballs to come between us.")

In 1806 **Jefferson** had to put down a party revolt to ensure the ascendancy of **Madison** over **Monroe** who was in Europe at the time. **Monroe** still contended with **Madison** for the presidency two years later. By this time, **Monroe** tended to favor England while **Madison** favored France. **Jefferson** told **Monroe**: "I see with infinite regret a contest between yourself and another, who have been very dear to each other, and equally so to me." After the election it took **Monroe** a few years and some behind-the-scenes work by **Jefferson** to work back into good standing with the Republican Party. In trying to get back into a position of influence **Monroe** needed to reconcile his faction with that of **Madison**. He said: "Mr. **Madison** is a Republican and so am I." He was elected governor of Virginia in 1811 and almost immediately was asked to be Secretary of State. His allies urged him to accept on the grounds that it would put him in line for the presidency and that he could re-tilt toward England.

John Quincy Adams almost alone among the Federalists supported **Jefferson** on the Louisiana Purchase. In 1808 he bolted the party and supported **James Madison** for the presidency. On these issues and others like the Embargo and Aaron Burr, **John Quincy Adams** alienated New England Federalists whom he believed wanted to dissolve the Union. He was reproved by his own mother. This was his drift to the Republican Party. As noted, the Massachusetts legislature voted to recall him from the Senate. This defeat of **Adams** put Massachusetts back in the Federalist column. But whereas the Federalists in 1801 had been the national party, the Federalists of 1808 were a pro-British party in secret alliance with England. **John Adams** also crossed party lines to support **Madison** in the War of 1812. This made him a figure of disdain to the Federalist Party. As noted, **Madison** appointed **Adams** minister to Russia.

As Acting Secretary of War in the War of 1812 **Monroe** moved to the non-Republican positions of a conscript army instead of state militias and a national bank to fund the war. He wrote **Jefferson** in 1814: "Our finances are in a deplorable state." He wrote **Madison** that a bank would "attach the commercial part of the community in a much greater degree to the Government; interest them in its operations..." **Monroe** was the first Republican leader to realize that it was not merely an agrarian party.

In general, the War of 1812 ended the Jeffersonian vision of an agrarian society. **Madison's** post-war program in 1816 included such Federalist policies as:

- A protective tariff for manufacturing
- A permanent army staff.
- New ships for the navy.
- Internal improvements. (He advised - at least as a gesture - a constitutional amendment,)

In his State of the Union in 1817 **Monroe** wanted a constitutional amendment to permit federally funded internal improvements. There was controversy over whether this was needed. **Monroe** consulted **Madison** about the precedent of **Jefferson** approving federal funding for the Cumberland Road. **Madison** said he couldn't remember discussing it with **Jefferson** but assumed **Jefferson** had signed it "doubtingly or hastily" and that other bills following it had been approved with less scrutiny than was "perhaps due to the case." In 1819 the Supreme Court upheld the constitutionality of the Bank of the United States in *McCulloch v Maryland.* In 1820 **Monroe** acknowledged to **John Quincy Adams** that the Bank was necessary to provide credit throughout the US and to maintain specie payments. Years later **Madison** said that his party "had been reconciled to certain measures and arrangements which may be as proper now as they were premature and suspicious when urged by the champions of Federalism." (In other words, he had been right when he opposed these measures and right when he supported them.) **John Tyler** did not go along. He announced that he would not run for re-election in 1820. One reason: he was in the minority and wrote his friend of "daring usurpations of this government - usurpations of a more alarming character than have ever before taken place even during the fearful period of '98-'99." It is remarkable that by 1820 time had passed him by but in twenty years party politics made him president. In 1841 in trying to persuade the Senate to override **Tyler's** veto of a bank bill Henry Clay criticized the veto by citing **Madison's** acceptance of the second Bank of the United States.

If the Jeffersonians were co-opted by Federalist principles and in turn co-opted the key Federalists like the **Adamses**, they retained the idea of extinguishing party divisions. For **Monroe,** this was a gradual project with stops and starts. As he was forming his cabinet, for example, **Jackson** advised him to pick a Federalist for Secretary of War. **Monroe** demurred. He told **Jackson** that they needed to depend on "decided friends, who stood firm in the day of trial." He also wrote **Jackson** that his goal was "to prevent the reorganization and revival of the federal party." He thought "that the existence of parties is not necessary to free government." **Monroe** believed "that the great body of the federal party are republican." **Jackson** went along with that, telling **Monroe**: "Now is the time to *exterminate* the monster called party spirit." **Monroe** took this thought into his first inaugural asserting that the American people "constitute one great *family* with a common interest." He stressed that "*discord* does not belong to our system." After a warm welcome in New England in 1817 **Monroe** wrote **Madison** that he was glad to give the Federalists the chance to "get back in the great family of the union." In 1822 he wrote **Madison** again that: "We have undoubtedly reached a new epoch in our political career which has been formed by the destruction of the Federal Party...by the general peace... the entire absence of all political excitement, and, in truth by the real prosperity of the Union.... Parties have now cooled down, or rather have disappeared from this great theatre, and we are about to make the experiment whether there is sufficient virtue in the people to support our free republican system of government." This was a look backwards and a denial of the reality of conflict and the corresponding need to manage it. A look forward was offered by **Martin Van Buren**.

Van Buren went to the Senate in 1821. He distrusted **Monroe** whom he thought had too many Federalists around him. **Van Buren** called **Monroe's** attempt to amalgamate the parties "**Monroe's** heresy." There are several points to be drawn from this. First, **Van Buren** sounded a lot like a young **Monroe** who when he was informed about Federalist machinations in the disputed election of 1800 wrote **Jefferson** asking if the Federalists could be capable of this "degree of boldness as well as wickedness." Second, **Van Buren's** criticism was exactly what one might expect a political person to feel in perceiving **Monroe's** desire for consensus. Third, **Van Buren** was abetted by **Thomas Jefferson**. **Van Buren** visited **Jefferson** in 1824 for several days. **Jefferson** confirmed his impression that **Monroe** had strayed from Jeffersonianism. He later wrote **Van Buren**, "Tories are still Tories, by whatever name they are called." **Van Buren** wrote back that he hoped to save **Jefferson's** country from "misrule."

In the 1825-29 period **Van Buren** was still in Senate, **John Quincy Adams** was president and **Van Buren** felt pretty much the same way. He watched **Adams** pick former Federalists for posts along with members of the new Republican Party. **Van Buren** objected and complained that **Adams** didn't care if his support came from "Jew or Gentile." In response to all this, **Van Buren** helped create the modern party system. In that period he was allied with regional politicos like **James Buchanan** of Pennsylvania and **Franklin Pierce** of New Hampshire. As **Buchanan** was later a quintessential Jacksonian Democrat his party arc is worth noting. He had been a Federalist critical of **James Madison**. Later, in the Pennsylvania legislature he wrote that he saw no "trace of the old distinction between Federal and Democrat...several of those elected as Federalists held to a considerable extent Democratic principles, while many of those who had been called Democrats held high-toned federal principles." In the early 1820s as a member of Congress from Pennsylvania **James Buchanan** left the Federalists for the Jacksonian Democrats. By 1825 **Buchanan** joined the group of Congressmen around **Andrew Jackson** after **Jackson's** defeat in the presidential election by **John Quincy Adams** and worked closely with **Van Buren**. For the rest of his life as Whigs, Know-nothings and modern Republicans emerged and in some instances declined, **Buchanan** held to the Democrat doctrines of "the Sovereignty of the People, the Rights of States, and a light simple government."

In the **John Quincy Adams** administration, **Adams**, Henry Clay and eventually Daniel Webster gathered around the old Madisonian program of National legislation to promote economic development. In his State of the Union address in 1825 **Adams** proposed programs like internal improvements such as roads, bridges, canals and highways, a type of planetarium to study the stars, a standard system of weights measures, a new Department of the Interior and American attendance at an international conference of Latin American states. He said: "...let us not be unmindful that liberty is power; that the nation blessed with the largest portion of liberty must in proportion to its members be the most powerful nation upon earth. While foreign nations less blessed with that freedom which is power than ourselves are advancing with gigantic strides in the career of public improvement were we to slumber in indolence or fold up our arms and proclaim to the world that we are palsied by the will of our constituents, would it not be to cast away the bounties of Providence and doom ourselves to perpetual inferiority?"

However, the **Adams** administration with its activism and elitism was out of step with the growing voter franchise. The response to this early-eighteenth-century paean to big government was that the original Republican Party of **Jefferson** broke into the National Republicans and the Democratic Republicans. The National Republicans favored **Adams'** programs and were aligned with Henry Clay's American System. The Democratic Republicans favored limited government along the lines of **Jefferson** and were led by **Van Buren** and **Jackson.** The Democratic Republicans or Democrats triumphed in 1828 and for the most part held power until the time of **Lincoln**. Jacksonian Democrats were typically for small government, white male suffrage and southern rights. Their ranks included **Van Buren**, **Polk**, **Pierce**, **Buchanan**, **Andrew Johnson** and wannabes like Stephen F. Douglas who helped establish the Compromise of 1850 and famously debated **Lincoln**.

Reading for the law in 1825 in Portsmouth New Hampshire a young **Franklin Pierce** supported efforts to build a pro-**Jackson** party in a Federalist stronghold. He had a modern concept of politics writing a friend, "A republic without parties is a complete anomaly." Also: "The citizens are convinced that Jeffersonian principles are the principles for a free people, and I trust they have no notion of renouncing their faith."

By 1828 the National Republicans in New York endorsed the Anti-Mason movement and **Fillmore** became a delegate to the first state-wide Anti-Masonic convention. **Fillmore** was also a delegate to Erie County's National Republican convention that endorsed **John Quincy Adams**. He was involved in a very complicated party fight trying to mediate between the Anti-Masons and the National Republicans. Ultimately the Jacksonian Democrats won the state under **Martin Van Buren** who was elected governor. Out of all this **Fillmore** went to the state assembly. In the early 1830s **Fillmore** worked to get the Antimasons and the National Republicans to blend into the new Whig Party. The Anti-Masons were a national force in the late 1820s and early 1830s. They included within their supporters Thaddeus Stevens – Massachusetts, William Seward - New York, **John Quincy Adams** – Massachusetts and others like **Millard Fillmore**.

As a young state legislator **Pierce** worked with the **Jackson** administration to bring about the first party nominating convention in 1832 that renominated **Jackson** for President and **Van Buren** for Vice President.

The political differences between the two second-generation political giants Henry Clay and **Andrew Jackson** defined the two party system. Clay wanted the federal government to work on behalf of economic development through such programs such as tariffs and federal expenditures. He called it the American System. It became the foundation of the Whig Party. **Jackson** was for a smaller federal government. This difference could be seen in 1836 as **Jackson** left office and two future Presidents - **Van Buren** the Democrat and **William Henry Harrison** the Whig - differed on:

- The Bank of the US. **Van Buren** - There should be no Bank "until the people give to Congress the right to establish one." **Harrison** - He thought the Bank had violated its charter and he would sign on to a new one only "if it were clearly ascertained that the public interest would materially suffer without it."
- Internal improvements - particularly of navigable streams above ports of entry. **Van Buren** - No. **Harrison** - Yes if Congress approved.
- Expunging of a Senate censure of **Andrew Jackson**. **Van Buren** – this was not the concern of a president but

in this instance the action was probably commendable. **Harrison** - No.

The first of these two were serious party differences. The last was just politics. **Van Buren** took the election but **Harrison** took the rematch four years later in the first genuine two-party campaign.

On the basis of his pro-tariff views **Fillmore** caught a wave and became part of the Whig surge and eventually the president. In judging candidates for the presidential election of 1840 and wanting to defeat **Van Buren**, **Fillmore** wrote a friend: "It must be recollected that we have to cement the fragments of many parties and it is therefore very important that we get a substance to which all can adhere, or at least that presents as few repellant qualities as possible. Into what crucible can we throw this heterogeneous mass of old national republicans, and revolting **Jackson** men; masons and antimasons; abolitionists, and pro-slavery men; bank men and anti-bank men with all the lesser fragments that have been, from time to time, thrown off from the great political wheel in its violent revolutions, so as to melt them down into one mass of pure Whigs of undoubted mettle?" **Fillmore** ended up using Winfield Scott as a stalking horse to defeat Henry Clay in New York and secure the Whig nomination for **William Henry Harrison**.

In sum, most partisan political conflict between 1834-56 was economic, such as:

- The proper level of responsibility of the federal government to build such infrastructure as turnpikes, canals, and railroads.
- The privileges awarded to shareholders in corporations, especially those that absolved them from any responsibilities for companies' debts.
- Banking and paper money.

Historians sometimes call this period the Second American Party System. The Jacksonian position came to be opposition to government money to support economic development, opposition to paper money, opposition to corporate privilege. Whigs nominated three generals in four elections. The party lasted effectively through the early 1850s. It was primarily held together by Clay and his ability to reach compromises, Webster's orations, the military nominees, the 1840 campaign and a loathing of **Jackson**.

Within the same party, of course, there were significant rivalries. **Jackson's** attitude toward **Buchanan** was dismissive. **Buchanan** has been rumored to have been gay and **Jackson** once called him "Aunt Nancy." **Jackson** also once called **Buchanan** "an inept busybody." **Jackson** appointed him ambassador to Russia but said later, "It was as far as I could send him out of my sight. ... I would have sent him to the North Pole if we had kept a minister there." **Polk** on **Buchanan** at the end of his term: "He is an able man...but sometimes he acts like an old maid."

James Polk and **Andrew Johnson** were both from Tennessee and both Jacksonian Democrats. In the Tennessee Senate in 1841, **Johnson** used parliamentary procedures to block the selection of two Whig US Senators, earning the praise of the governor **Polk** and **Jackson**. But tensions arose. **Polk** was of the upper class. **Johnson** was a backwoods politician who learned to read and write as an adult. **Johnson** once gave him unsolicited advice on an issue but qualified it by the phrase "unless I am rong." **Polk** ignored the advice. **Polk's** negative feelings toward the younger **Johnson** persisted. After a meeting with him, **Polk** wrote that **Johnson** was a "demogue...I would almost prefer to have two Whigs here."

As a Jacksonian Democrat, **Andrew Johnson** saw democracy as a cure. He came along at a time when incipient unions were making demands for equal citizenship. **Andrew Johnson** became an alderman about the time **Andrew Jackson** became president. In retirement, **Jackson** would send **Johnson** words of approval as **Nixon** would for **George HW Bush** in another century. **Jackson** and **Johnson** both valued states rights but put the union over Nullification or Secession. **Johnson** as a young politician read aloud at a dinner **Jackson's** famous 1830 toast: "Our Federal Union it must be preserved." As noted, he used it as president years later.

In 1844 six presidents were involved. **Polk** went to the 1844 Democrat convention hoping to be selected as **Van Buren's** running mate. (**Polk** had received 1 electoral college vote for vice –president in 1840 when the Democrats failed to nominate anyone.) **Andrew Johnson** was at first reluctant to support **Polk** for vice president because of **Polk's** support for **Van Buren**. **Polk** organized his state delegation to support himself for vice president but no one for president, a move that strained relationships with **Van Buren**. At one point **Buchanan** dropped out sensing a **Van Buren** win. **Polk** wrote **Jackson**: "*Ohio* I regard to be the *pivot*, upon which the question of the Vice Presidential nomination will turn." **Jackson** wrote a letter on his behalf. In the maneuvering for the Vice Presidency it began to occur to **Polk's** friends that he should aim for the presidency. The issue of President **Tyler** secretly negotiating for Texas began to emerge. When **Van Buren** renounced annexation of Texas in 1844 **Jackson** wrote him that it would be "impossible" to elect him and turned to **Polk.**

Polk as noted defeated **Van Buren** at the Democrat convention only because of the two-thirds rule. He then entered the race against Henry Clay of the Whigs. The incumbent **Tyler** encouraged a third party appealing to states' rights Whigs, expansionists, and Jacksonian populists. There was a move to get **Jackson** to assure **Tyler** that if he did drop out of the race **Tyler's** associates would be welcomed back into the party and treated well and considered for future government jobs. **Polk** wrote an associate: "I believe Gen. **Jackson** is the only man in the country whose advice Mr. **Tyler** would take." **Jackson** distanced himself from the idea in a letter to **Polk**: "Why my dear friend such a letter from me or any other of your conspicuous friends would be seized upon as a bargain & intrigue for the presidency. Let me say to you that such a letter would damn you & destroy your election." Yet **Jackson** sent a more circumspect message to a friend of **Tyler's** and it worked to get **Tyler** out of the race and to get him to ask his friends to support **Polk**. **Van Buren** also endorsed **Polk** who went on to win a close election over Clay. As he left office in 1845 **Tyler** who had been effectively expelled from the Whig Party threw a lavish banquet for the incoming **Polk**. When complimented on the celebration **Tyler** joked, "They cannot say *now* that I am a President *without a party*." **Polk** had one of the most consequential presidencies in history, expanding the US to California.

In the Black Hawk War of 1832, Private **Abraham Lincoln** was in camp under Colonel **Zachary Taylor**. Fifteen years later as **Taylor** became famous during the Mexican-American War, Whig Party leaders began to see him as a possible president and **Lincoln** joined a pro-**Taylor** group in Congress. **Taylor** danced around the issue of party. In 1847 he said he would be available for the presidency but added "In no case can I permit myself to be the candidate of any party, or yield myself to party schemes." He backed off this statement amidst criticism and declared himself a Whig, which he inaccurately identified with **Thomas Jefferson**. In 1848 in a letter propelling his candidacy **Taylor** wrote: "I am a Whig but not an ultra Whig. If elected I would not be the mere president of a party..." **Taylor**, like other career-generals-turned-presidents - **Washington**, **Grant** and **Eisenhower** – had learned a nationalism in the army that left him somewhat disdainful of parties. He said that his election "would be the most signal rebuke ever ministered to a party under similar circumstances." **Taylor** made no promises about what he would do as president other than "support the Constitution as near as practicable, as was construed by our first chief magistrate."

That year the Democrat Party was split between **Polk** and **Van Buren** factions. In addition to patronage the factions were split over the extension of slavery. The Whigs nominated **Taylor** (and **Millard Fillmore**), the Democrats nominated Lewis Cass and the Free Soil party nominated **Van Buren** and Charles Francis Adams representing the forces opposed to the extension of slavery (and also reconciling the two families of once-feuding ex-presidents). There is some indication that **Van Buren** may have been reluctant to run and would have wanted **Pierce** to be nominated by the Free Soilers.

President **Polk** hated **Taylor** and turned on **Van Buren**, declaring that his third-party candidacy "is a most dangerous attempt to organize Geographical parties upon the slave question. Mr. **Van Buren's** course is selfish, unpatriotic, and wholly inexcusable." Later, he wrote, "Mr. **Van Buren** is the most fallen man I have ever known." **Polk's** fears were justified. The **Van-Buren**/Adams ticket got enough votes in New York to swing the election to the Whigs of **Taylor** and **Fillmore**. (This point could be debated. Some recent scholarship indicates that **Taylor** would have probably won the election of 1848 even if **Van Buren** was not in the race.) The Free Soil Party got ten percent of the vote, prefiguring the Republican Party.

By 1850 both parties had a North-South orientation with the Democrats more beholden to the South and with the Whigs teetering on collapse. **Andrew Johnson,** seeing the break-up of the Whig party observed in 1853 that the consequences would also be bad for the Democrats: "The Whig party is now disbanded leaving the (Democratic) party without external pressure to keep it together." But the Democrats own collapse was forestalled by the competition from two new parties. The American Party (also called the Know-Nothings, a reference to its member's penchant for secrecy) emerged as an anti-Catholic party. **Fillmore's** move to the American Party in 1855 was in keeping with his association with the Antimasonic Party earlier and with his desire to find a national party. **Abraham Lincoln** criticized **Fillmore's** new party: "When the Know-Nothings get control (the Declaration) will read, 'All men are created equal, except Negroes and foreigners and Catholics.'" The success of the American Party in the 1854 congressional elections in the Whig's northern base helped persuade people like William Seward and **Lincoln** to give up on the Whigs for a new, more resolutely anti-slavery party and the Republican Party emerged. By 1855 most Whigs went into the American Party or the Republicans.

Preserving the Democratic Party was a top objective of President **Pierce** in the years 1853-57 as he wrestled with slavery and sectional hatreds. In the 1856 election, **Fillmore** as a third party candidate may have helped **Buchanan** win much as **Van Buren** had assisted **Taylor** eight years earlier. But the real news was this: the tally showed that the Republicans, not the Know-Nothings, were the party of the future.

In the 1850s a young **Rutherford B Hayes**, a reform-minded Whig lawyer had no philosophical difficulties moving into the new Republican Party. **Lincoln** came to Cincinnati in 1859 to campaign for Republicans. **Hayes** met him and showed him to his hotel. **Hayes** advised **Lincoln** on the political mix of Republicans and the Know-Nothings. **Hayes** thought that if **Lincoln**, "an old Clay Whig, of Kentucky parentage, with a wholesome dislike of Locofocoism" (a radical off-shoot of the Democrat party) were cautious "as to our peculiar position" he would do well. Some years later **Hayes** recalled "that the presidential bee had already begun to buzz around" **Lincoln**. When **Lincoln** later spoke in Cincinnati **Hayes** thought "Here is Henry Clay over again."

Ulysses S. Grant also moved easily into the Republican Party. An early biographer said of **Grant**: "**Grant** is a Douglas Democrat, but is converted to Republicanism." (**Grant's** father had lived with the family of abolitionist John Brown. He was a Jacksonian Democrat who turned to the Whigs in the 1830s appreciating its pro-business and free labor policies. He went to the Republicans in the 1850s before his son did.)

For his part, Democrat President **James Buchanan** demonized the Republican Party as a threat to the South making secession more likely when **Lincoln** was elected. **Buchanan** also fought with his own party. In late 1857 **Buchanan** argued with Senator Stephen Douglas over his pro-southern policies in Kansas. He reminded Douglas that Senators who opposed **Jackson** were marginalized. Douglas sounded the death knell of the Democrat Party of the antebellum era with all its temporizing on slavery by responding: "Mr. President, **Andrew Jackson** is dead." By 1858 **Buchanan** had split the Democrat Party. That year campaigning for the Senate **Lincoln** said that "**James**" (**Buchanan**), "Roger" (Taney), "**Franklin**" (**Pierce**) and his opponent "Stephen" (Douglas) had conspired to protect slavery throughout the US. The Democrats elected only one president – **Cleveland** – in the next fifty years.

The Republican Party became the party of the union. In 1861 **Grant** told the town of Galena Illinois: "There are but two parties now,

Traitors and Patriots and I want hereafter to be ranked with the latter, and I trust, the stronger party."

In 1864 **Grant** was told that some Republicans wanted to run him for president against **Lincoln**. He hit his chair arms and cried, "They can't do it! They can't compel me to do it!" He added. "I consider it as important to the cause that he should be elected, as that the army should be successful in the field." (With **Lincoln's** re-election **Buchanan** said of the losing candidate: "It is fortunate both for himself and the Democratic party that he was not elected.")

Lincoln figured that without the support of the War Democrats he could not win the Civil War. This political reality produced stress between him and the Radicals in his own party and led to the last Jacksonian President, **Andrew Johnson**. **Johnson's** trajectory in those few years is instructive. He was a patriot who put the country over party. In 1864 **Andrew Johnson** as military governor of Tennessee sent a message to Tennessee's congressman: "I would give some of the faultfinders to understand that the real Union men will be for **Abraham Lincoln** for President. The war must be closed under **Lincoln's** administration." **Lincoln** picked him for a running mate and he ascended to the presidency determined to carry out **Lincoln's** post-war objectives.

In 1865 Congressman **Garfield** met with President **Johnson** and had what **Garfield** called a "full and free" conversation. **Garfield** wrote: "Some foolish men among us are all the while bristling up for a fight and seem to be anxious to make a rupture with **Johnson**. I think we should assume that he is with us, treat him kindly, without suspicion, and go on in a firm, calmly considered course, leaving him to make the breach with the party if any is made. I doubt if he would do it under any such circumstances."

A Republican goal in Reconstruction was to get Black votes to secure a two-party system in the South. (A century later a Democrat **JFK** described Reconstruction as "a black nightmare the South could never forget" in his Pulitzer-prize winning *Profiles in Courage*.)

In 1866, **Johnson** saw both parties going to the extremes and tried to start a Union party which failed.

Johnson tried to defeat the Radical Republicans in the 1866 Congressional elections by a campaign trip that was unusual for the era. It was a three-week trip by train from Washington DC to New York, to Chicago, to St. Louis, and east through the Ohio River valley back to Washington DC. It was called the "Swing Around the Circle." **Grant**, William Seward and George Armstrong Custer accompanied **Johnson**. (In the next decade, Custer and his entire unit were wiped out by Indians in the Battle of Little Big Horn. **Grant** by then in his last year in office told a reporter: "I regard Custer's Massacre as a sacrifice of troops, brought on by Custer himself; that was wholly unnecessary— wholly unnecessary.") So did the Mexican ambassador. **Fillmore**, meeting with **Johnson** in Buffalo, said that in 1861 **Johnson** "stood like a rock in the midst of an ocean against which the waves of rebellion dashed in vain." **Buchanan** observing the trip said "I do not like the progress to Chicago. I think it is ill-judged." He thought **Johnson** would be indentified with Stephen F. Douglas' views of repeal of the Missouri Compromise and popular sovereignty. **Grant**: "I am disgusted with this trip. I am disgusted at hearing a man make speeches on the way to his funeral." **Grant** wrote his wife that the speeches were a "national disgrace." But he told her: "Of course, you will not show this letter to anyone for as long as Mr. **Johnson** is President I must respect him as such, and it is in the country's interest that I should also have his confidence." The fall elections showed that the trip was largely a failure.

In the 1867 elections, however, Democrats generally did very well with the exception of the Republican **Hayes** winning the governorship in Ohio. This caused more talk of a resumption of the Civil War and temporarily quelled talk on impeachment. William Tecumseh Sherman in a letter to his brother in 1867: "If the President is impeached and the South reduced to territories, the country will, of course, relapse into a state of war, or quasi-war, and what good it will do passes my comprehension."

In 1868, after impeachment and Senate acquittal, **Andrew Johnson** was a candidate for the Democratic nomination even though he had been elected with **Lincoln** on the "Union" ticket in 1864. In 1872 the Liberal Republicans arose in opposition to **Grant's** second term. Charles Francis Adams competed for the nomination but lost to Horace Greeley. This new party stood for civil service reform, reduction of the tariff, withdrawing troops from the South. **Grant** came to dismiss them as a threat telling **James Garfield** that they reminded him of howling prairie wolves he had encountered while serving under **Zachary Taylor** in Texas which he had estimated to number about a hundred but came to discover that two wolves were making all the noise. However, the Liberals had some influence as their platform was adopted by **Hayes** in 1877 when he got to the presidency. In 1872, though, **Hayes** stayed with the Republicans and **Grant**. In 1876 Charles Francis Adams of the Liberal Republicans supported the Democrat Samuel Tilden. The Democrats in Massachusetts nominated Adams for governor. This son and grandson of presidents was by then a figure of the past.

In 1876 **Arthur** was not a follower of **Hayes** but as a good party man supported him. After the election, however, as noted, **Hayes** moved to fire **Arthur** from head of the New York Custom House and replace him with **TR's** father provoking an intra-party fight.

At the 1880 Republican convention **Benjamin Harrison** favored James G. Blaine over **Grant**. At a crucial point he shifted to **James Garfield**. In the election **Garfield,** in an attempt at reconciling factions within the party between the liberal Republicans and the regular Republicans, went to a hotel on Fifth Avenue in New York for a crucial meeting with leaders from the regular faction. After the "Fifth Avenue" meeting **Garfield** realized that he may have misled them into thinking they would get to make appointments to federal jobs in New York. He wrote **Hayes**: "If I finished the N.Y. trip without mistakes, I shall be glad." (In 1960 **Richard Nixon** met with Nelson Rockefeller at his apartment on Fifth Avenue in New York to try to work out party differences. The agreement they reached was called the "Treaty of Fifth Avenue." In 1963 **Nixon** moved to New York and into that apartment building, became Rockefeller's neighbor and launched his comeback that got him to the presidency in a few years.) **Arthur,** running for Vice President, was a major factor in the Republican victory by his fundraising and management skills. **Benjamin Harrison** said at that time of the Republican Party: "It has always sympathized with and aided the efforts of every class of people who were seeking a larger liberty and a more perfect sphere for the development of their powers."

Parties of course lose their focus. The Federalists did, the Jeffersonians did, and the Whigs did. The Jacksonians regrouped. The Republicans were not immune. For the Republicans it was a twenty-eight year process. In 1884, with **Garfield** dead and **Arthur's** health compromised (he died within two years after leaving the White House) the Republicans turned to James G. Blaine causing a group of Republicans –the "Mugwumps" – to support the Democrat **Cleveland.** As a young journalist, **Warren Harding** gave credit to a young **TR** for not bolting the Republican Party in 1884. What followed were two terms of **Grover Cleveland** broken by a single term of **Benjamin Harrison**.

Toward the end of his life **Benjamin Harrison** wrote, "In the old Republican days the subject of slavery and of the saving of the Union made appeals to the consciences and liberty-loving instincts of the people. These later years have been full of talk about commerce and dinner pails, but I feel sure that the American conscience and the American love of liberty have not been smothered. They will break through this crust of sordidness and realize that those only keep their liberties who accord liberty to others." The reference to "dinner pails" was a swipe at a **McKinley** campaign slogan which touted the **McKinley** presidency as helping cause a "full dinner pail."

Some journalists regarded **McKinley's** win in 1896 over William Jennings Bryan as vindication of **Cleveland** who had not supported his fellow Democrat Bryan. **Woodrow Wilson** also crossed party lines and voted for **McKinley** over Bryan. The historical memory of **McKinley** quickly disappeared after his assassination in 1901 and he came to be seen as a prelude to the more dynamic **TR**. But one of the achievements for which he should be remembered is that he solidified the Republican Party by winning twice and broadening the base. The split that came a decade later was not fatal due in some part to this work.

The historic split in the Republican Party began to emerge in 1904 when upon his re-election **TR** announced that he would not seek another term. Four years later he was succeeded by **Taft**. Although a break-up was probably inevitable, **Taft's** discharge as Chief of the Department of Forestry of Gifford Pinchot was an early blow to his relationship with **TR**. **TR** had resisted the Mugwumps who bolted the party in 1884 but became the greatest party splitter ever in 1912 when he challenged **Taft**. When the *Titanic* sunk in the midst of the primary campaign Henry Adams wrote: "The *Titanic* is wrecked. So is **Taft**; so is the Republican Party." **Taft** won the nomination and in his acceptance speech referred to **TR** as "the leader of former Republicans who have left their party." **Harding** excoriated **Roosevelt**.

TR formed the Progressive Party and told his supporters: "We stand at Armageddon and we battle for the Lord." **Coolidge** remained loyal to **Taft** and spoke out against **TR's** support for the recall of judicial decisions. **Herbert Hoover** supported **TR** and contributed one thousand dollars to his campaign. That year **Taft** said he wanted to get nominated to keep **TR** from wrecking the Republican Party. Someone said it was probably too late and **Taft** explained, "I don't mean wrecking it in an election. I mean warping it away from its purpose and changing its character. I mean changing it to a radical party from a party of moderate liberalism." After his 1912 defeat, **Taft** said: "The vote for Mr. **Roosevelt**, the third party candidate, and for Mr. Debs, the Socialist candidate, is a warning that their propaganda in favor of fundamental changes in our constitutional representative Government has formidable support... It behooves Republicans to gather again to the party standard and pledge anew their faith in their party's principles and to organize to defend the constitutional government handed down to us by our fathers.... Let us close ranks and march forward to do battle for the right and the true."

Taft's role in that campaign of moving the Republican Party to the right was one of the most important results of his presidency.

Harding, Coolidge, Reagan, and **George W Bush** are clearly of the party of **Taft**. The other twentieth century Republican presidents fit less obviously into this wing of the party:

- **Hoover: FDR** advisor Rex Tugwell said in 1974: "We didn't admit it at the time, but practically the whole New Deal was extrapolated from programs that **Hoover** started." (In June 1940 John L Lewis president of the Mineworkers spoke to the NAACP. He claimed that **Hoover** had been unfairly blamed for depression. He said that the recovery was well underway in 1932 but was sabotaged by **FDR** and the New Deal.) **Hoover** may have later moved rightward: he called **Eisenhower** "a very expensive president" reflecting **Eisenhower's** evolution of the New Deal.
- **Eisenhower**: In 1953, **LBJ** described **Eisenhower's** first inaugural address as "a very good statement of Democratic programs of the last twenty years." **Eisenhower** defeated **Taft's** son to win the Republican nomination in 1952.
- **Nixon: Jimmy Carter** called **Nixon's** foreign policy "good and productive."
- **Ford: Ford** was challenged from the right by **Reagan** in 1976 and nearly denied the nomination.
- **George HW Bush:** The conservatives in the party were lukewarm toward him. He opposed **Reagan** in the 1980 primaries and in 1992 he faced a right-wing primary challenge. His background was east-coast affluent (plus war hero). As a young man **George HW Bush** stayed out of political discussions that focused of party labels. He told his wife, "Labels are for cans."

TR's split of the Republican Party had many consequences. One, unnoticed at the time, was a localized effect of a divided Republican Party: the split helped Democrat **FDR** get elected to the New York state legislature that year in a Republican district in 1910 and re-elected in 1912.

Wilson, the winner in 1912, saw the value of party and said in his inaugural address: "The success of a party means little except when the nation is using that party for a large and definite purpose. No one can mistake the purpose for which the nation now seeks to use the Democratic Party."

In the next four years **Wilson**:

- Signed legislation reducing the tariff.
- Authorized federal income tax.
- Created Federal Reserve to regulate money supply.
- Strengthened the Sherman Anti-Trust Act to curb corporations.
- Created the Federal Trade Commission.
- Signed laws for government loans to farmers.
- Signed laws for restrictions on child labor.
- Signed laws for Workers Compensation for government contractors.
- Signed laws for an eight-hour day for interstate railroad employees.
- Put in higher taxes on wealthy.

By the time **Wilson** ran for re-election he had put in place every major plank of the 1912 Progressive Party platform.

In 1916 **Taft** urged Charles Evans Hughes to run for the Republican nomination to block **Theodore Roosevelt. Taft** was concerned about any **Roosevelt** appointments to the court.

In early 1920 a movement to elect **Herbert Hoover** began but it was not clear if he belonged to either party. He said: "There are about forty live issues in this country in which I am interested, and before I cannot answer whether I am a Democrat or Republican, I shall have to know how each party stands on these issues."

It is hard to imagine now but in the 1920s **Coolidge** was a powerful cultural influence. Former President and Chief Justice **William Howard Taft** wrote Treasury Secretary Andrew Mellon in 1924: "that the welfare of the country is critically dependent on the success of President **Coolidge**. The Republican Party has no chance without him. I don't remember a case in which a party is so dependent on a man." The **Coolidge** and **Hoover** administrations held the center of the country until the coming of the New Deal and Democrat control of the presidency for the next twenty years through **FDR** and **Truman**.

FDR in the election of 1932 effected a realignment of American politics. In the 1936 campaign **FDR** likened himself to one of the original Democrats, **Andrew Jackson**: "**Jackson** fought for human rights in his many battles to protect the people against autocratic or oligarchic aggression. ... They loved him for the enemies he had made."

But **Franklin Roosevelt** grew weary of the southern conservative influence in the Democratic Party and is known to have considered teaming up with his 1940 Republican opponent Wendell Wilkie to develop a postwar liberal party with conservatives and isolationists on the other side. It was not to be.

FDR's New Deal made only one mark on the Constitution: the 22nd amendment which limited the terms of the president. A summary of the changes to the Constitution from other eras is as follows:

- The first ten amendments, the Bill of Rights, came from the great debate over ratification.
- The Civil War brought about another set of amendments.
- The Progressives amended the constitution several times establishing an income tax, prohibiting the sale of alcohol and establishing the direct election of senators.

Modern liberalism has, ever since the New Deal, had an uncertain foundation. Seeing the end of this period, **LBJ** said: "**Roosevelt** is gone. We never finished what he started out to do, and I'm not sure, the way the country seems to be going, that we're going to do much about the things that most need doing. The economizers are in the saddle, and after November, they'll have the reins. "We ought to be doing something for our schools, but we won't. We ought to be doing something for our old folks, but we won't. ..I don't know what I can do, or anybody can do. We don't seem to have the ideas like we used to have, and if we had the ideas, I'm not sure we could get the votes."

But of course **Eisenhower** did not revoke the New Deal. He was a centrist. In 1951 **Eisenhower** was closer to the Democrats on foreign policy than he was to Bob Taft and closer to the Republicans on domestic policy. When **Truman** tried to get him to commit to run in 1952 as a Democrat, **Eisenhower** responded: "You can't join a party just to run for office. What reason have you to think I have ever been a Democrat? You know I have been a Republican all my life and that my family have always been Republicans." When **Truman** pressed, **Eisenhower** demurred saying his differences with the Democrats over domestic matters particularly labor issues were too great.

In January of 1952 **Truman** gave Congress his budget with a $14B deficit. In February 1952 **Hoover** joined with Bob Taft in a statement that "American troops should be brought home" from Europe. These two events pressured **Eisenhower** to enter the contest for the Republican nomination. In essence, then, in 1952 **Eisenhower** was trying to save the country from **Truman** and Taft. By early in the **Eisenhower** years Taft died and **Nixon** took on the critical role of keeping the Republican Party united behind **Ike**. (Joseph McCarthy put out the word that he was "sick and tired of the constant yack-yacking from that prick **Nixon**.") During his time in office **Eisenhower** was consistently popular but he relied on his Vice President's political skills within the party even though parts of **Nixon's** personality irritated him. At one point he drafted a letter to **Nixon**: "I am constantly working to produce a bipartisan approach, and I rather think that keeping up attacks on (former Secretary of State under **Truman**) Acheson will, at this late date, hamper our efforts." **Ike** did not send the letter.

Reagan who had campaigned for **Truman** in 1948 crossed party lines in 1952 and 1956 to endorse **Eisenhower**. In 1960 **Reagan** endorsed **Nixon** and discussed changing parties. But **Nixon** asked him to stay a Democrat.

In 1960 **Eisenhower** thought **Lyndon Johnson** "would be the best Democrat of them all as President from the viewpoint of responsible management of the national interest." **Eisenhower** later said to **Johnson**: "You were my strong right arm when I was President."

Nixon ran for president in two very different times, 1960 and 1968. In 1968 **LBJ** declined to run for re-election. He favored Vice President Hubert Humphrey for the Democrat nomination. He urged New York Governor Nelson Rockefeller to run for the Republican nomination against **Nixon**.

After the 1968 Republican convention, **Nixon** visited **LBJ** and secretly told him that he would not criticize **LBJ's** conduct of the war provided that **LBJ** did not soften his bargaining position with the North Vietnamese which might allow Humphrey to emerge with the peace mantle. **Johnson** told his security team later that "the GOP may be of more help to us than the Democrats in the next few months." **Nixon** effectively neutralized **LBJ** who offered little help to Humphrey. **LBJ** cited as precedent **Eisenhower's** limited role in the **Nixon** campaign of 1960. Right before the election **LBJ** heard that **Nixon** allies had encouraged the South Vietnamese government to hold out in peace talks then underway. **Nixon** called **Johnson** to deny this. **LBJ** in retirement told an aide to let the **Nixon** White House know that he would not divulge this.

The Vietnam War and the abandonment of **Lyndon Johnson** by the Democrats embittered him. In 1969 **Lyndon Johnson** gave indirect support to **George HW Bush** when he declared for the US Senate in Texas. (In that election **George HW Bush** was angry at **Nixon** for reaching out to John Connolly a conservative Democrat who was backing his opponent.) In 1972 **Johnson's** endorsement of Democrat candidate George McGovern was muted.

In 1971 **Nixon** hoped his Vice President, Spiro Agnew, would step down to return to the private sector to earn money. He felt he couldn't push Agnew out since that might risk the right wing uniting around **Reagan** to try to take the nomination away from him (**Nixon**).

In 1992 when Texas billionaire H. Ross Perot began a third-party challenge to **George HW Bush, Nixon** worried about **Bush**: "What concerns me is that he still may not realize how serious the Perot challenge is." **Clinton** privately called himself an **Eisenhower** Democrat and his policies - free trade, cutting the capital gains taxes - contributed to a time of prosperity. In the 2010 midterms a Gallup poll showed **Clinton** to be a more persuasive campaigner than **Obama**. **Clinton** worked hard on behalf of Democrats in close races.

What is the point of all this?

The American two-party system, although not created by the Constitution and odious to many of the Founders is actually a pillar of our system. In modern times it manages a diversity of opinions and views.

It is also a lens through which to analyze one of the key drivers of American history: race, particularly black-white relations. In many ways, the party of **Martin Van Buren**, the Jacksonian Democrats, managed the issue of slavery by electing a series of men who would not tamper with the institution: **Jackson**, **Van Buren**, **Polk**, **Pierce** and **Buchanan**. **Tyler**, though elected with **William Henry Harrison** fit this mold. **Andrew Johnson**, though elected with **Lincoln**, also fit this mold.

The modern Republican Party emerged as an antislavery party. The race difference between the parties was set as early as 1865 when 51 of the 65 Democrats in the Congress voted against the Thirteenth Amendment abolishing slavery. It passed as every Republican voted for it. Its post-Civil War elected presidents – **Grant, Hayes, Garfield**, and **McKinley** - all had Black support as leaders of the "party of **Lincoln**."

We turn now to the topic of race and how the presidents have interacted over it.

Chapter 11

Race

Overall context

I believe it was the historian Joseph Ellis who wrote that with all the talent that they possessed, one issue that the Founders did not solve was slavery. At best they established national unity until the issue could be resolved in blood some seventy years later. Whatever the truth of that, one cannot discuss the interaction of the presidents without a review of race relations. This analysis will focus on Black-White relations.

Moving Forward

After the Revolution the Massachusetts Supreme Court ruled slavery illegal basing the decision on language **John Adams** had written in the state constitution. In 1784 **Jefferson** wrote a provision into the Ordinance of 1784 ending slavery in all newly- created states by 1800 but it failed by one vote. **Jefferson**: "the fate of millions unborn (was) hanging on the tongue of one man, and Heaven was silent in that awful moment."

Under the Articles of Confederation each state had an equal vote. At the Constitutional Convention of 1787 the three-fifths rule was a concession to the South. The three-fifths rule meant, for example, that a man who had one hundred slaves would count as 61 people - himself plus three-fifths of one hundred slaves. There were about seven hundred thousand slaves in the South. This gave that region at least another dozen members of the original Congress and that many electoral votes. During this part of the debate the delegates from Virginia - **Washington** and **Madison** - were mostly silent. The impact of the three-fifths rule grew as the slave population increased.

Here's an example of the three-fifths compromise and its distortive effect on American politics: The Twenty-third Congress convened in December of 1833 with 240 members. The slave states had 98 representatives rather than 73 to which they would have been entitled had only the nonslave population been counted. Of the 240 about 140 were Democrats.

Jefferson had three opportunities to change the course of history and end slavery: First, in his home state in the Revolutionary War era. Several prominent Virginians did free their slaves but **Jefferson** and **Madison** did not. Second, in the Ordinances of 1784-85; last in the Louisiana Purchase. A 1998 DNA test showed that one of **Jefferson's** slaves, Sally Hemmings, had a child fathered by a member of **Jefferson's** family, possibly **Jefferson**. The child was conceived when **Jefferson** was in his 60s. When the story of Sally Hemmings was first reported by pamphleteer James Callender, **John Adams** noted privately: "Callender and Sally will be remembered as long as **Jefferson** as blots on his character." (In Dusseldorf in 1788 Jefferson had seen a 1699 painting by Dutch artist Adriaen van der Werff of the Biblical patriarch Abraham taking the servant Hagar to bed. He wrote that the painting was "delicious. I would have agreed to have been Abraham though the consequence would have been that I should have been dead five or six thousand years." **Jefferson** saw this picture at about the time he is said to have started his relationship with Sally Hemmings.)

Monroe's attitude toward his "workforce" crept in through his rhetoric. While ambassador to France in 1796 he got a rebuke from Secretary of State Timothy Pickering over his handling of the fall-out from the Jay Treaty. **Monroe** wrote **Madison** comparing the rebuke to a note sent by an "overseer on the farm to one of his gang."

In 1800 Virginia Governor **Monroe** wrote **Thomas Jefferson** about rumors of a slave revolt - "a negro insurrection" - in Virginia. The revolt fizzled as some slaves betrayed it. **Monroe** called out the militia and hunted down the leaders. He wrote **Madison** that "this alarm has kept me much occupied." As trials and executions ensued and more were waiting trial **Monroe** wrote **Jefferson**: "It is unquestionably the most serious and formidable conspiracy we have ever known of the kind." He went on that he was not sure "whether mercy or severity is the better policy in this case" but he allowed that "when there is cause for doubt it is best to incline to the former." **Jefferson's** advice: "Whether to stay the hand of the executioner is an important question. There is strong sentiment that there has been hanging enough. The other states and the world at large will forever condemn us if we indulge a principle of revenge." But **Jefferson** added: "I hazard these thoughts for your own consideration only, as I would be unwilling to be quoted in this case." This from **Jefferson** of the Declaration in 1776 and who applauded Shay's Rebellion in 1787 with his: "I like a little rebellion now and then." **Monroe** issued some pardons but in the end twenty-seven men were hanged including the leader Gabriel Prosser. In 2007 the Governor of Virginia pardoned Prosser and his followers.

In 1801 **Thomas Jefferson** wrote **James Monroe** generally supporting **Monroe's** expatriation plan for freed Blacks but he opposed **Monroe's** plan for some western territory of America in favor of some Caribbean place: "Nature seems to have formed these islands to become the receptacle of blacks transplanted into this hemisphere." In 1806 the Congress passed and **Jefferson** signed a law prohibiting trade with the Black republic of Haiti. It was to appease Napoleon but also racism-based and founded on southern fears. Henry Adams later wrote that this law "might claim distinction among the most disgraceful statutes ever enacted by the United States government."

Secretary of State **John Quincy Adams** was asked by a British official if there was a greater evil than slavery and he responded, "Yes. Admitting the right of search by foreign officers of our own vessels upon the seas in time of peace: for that would be making slaves of ourselves." The Treaty of Ghent ending the War of 1812 condemned slave trading and US law had outlawed it but **Adams** and **Monroe** did not want to cede authority to foreign inspections.

In 1818 Secretary of State **John Quincy Adams** negotiated with the Spanish government for the obtaining of Florida and the definition of the southern and western boundaries of the Louisiana Purchase. **Monroe** counseled **Adams** to draw in **Jackson** by seeking his input. **Adams** got **Jackson** to agree that getting Florida was more important than getting Texas even though **Jefferson** wanted Texas included. **Monroe** supported this outcome assuming that the US would eventually deal with a new Mexican government on the matter of Texas and because as he wrote **Adams,** Texas "involved difficulties of an internal nature which menace the Union itself." This was a reference to slavery and northern concern over its spread. The treaty extended the US to the Pacific (Oregon north of the 42nd parallel) and **Adams** regarded it as the "most important event" of his life. A generation later, the Democrat convention that nominated **Polk** in 1844 asserted that **Adams** had "criminally" given up Texas in these negotiations.

In 1820, slavery again roiled American politics over the application for statehood of Missouri when an amendment to the admissions bill was proposed. This amendment would have required the manumission of slaves at 21 with no further introduction of slavery as a condition of Missouri's admission into the US as a state. **Jefferson** responded to the crisis as follows: "This momentous question, like a fire bell in the night, awakened and filled me with terror. I considered it at once as the Knell of the Union." **Jefferson** wrote **Monroe** during the crisis that "this is as close as we have come to dissolving our union since our founding." **Monroe** agreed and wrote **Jefferson**: "I have never known a question so menacing to the tranquility and even the continuance of the Union as the present one." **John Quincy Adams** entered in his diary: "I take it for granted that the present question is a mere preamble – a title page to a great, tragic volume."

The Missouri Compromise was created in the Congress to fend off the amendment. It admitted Maine carved out from northern Massachusetts as a free state, allowed slavery in Missouri and prohibited slavery in new states taken from the Louisiana Purchase north of the 36•30' line. What follows are the reactions of seven of our presidents.

Jefferson opposed the Missouri Compromise. He expressed the hope in what he called "diffusion" - that slavery spreading over a greater surface of territory would lead to emancipation. When **John Adams** heard this he opined that **Jefferson** had temporarily lost his mind. His son was on the same page. **John Quincy Adams** may have had **Jefferson** or **Madison** in mind when he said of Virginians: "This Missouri question has betrayed the secret of their souls." **John Quincy Adams** in his diary: "In the abstract (southerners) say that slavery is an evil. But when probed to the quick on it they show at the bottom of their souls pride and vainglory in their condition of martyrdom."

From the Congress **Tyler** opposed the Compromise. Decades later he said of it: "I believed it to be unconstitutional. I believed it to be... the opening of the Pandora's Box, which would let out upon us all the present evils which have gathered over the land. I never would have yielded to the Missouri Compromise. I would have died in my shoes, suffered any sort of punishment you could have inflicted upon me, before I would have supported it."

Madison advised **Monroe** to accept the Missouri Compromise. Even though he doubted the constitutional authority of Congress to prohibit slavery in the territories he did not see it as in conflict with the Constitution. **Monroe** thought the Compromise was necessary for the preservation of the Union. He feared parties based on sections. He wrote **Jefferson** that the plot to disunion had been stopped "by the patriotic devotion of several members in the non slave-holding states, who preferred the sacrifice of themselves at home, to a violation of the obvious principles of the Constitution..."

Ultimately **John Quincy Adams** supported the Missouri Compromise "believing that it was all that could be effected under the present Constitution, and from an extreme unwillingness to put the Union at hazard." For the next generation of politicians like **Abraham Lincoln** the Missouri Compromise came to have near-constitutional status and it was their best hope to contain and eventually extirpate slavery. The Missouri Compromise postponed a showdown in which the North would not have been able to keep the South - especially if the South was allied with England - in the Union. Forty years later this was different.

In 1829 **Madison** and **Monroe**, long out of office, were delegates to a convention dealing with reapportionment in Virginia. Districts were apportioned by population including slaves for representative purposes. This favored the eastern part of the state. The two ex-Presidents tried two compromises:

- Keeping the current model for the Virginia Senate and changing the House to one based only on the white population.
- The three-fifths compromise.

Tyler, also a member of the convention, opposed both and both failed. The slavocracy won. What this meant in arithmetic terms is that Blacks were counted as 5/5 of a person for voting representational purposes. But since of course they could not vote themselves, this just gave more power to the Whites.

In 1838, some three years before he assumed the presidency, **Tyler** was elected president of the Virginia Colonization Society. He supported emigration of free Blacks to Liberia predicting that Blacks would spread out from there over Africa: "and Monrovia will be to Africa what Jamestown and Plymouth have been to America." Within the US, **Tyler** had the same curious argument that **Jefferson** had had that if slavery expanded geographically it would gradually become extinct.

Madison sold some of his slaves in 1834 at age 83 and he said they were relieved because of "their horror of going to Liberia." If he had freed his slaves at his death it would have impoverished his widow. This is how other Presidents before the Civil War handled their slaves upon their own death:

- **George Washington** - In a secret will written six months before he died, he ordered that his and his wife's slaves be freed upon her death "without evasion, neglect or delay."
- **Thomas Jefferson** – He could not manumit his slaves because he had mortgaged them to pay debts.

- **James Monroe** – He was in the same situation as Jefferson.
- **James K. Polk** – He wrote a new will in 1849 expressing an intention to free his slaves upon the deaths of himself and his wife but he gave his wife discretion (unlike **Washington**). He died that year. His wife died in 1891 long after her preferences in the matter of the freedom of other human beings was moot.(Note: As he moved victoriously through Tennessee in 1862 General **Ulysses S. Grant** paid a courtesy call on the widow of **James K Polk.** It was the new era visiting the old.)

John C. Calhoun wrote in the 1830s: "The soundest friends of slavery...were in the Democratic party" and forty years and a Civil War later, running for the Democrat nomination for president, Samuel Tilden assured the South that earlier antislavery comments were "youthful indiscretions." In 1830 Congressman **Buchanan** said that if the US emancipated slaves "they would become masters.... Is there any man in this Union who could for a moment indulge the horrible idea of abolishing slavery by the massacre of the high-minded and the chivalrous race of men in the South?" This was not the universal opinion. A Whig, **William Henry Harrison** in 1833 wrote that: "We might look forward to a day...when a North American sun would not look down upon a slave." (**Harrison** was born in Virginia into a slave-holding family. The twentieth century civil rights leader William Francis White who was the president of the NAACP traced his ancestry to **Harrison** claiming to be his great-grandson.)

But protecting slavery in the South was at the core of the new Democratic Party. In 1836 as he prepared to run for president, **Martin Van Buren** needed to hold the party together over slavery. He worked with his allies and future Presidents **James Buchanan** in the Senate, Speaker of the House **James K Polk** and congressman **Franklin Pierce** to establish and enforce the notorious gag rule. It allowed for anti-slavery petitions to be presented but then immediately tabled never to be discussed. It declared that slavery in the states was off-bounds for Congress on Constitutional grounds. All anti-slavery petitions were to be tabled. When the rule was reported in Congress, **Polk** saw **John Quincy Adams** rise to attack it and immediately recognized another member of Congress whom he knew would call the question. **Pierce** took this position as a compromise to the position of some Southerners not to receive petitions at all which he saw as a violation of the Constitutional right to petition. **John Quincy Adams** and **Fillmore** opposed the gag rule over the years. As a candidate for president, **William Henry Harrison** supported the gag rule. The gag rule was later amended that Congress would not even receive anti-slavery petitions. It was in place until 1844. **Andrew Johnson** voted to support the gag rule but also voted to allow an abolitionist congressman to present a petition.

In 1840-41 in the *Amistad* case involving thirty-nine slaves who had taken over a Spanish vessel on the way to plantations in Cuba, **John Quincy Adams** represented the slaves in an American courtroom. He attacked the policies of the **Van Buren** administration. As **John Quincy Adams** escalated his vigorous attacks on slavery in his later years, **Jackson** wrote: "He must be demented, if not, then he is the most reckless and depraved man living." This from the father of the Democratic Party.

Tennessee's state constitution had a three-fifths clause that mimicked the federal constitution. It gave disproportionate power to counties with more slaves. **Andrew Johnson** was a state senator from East Tennessee where slaves were few. He tried unsuccessfully to eliminate this clause in the early 1840s.

The Whig Party was better on the slavery issue but nowhere near an anti-slavery party. Running for re-election to Congress in 1838 **Fillmore** got a questionnaire as did other Whig candidates from the Abolitionist movement that was forming. He worried because he saw the divisive threat to Whig victory. The questions were:

- Do you believe that petitions to congress on...slavery and the slave trade, ought to be received...and...considered...?
- Are you opposed to the annexation of Texas...?
- Are you in favor of congress... (abolishing) the...slave trade between the states?
- Are you in favor of immediate...abolition of slavery in the District of Columbia?

Fillmore's first reaction was "The Philistines are upon us." But he then answered each question with a yes.

Fillmore's slight abolitionism helped defeat his vice presidential aspirations in 1844. Running for Vice President in 1848 he said that he "regarded slavery as an evil, but one with which the National Government had nothing to do. That by the Constitution of the United States the whole power over that question was vested in the several states where the institution was tolerated. If they regarded it as a blessing, they had a constitutional right to enjoy it;" This was a standard dodge in that era.

In 1841, when **Tyler** ascended to the presidency, **John Quincy Adams** thought of him as "a political sectarian of the slave driving Virginian, Jeffersonian School... with all the interests and passions and vices of slavery rooted in his moral and political constitution." **Polk** missed the significance of slavery. He focused on preventing concentration of power at the federal level or with big business, keeping tariff rates just high enough to sustain a national government, trying to maintain currency stability without a national bank, and national expansion.

Monroe's concerns over Texas from 1818 resurfaced in 1844. **John Quincy Adams** wrote as the treaty of annexation of Texas was sent to the Senate: "This was a memorable day in the annals of the world. The treaty for the annexation of Texas to this Union was this day sent into the Senate; and with it went the freedom of the human race." **Hayes** went to Harvard Law School in 1843-45. While in Boston he heard **John Quincy Adams** speak on slavery in the South and considered him "a deluded old man." He said **Adams'** speech contained "much abolitionism" and was "unreasonable and very unfair." But he acknowledged: "I do not wonder that he is regarded as a dangerous adversary in a mere personal encounter. He is quick, sharp, fearless, and full of the wit and the learning of the ages." (Thus **Washington** the first President who was born in 1732 and **Hayes** the nineteenth president who died in 1893 observed **John Quincy Adams** in action and gave opinion.)

On his deathbed **Andrew Jackson** told his household which included slaves: "I hope to meet you all in Heaven - yes, all in Heaven, white and black." He added: "Christ has no respect to color." (In the next decade, another Jacksonian, **Franklin Pierce** and his wife attended church at a mixed-race congregation.)

In 1846 two measures were introduced in the Congress greatly agitating the slavery question. **Andrew Johnson** introduced what eventually became the Homestead Act offering land at cheap prices in the West. It was pilloried by slave interests. **Polk** said that **Andrew Johnson's** Homestead plan was "not worthy of an answer." **Johnson** persisted. In 1860 he was indignant that **Buchanan** vetoed his Homestead Bill. He said the veto message was "monstrous and absurd." Later that year **Lincoln** won running on "Free land and free labor" and the bill was finally passed in 1862. Also in 1846 the Wilmot Proviso was introduced into a fractious House debate over a two million dollar appropriation for **Polk** to use in possible negotiations with Mexico. It would have prevented slavery in any territories taken from Mexico. In one sense it was odd. No one was suggesting slavery in those territories. But it ignited the issue. **Polk** called it a "mischievous and foolish amendment." He went on: "What connection slavery had with making peace with Mexico it is difficult to conceive."

John Quincy Adams said from the Congress that he would vote for the appropriation since it was in line with his antiwar position: "... we have whipped (Mexico) already more than the most cruel task-master ever whipped a slave, without cause and without necessity... And one of the reasons why I shall heartily vote for ....this bill is that ....instead of whipping Mexico, the President shows a desire to make peace with that republic." He thought the Wilmot Proviso was not needed because there was no slavery in the territory but he voted for it on the point of principle. Over the next few years it passed repeatedly in the House and failed in the Senate. Like the gag rule, its failure may have attributable to the three-fifths compromise which continued to give the South outsized strength in the Congress (and the Electoral College). In 1848 the Free Soil ticket of **Martin Van Buren** aligned with the Proviso and held for limiting slavery to where it already existed. By mid-1849 there was concern that President **Taylor** of the Whigs was moving toward the Wilmot Proviso. He told a meeting of the Free-Soil Party that "the people of the North need have no apprehension of the further expansion of slavery." His death mooted that question.

The Wilmot Proviso was one of those turning points. It politicized slavery and led to making the Democrats a southern white party for over one hundred years.

By 1850 sectional tensions pulled the US toward the brink of war. The Compromise of 1850 resulted. The Compromise entailed a series of bills, one of which was a strong Fugitive Slave Act requiring northerners to return runaway slaves, with officials who refused to do so subject to fines. As president, **Taylor** was opposed to strengthening the Fugitive Slave Act which divided him from Henry Clay who saw it as part of a compromise. **Taylor's** death ensured the passage of the Compromise as **Fillmore** supported the bills. **Fillmore** called it the "a final settlement" of the slavery question. He added: "God knows that I detest slavery but it is an existing evil, for which we are not responsible, and we must endure it, till we can get rid of it without destroying the last hope of free government in the world."

Tyler favored the Compromise of 1850. In 1852 **Hayes** thought that it had resolved the slavery issues and his reaction to **Pierce's** win that year was a nonchalant, "Who cares?" As a teenager **Benjamin Harrison** supported the Compromise of 1850. The Compromise of 1850 was barely endorsed at the last Whig convention on 1852. **Abraham Lincoln** was known to approve of the Compromise. Daniel Webster championed it. A century later, **John F. Kennedy** credited Daniel Webster for supporting the Compromise even though Webster had advocated the South's position on the Fugitive Slave law. In 1852 **Pierce** assured Southerners that he supported the Compromise of 1850 particularly the Fugitive Slave Act as did **James Buchanan**. In his 1853 inaugural address **Pierce**, citing the Constitution and the Compromise of 1850 said, "I ferverently hope that the (slavery) question is at rest and that no sectional or fanatical excitement may again threaten the durability of our institutions or obscure the light of our prosperity." That of course was the hope of the Democratic Party back to **Van Buren** (who had rejected this position by 1848) but it did not work out that way. However, like the Missouri Compromise three decades earlier, the Compromise of 1850 may have bought crucial time for the forces that ultimately ended slavery. In the decade after 1850 the North's development -railroads and industry - increased its military advantage.

In the 1850s the status of the Spanish colony of Cuba brought additional stress to the slavery question in the US. In 1854 **Buchanan** as the ambassador to England worked at **Pierce's** direction to develop the Ostend Manifesto, essentially a white paper issued from a small town in Belgium by that name. It set a price of 10 million dollars for the US to buy Cuba from Spain and asserted that if Spain would not sell Cuba the US would be justified for its own protection to take it by force. **Buchanan** was alluding to the southern fear of a slave revolt in Cuba. **Pierce** rejected the conclusion that the US would be justified in seizing Cuba. It was practical end of the philosophy of Manifest Destiny.

Also in 1854 the Kansas-Nebraska Act passed calling on states to vote ("popular sovereignty") on the question of slavery within their borders. It passed with President **Pierce's** support. It destroyed the Missouri Compromise of 1820 and led to the Civil War.

Pierce was siding with the South. He was moving the Democratic Party to a position that the vote of white citizens in a territory could determine the existence of slavery. The Kansas-Nebraska Act of 1854 like the Compromise of 1850 was meant to settle the slavery question. This time the resolution was popular sovereignty. It:

- Effectively repealed the Missouri Compromise of 1820 which for a generation of people (including **Lincoln**) had near constitutional status and was seen as a way to confine and eventually end slavery. They saw Kansas-Nebraska as a betrayal.

- Moved the authority of slavery from the Congress to the territories.
- Led to bloodshed.

As a young man **Hayes** opposed the Kansas-Nebraska Act and defended Blacks in court in cases arising under the Fugitive Slave Law. In 1856 he supported the Republican John C. Fremont. He wrote that his politics were "For free States and against new slave States." He became a Republican. He wrote of how a Republican torchlight parade "was assailed by **Fillmore** and **Buchanan** rowdies." (A young **Grover Cleveland** marched in a torchlight parade cheering the win of **James Buchanan** that year.)

The Kansas-Nebraska Act helped propel the Republican Party and destroy the Democratic Party. The issue was slavery in the territories with the Democrats were on record for congressional non-interference. In 1856 the Republicans as noted had for its platform the elimination of "those twin relics of barbarism, polygamy and slavery" from the territories. (Polygamy was a reference to the Mormons of Utah.)

In 1857 **Buchanan** advocated that Kansas be admitted as a slave state. **Hayes** in Cincinnati saw this as a blunder, writing: "Farewell, Mr. **Buchanan**." From 1860 - 1908, the Democrats only won two presidential elections and lost twelve. People in the South referred to the Black Republican party.

Lincoln opposed the Kansas-Nebraska Act and it brought him back into politics much as the Jay Treaty has revived **Jefferson** sixty years before. For **Lincoln** on the back-country Illinois circuit, the Act roused him "as he had never been before" as it showed that slavery was not on the road to extinction. He later said the Act "took us by surprise" and "We were thunderstruck and stunned." **Lincoln's** position at that time was that of the Missouri Compromise or even the Compromise of 1850 - to allow slavery but to stop its spread. Former President **John Tyler** supported the Kansas-Nebraska Act.

Chester Alan Arthur's father was a Baptist minister who often preached against slavery and after college **Arthur** worked for an abolitionist lawyer who opposed the Fugitive Slave Act. As a lawyer and Free Soiler **Arthur**, 27, moved to Kansas in 1856 to help bring Kansas into the union as a free state under the popular sovereignty of the 1854 Kansas-Nebraska Act. He was out of place and returned to New York soon and joined the Republican Party. Back in New York still before the war, **Arthur** worked for Black rights winning nondiscriminatory treatment for Blacks on New York City streetcars. As president in the 1880s he allied with the Readjustors in Virginia a party that opposed the Democrats on a platform of debt realignment and racial equality.

As president, **James Buchanan** was presented with a mini-Civil-War in Kansas. Using a flawed analogy, he cited **Madison's** refusal to attack the Hartford Convention during the War of 1812 – a "wise example" - as his reason for not attacking the anti-slavery elements based in Topeka Kansas. **Buchanan** therefore effectively branded the anti-slavery side as potentially treasonous.

Lincoln avoided extremes in most areas of his life. He didn't associate with the temperance movement and he never joined a church. He was not part of the abolitionist movement. In 1860 he was a compromise candidate to get the Republican nomination beating out the more abolitionist minded senators William Seward and Salmon P. Chase. That year he defeated a divided Democratic Party. He stood only for the nonexpansion of slavery. He supported a proposed Constitutional amendment that would have prohibited the federal government from interfering with slavery in the states. He pledged to support the Fugitive Slave Law. He was for compensating slaveholders and thought that emancipation would be gradual, taking up to 35 years.

Lincoln developed the most sophisticated thoughts of any of the past or future Presidents at that time on slavery. He said that at the time the Constitution was adopted, "the plain unmistakable spirit of that age, toward slavery, was hostility to the principle, and toleration only by necessity." He added that when Virginia ceded its northwest territory to the US it was with the understanding that slavery would be prohibited. He also attacked slavery from the Declaration of

Independence. **Lincoln's** view in 1858 was similar to that of most Republicans: "I have no purpose directly or indirectly to interfere with the institution of slavery in the states where it exists. I believe I have no lawful right to do so, and I have no inclination to do so." And: "I have no prejudice against the Southern people. They are just what we would be in their situation. If slavery did not exist amongst them, they would not introduce it. If it did now exist amongst us, we should not instantly give it up."

Garfield's views developed because of the Civil War. In 1855 at age 24 he heard a speech on the Kansas-Nebraska Act and admitted that he did not understand the issue. After Fort Sumter State Senator **Garfield** wrote that the war would be ultimately fought over slavery. "The war will soon assume the shape of Slavery vs. Freedom." He was correct and in that war everything changed.

In 1862 **Andrew Johnson** as military governor of Tennessee considered gathering a group of Black troops. **Lincoln** responded: "I am told that you have at least thought of raising a Negro military force. In my opinion the country needs no specific thing so much as some man of your ability and position, to go to work. When I speak of your position, I mean that of an eminent citizen of a slave state, and himself a slaveholder."

The Republican Party lost ground to the Democrats in the mid-term elections of 1862, potentially endangering the Emancipation Proclamation. **Lincoln** in 1862 while he was preparing to issue it delayed at Seward's suggestion until a Union victory. During that time, he discussed emigration with Black leaders. "You and we are different races. We have between us a broader difference than exists between almost any other two races." He was criticized and wrote: "If I would save the Union without freeing any slave I would do it, and if I could save it freeing all the slaves I would do it; and if I could save it by freeing some and leaving others alone I would also do that. What I do about slavery, and the colored race, I do because it helps to save the Union;" When **Lincoln** did issue the Emancipation Proclamation it was bitterly criticized by **Franklin Pierce**: "...what will the world say of a proclamation emanating from the President of the United

States not only in defiance of the fundamental law of the Country for the upholding of which he ought to have been willing to shed his own blood, but in defiance of all human & Divine which invited the black race in six entire states and in parts of several others to use with all the barbaric features which must be inseparable from a successful servile insurrection to slay & devastate without regard to age or sex, without any condition of restraint … Yes and one other, that the women and children brutally violated & slaughtered shall be white women and children."

After the Emancipation Proclamation a union recruitment campaign to get Blacks into the army ensued with **Grant's** support. When he heard of atrocities committed by Confederates against Black POWs he wrote the Confederate general in the area: "I can assure you that these colored troops are regularly mustered into the service of the United States. The Government and all Officers under the Government are bound to give the same protection to these troops as they do any other troops." Later **Grant** said that he was bound "to protect all persons received into the army of the United States, regardless of color or nationality."

In an 1864 campaign speech **Johnson** compared slave owner exploitation of female slaves unfavorably with polygamy. In 1864 Democratic newspapers accused **Lincoln** of continuing the war for the sole purpose of freeing the slaves. In the spring of 1864, the Thirteenth Amendment abolishing slavery passed the Senate by the two-thirds requirement but failed to get the two-thirds requirement in the House where on a near party line vote Republicans supported abolition and Democrats opposed it. **Lincoln** worked the lame duck Congress in January using the results of the election, patronage and pressure to shift enough Democrats to pass it. As the Civil War progressed **Johnson** came to oppose slavery. **Lincoln**: "I see that you have declared in favor of emancipation, for which, may God bless you."

Frederick Douglass later judged **Lincoln** in his historical context: "From the genuine abolition view, Mr. **Lincoln** seemed tardy, dull, cold and indifferent, but measuring him by the sentiment of his country - a sentiment he was bound as a statesman to consult - he was swift, zealous, radical, and determined."

Lincoln's reconstruction plan that he announced to Congress in late 1863 was for a general amnesty for all who would pledge future loyalty to the US with the exception of the highest ranking Confederates. The loyalty oath would require acceptance of the Thirteenth Amendment. He held that the states had rebelled but not left the Union. He held that state governments would be re-established when 10 percent of the voters made the loyalty oath. But **Lincoln's** plan did not address the future status of the Blacks. In 1864 the Radical Republicans put their reconstruction ideas into the Wade-Davis bill:

- State governments would be re-established when 50 percent of the voters made the loyalty oath.
- The category of ineligible Confederates was expanded.
- The Confederate states were like conquered provinces.
- No mention of Black suffrage.

Lincoln pocket-vetoed Wade-Davis as too harsh saying that "there is too much disposition, in certain quarters, to hector and dictate to the people of the South, to refuse to recognize them as fellow citizens. Such persons have too little respect for Southerners' rights. I do not share feelings of that kind."

In 1864 Louisiana, Arkansas and Tennessee had been re-established under **Lincoln's** ten percent plan. As president, **Johnson** sought to apply that policy to the other eight states which **Johnson** like **Lincoln** saw as having never left the union. But to placate Radical Republicans **Johnson** required the states to abolish slavery and repudiate their war debt.

Assigning more blame to southern leaders than to ordinary southern Whites was foundational to both **Lincoln's** and **Johnson's** views of post-war reconstruction. In 1866 **Johnson** vetoed the Freedmen's Bureau which was sustained and the Civil Rights Act of 1866 which was overridden. This was the start of his struggles with Congress.

He later said: "There is not a principle of (**Lincoln's**), in reference to the restoration of the Union, from which I have departed - not one..."

In 1867 **Johnson** vetoed and the Congress overrode a law to allow Black suffrage in Washington DC. **Grant** supported the veto in the cabinet because he thought it was a "very contemptible business" for member of Congress to impose Black suffrage when their own states prohibited it.

Grant proved in time to be a great defender of Blacks. He acted from sincere motives. After he left the army in 1854 he had taken up farming in Missouri on land given to him by his slaveholding father-in-law. He did not take slaves; he hired local Blacks when he needed workers at above market rates and freed the one slave his father-in-law had given him who was worth about fifteen hundred dollars. He was an unsuccessful farmer. Health problems, bad weather and the Panic of 1857 ruined him. In the election of 1868, **Grant** received a minority of White votes and was the best guarantor of the constitutional amendments which had come out the Civil War.

Grant had to reconcile with the South and in that he was following **Lincoln**. However, he stood for the achievement of civil rights for Blacks, more than any American Presidents for the next many decades. He had to deal with the protection of former slaves, maintaining the Republican Party, and a depression. The Ku Klux Klan was set up after the Civil War to destroy the Republican Party in the South. The passage of the Fifteenth Amendment giving Blacks the right to vote brought this from **Grant**: "A measure which makes at once Four Millions of people, heretofore declared by the highest tribunal in the land not citizens of the United States, nor eligible to become so, voters in every part of the land...is indeed a measure of grander importance than any other one act of the kind from the foundation of our government to the present day." He added: "To the race more favored heretofore by our laws I would say withhold no legal privilege of advancement to the new citizen... I repeat that the adoption of the 15th Amendment to the Constitution completes the greatest civil change, and constitutes the most important event that has occurred, since the nation came into life." The **Grant**

administration prosecuted the KKK nearly out of existence until it revived in 1915. (The Democrat National Convention of 1924 debated and dropped an anti-Klan resolution.) **Grant** wrote in his *Memoirs* about the Southern Cause that he believed it was "one of the worst for which a people ever fought, and one for which there was the least excuse." Frederick Douglass said: "To **Grant** more than any other man the Negro owes his enfranchisement..."

In South Carolina by October of 1876, a campaign of terror took place led by Confederate General Wade Hampton. The governor requested federal intervention. **Grant** declared a state of insurrection and sent troops. **Grant** also sent troops to Louisiana to protect voting. When he thought the Democrats had won the 1876 election **Garfield** wrote: "It now appears that we were defeated by the combined power of rebellion, Catholicism and whiskey, a trinity very hard to conquer... We shall have a hard, uncomfortable struggle to save the fruits of the great war..." As noted, this election is often seen as one which the Republicans stole but it must also be acknowledged that the Democrats suppressed Black votes in the South. The Republican Party was mostly Black in the South in 1876 with Whites leaving for reasons of social shunning. In South Carolina in the 1876 election Blacks outnumbered whites 5-3 and uniformly voted for the Republicans yet the first returns gave the state to the Democrats.

During the Civil War **Hayes** who as a college student had dismissed **John Quincy Adams'** anti-slavery speeches wrote "the negroes expect the North to set them free and see no need of risking their lives to gain what will be given them by others." His views began to change, however. As young non-West Point officers he and **Garfield** thought that some of the generals' lack on military zeal toward the enemy was due to ambivalent views toward slavery. **Hayes** wrote that **Garfield** "speaks of want of sympathy among army officers with the cause of the war." In 1867 when he ran for governor of Ohio, **Hayes** stood against his Democrat opponent on the issue of voting rights for Blacks. **Hayes**: "Color ought to have no more to do with voting than size." As President, **Hayes** appointed Frederick Douglass as Marshal of the District of Columbia.

In 1872 **Rutherford B Hayes** spoke on the Fifteenth Amendment: "Notwithstanding the predictions of our adversaries, that to confer political rights upon colored people would lead to a war of races, white people and colored people are now voting side by side in all of the old slave States, and their elections are quite as free from violence and disorder as they were when the whites alone were the voters...." The Democrat victories in the off-year elections of 1874 were a reaction against Reconstruction and the Fifteenth Amendment. This drew **Hayes** back into politics. He ran for a third nonconsecutive term of governor of Ohio, defeating the father of **William Howard Taft** at a state nominating convention. **Hayes** was already aiming at the presidency.

In 1877 **Hayes** who had removed federal troops from the South used them to restore order in a national strike. He received widespread support. But **Grant** was disdainful saying, "During my two terms in office, the whole Democratic press and the morbidly honest and 'reformatory' portion of the Republican press, thought it horrible to keep US troops stationed in the southern states, and when they were called upon to protect the lives of negroes - as much citizens under the Constitution as if their skins were white - the country was scarcely large enough to hold the sound of indignation belched forth by them for several years. Now, however, there is no hesitation about exhausting the whole power of the government to suppress a strike on the slightest intimation that danger threatened." However, **Hayes**' record on race relations was decidedly positive. WEB DuBois was "especially grateful" to **Hayes** for his post-presidential efforts and "tireless energy and single heartedness for the interests" of Blacks. Running for the presidency in 1880, Civil War veteran **James Garfield** said: "We have seen white men betray the flag and fight to kill the union, but in all that long and dreary [civil] war you never saw a traitor under a black skin. In all that period of terror and distress, no union soldier was ever betrayed by any black man anywhere and so long as we live we'll stand by these black allies of ours."

In 1872 **Benjamin Harrison** lost a race for the Republican nomination for governor of Indiana. At the convention he argued that the Republican mission would not be fulfilled "until the humble cabin of the negro is made safe against the midnight assaults of barbarian Democrats." In 1876 running for governor again **Harrison** responded to the plight of ex-slaves in the South. "We entered into an obligation solemn as a covenant with our God to save these people from the dastardly outrages that their rebel masters are committing upon them in the South." **Harrison** praised **Grant's** assignment of federal troops to South Carolina to prevent violence. In the 1880s in the Senate **Benjamin Harrison** supported federal aid for education but he put in a provision that a state would not get federal money unless they could prove that they provided "free common schools for all its children of school age, without distinction of race and color." **Harrison**: "Unless the black boy and girl in the South can share equally in the privileges of education, then I am opposed to the bill, because it will not reach the evil that we are endeavoring to eradicate." The Senate passed the bill but the House did not.

Republican presidents continued to stand by Blacks. In 1883 the Supreme Court ruled the Civil Rights Act of 1875 unconstitutional. **Arthur** called for legislation to redress the court decision. **TR** was the first president to appoint Blacks to federal positions. He was called the "Black Man's Buddy." In 1909 Booker T. Washington expressed "disappointment" in the lack of Blacks appointed by **Taft**. **Taft** was in this regard somewhat of an exception to his Republican predecessors and yet he still failed to penetrate the Democrat South

In 1893 **Woodrow Wilson** wrote of slavery that "domestic slaves were dealt with indulgently and even affectionately by their masters." He had also written that the Ku Klux Klan of the post-Civil War era engaged in "pranks," "mischief" and "frolicking." **Wilson** acknowledged that the Klan did harass Blacks but that their fears of the Klan were "comic." Early in his first term, **Wilson** ordered the segregation of the civil service over the objections of the NAACP. In his private notes **Wilson** wrote that Blacks were an "inferior" race.

At Whittier College in the 1930s **Nixon** sponsored a Black student to be a member of a campus club. In doing so he showed his Quaker heritage. At Yale in the late 1940s **George HW Bush** did volunteer work for the United Negro College Fund. As a Grand Rapids Michigan, Congressman **Ford** was a member of the NAACP.

Truman, a White southerner, became the first Democrat president to support Black rights. Arguing for the extension of the Fair Employment Practices Commission he said: "Discrimination in the matter of employment against properly qualified persons because of their race, creed or color is not only un-American in nature, but will eventually lead to industrial strife and unrest. The principle and policy of fair employment should be established permanently as part of our national law."

In 1948 **Truman** put forth a program for civil rights legislation. It included creation of a Civil Rights Division in the Department of Justice, creation of a Civil Rights Commission, a federal antilynching law, elimination of poll taxes and legislation for fair employment practices, voting rights, and prohibition of discrimination in housing, education, transportation and health care. It was widely opposed in the South. **LBJ**, running for the Senate, called it "a farce and a sham - an effort to set up a police state in the guise of liberty."

However, **LBJ's** attitudes changed too. In the Senate he got the 1957 Civil Rights Act passed with Vice President **Richard Nixon's** help. *(*Martin Luther King complimented **Nixon** for helping with the passage saying that **Nixon** showed "assiduous labor and dauntless courage.")

In 1960 during the presidential debates, **Nixon** made a strong statement on civil rights and criticized **JFK** for picking as his running mate **LBJ**. **Nixon's** running mate said that **Nixon** would appoint a Black to the cabinet. **JFK** labeled this commitment "racism in reverse at its worst." **Nixon** temporized, causing Jackie Robinson an important supporter to say, "This did not sit well with me." (Jackie Robinson's middle name was **Roosevelt** in honor of **TR**.) **Nixon** lost that election. If he had done as well among Blacks as he and **Eisenhower** did four years earlier he would have carried enough states to win. His inaction when Martin Luther King was arrested in contrast to **JFK's** calling of Coretta Scott King was a crucial lapse. Still, in 1960, one-third of all Blacks voted for **Nixon**; in 2004 only one in ten of a richer Black population voted for **George W Bush.**

JFK's response to Martin Luther King's March on Washington speech in 1963 which he watched on television from the White House: "He's damn good." In 1963 five days after **John F. Kennedy** was killed, **LBJ** urged passage of the Civil Rights Act as a tribute to **JFK**: "No memorial oration or eulogy could more eloquently honor President **Kennedy's** memory than the earliest possible passage of the civil rights bill for which he fought so long."

Pushing southern senators to drop the filibuster of the Civil Rights Act in 1964, **Johnson** told them: "You've got a southern president and if you want to blow him out of the water, go right ahead and do it, but you boys will never see another one again. We're friends on the q.t. Would you rather have me administering the civil rights bill, or do you want to have **Nixon**...?" **George HW Bush** ran for the Senate in Texas in 1964 coming out against the Civil Rights Act of 1964. After his 1964 defeat **Bush** apologized to his supporters for running a campaign that tolerated the positions of the extreme right John Birch Society and racists. **Eisenhower**, **Richard Nixon** and **Gerald Ford** campaigned for **George HW Bush** for Congress in Houston in 1966 as he defeated a more conservative Democrat who race-baited him on open housing.

In Congress **George HW Bush** supported the Philadelphia Plan with required that goals be set to hire minorities on federally funded construction projects.

In the day or so after Martin Luther King's murder in 1968 race riots broke out. **LBJ** told a group in the White House: "If I was a kid in Harlem I know what I'd be thinking right now: I'd be thinking the whites have declared open season on my people, and they're going to pick us off one by one unless I get a gun and pick them off first." In the wake of the assassination, **Johnson** asked Congress to pass the Fair Housing law, writing **Gerald Ford** a letter urging him to ask "What more can I do to achieve brotherhood and equality among all Americans?" Congress passed the bill. **George HW Bush** voted for it.

In 1971, Governor **Jimmy Carter** said he would support a state wide boycott of school busing for integration purposes in Georgia if no remedy to the objections whites could be found. In this he aligned with Governor George Wallace who ordered the Alabama school districts to defy court-ordered busing. As President, **Carter** supported affirmative action much as **Nixon** had. In 1979 **Carter** fired his ambassador to the UN Andrew Young for having an unauthorized meeting with a representative of the Palestine Liberation Organization. Jesse Jackson objected: "So the President has apparently decided to sacrifice Africa, the Third World and Black Americans. I think it's tragic."

In 1991 Jackson compared **George HW Bush** to George Wallace: "George Wallace stood in the door of the schoolhouse and said no to desegregation - segregation today, segregation tomorrow, segregation forever. He promised white America protection from Blacks and drove a wedge of hatred deep into the heart of the nation. Today, **George Bush** stands in the door of the White House and says no to quotas, no today, no tomorrow, no forever. He promises to protect white America from Blacks and women entering the workforce. He promises to protect corporations from lawsuits for discrimination, putting the burden of proof on the victim."

In 1992 **Clinton** criticized a rap singer at a convention of the Rainbow Coalition, Jackson's organization. The rap singer was known at the time for violent and anti-white verses. She had performed the day before **Clinton** spoke. Jackson was outraged at **Clinton's** criticism of her. He called it a "sneak attack" that showed "a character flaw." **Clinton** told his colleagues that her appearance was an example of Jackson's "dirty, double-crossing back-stabbing."

Clinton was sometimes called the first Black president.

In the 2008 campaign **Bill Clinton** complained to Ted Kennedy that **Barack Obama** was exploiting race. In lobbying Senator Edward

Kennedy to endorse his wife Hillary for President, former President **Clinton** angered the liberal icon by belittling **Obama**. Telling a friend about the conversation later, Kennedy recalled that **Clinton** had said "a few years ago, this guy would have been getting us coffee." A spokesman for the former president declined to comment on the claim. **Obama** responded to these sorts of issues by saying: "I think **Bill Clinton** and Hillary have historically and consistently been on the right side of civil rights issues." However, some **Obama** supporters questioned **Clinton's** racial insensitivity enraging **Clinton** who complained bitterly to **George W Bush**. **Bush** would even call **Clinton** on bad days in the campaign. **Bush** later said: "Those are the days when you need friends to call you, but sometimes they never do."

During a speech by **Obama** before Congress in 2009, a congressman shouted out "you lie." He later apologized and **Obama** accepted the apology. Within a few days **Carter** said the congressman's shout was "based on racism. ... There is an inherent feeling among many in this country that an African-American should not be president." A day later he added, "I think an overwhelming portion of the intensely demonstrated animosity toward President **Barack Obama** is based on the fact that he is a Black man, that he's African-American." **Carter** added: "I live in the South, and I've seen the South come a long way, and I've seen the rest of the country that shares the South's attitude toward minority groups at that time, particularly African-Americans."

What is the point of all this?

In one instance, the point is obvious. As our society has changed so have the Presidents. In the other, it is also obvious. In the US race remains at the beginning of the twenty-first century a vexing issue.

Chapter 12

Summary

The forty-three Presidents have interacted both with their contemporaries and also across time. I have looked at one aspect of their biographies: what presidents said to and about each other and how they handled similar issues and events to examine vital national themes such as race, the Constitution, religion, national unity and more.

A non-exhaustive list of the scholars and writers I have read to describe the presidential interactions includes:

Stephen Ambrose, Harry Ammon, Judith Icke Anderson, Louis Auchincloss,

Jean H. Baker, Dan Balz and Haynes Johnson, Fred Barnes, Robert L. Bartley, Michael Beschloss, Conrad Black, Paul F. Boller, Jr., Garry Boulard, Walter R. Borneman, Bill Bryson, James MacGregor Burns, H.W. Brands, Douglas Brinkley, Richard Brookhiser, Patrick J. Buchanan, Josiah Bunting III, Charles W. Calhoun, Lou Cannon, Robert A. Caro, Richard J. Carwardine, James Chace, Winston Churchill, Freeman Cleaves, Christopher and James Lincoln Collier, Robert Dallek, John W. Dean, Thomas M. DeFrank, David Herbert Donald, Hedley Donovan, Elizabeth Drew, Susan Dunn, William Dusinberre, HJ Ekenrode, John SD Eisenhower, Joseph J. Ellis, Bruce Feiler, Carol Felsenthal, Paul Finkelman, Thomas Flemming, Daniel J. Flynn, Claude M. Fuess, David Gelernter, Jeff Gerth and Don Van Natta, Nancy Gibbs and Michael Duffy, Doris Kearns Goodwin, Lewis L. Gould, Henry F. Graff, David Greenberg, Jan Crawford Greenburg, Holman Hamilton, Gary Hart, George C. Herring, Seymour M. Hersh, Michael F. Holt, Ari Hoogenboom, Edwin P. Hoyt, James Humes, Walter Isaacson, David E. Johnson and Johnny R. Johnson, Paul

Johnson, Zachary Karabell, Roger G. Kennedy, Jeane J. Kirkpatirck, Adrienne Koch, Charles Lachman, Edward J. Larson, Margaret Leech, William E. Leuchtenburg, Edward G. Longacre, Jeremy Lott, Rich Lowry, William Manchester, Alf J. Mapp, Jr., Gary May, Donald R. McCoy, David McCullough, George McGovern, Jon Meacham, Robert W. Merry, John Micklethwait and Adrian Wooldridge, Candice Millard, Paul Moreno, Edmund Morris, Roy Morris, Mark Moyar, Timothy Naftali, Paul C. Nagel, Jim Newton, Niels C. Nielson, John Niven, Barbara Olson, Herbert S. Parmet, Rick Perlstein, James M. Perry, Norma Lois Peterson, Kevin Phillips, David Pietrusza, Norman Podhoretz, Nick Ragone, Robert J. Rayback, Richard Reeves, William H. Rehnquist, Robert V. Remini, James David Robenalt, Gretchen Rubin, Larry J. Sabato, Nathan Schachner, Larry Schweikart and Michael Allen, John Seigenthaler, Peter Schweizer and Rochelle Schweizer, Jack Shepherd, Brooks D. Simpson, Jean Edward Smith, Richard Norton Smith, Kevin Starr, David O. Stewart, John M. Taylor, Lately Thomas, Tevi Troy, Margaret Truman, Harlow Giles Unger, Carl Van Doren, Peter A. Wallner, Joan Waugh, Ted Widmer, Doug Wead, Barry Werth, Sean Wilentz, Garry Wills, Jay Winik, Robert W. Winston, Gordon S. Wood and Julian E. Zelizer.

Also, I have read books devoted to other topics which discuss the Presidents. Among them: Eugene E. Campbell (the Mormon Church) and John R. Commons (the American labor movement), John J Miller and Mark Molesky (US-French relations), Stephen Prothero (religious life in the US) and Stephen Thernstrom and Abigail Thernstrom (race relations in the US),

Finally and most important, I owe a great deal to the paramount US historians of the nineteenth and twentieth centuries: Henry Adams and Arthur M. Schlesinger, Jr.

I have mentioned each US president – at an average of about 175 times per president. **Thomas Jefferson** at 466 and **Warren Harding** at 62 are the extremes.

Things are the way they are now often for reasons having to do with humans making choices. Think of people who have lived before us.

Their future is our past and present. **Lincoln's** decision to prevent the break-up of the US by force and his maneuvering to get the rebels to fire the first shot probably ensured that the US would become a great power and decisively affected the geopolitical world in two world-wide wars in the next century. **Eisenhower** exhibited this understanding when he would show visitors around Gettysburg and then ask what would be the historical reputation of *George Washington* if the North had not won that battle. We have been fortunate for many things in the US, one of which is that most presidents grasped that they were part of a very select fraternity.

Addendum

At my count, I have mentioned the presidents of the US as follows:

George Washington - 275
John Adams - 153
Thomas Jefferson – 466
James Madison - 238
James Monroe - 257
John Quincy Adams – 249
Andrew Jackson - 277
Martin Van Buren - 141
William Henry Harrison - 136
John Tyler - 114
James Knox Polk - 143
Zachary Taylor - 96
Millard Fillmore - 103
Franklin Pierce 133
James Buchanan - 118
Abraham Lincoln – 326
Andrew Johnson -106
Ulysses S. Grant - 246
Rutherford B Hayes - 171
James Garfield – 122
Chester Alan Arthur – 83
Grover Cleveland – 86
Benjamin Harrison - 64
William McKinley – 75
Theodore Roosevelt – 241
William Howard Taft – 143
Woodrow Wilson – 114
Warren Harding – 62
Calvin Coolidge – 102
Herbert Hoover - 145
Franklin Roosevelt - 174

Harry Truman - 215
Dwight Eisenhower - 273
John F. Kennedy – 267
Lyndon Johnson - 208
Richard Nixon - 329
Gerald Ford - 174
Jimmy Carter - 126
Ronald Reagan - 208
George HW Bush - 148
Bill Clinton - 191
George W Bush - 113
Barack Obama - 106

Printed in the United States
By Bookmasters